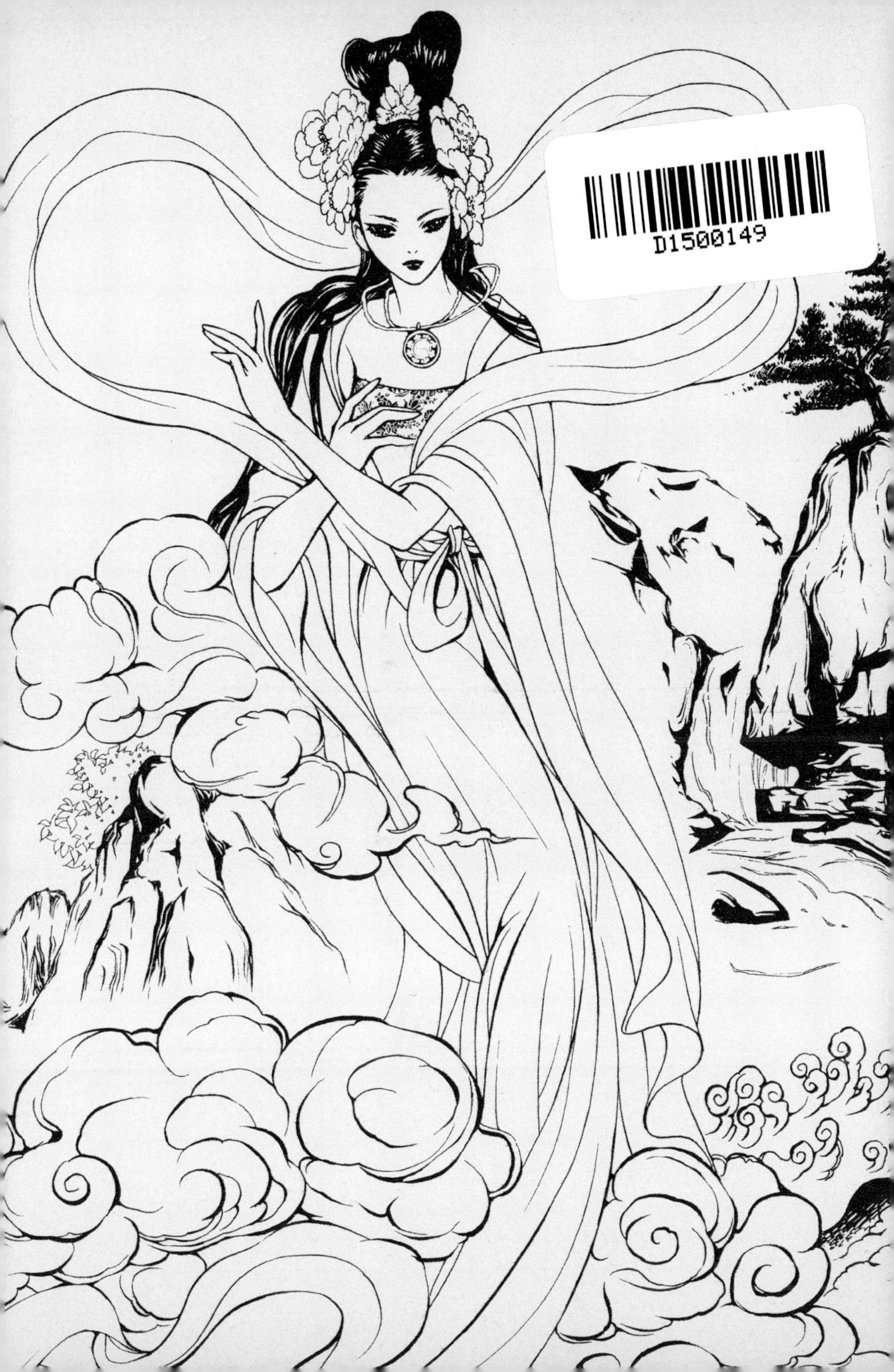

One thousand and one nights

vol. 4

Han SeungHee
Jeon JinSeok

Yen Press

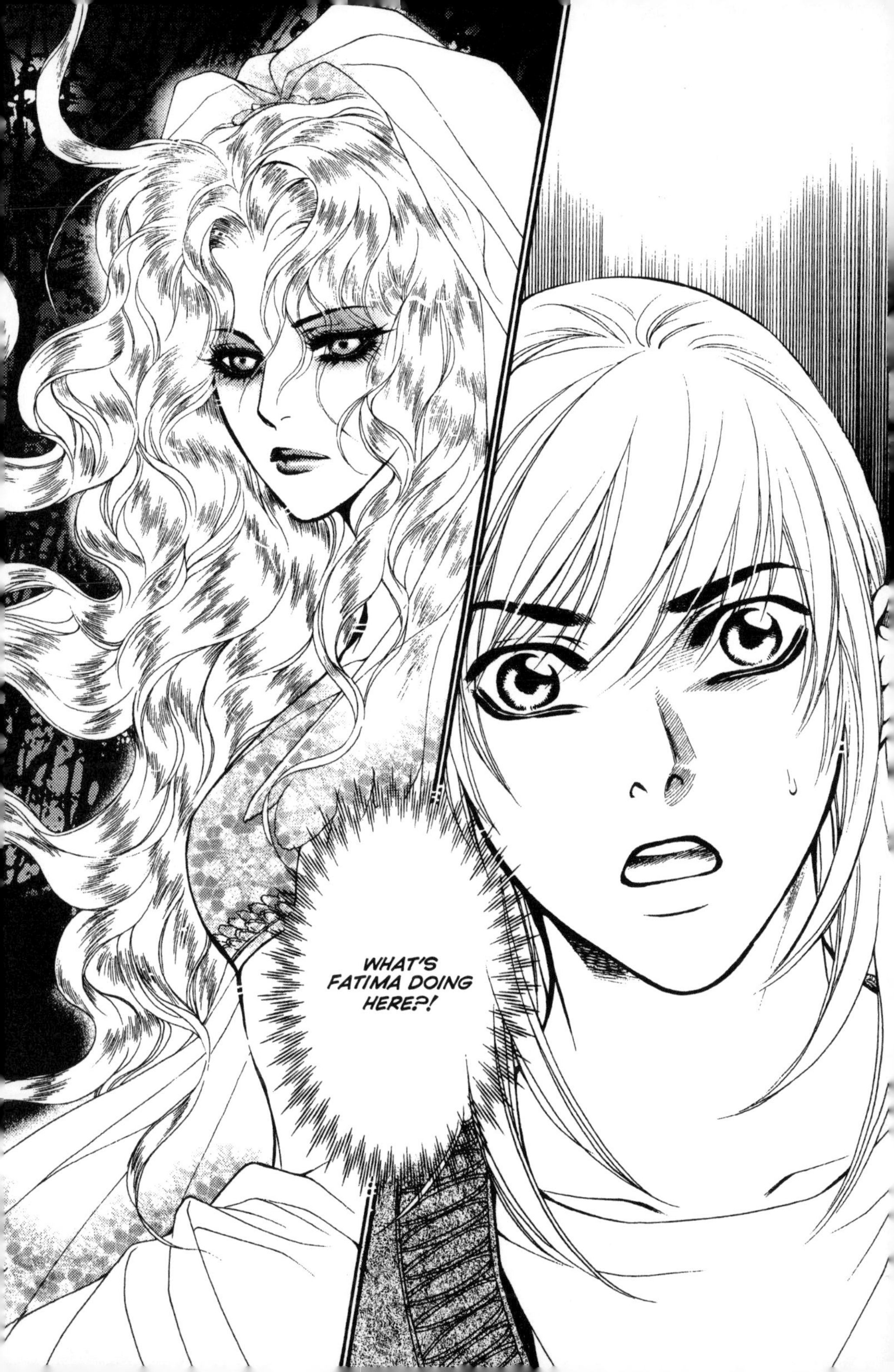
WHAT'S FATIMA DOING HERE?!

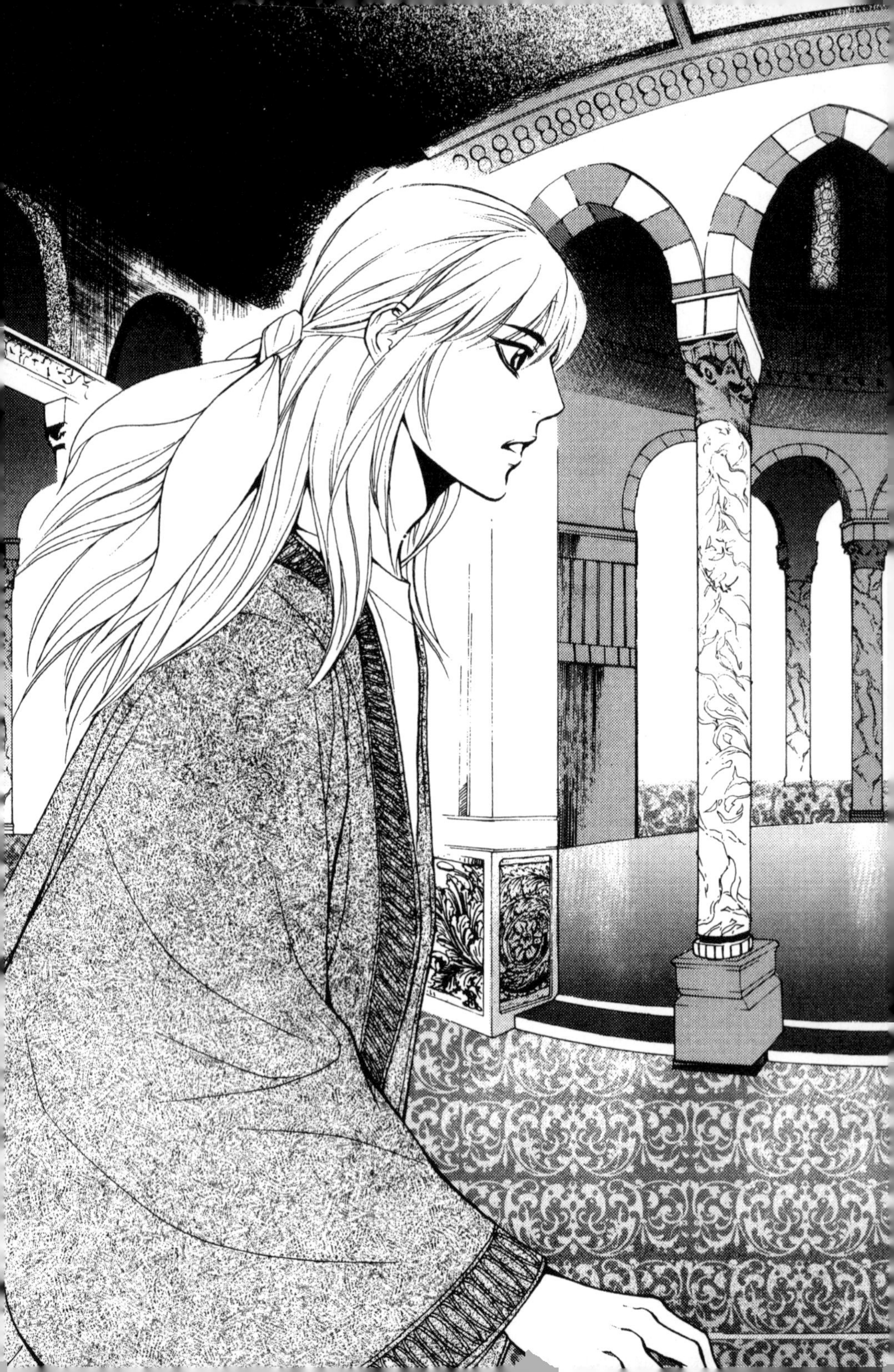

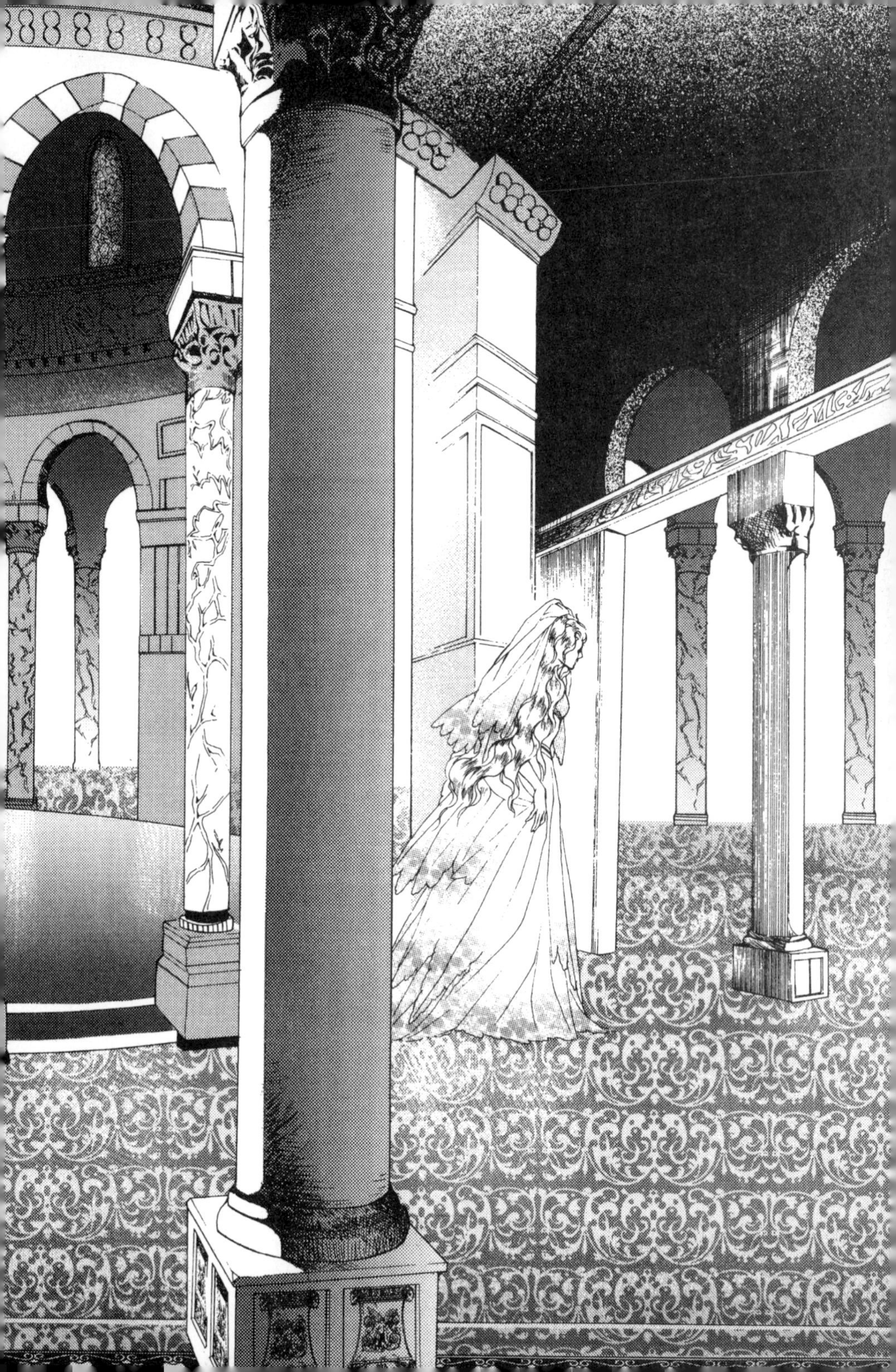

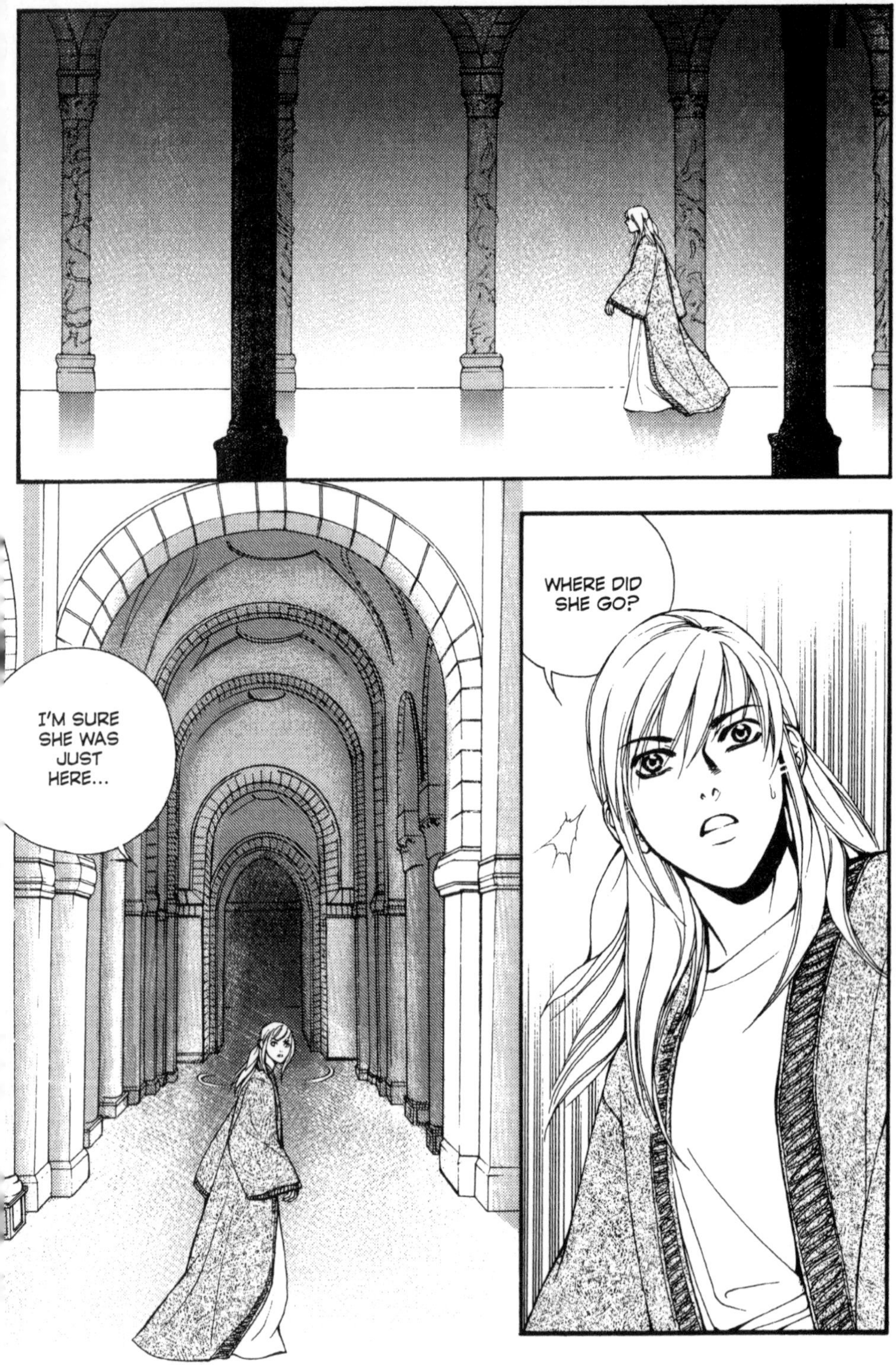
I'M SURE SHE WAS JUST HERE...
WHERE DID SHE GO?

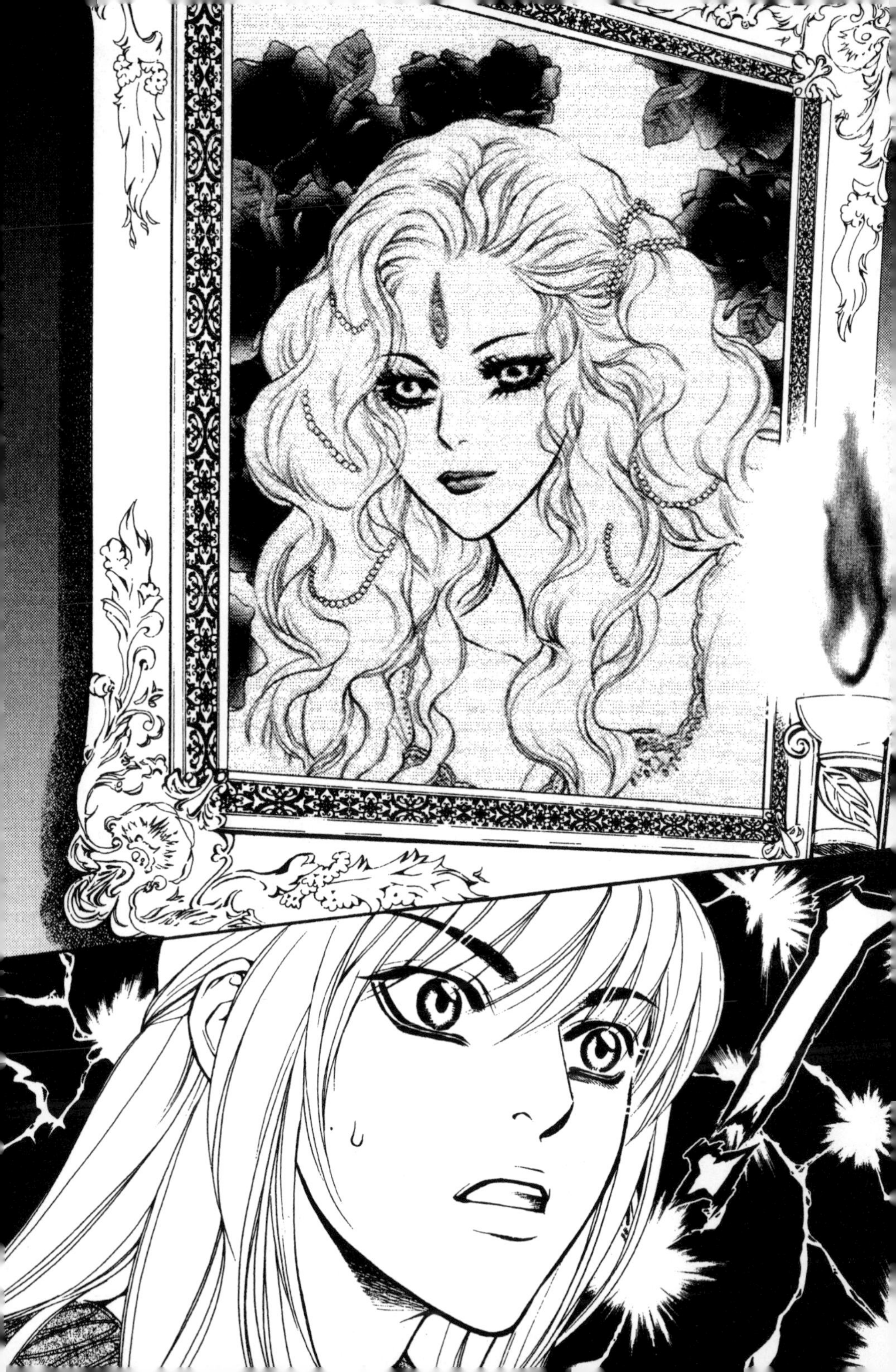

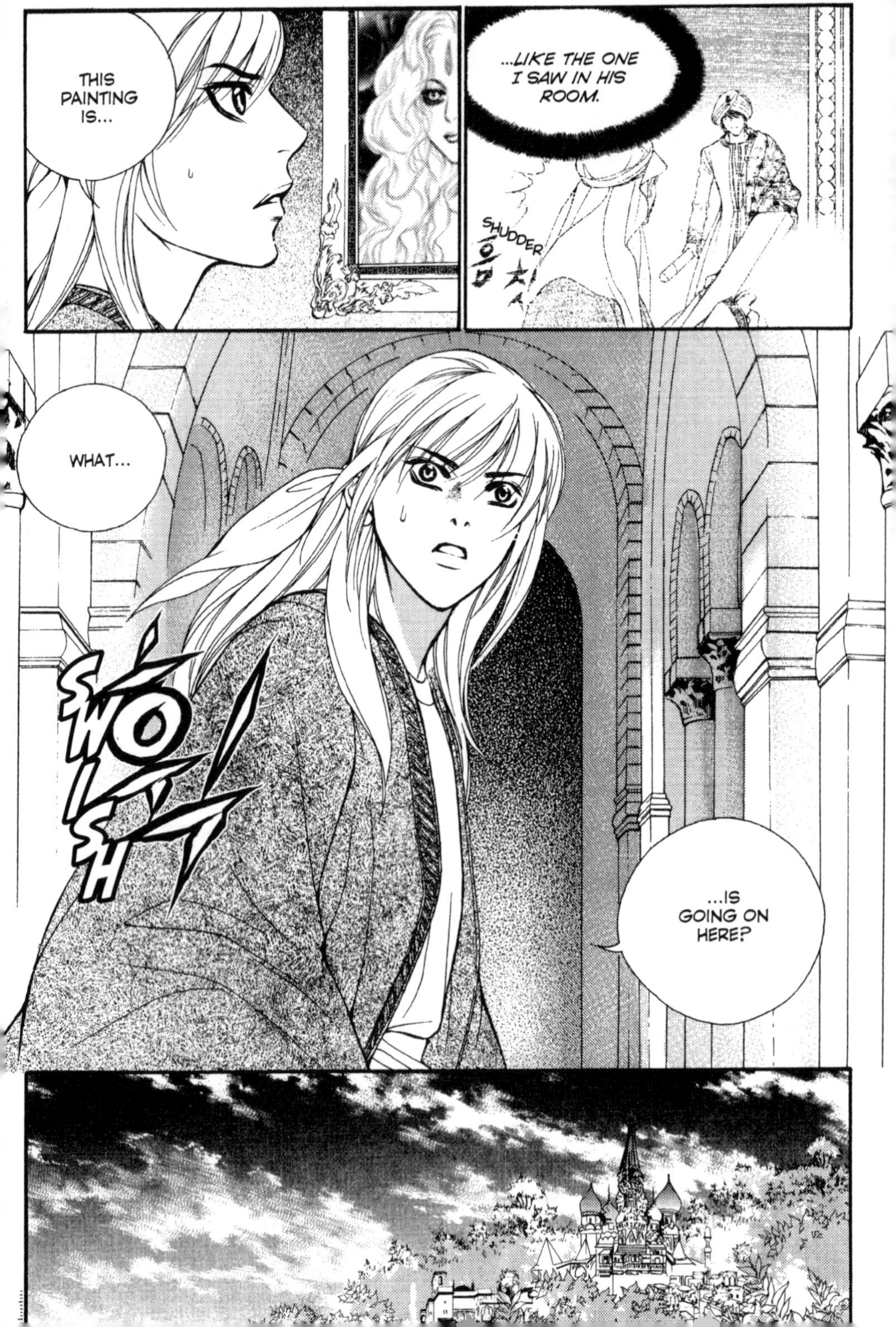
THIS PAINTING IS...
...LIKE THE ONE I SAW IN HIS ROOM.
SHUDDER
WHAT...
SWISH
...IS GOING ON HERE?

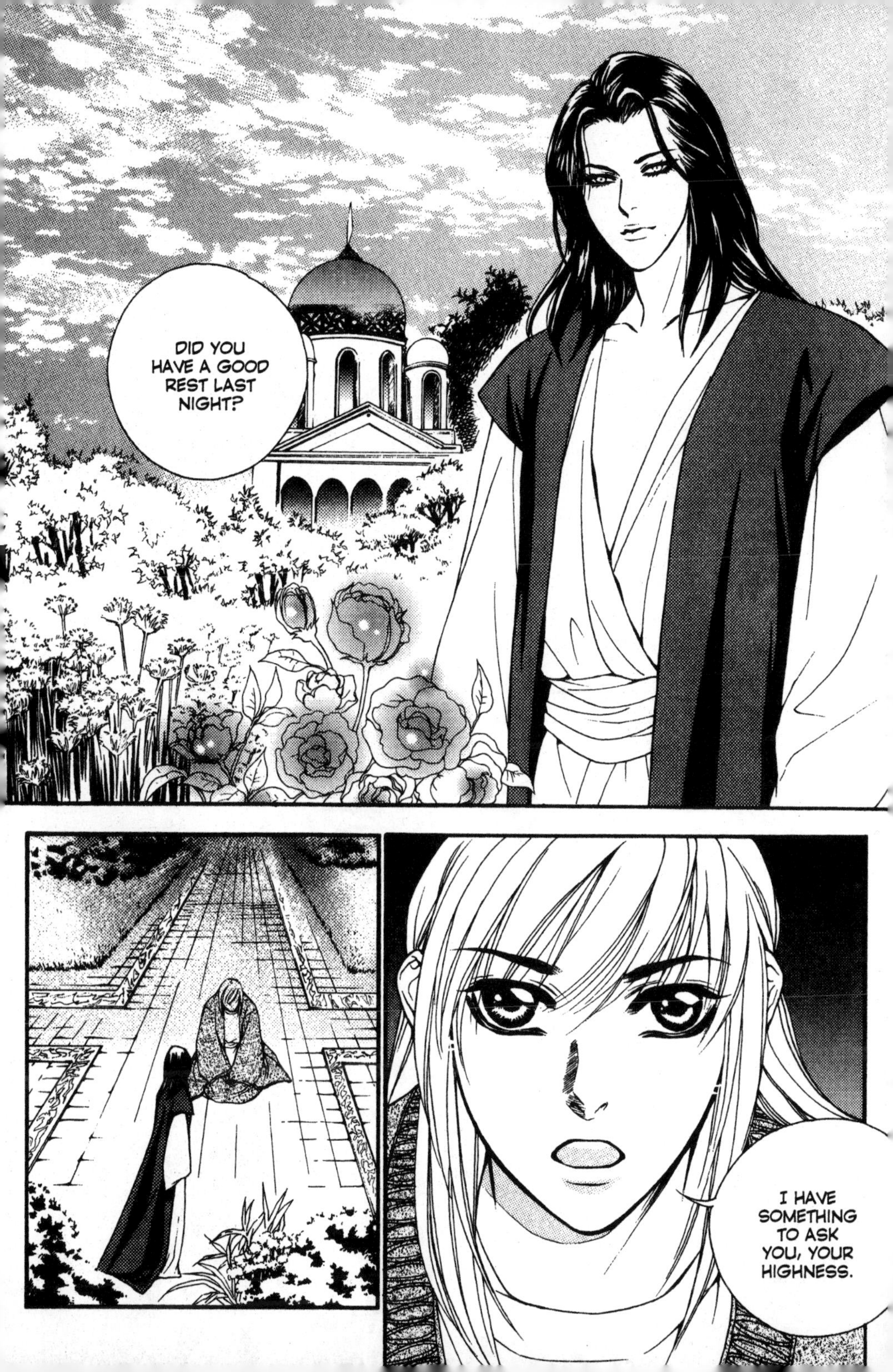
DID YOU HAVE A GOOD REST LAST NIGHT?
I HAVE SOMETHING TO ASK YOU, YOUR HIGHNESS.

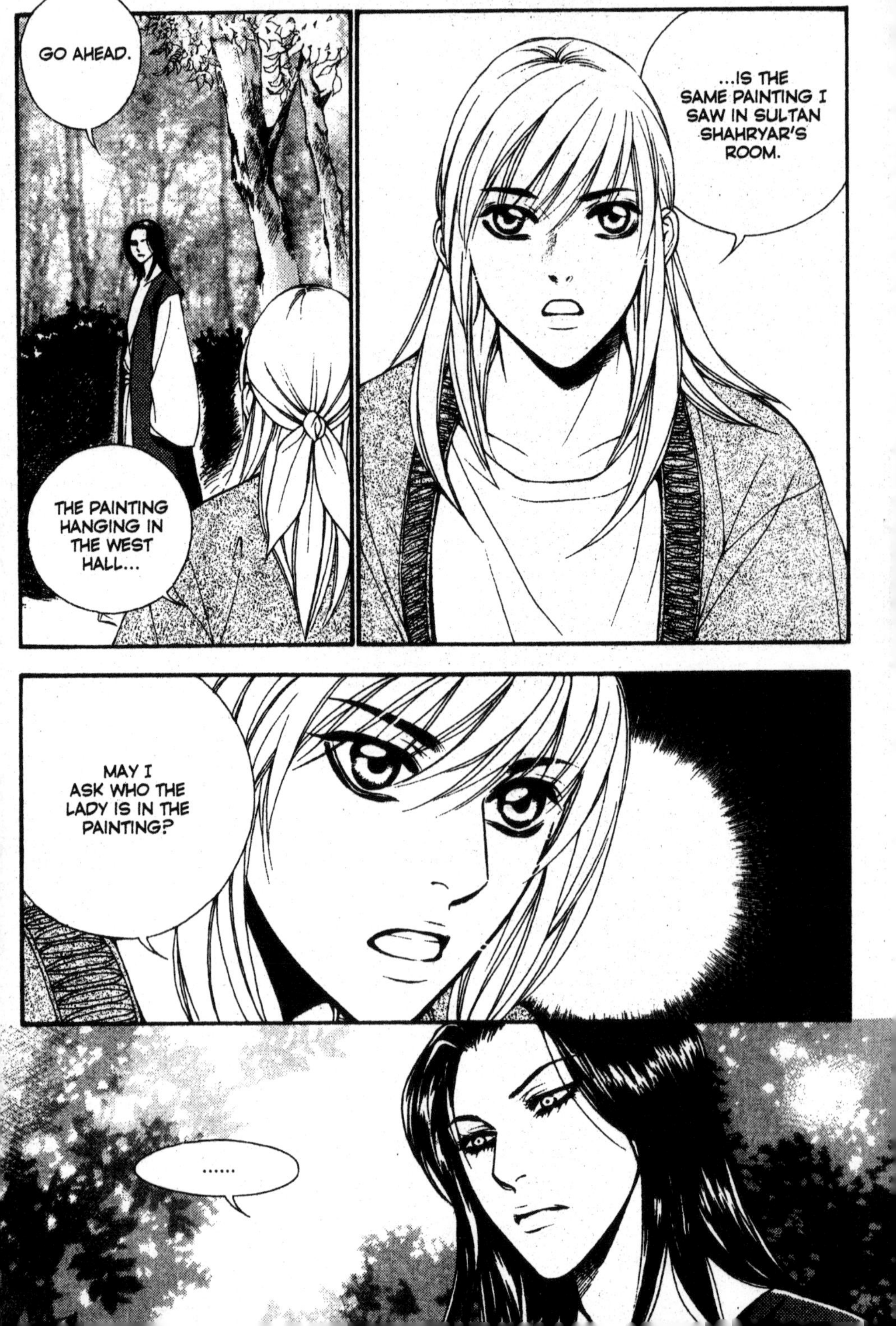
GO AHEAD.
THE PAINTING HANGING IN THE WEST HALL...
...IS THE SAME PAINTING I SAW IN SULTAN SHAHRYAR'S ROOM.
MAY I ASK WHO THE LADY IS IN THE PAINTING?
......

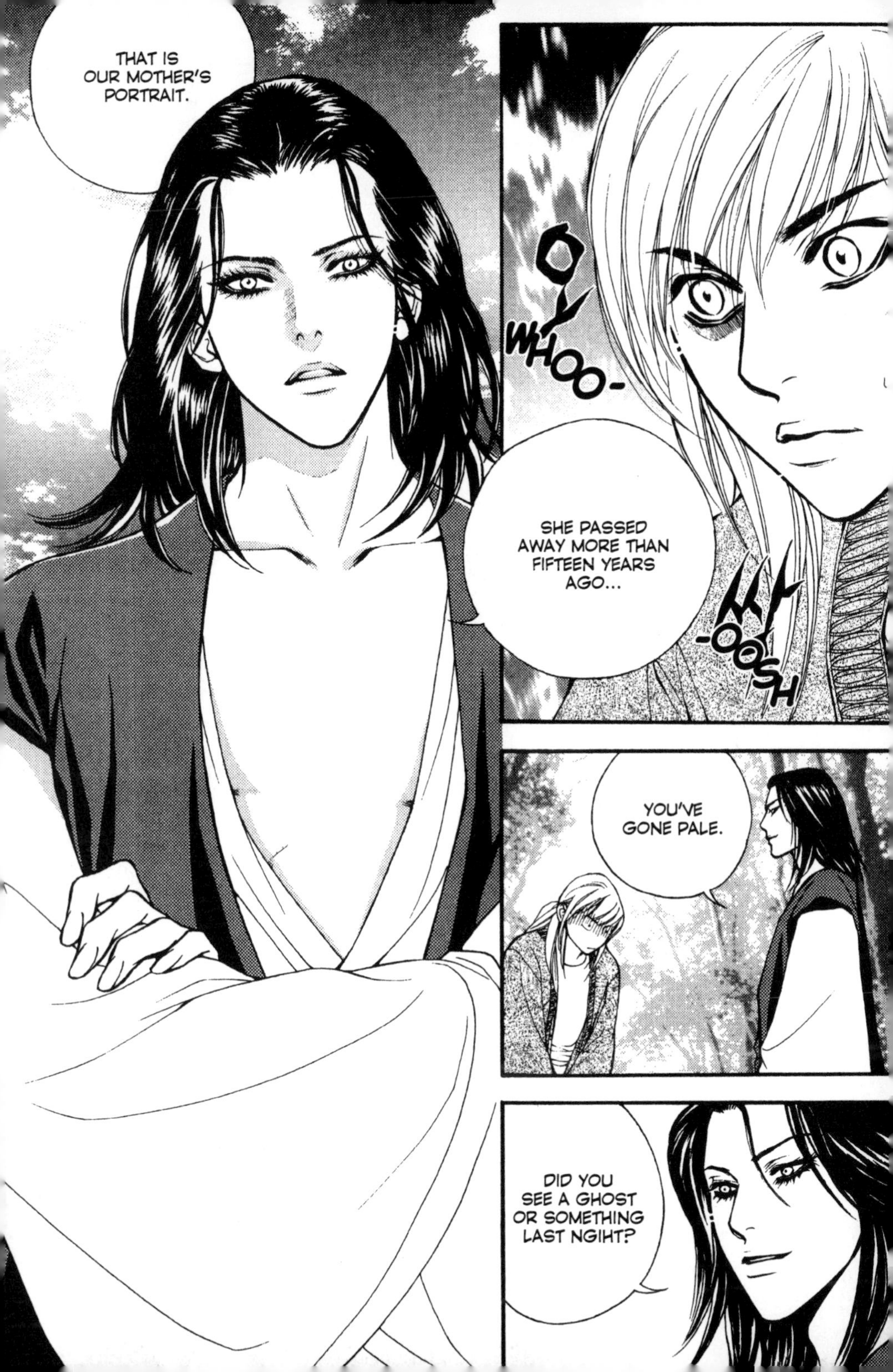
THAT IS OUR MOTHER'S PORTRAIT.
WHOO-
SHE PASSED AWAY MORE THAN FIFTEEN YEARS AGO...
-OOSH
YOU'VE GONE PALE.
DID YOU SEE A GHOST OR SOMETHING LAST NGIHT?

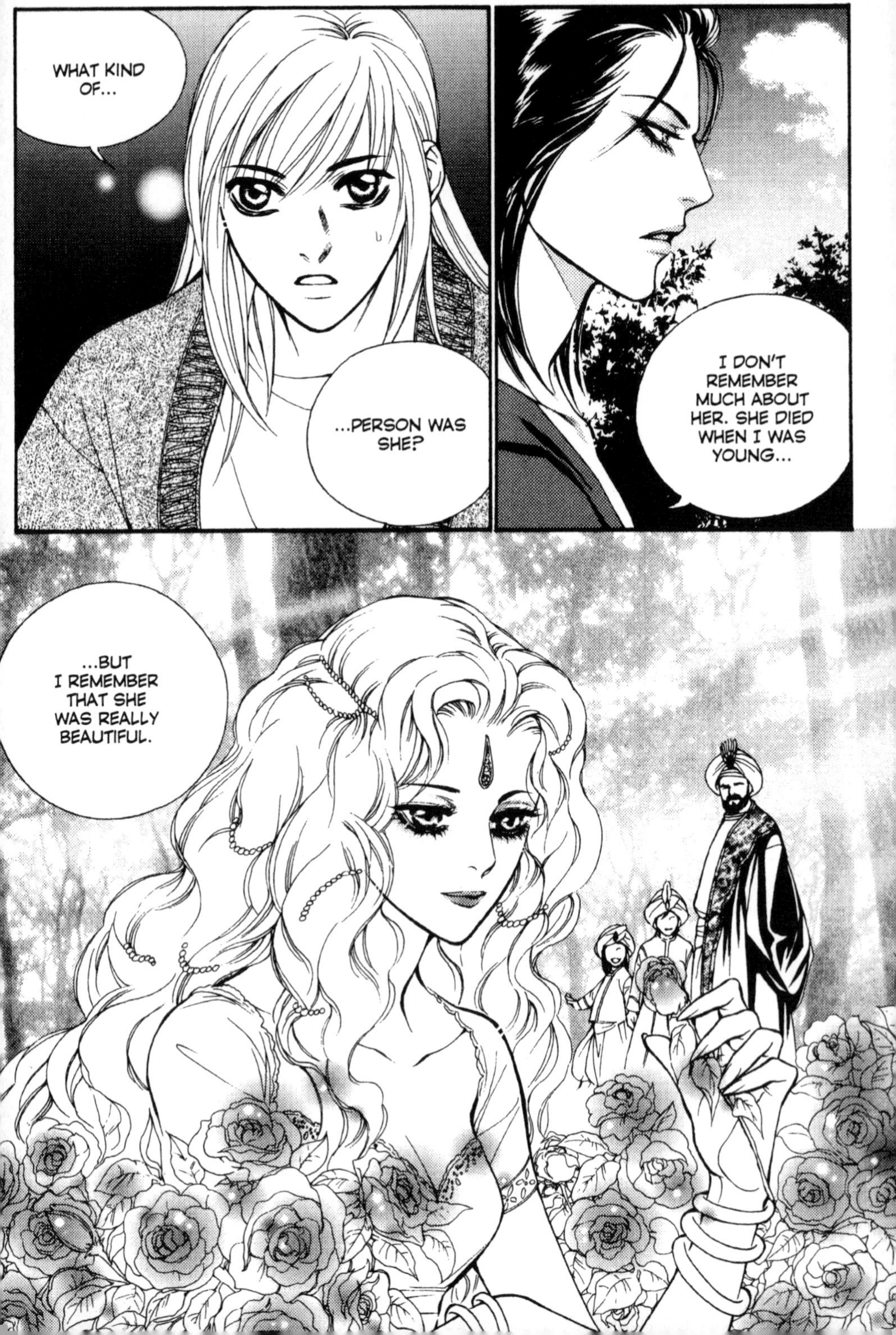
WHAT KIND OF...
...PERSON WAS SHE?
I DON'T REMEMBER MUCH ABOUT HER. SHE DIED WHEN I WAS YOUNG...
...BUT I REMEMBER THAT SHE WAS REALLY BEAUTIFUL.

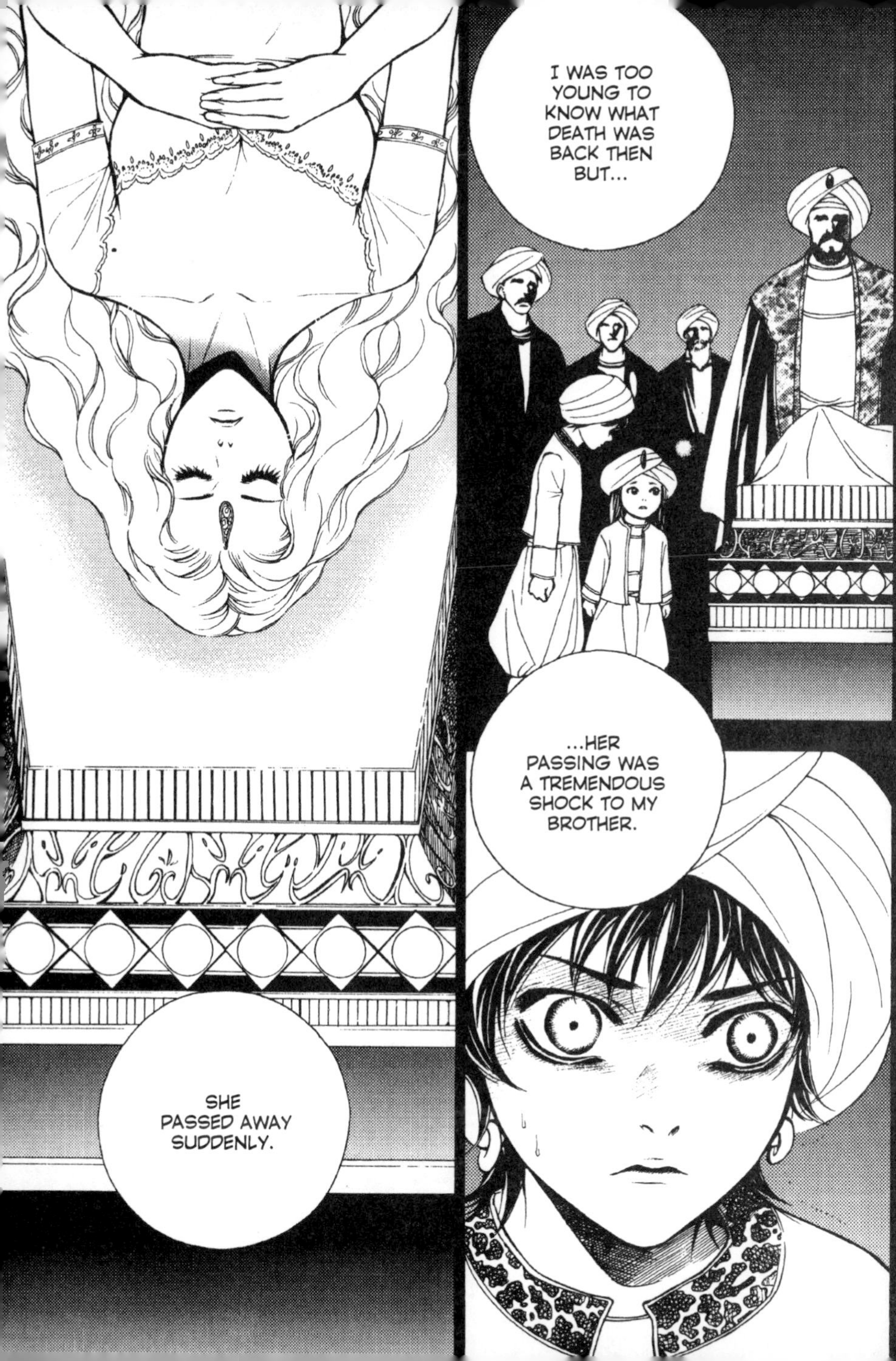
SHE PASSED AWAY SUDDENLY.
I WAS TOO YOUNG TO KNOW WHAT DEATH WAS BACK THEN BUT...
...HER PASSING WAS A TREMENDOUS SHOCK TO MY BROTHER.

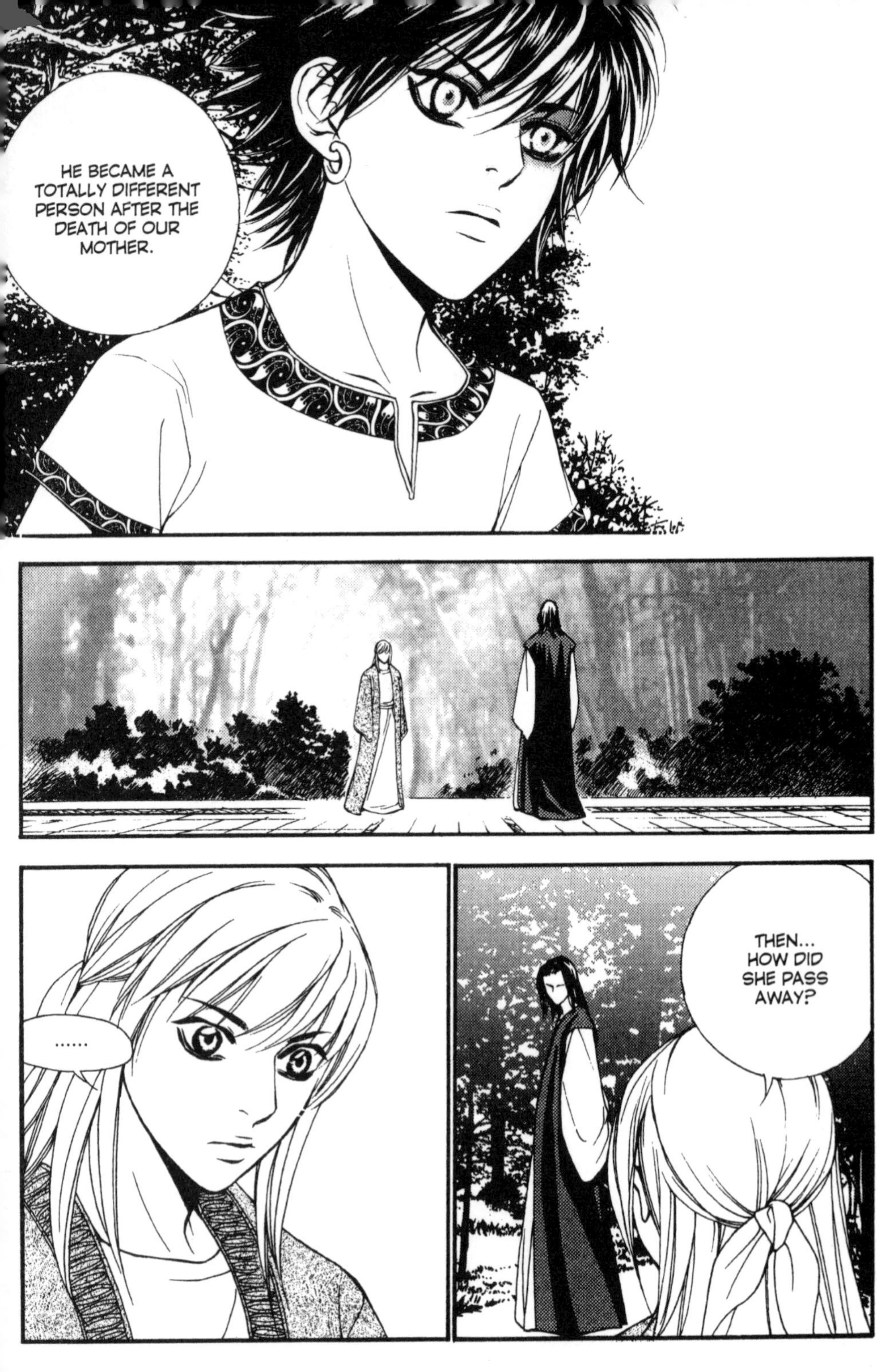
HE BECAME A TOTALLY DIFFERENT PERSON AFTER THE DEATH OF OUR MOTHER.
......
THEN... HOW DID SHE PASS AWAY?

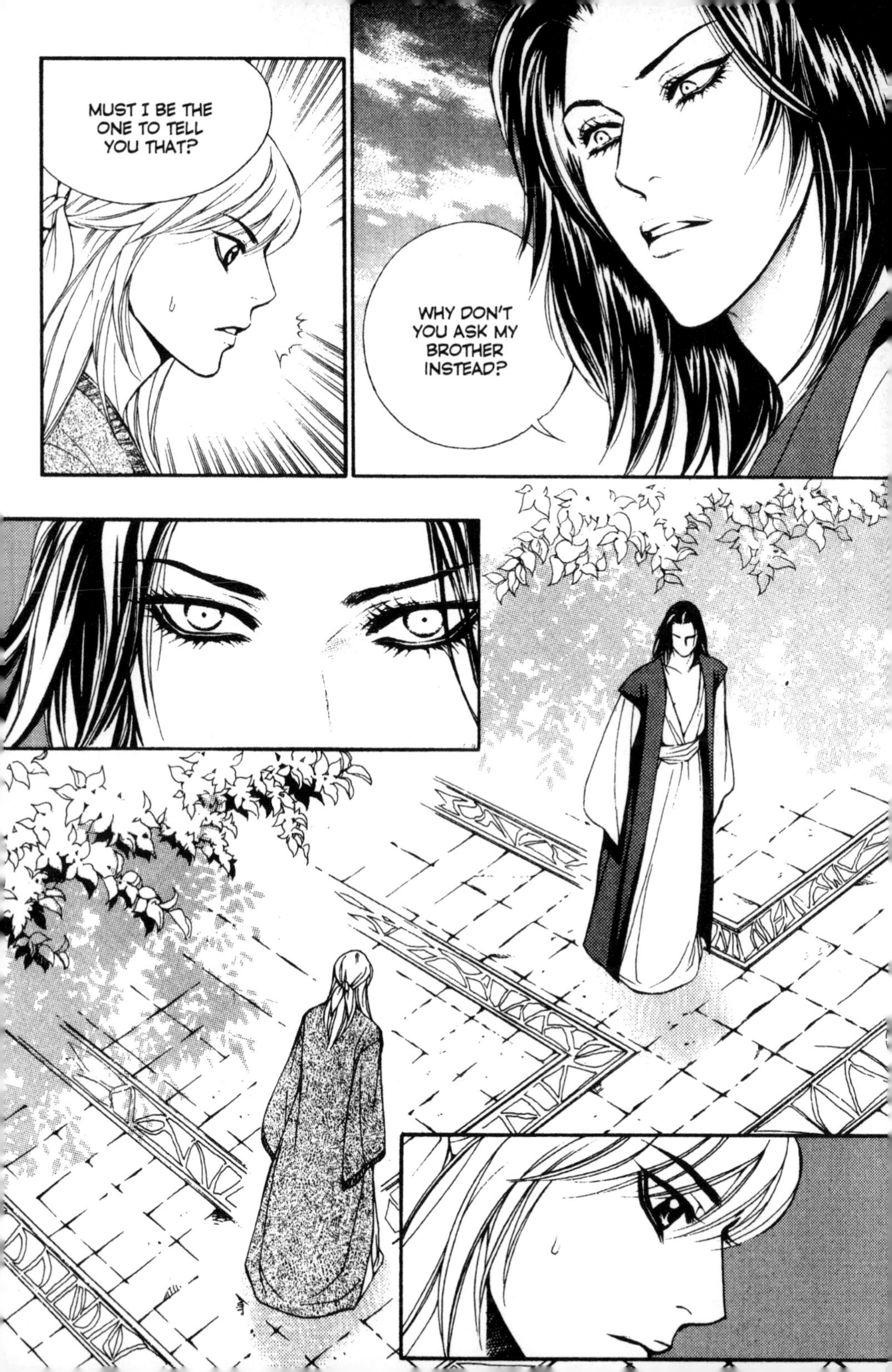
MUST I BE THE ONE TO TELL YOU THAT?
WHY DON'T YOU ASK MY BROTHER INSTEAD?

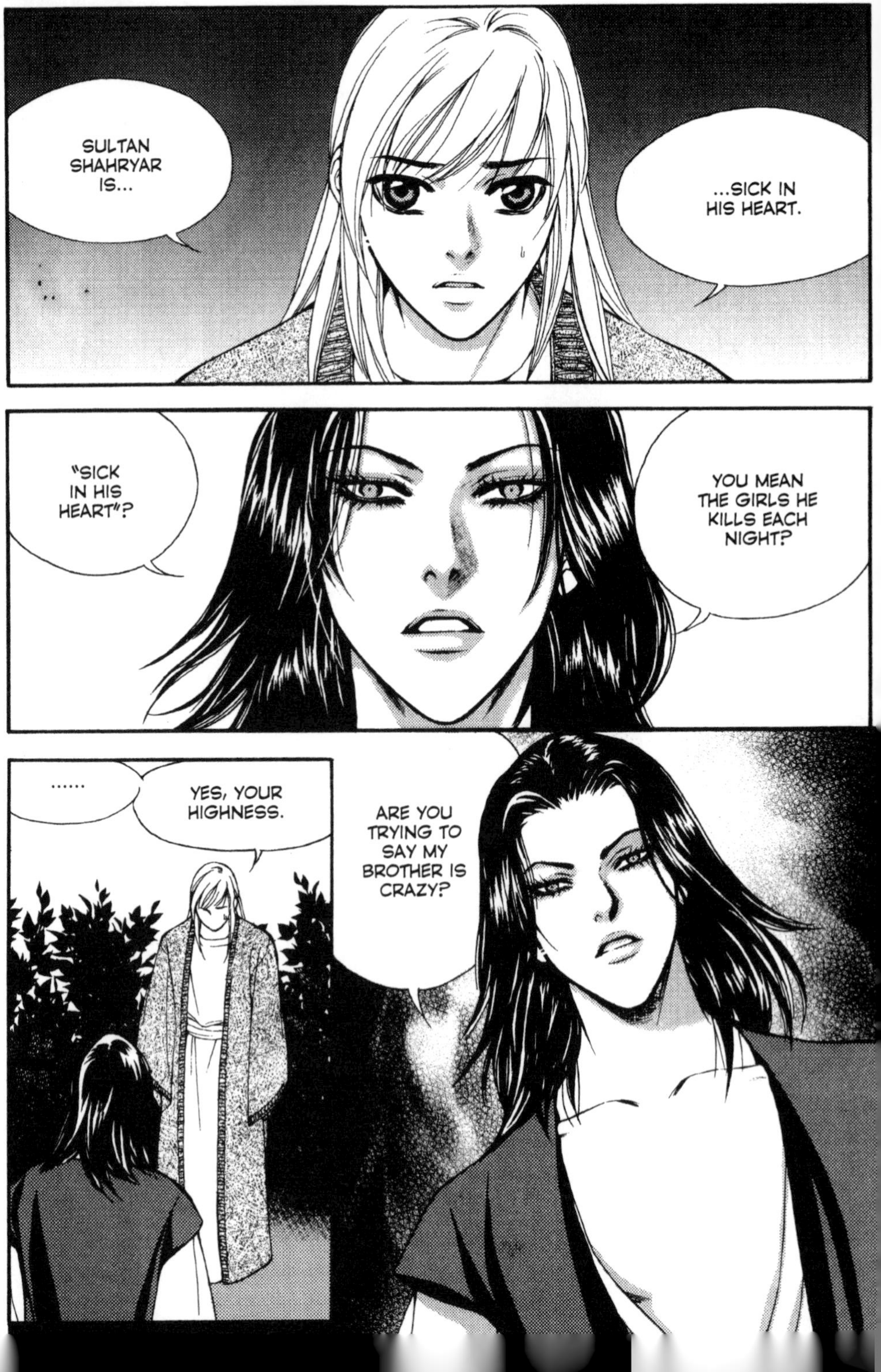
SULTAN SHAHRYAR IS...
...SICK IN HIS HEART.
"SICK IN HIS HEART"?
YOU MEAN THE GIRLS HE KILLS EACH NIGHT?
......
YES, YOUR HIGHNESS.
ARE YOU TRYING TO SAY MY BROTHER IS CRAZY?

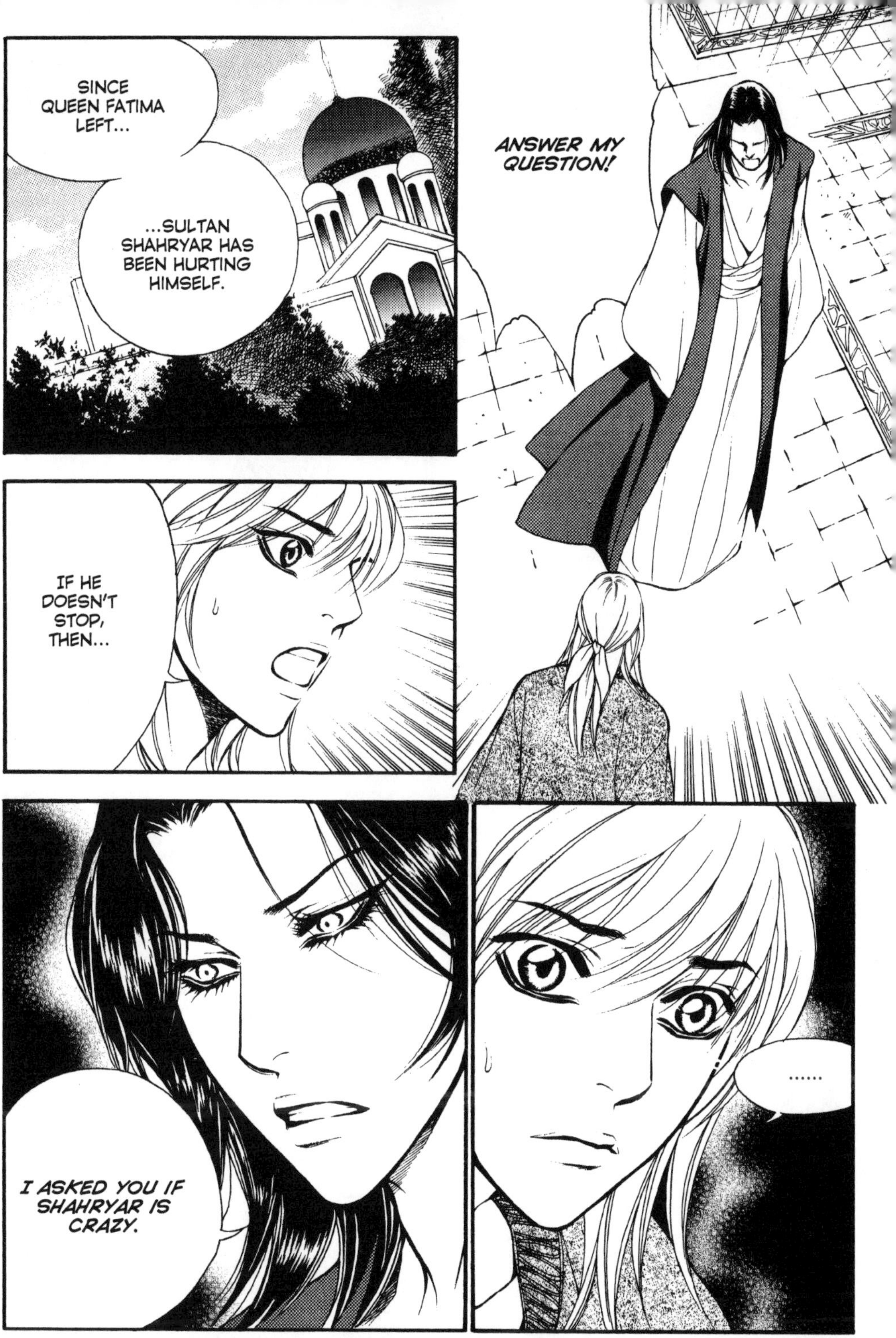
SINCE QUEEN FATIMA LEFT...
...SULTAN SHAHRYAR HAS BEEN HURTING HIMSELF.
IF HE DOESN'T STOP, THEN...
ANSWER MY QUESTION!
I ASKED YOU IF SHAHRYAR IS CRAZY.
......

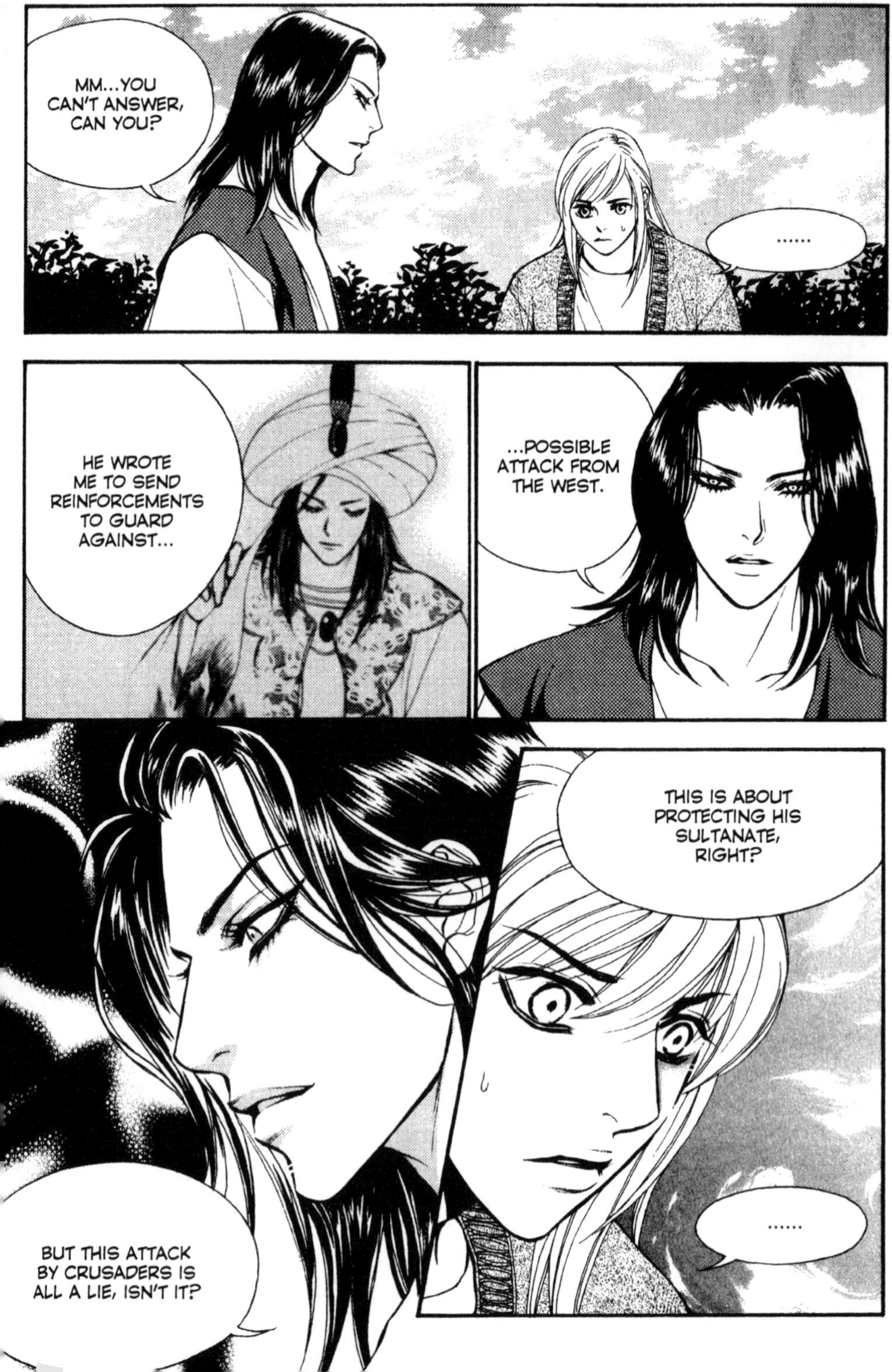
MM...YOU CAN'T ANSWER, CAN YOU?
......
HE WROTE ME TO SEND REINFORCEMENTS TO GUARD AGAINST...
...POSSIBLE ATTACK FROM THE WEST.
THIS IS ABOUT PROTECTING HIS SULTANATE, RIGHT?
BUT THIS ATTACK BY CRUSADERS IS ALL A LIE, ISN'T IT?
......

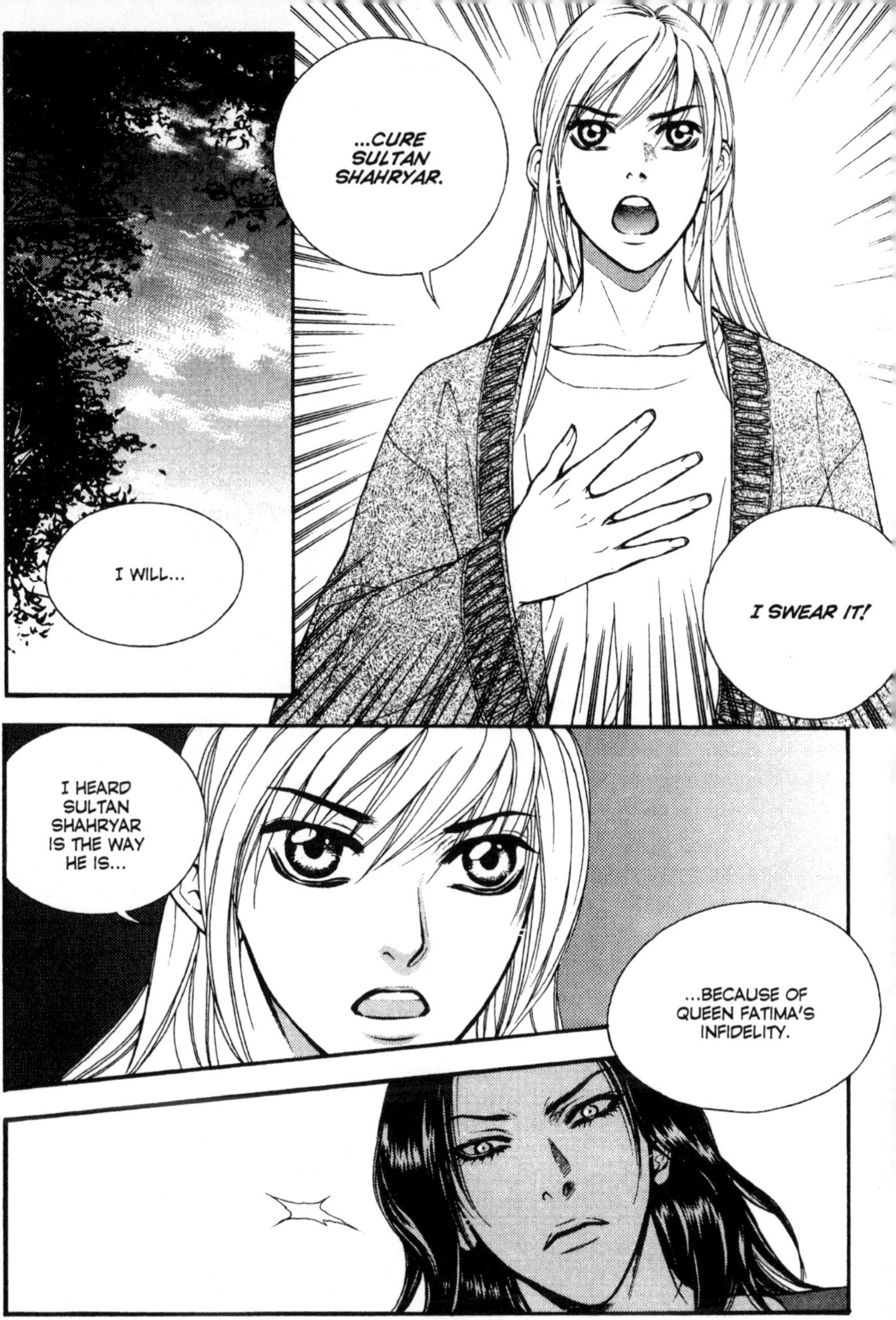
I WILL...
...CURE SULTAN SHAHRYAR.
I SWEAR IT!
I HEARD SULTAN SHAHRYAR IS THE WAY HE IS...
...BECAUSE OF QUEEN FATIMA'S INFIDELITY.

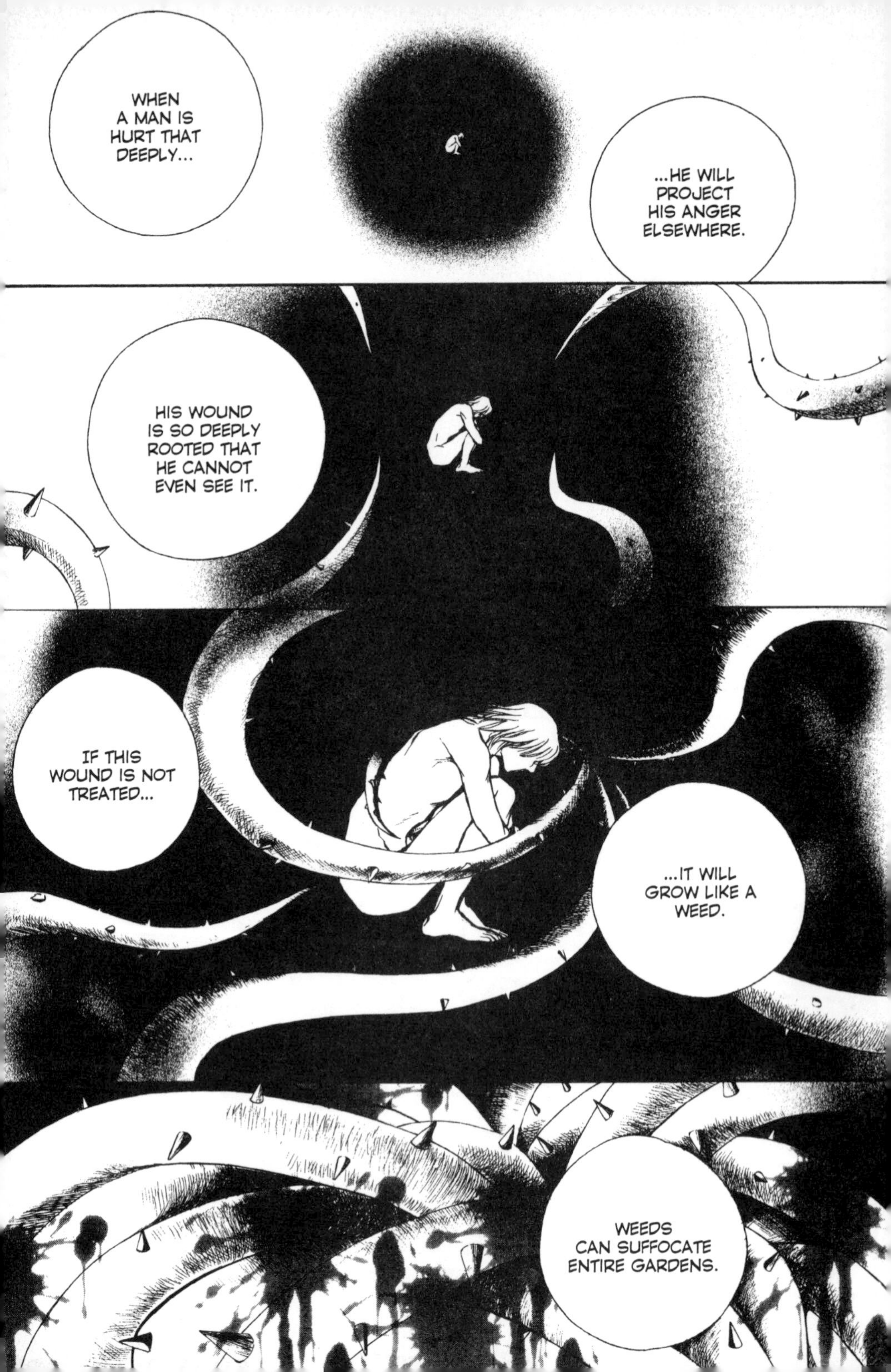
WHEN A MAN IS HURT THAT DEEPLY...
...HE WILL PROJECT HIS ANGER ELSEWHERE.
HIS WOUND IS SO DEEPLY ROOTED THAT HE CANNOT EVEN SEE IT.
IF THIS WOUND IS NOT TREATED...
...IT WILL GROW LIKE A WEED.
WEEDS CAN SUFFOCATE ENTIRE GARDENS.

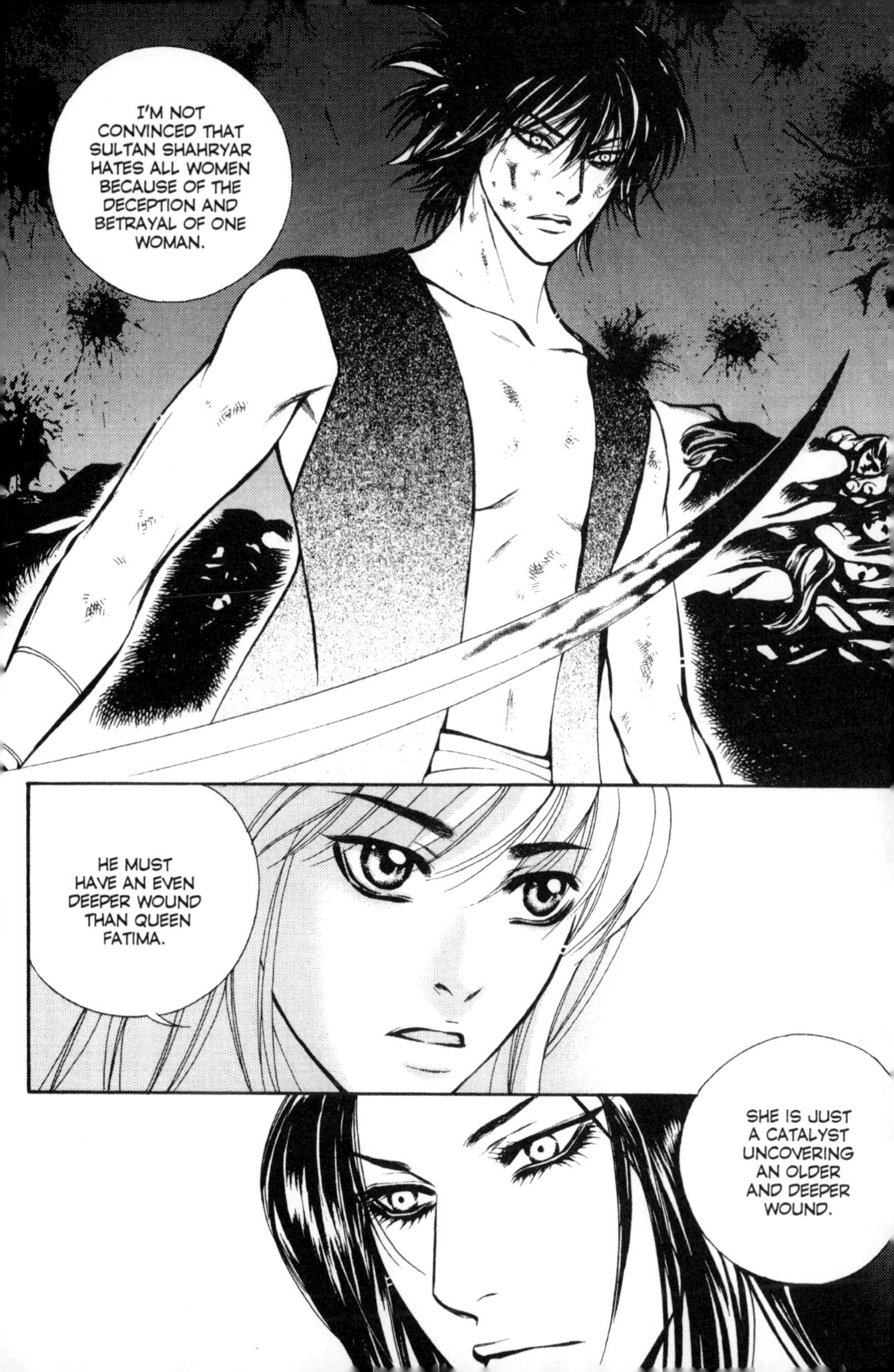
I'M NOT CONVINCED THAT SULTAN SHAHRYAR HATES ALL WOMEN BECAUSE OF THE DECEPTION AND BETRAYAL OF ONE WOMAN.
HE MUST HAVE AN EVEN DEEPER WOUND THAN QUEEN FATIMA.
SHE IS JUST A CATALYST UNCOVERING AN OLDER AND DEEPER WOUND.

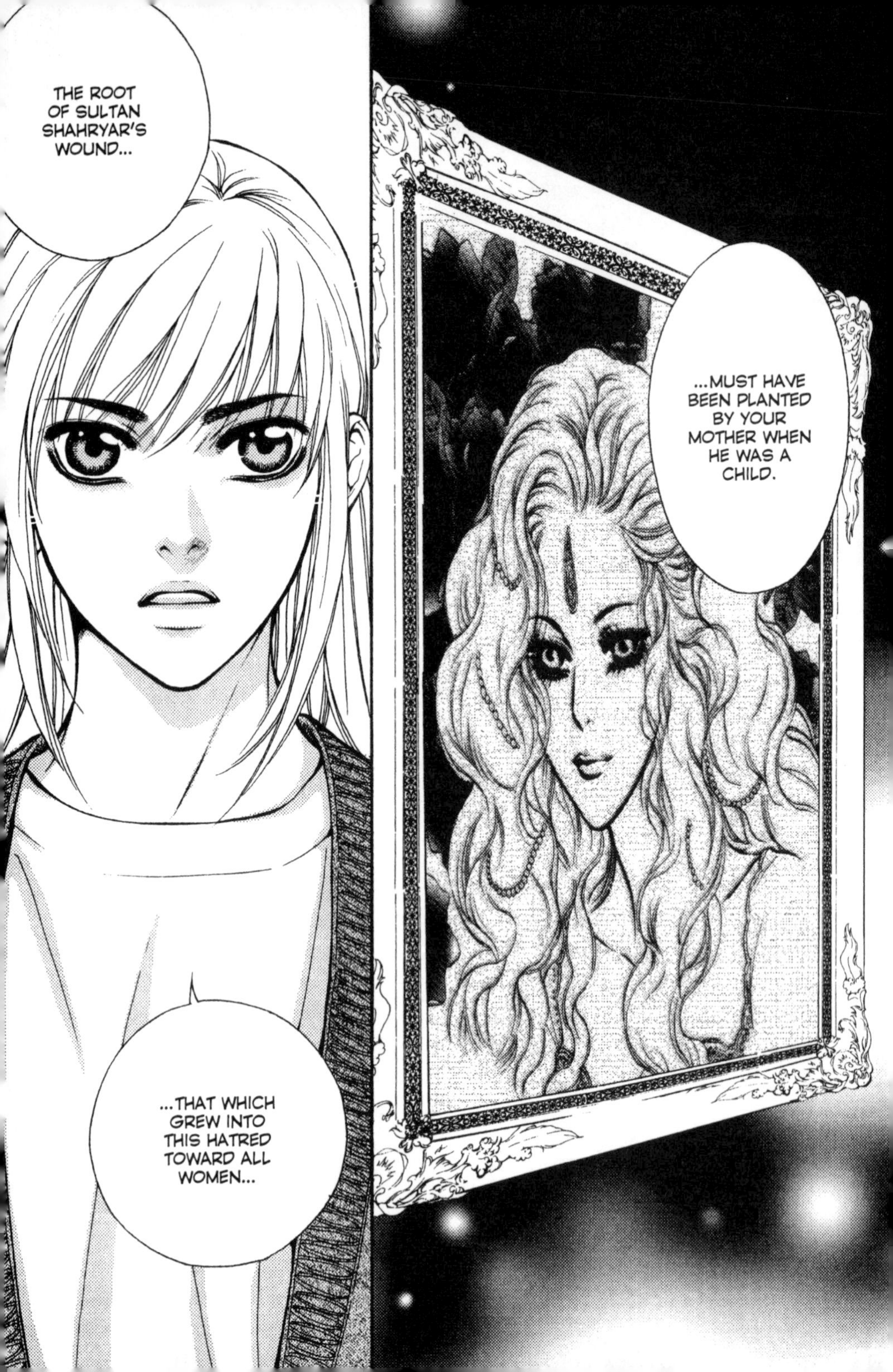
THE ROOT OF SULTAN SHAHRYAR'S WOUND...
...THAT WHICH GREW INTO THIS HATRED TOWARD ALL WOMEN...
...MUST HAVE BEEN PLANTED BY YOUR MOTHER WHEN HE WAS A CHILD.

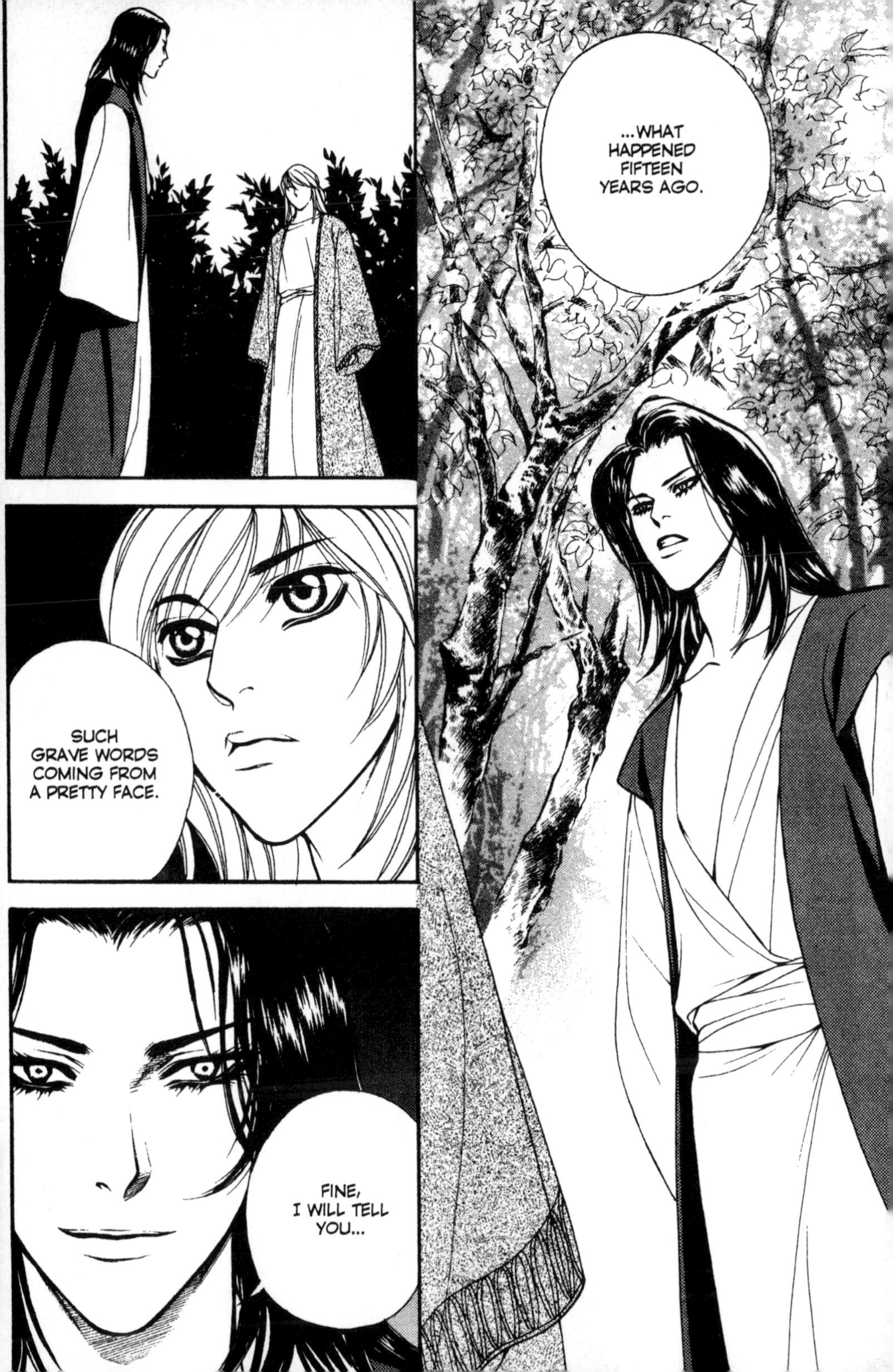
SUCH GRAVE WORDS COMING FROM A PRETTY FACE.
FINE, I WILL TELL YOU...
...WHAT HAPPENED FIFTEEN YEARS AGO.

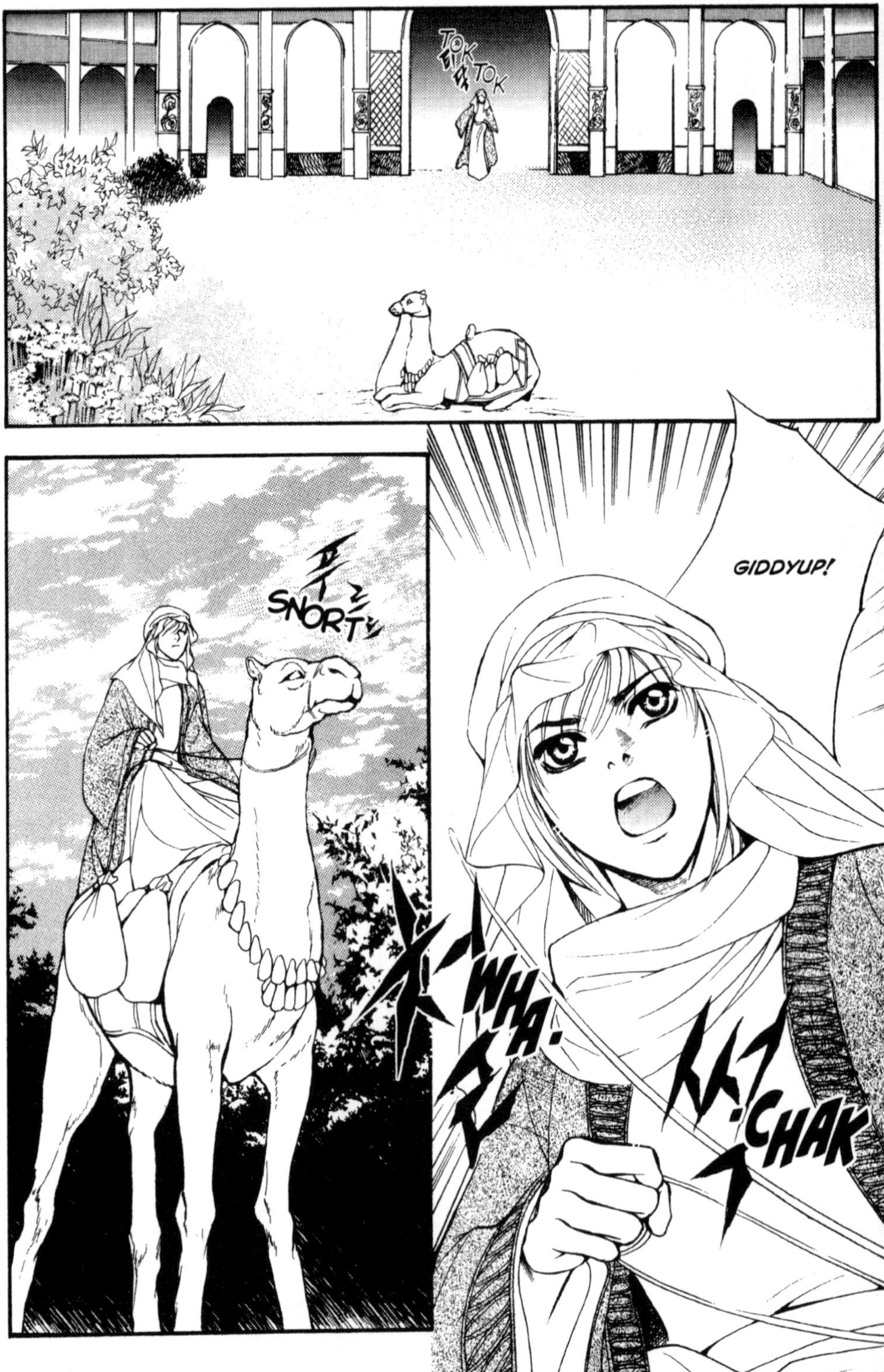
TOK TOK
SNORT
GIDDYUP!
WHA!
CHAK

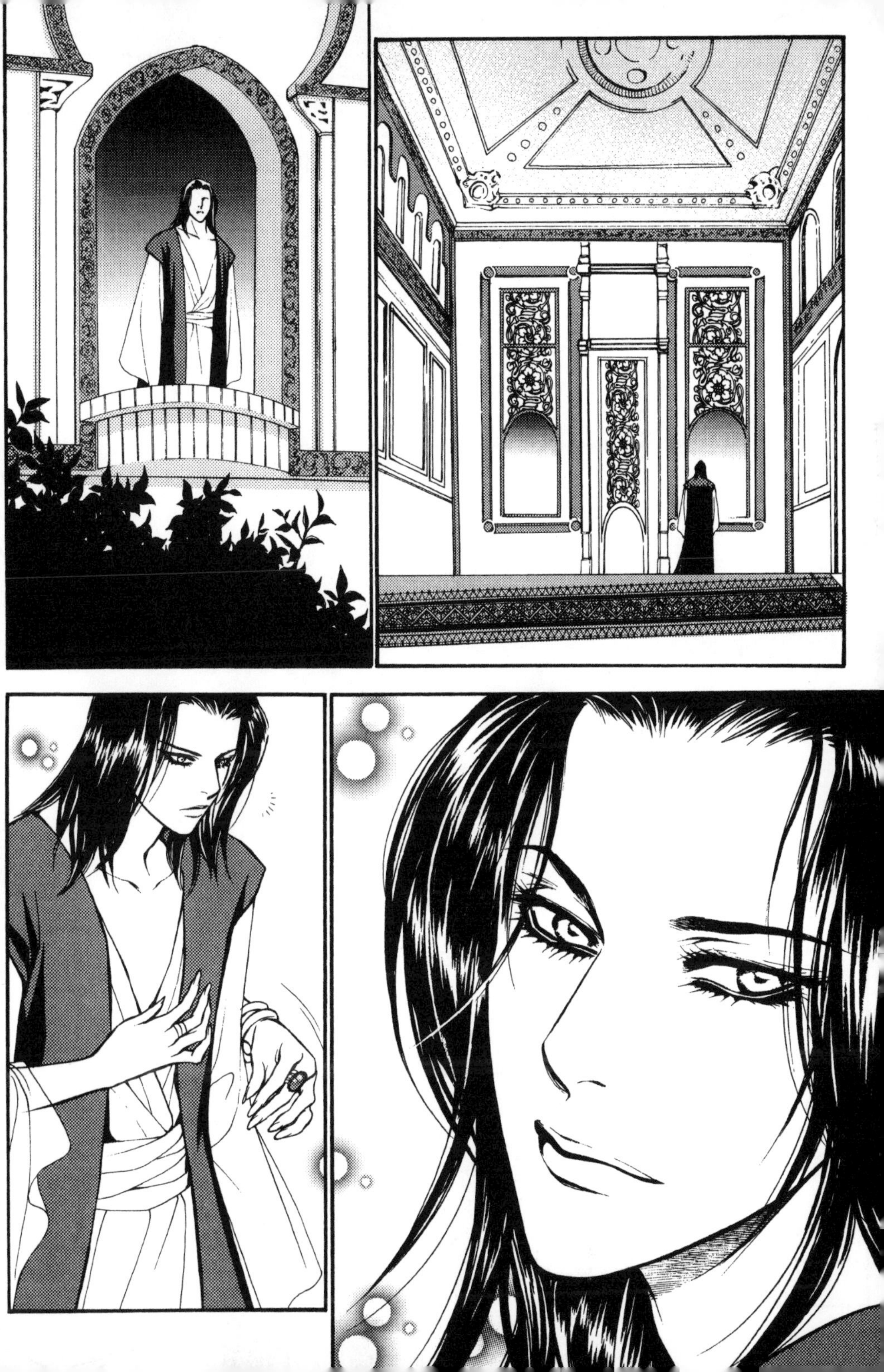

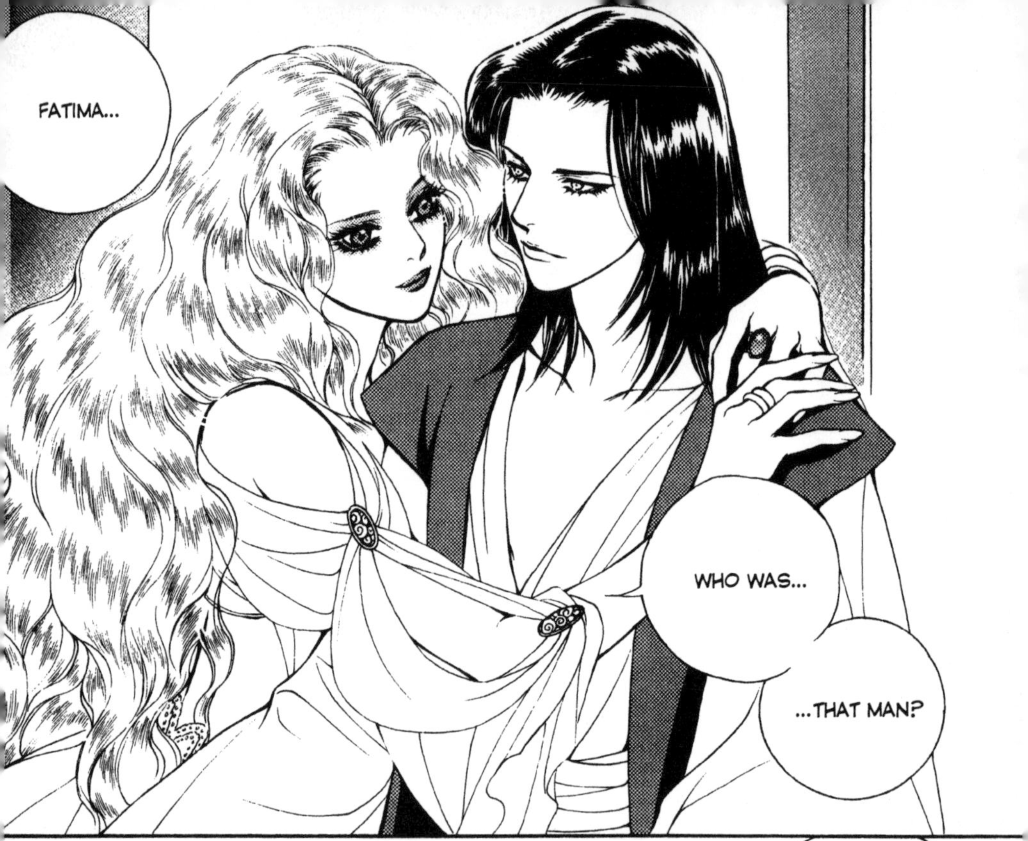
FATIMA...
WHO WAS...
...THAT MAN?
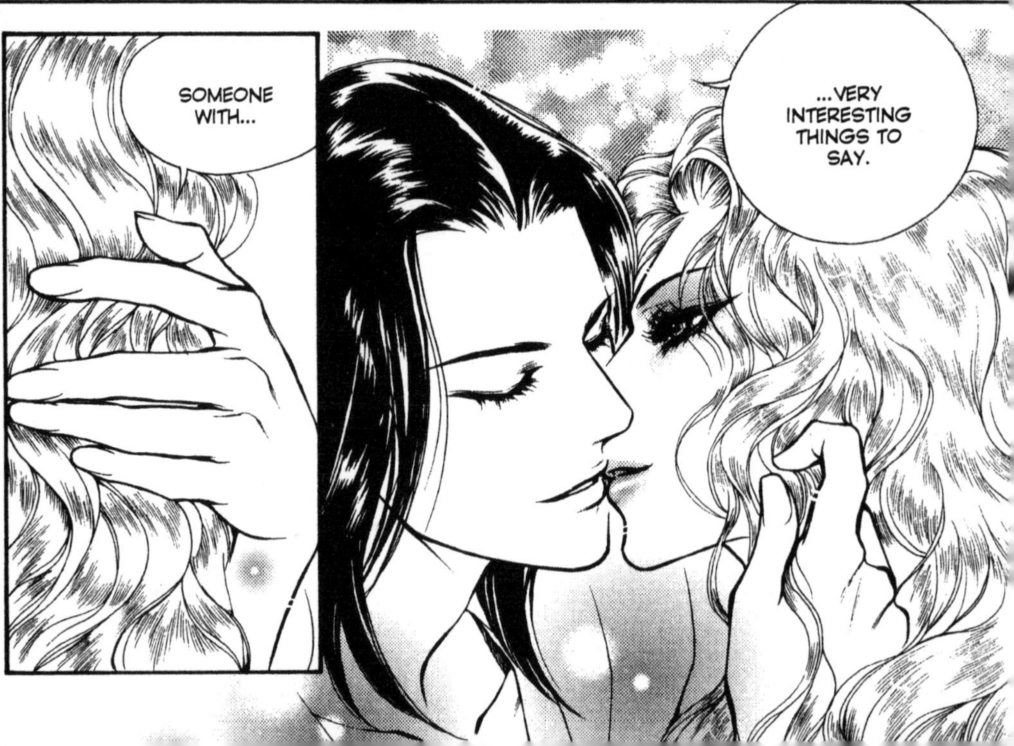
SOMEONE WITH...
...VERY INTERESTING THINGS TO SAY.

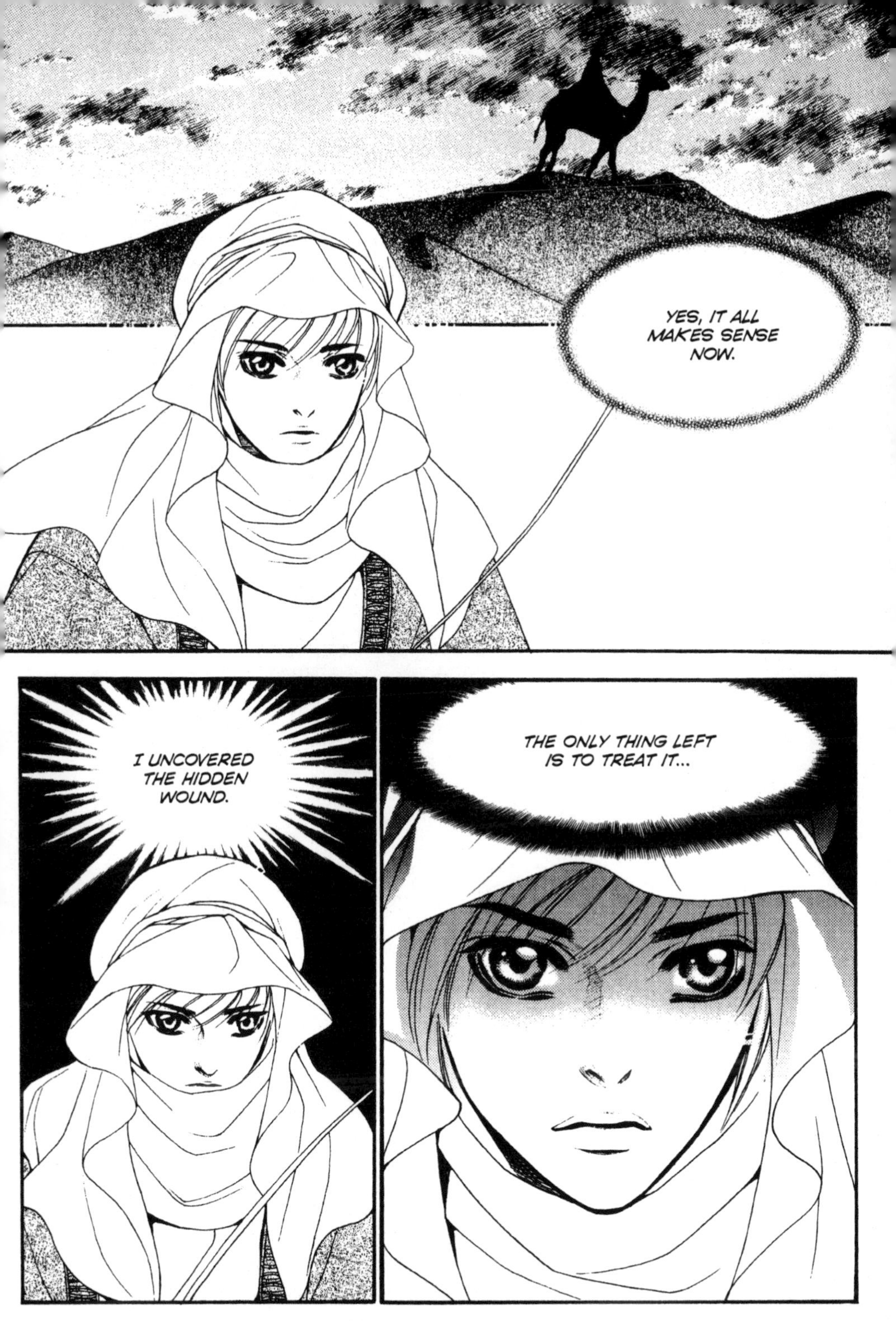
YES, IT ALL MAKES SENSE NOW.
I UNCOVERED THE HIDDEN WOUND.
THE ONLY THING LEFT IS TO TREAT IT...

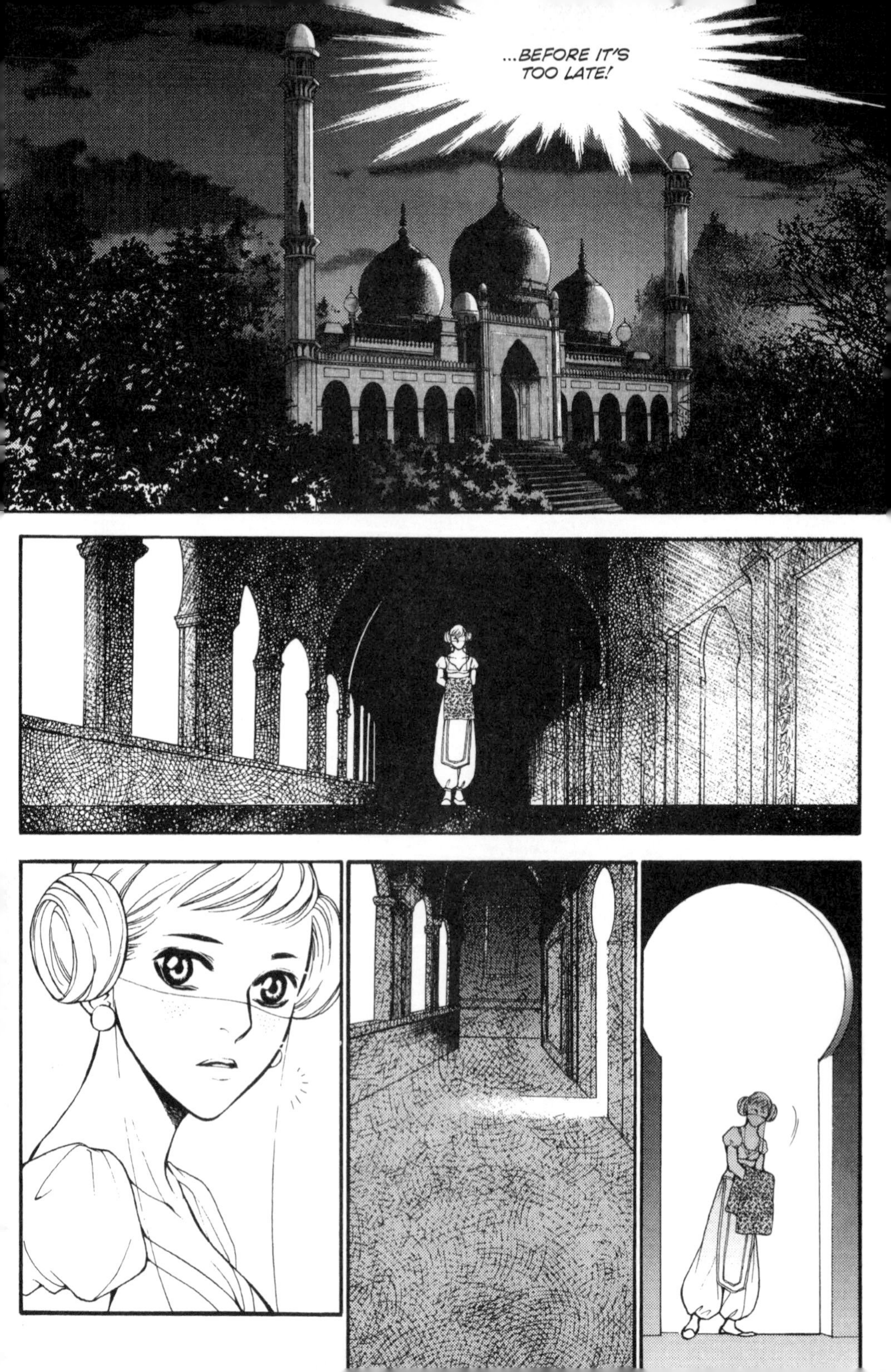
...BEFORE IT'S TOO LATE!

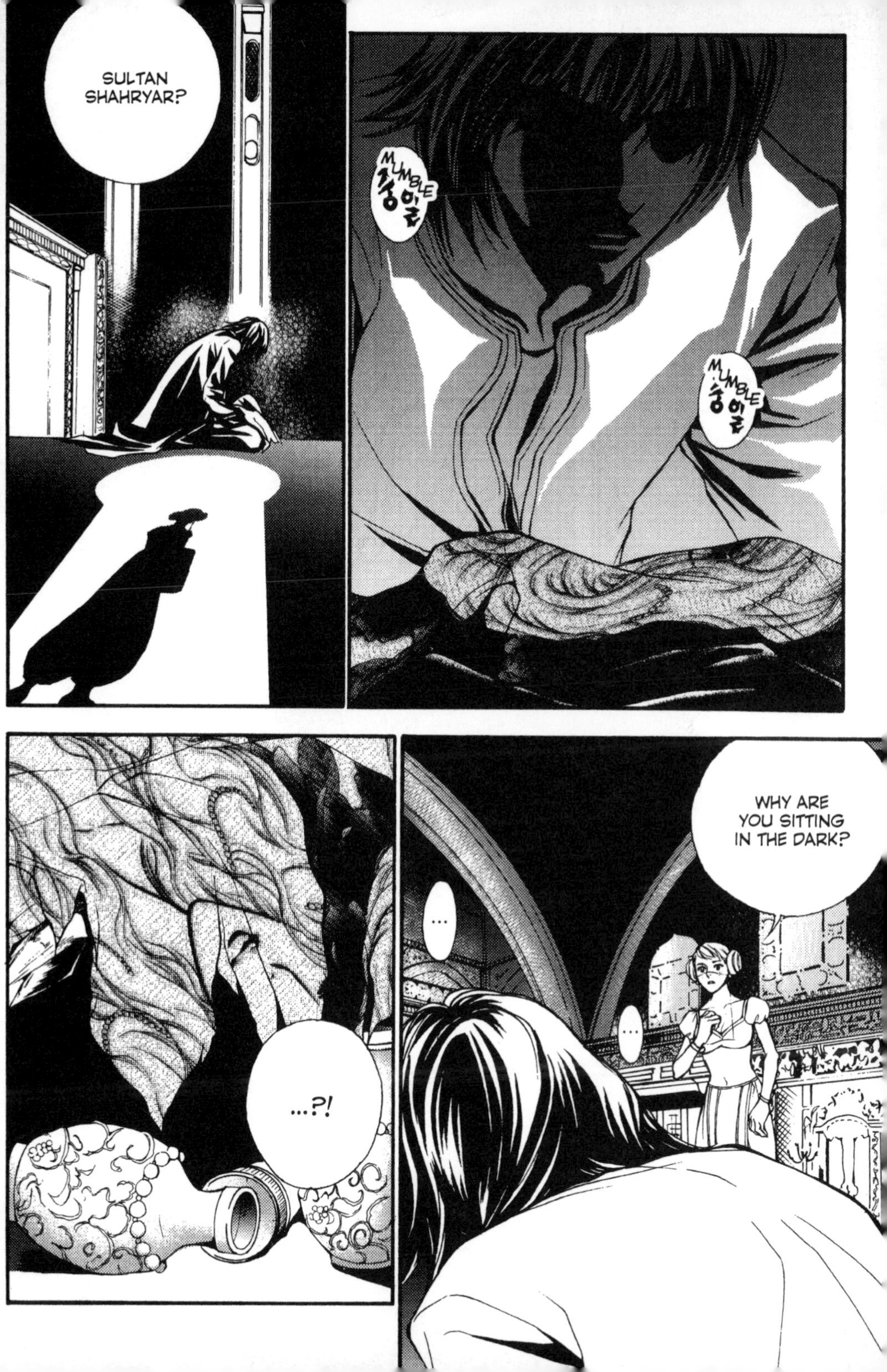
SULTAN SHAHRYAR?
MUMBLE
MUMBLE
...?!
WHY ARE YOU SITTING IN THE DARK?
...
...

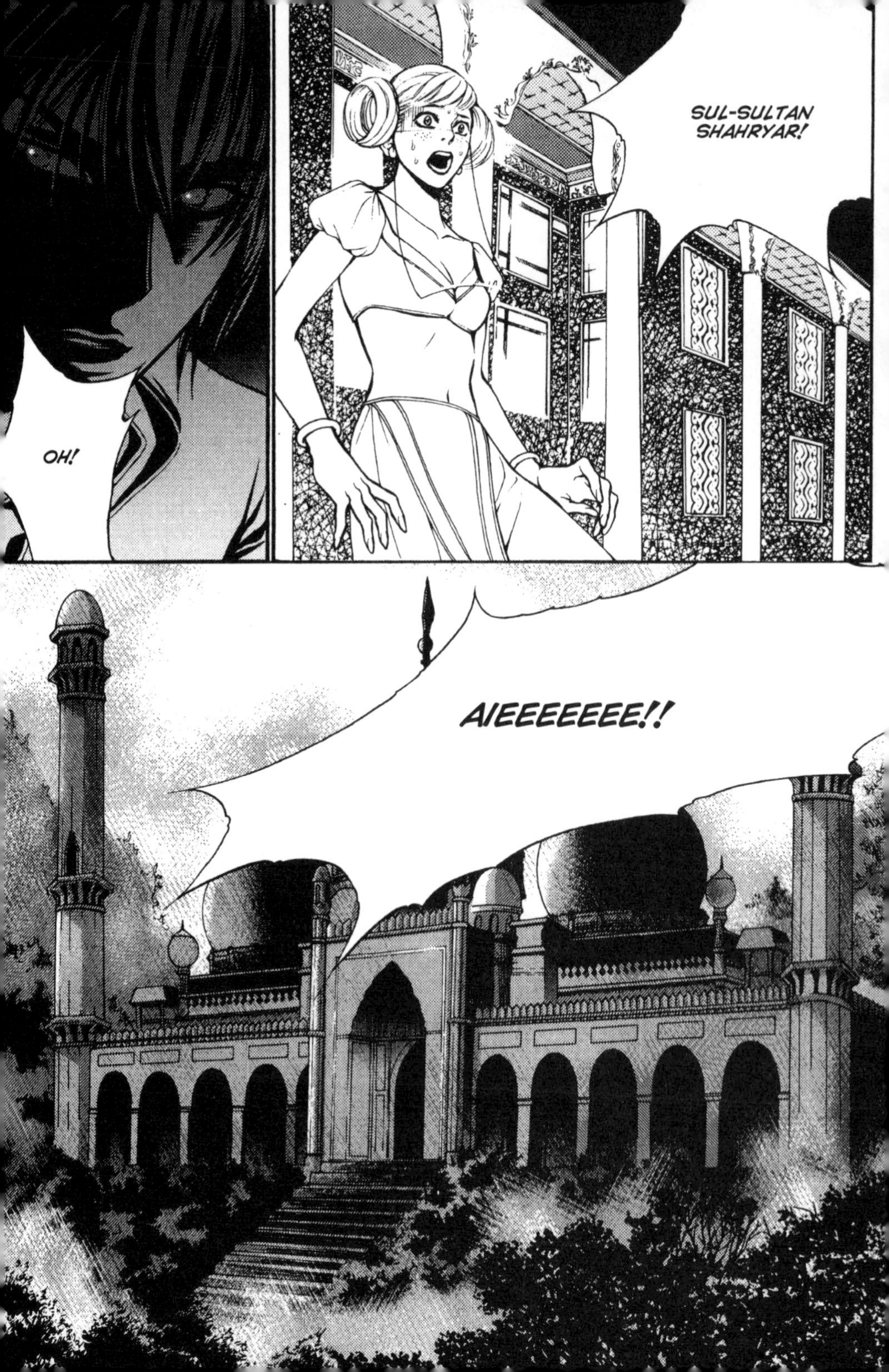
OH!
SUL-SULTAN SHAHRYAR!
AIEEEEEEE!!

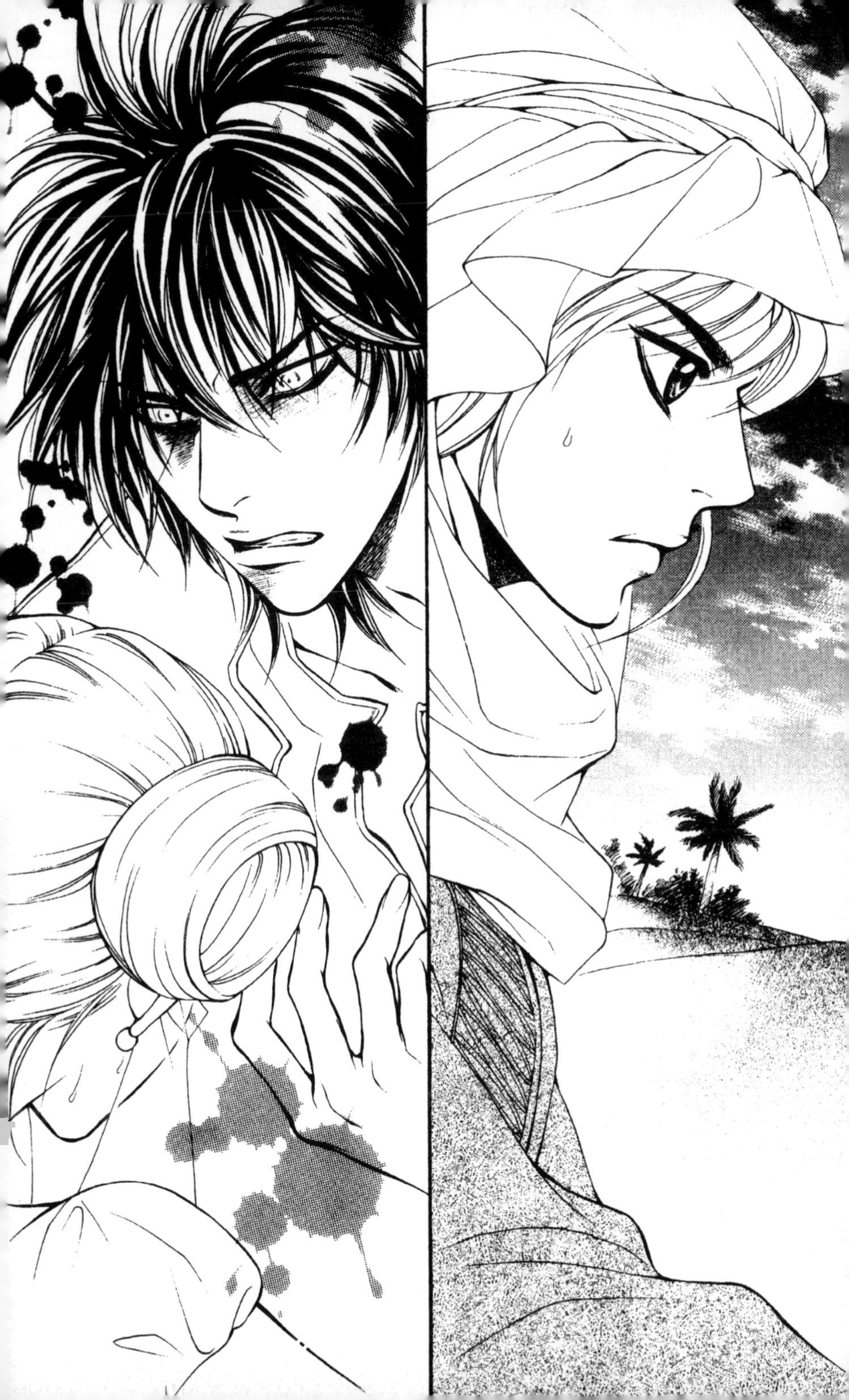

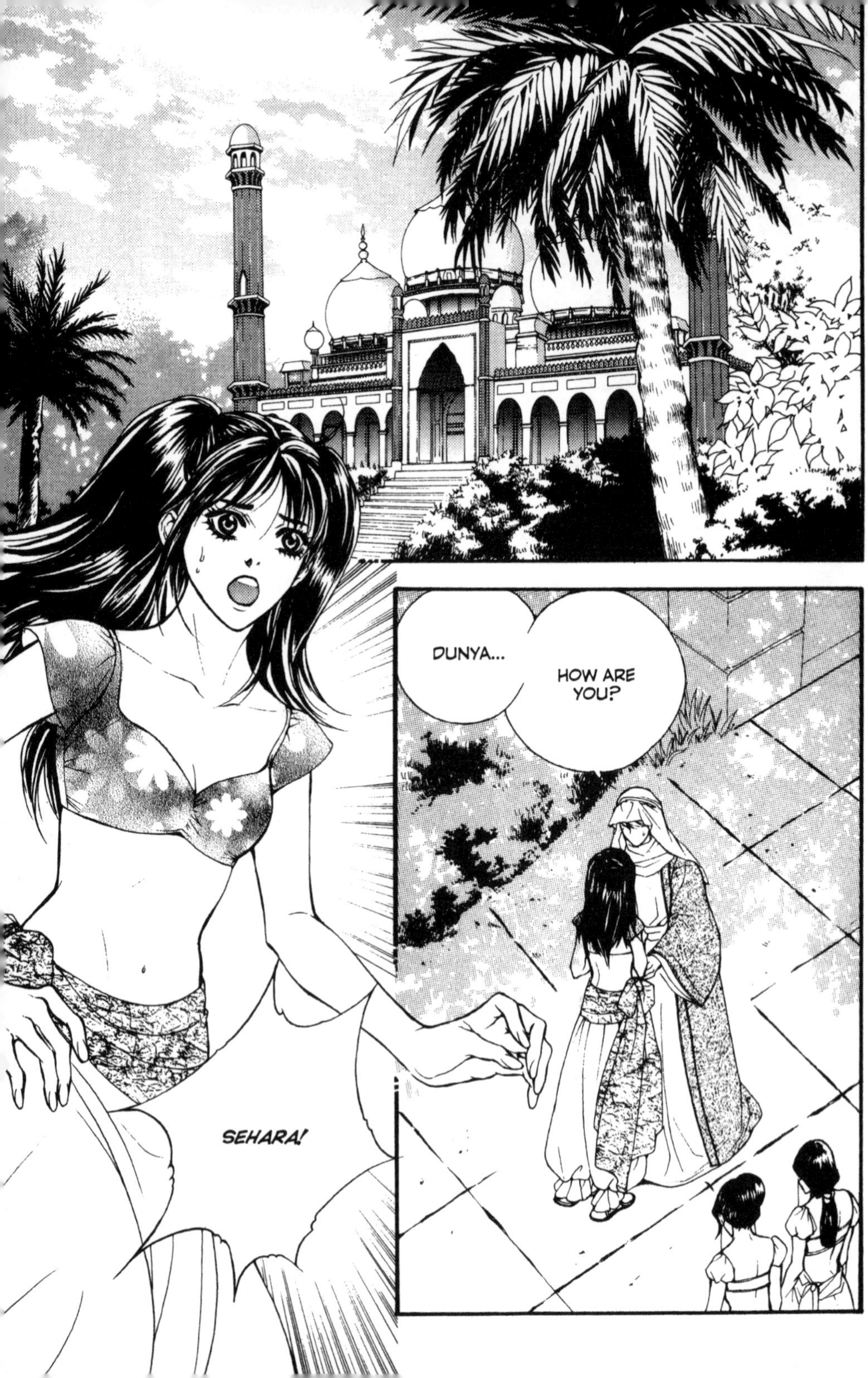
SEHARA!
DUNYA...
HOW ARE YOU?

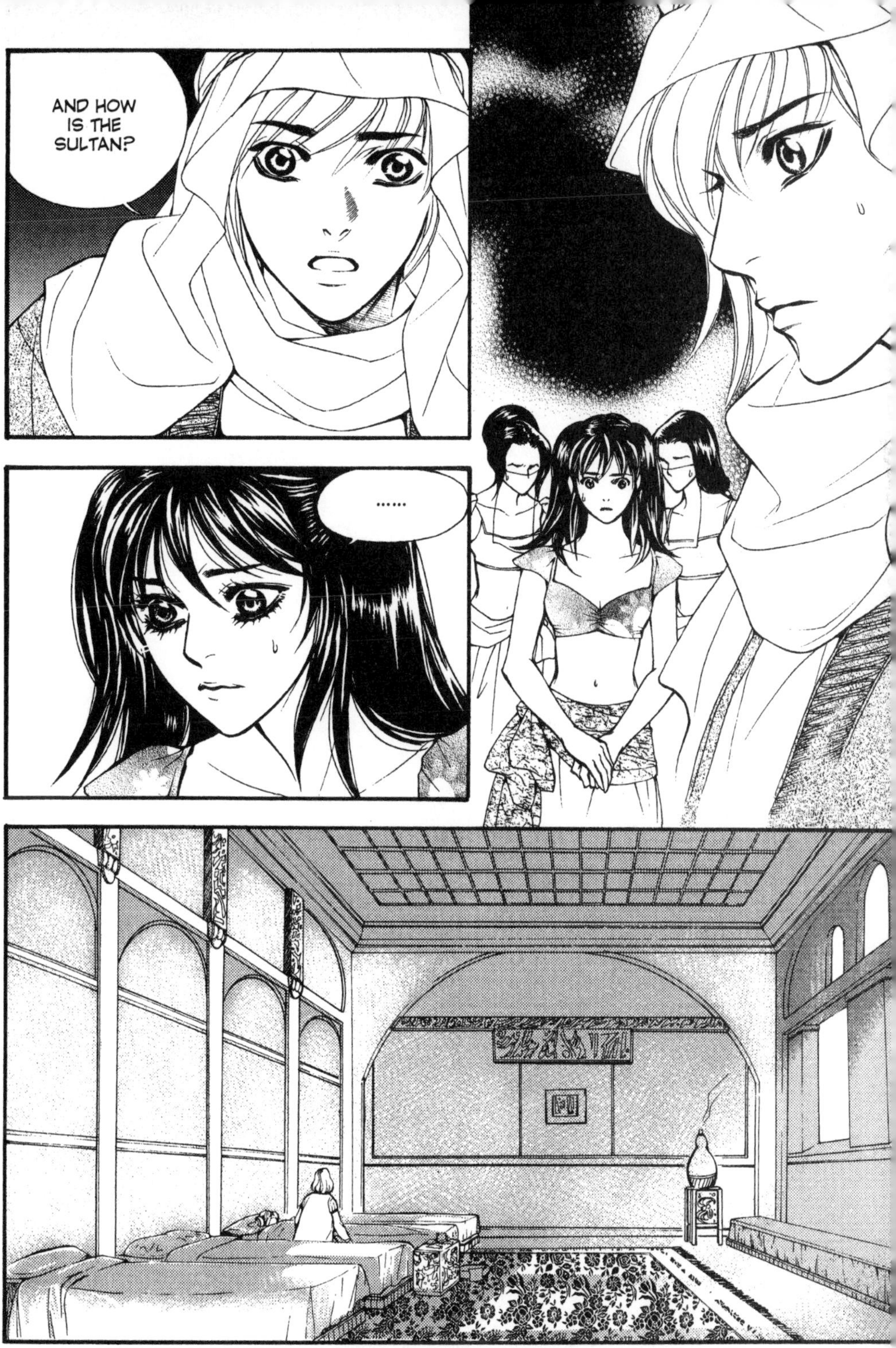
AND HOW IS THE SULTAN?
......

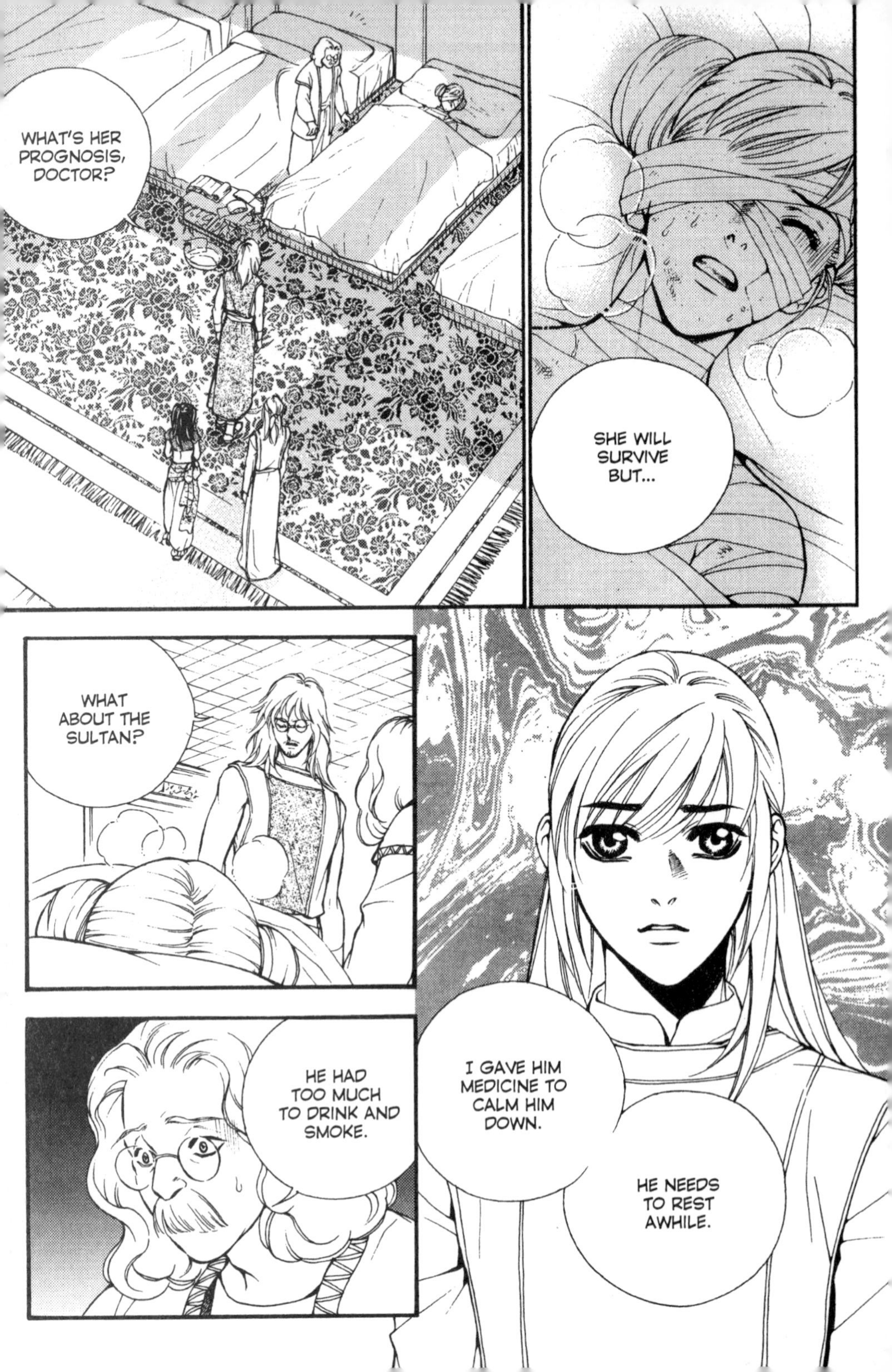
WHAT'S HER PROGNOSIS, DOCTOR?
SHE WILL SURVIVE BUT...
WHAT ABOUT THE SULTAN?
HE HAD TOO MUCH TO DRINK AND SMOKE.
I GAVE HIM MEDICINE TO CALM HIM DOWN.
HE NEEDS TO REST AWHILE.

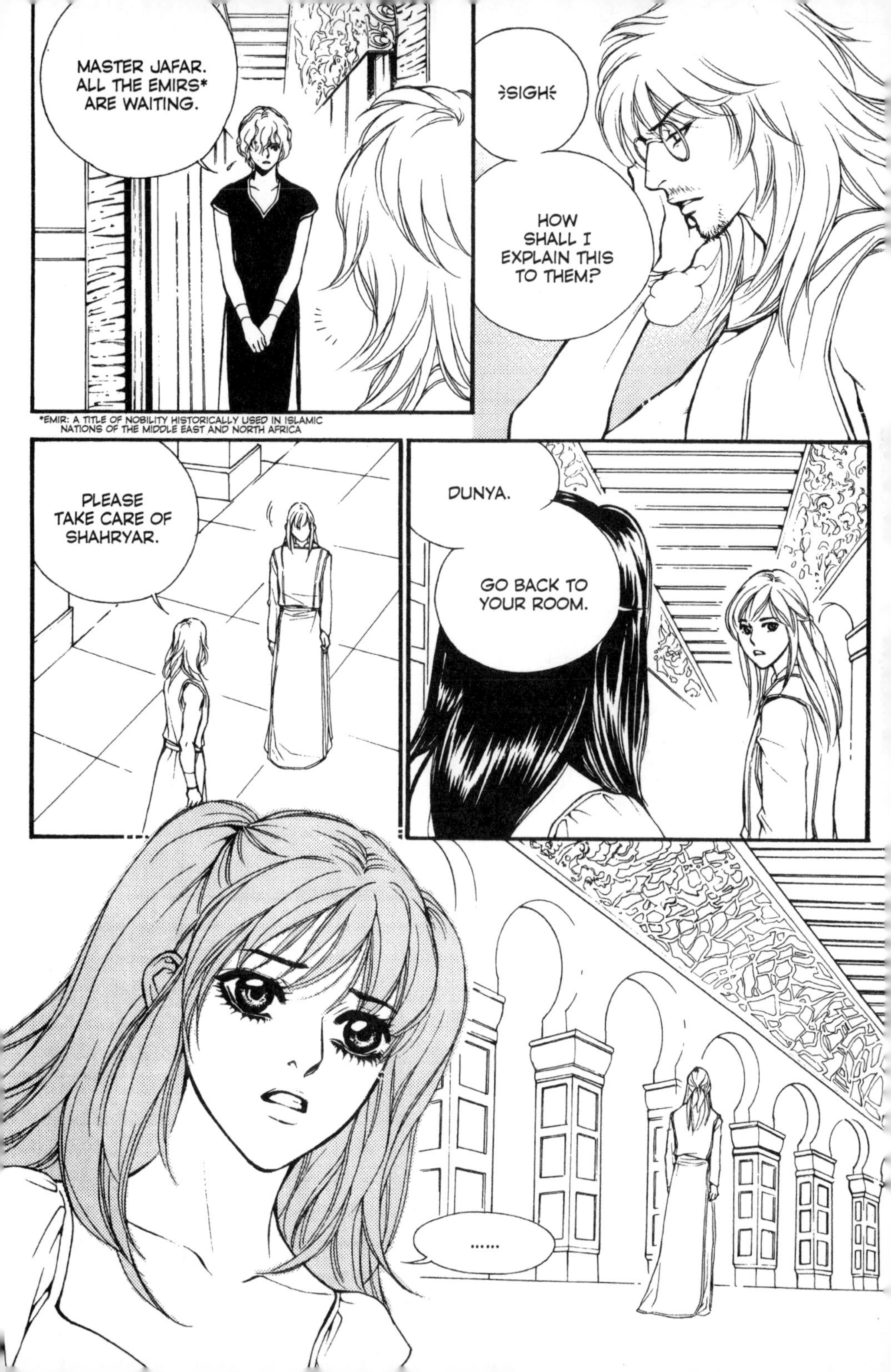
MASTER JAFAR. ALL THE EMIRS* ARE WAITING.
SIGH
HOW SHALL I EXPLAIN THIS TO THEM?
*EMIR: A TITLE OF NOBILITY HISTORICALLY USED IN ISLAMIC NATIONS OF THE MIDDLE EAST AND NORTH AFRICA
PLEASE TAKE CARE OF SHAHRYAR.
DUNYA.
GO BACK TO YOUR ROOM.
......

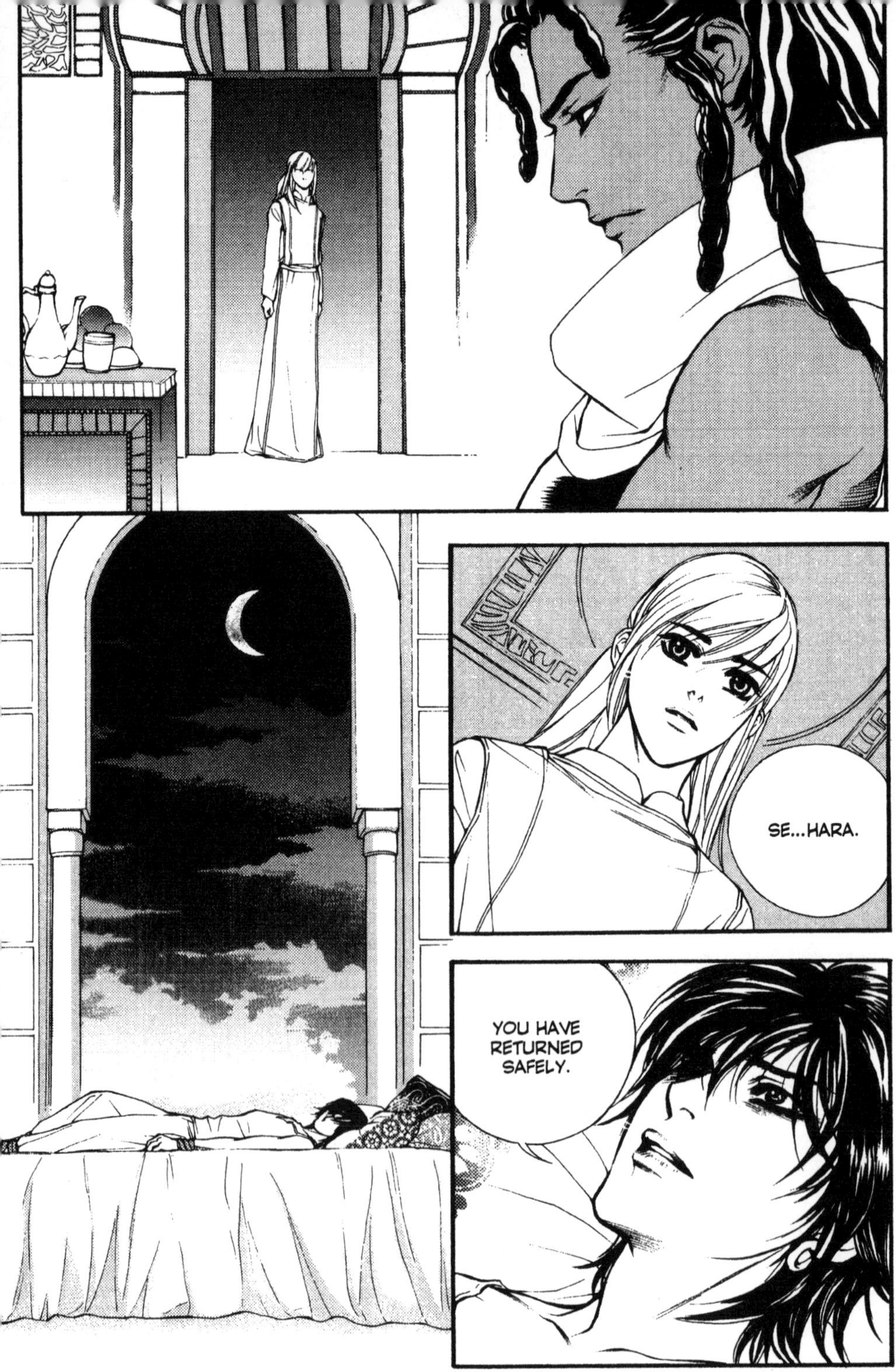
SE...HARA.
YOU HAVE RETURNED SAFELY.

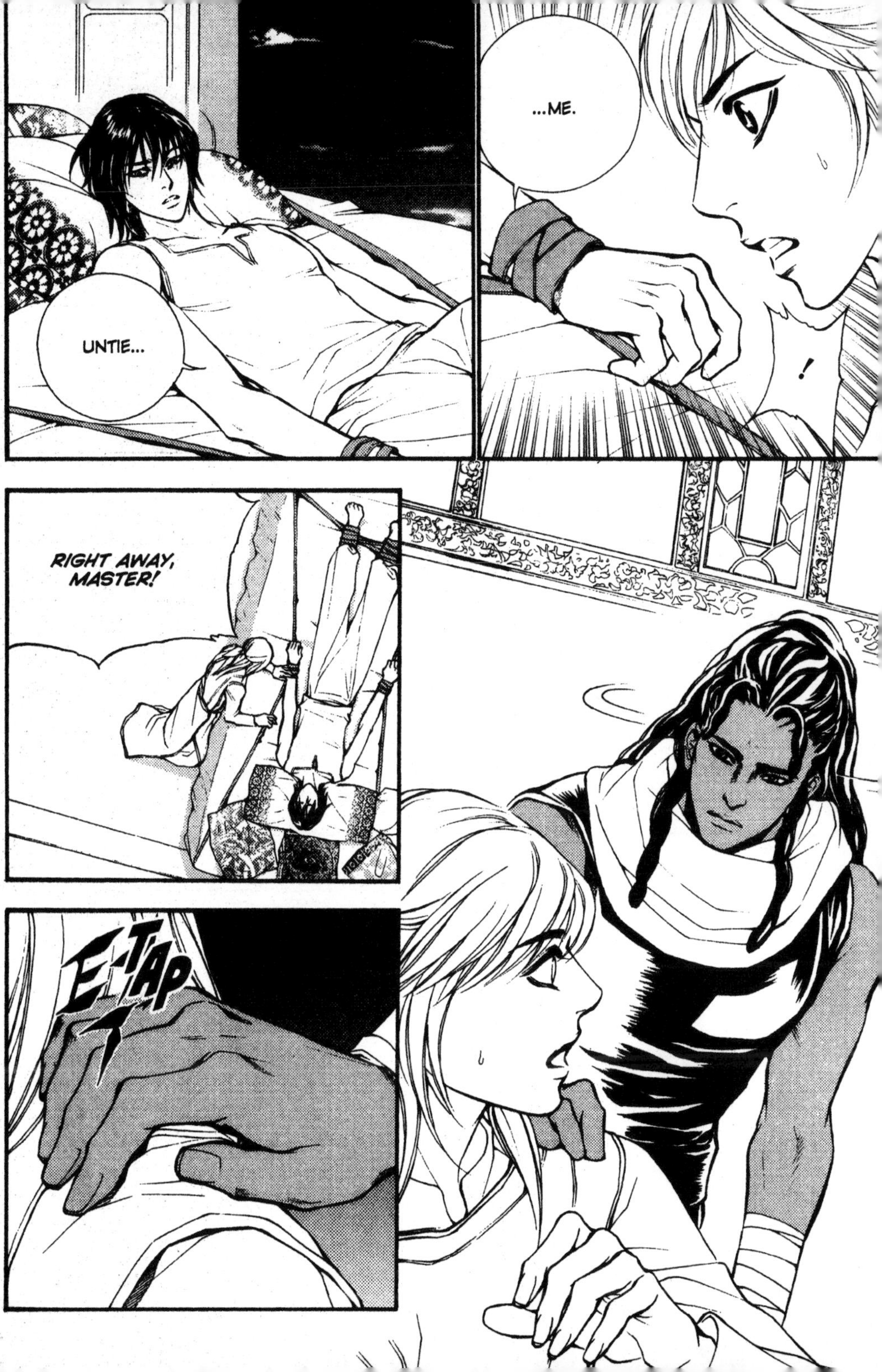
UNTIE...
...ME.
!
RIGHT AWAY, MASTER!
TAP

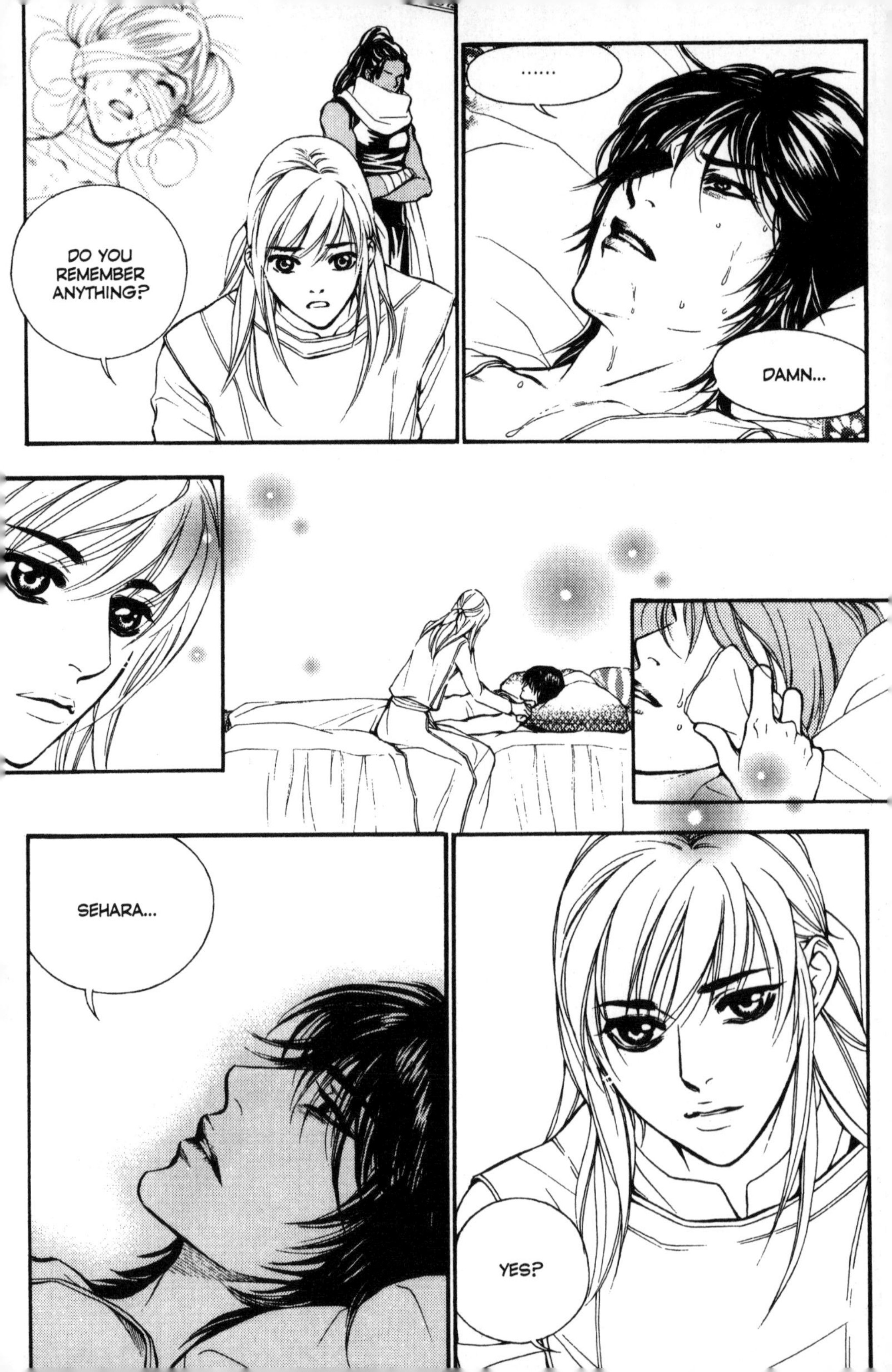
DO YOU REMEMBER ANYTHING?
....
DAMN...
SEHARA...
YES?

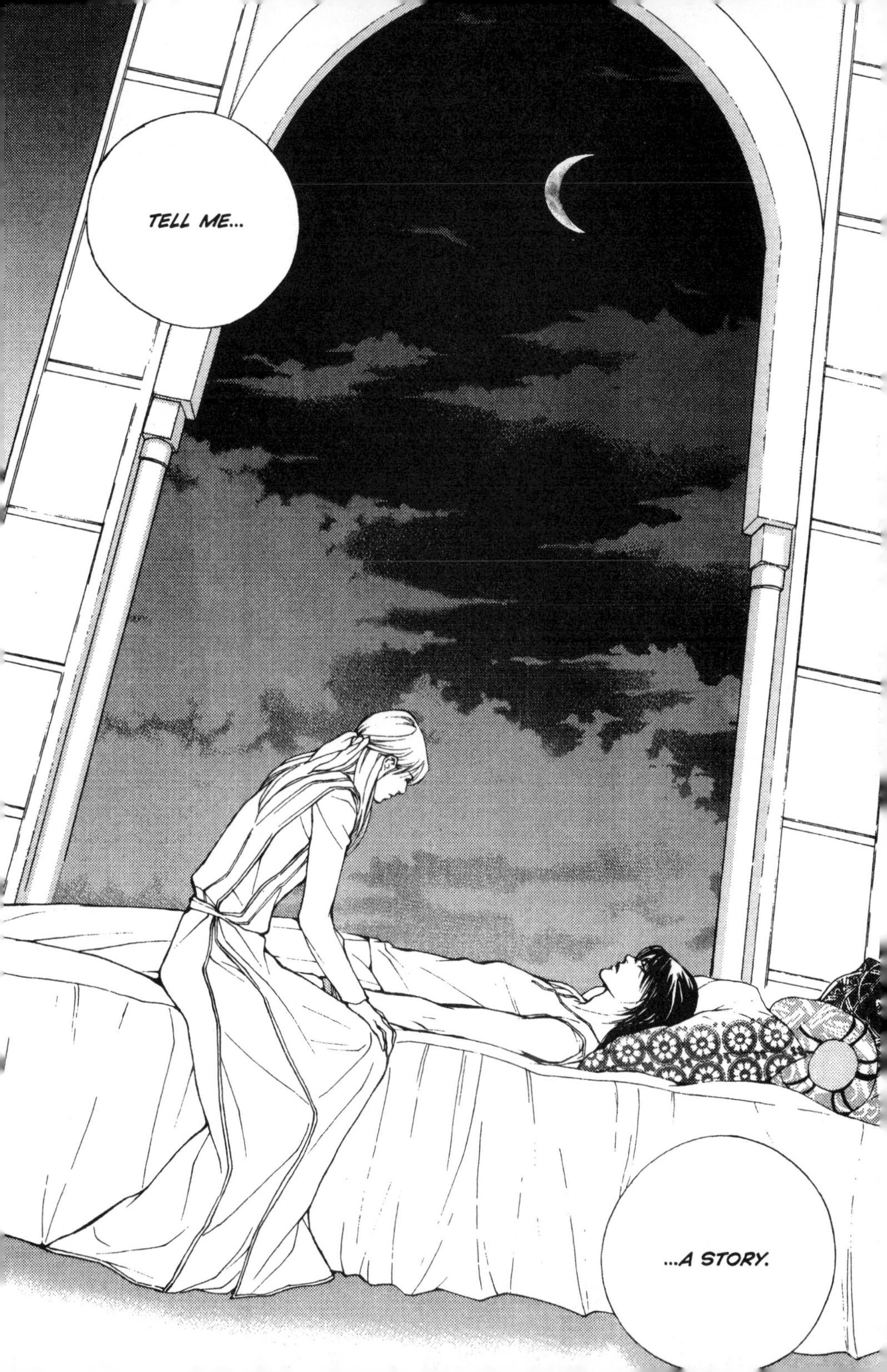
TELL ME...
...A STORY.

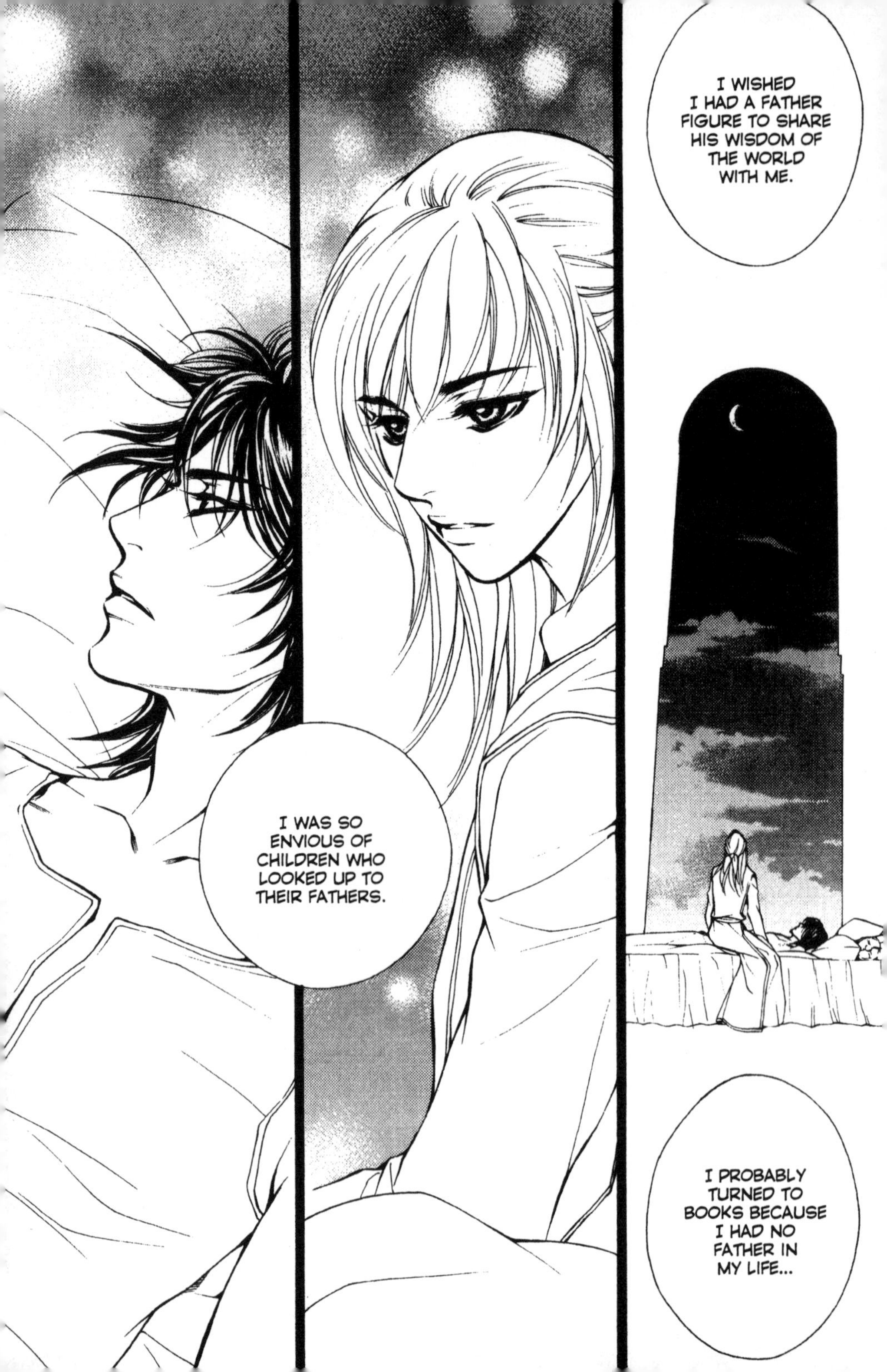
I WAS SO ENVIOUS OF CHILDREN WHO LOOKED UP TO THEIR FATHERS.
I WISHED I HAD A FATHER FIGURE TO SHARE HIS WISDOM OF THE WORLD WITH ME.
I PROBABLY TURNED TO BOOKS BECAUSE I HAD NO FATHER IN MY LIFE...

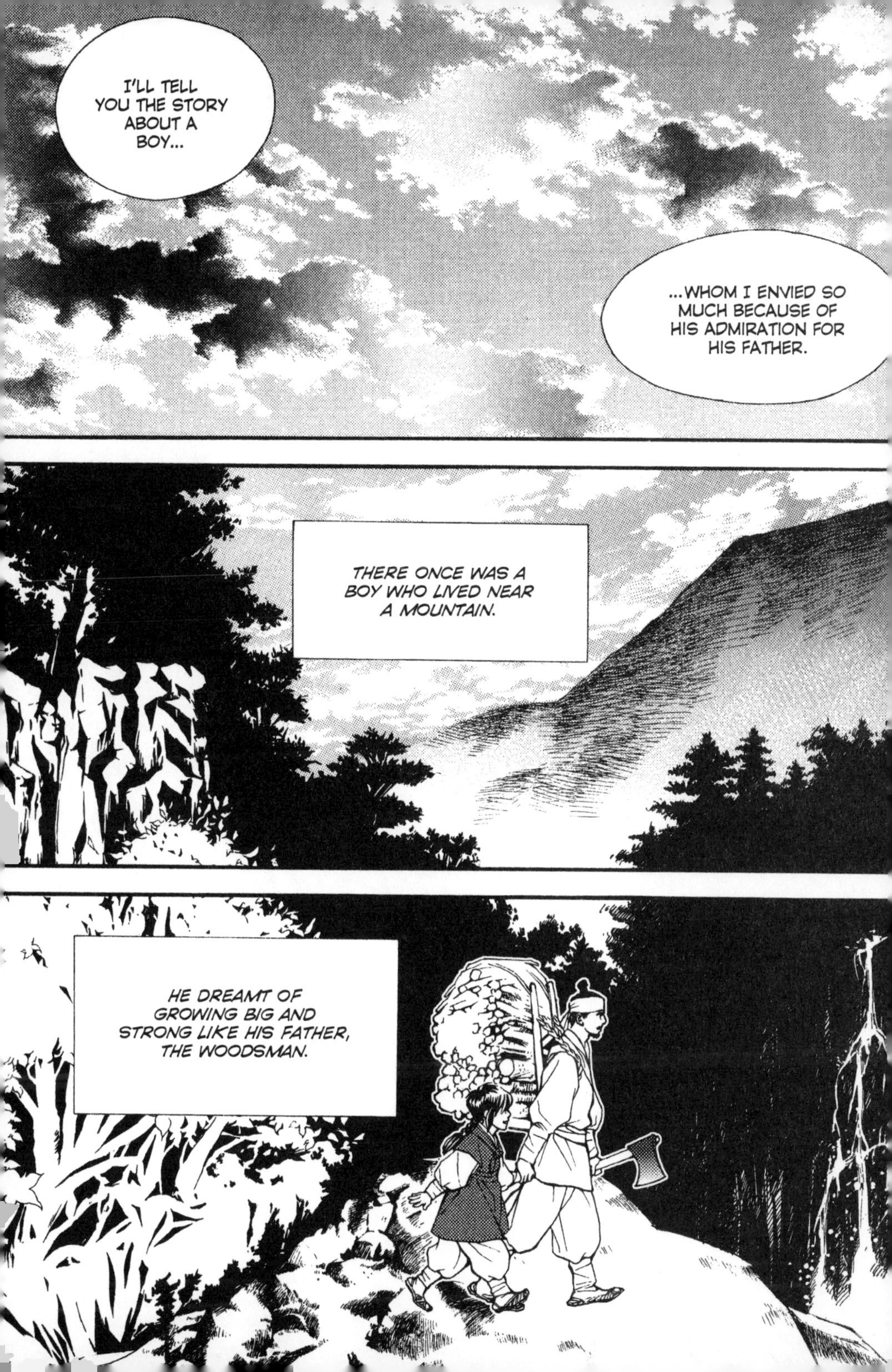
I'LL TELL YOU THE STORY ABOUT A BOY...
...WHOM I ENVIED SO MUCH BECAUSE OF HIS ADMIRATION FOR HIS FATHER.
THERE ONCE WAS A BOY WHO LIVED NEAR A MOUNTAIN.
HE DREAMT OF GROWING BIG AND STRONG LIKE HIS FATHER, THE WOODSMAN.

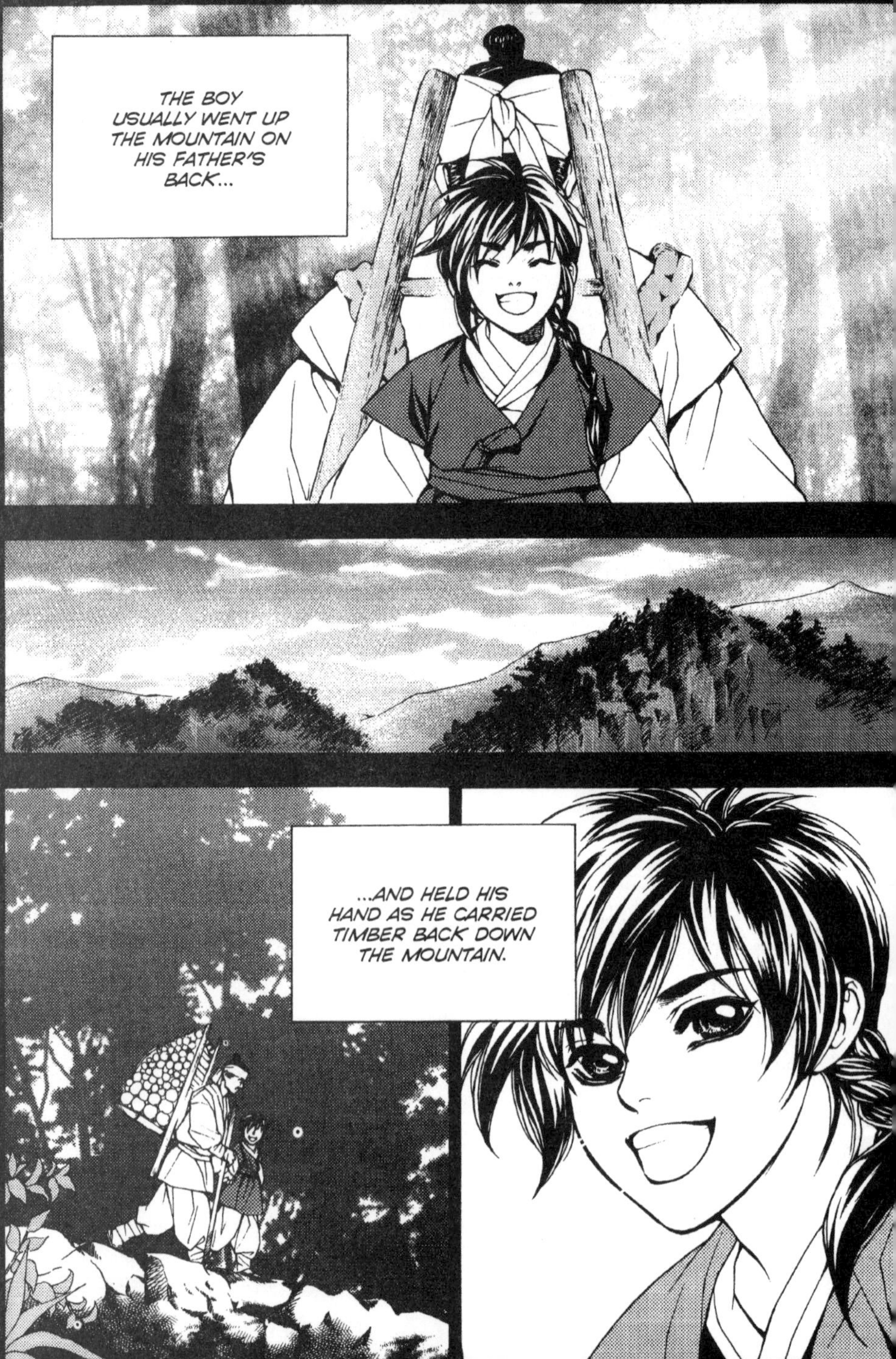
THE BOY USUALLY WENT UP THE MOUNTAIN ON HIS FATHER'S BACK...
...AND HELD HIS HAND AS HE CARRIED TIMBER BACK DOWN THE MOUNTAIN.

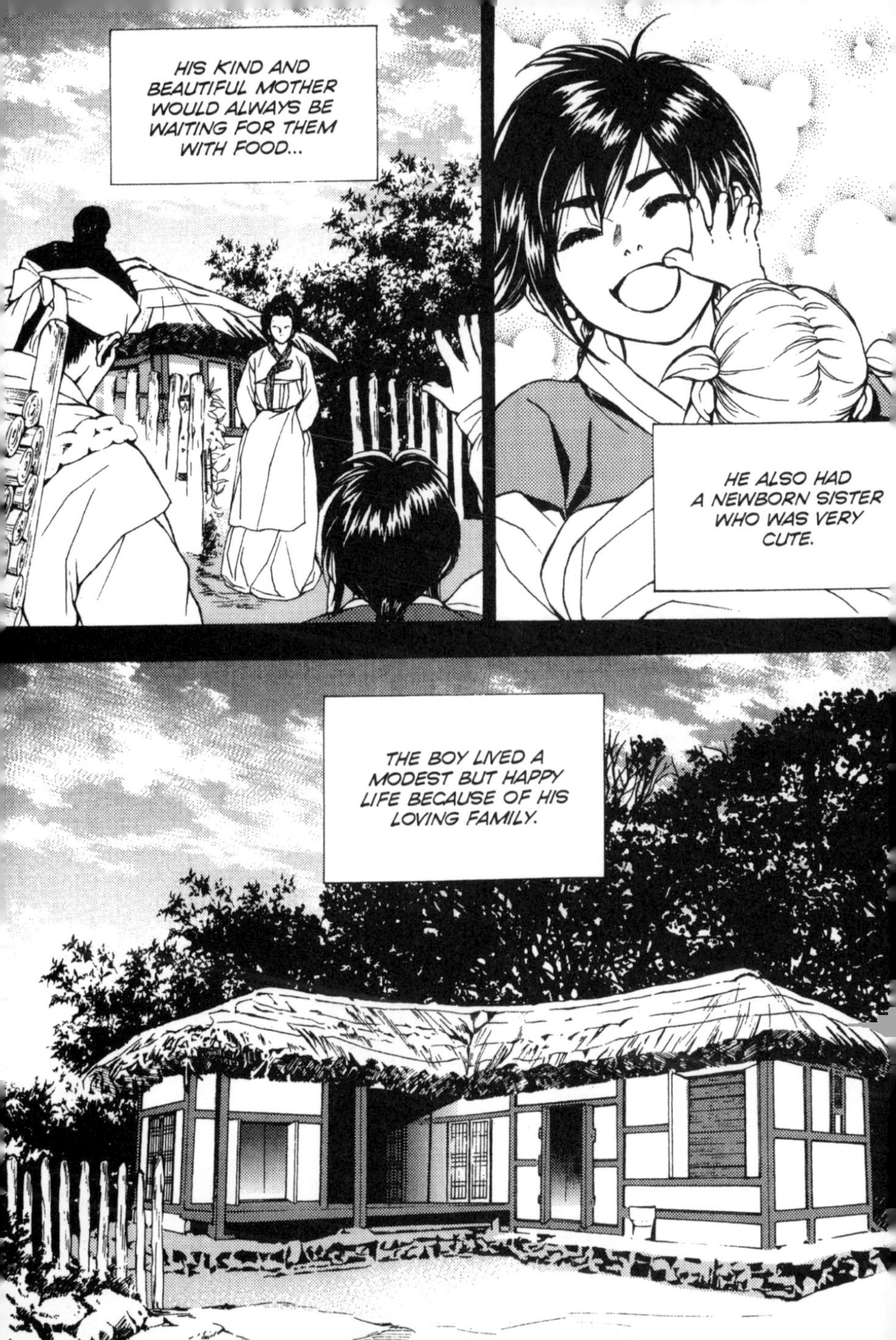
HIS KIND AND BEAUTIFUL MOTHER WOULD ALWAYS BE WAITING FOR THEM WITH FOOD...
HE ALSO HAD A NEWBORN SISTER WHO WAS VERY CUTE.
THE BOY LIVED A MODEST BUT HAPPY LIFE BECAUSE OF HIS LOVING FAMILY.

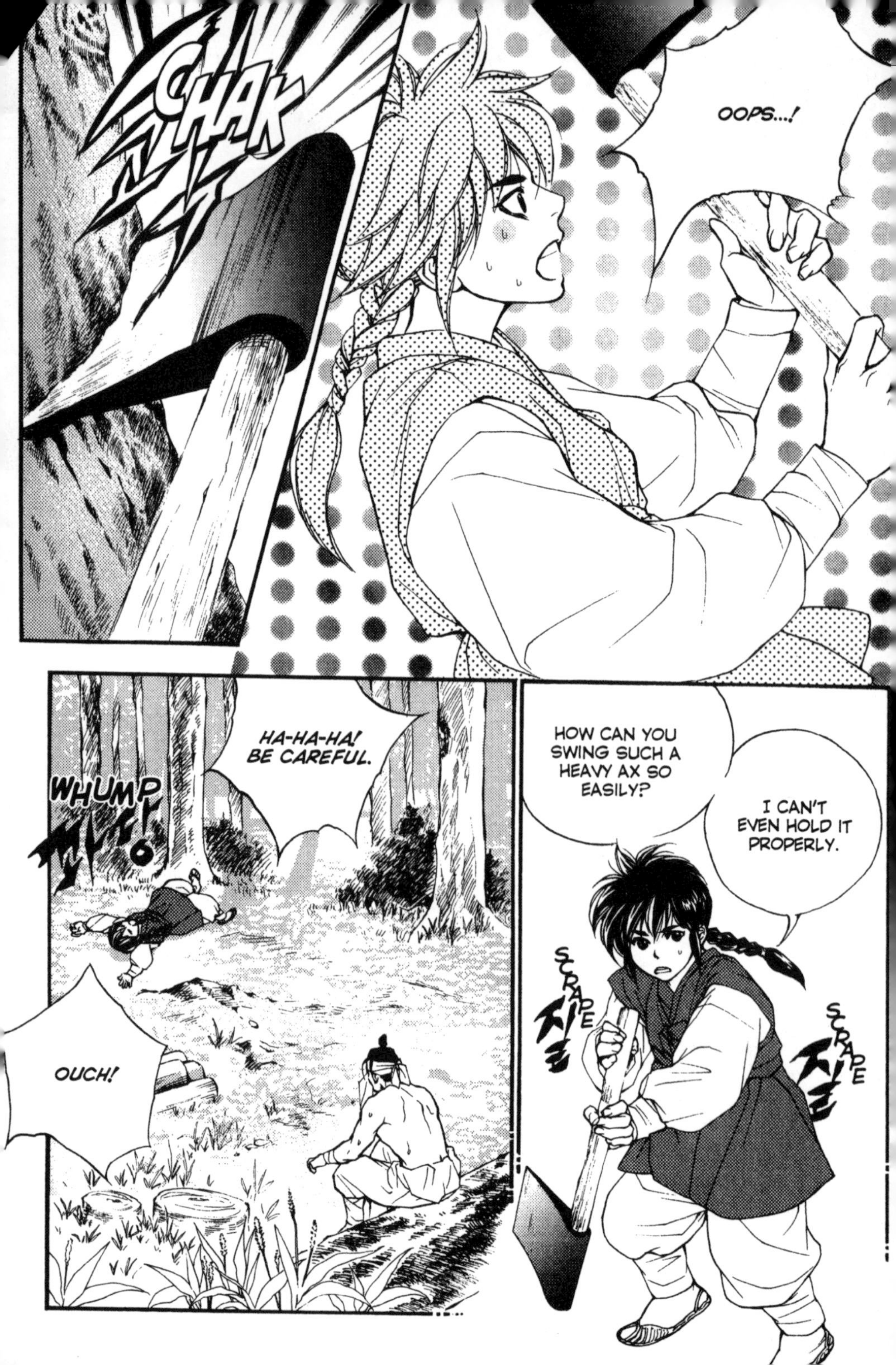
CHAK
OOPS...!
HA-HA-HA! BE CAREFUL.
WHUMP
OUCH!
HOW CAN YOU SWING SUCH A HEAVY AX SO EASILY?
I CAN'T EVEN HOLD IT PROPERLY.
SCRAPE
SCRAPE

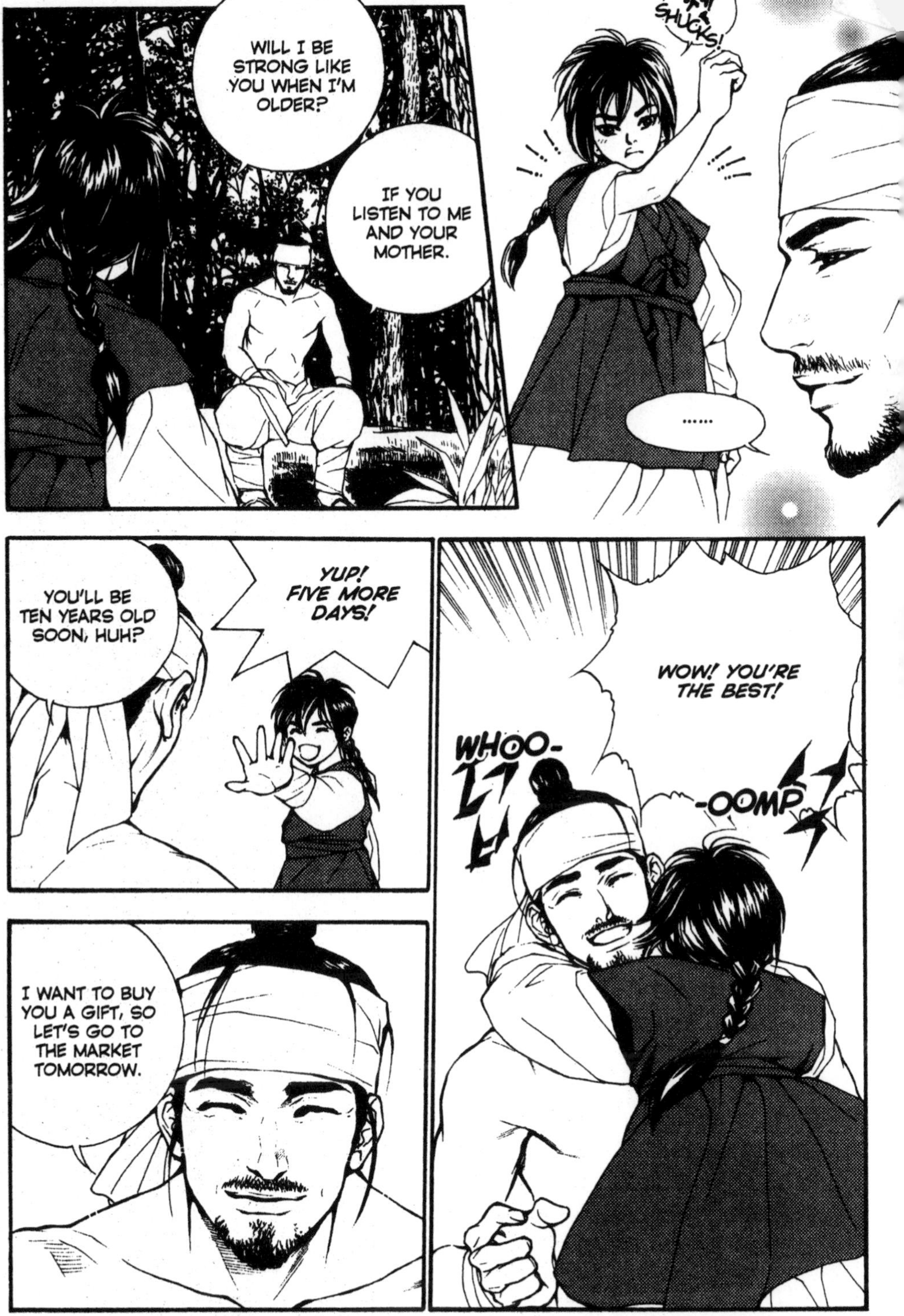
WILL I BE STRONG LIKE YOU WHEN I'M OLDER?
IF YOU LISTEN TO ME AND YOUR MOTHER.
SHUCKS!
......
YOU'LL BE TEN YEARS OLD SOON, HUH?
YUP! FIVE MORE DAYS!
I WANT TO BUY YOU A GIFT, SO LET'S GO TO THE MARKET TOMORROW.
WOW! YOU'RE THE BEST!
WHOO-
-OOMP

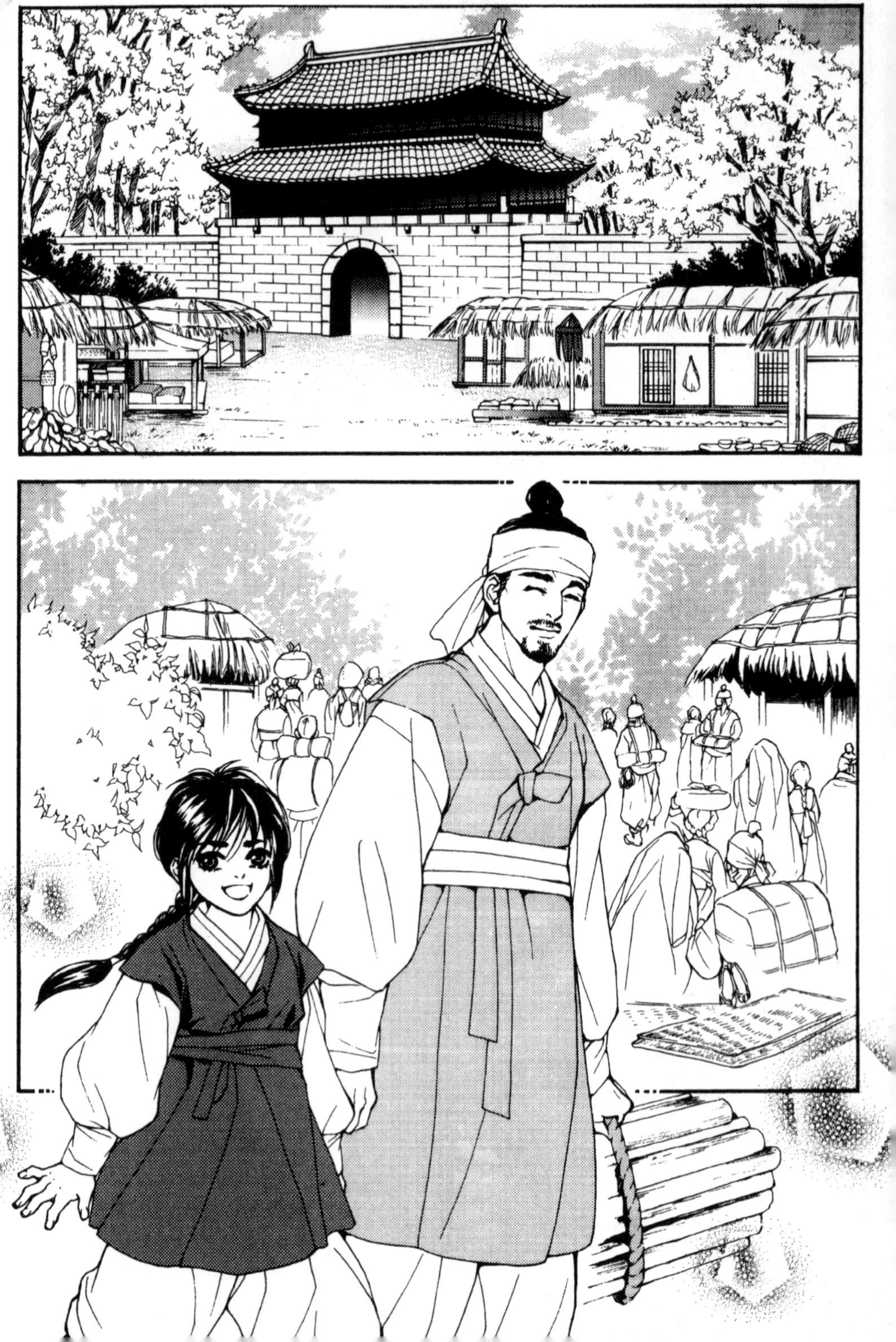

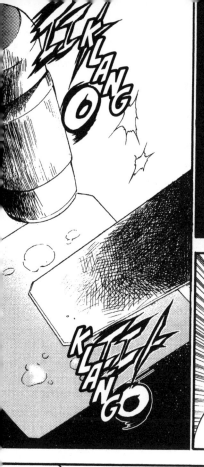

WOW!

LOOK AT YOU! SO BIG NOW!

HERE.

HUZZAH!

THIS IS THE BEST KIND OF WOOD FOR AN AX HANDLE...

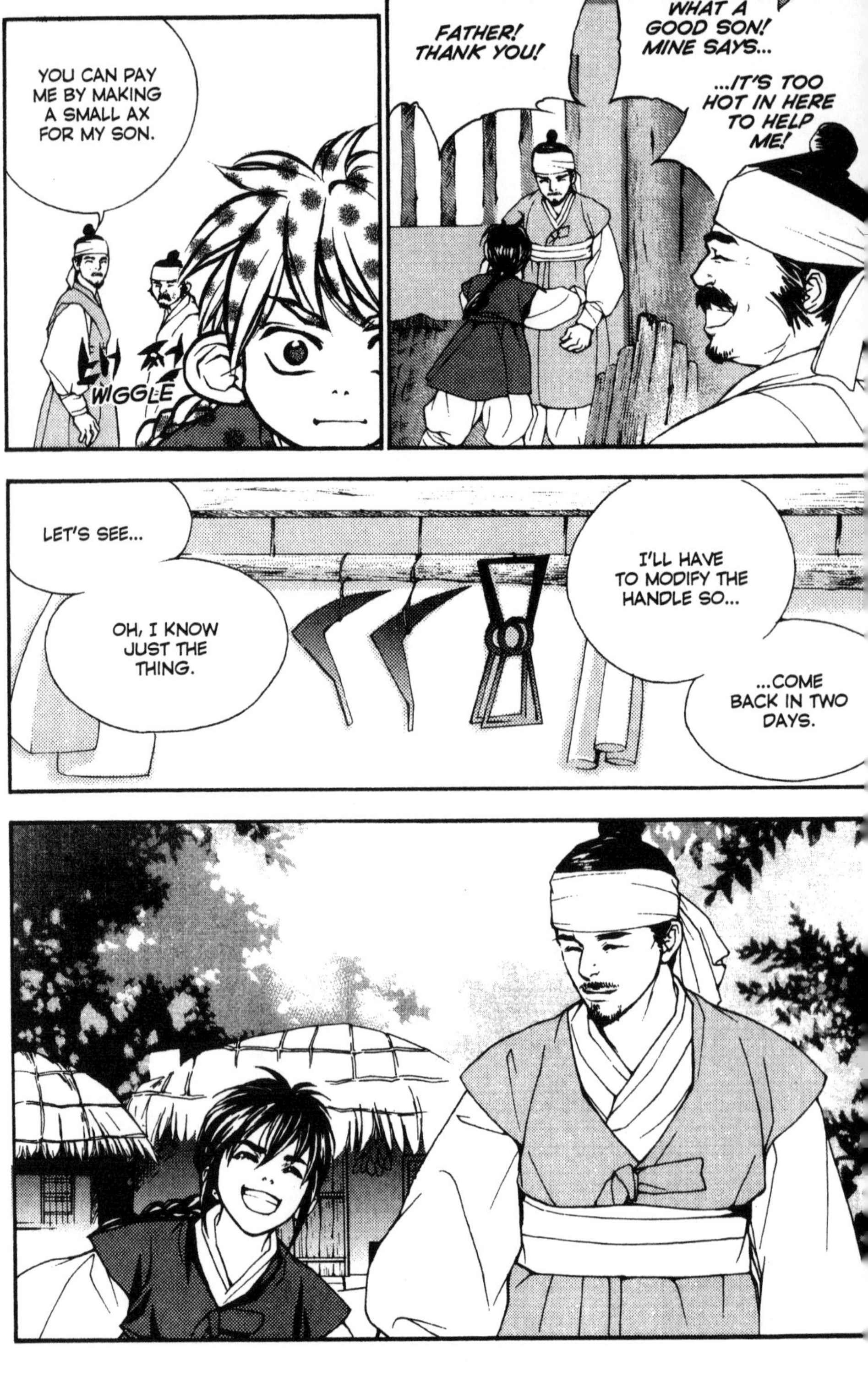
YOU CAN PAY ME BY MAKING A SMALL AX FOR MY SON.
WIGGLE
FATHER! THANK YOU!
WHAT A GOOD SON! MINE SAYS...
...IT'S TOO HOT IN HERE TO HELP ME!
LET'S SEE...
OH, I KNOW JUST THE THING.
I'LL HAVE TO MODIFY THE HANDLE SO...
...COME BACK IN TWO DAYS.

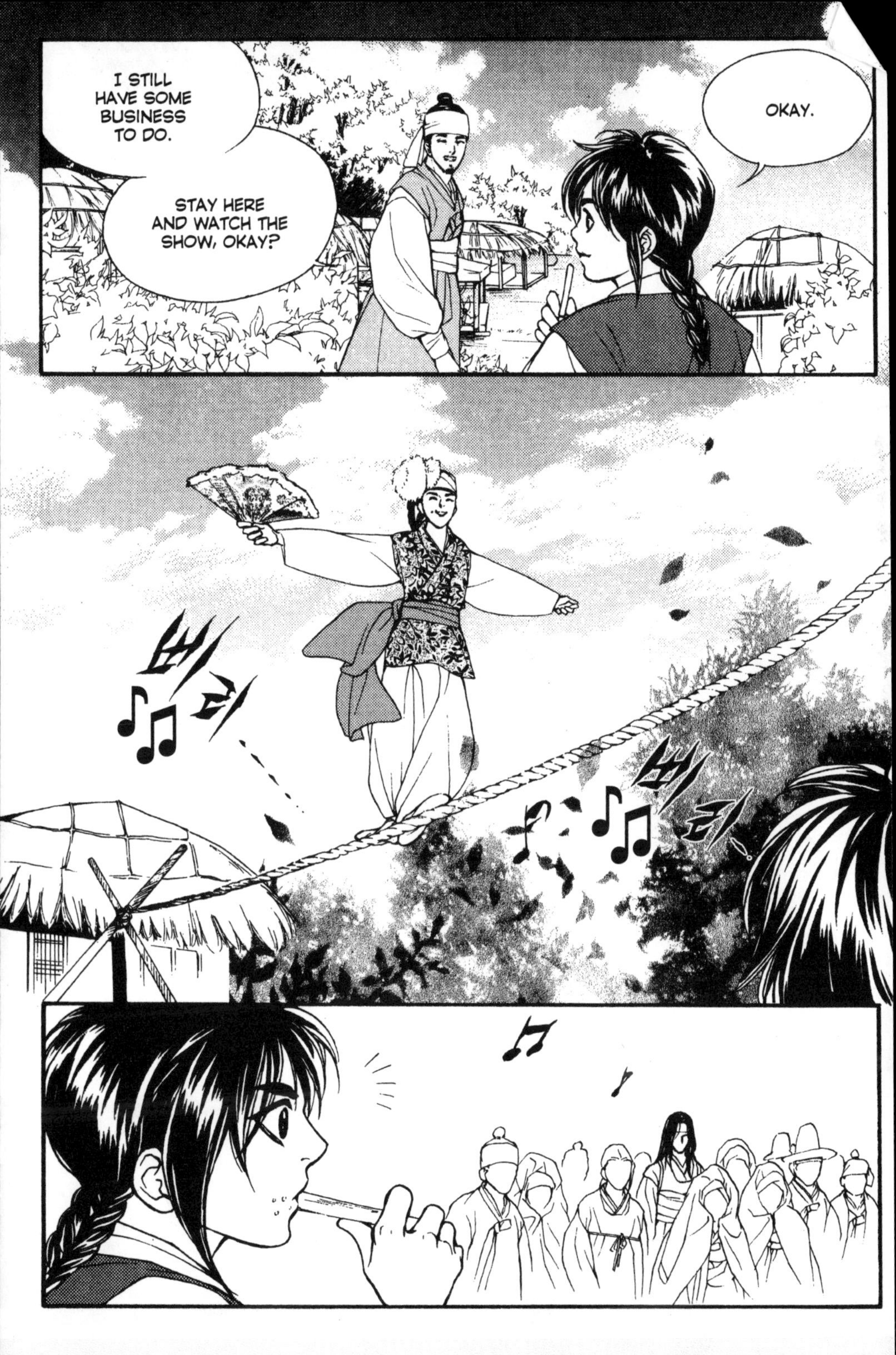
I STILL HAVE SOME BUSINESS TO DO.
STAY HERE AND WATCH THE SHOW, OKAY?
OKAY.
삐리
삐리

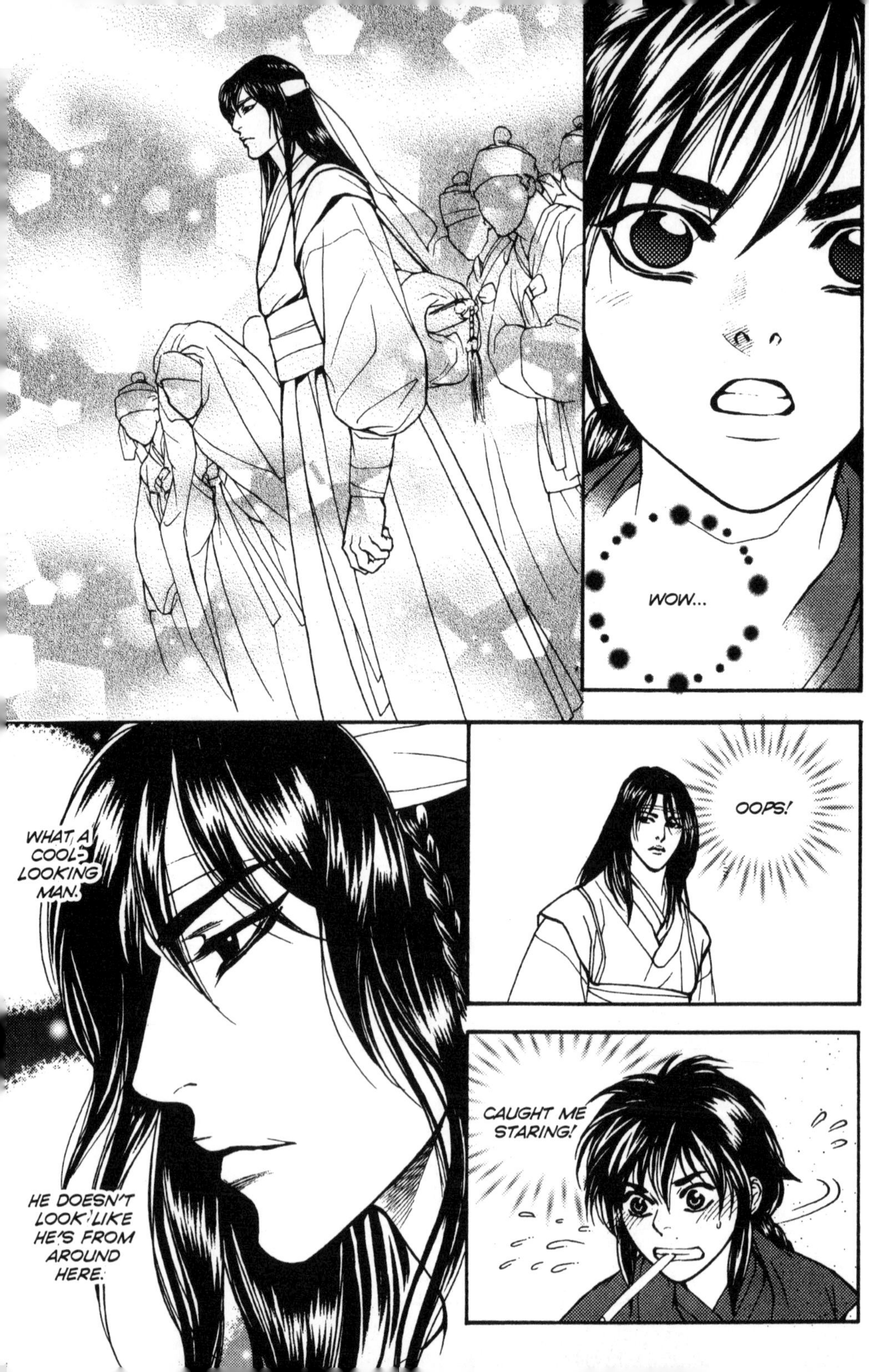
WOW...
WHAT A COOL-LOOKING MAN.
HE DOESN'T LOOK LIKE HE'S FROM AROUND HERE.
OOPS!
CAUGHT ME STARING!

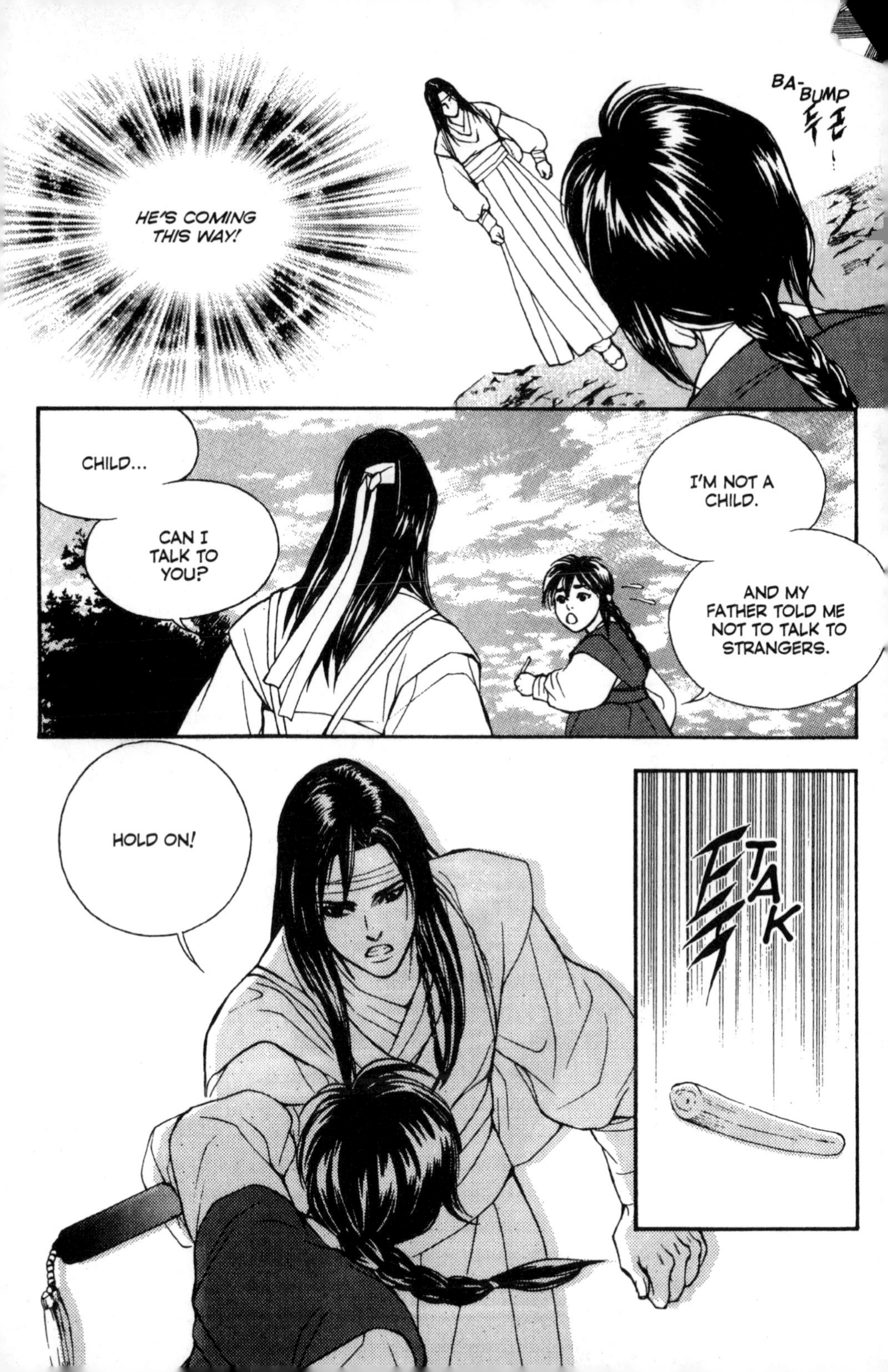
HE'S COMING THIS WAY!
BA-BUMP
두근
CHILD...
CAN I TALK TO YOU?
I'M NOT A CHILD.
AND MY FATHER TOLD ME NOT TO TALK TO STRANGERS.
HOLD ON!
TAK

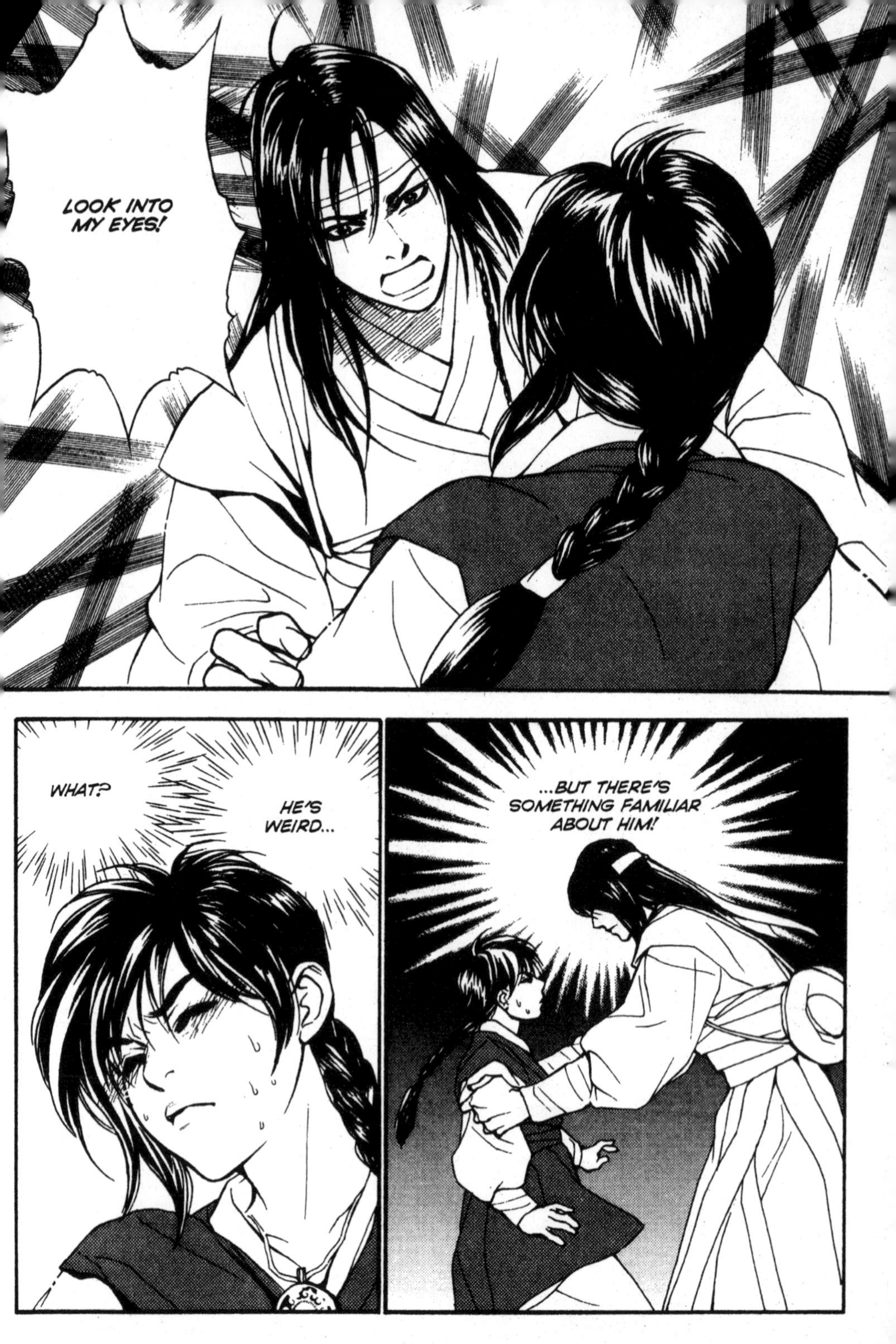
LOOK INTO MY EYES!
WHAT?
HE'S WEIRD...
...BUT THERE'S SOMETHING FAMILIAR ABOUT HIM!

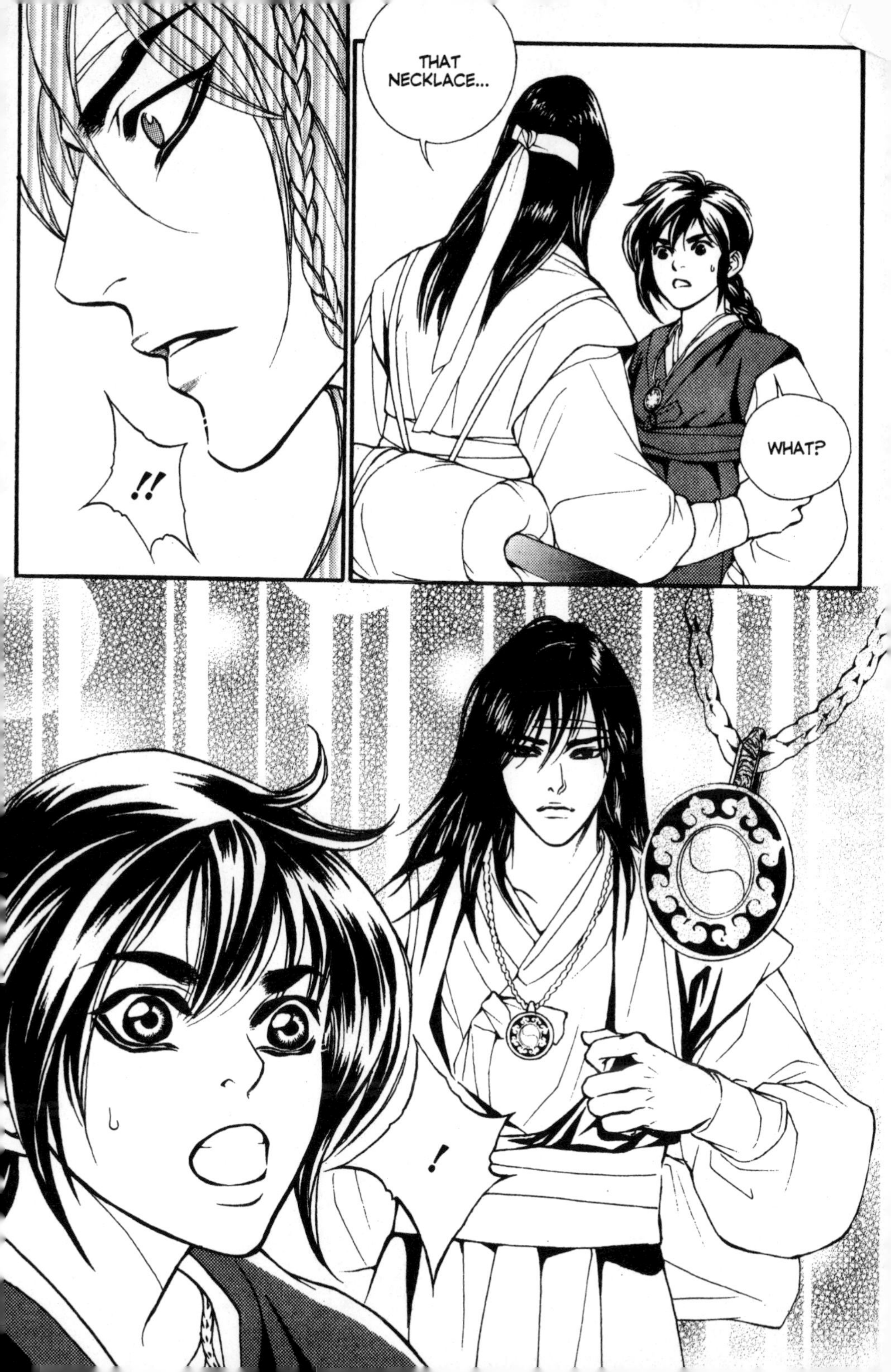
!!
THAT NECKLACE...
WHAT?
!

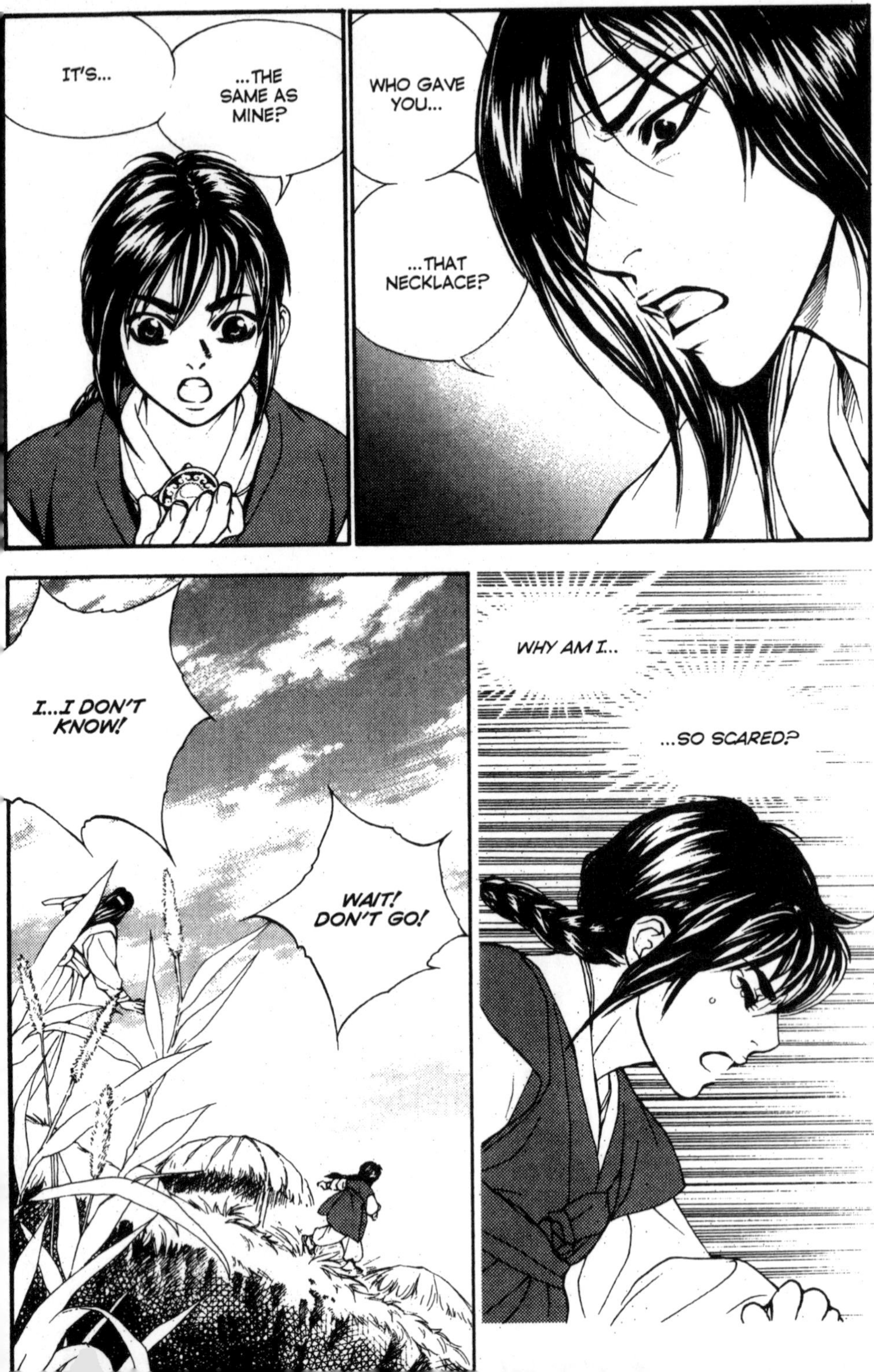
IT'S...
...THE SAME AS MINE?
WHO GAVE YOU...
...THAT NECKLACE?
I...I DON'T KNOW!
WAIT! DON'T GO!
WHY AM I...
...SO SCARED?

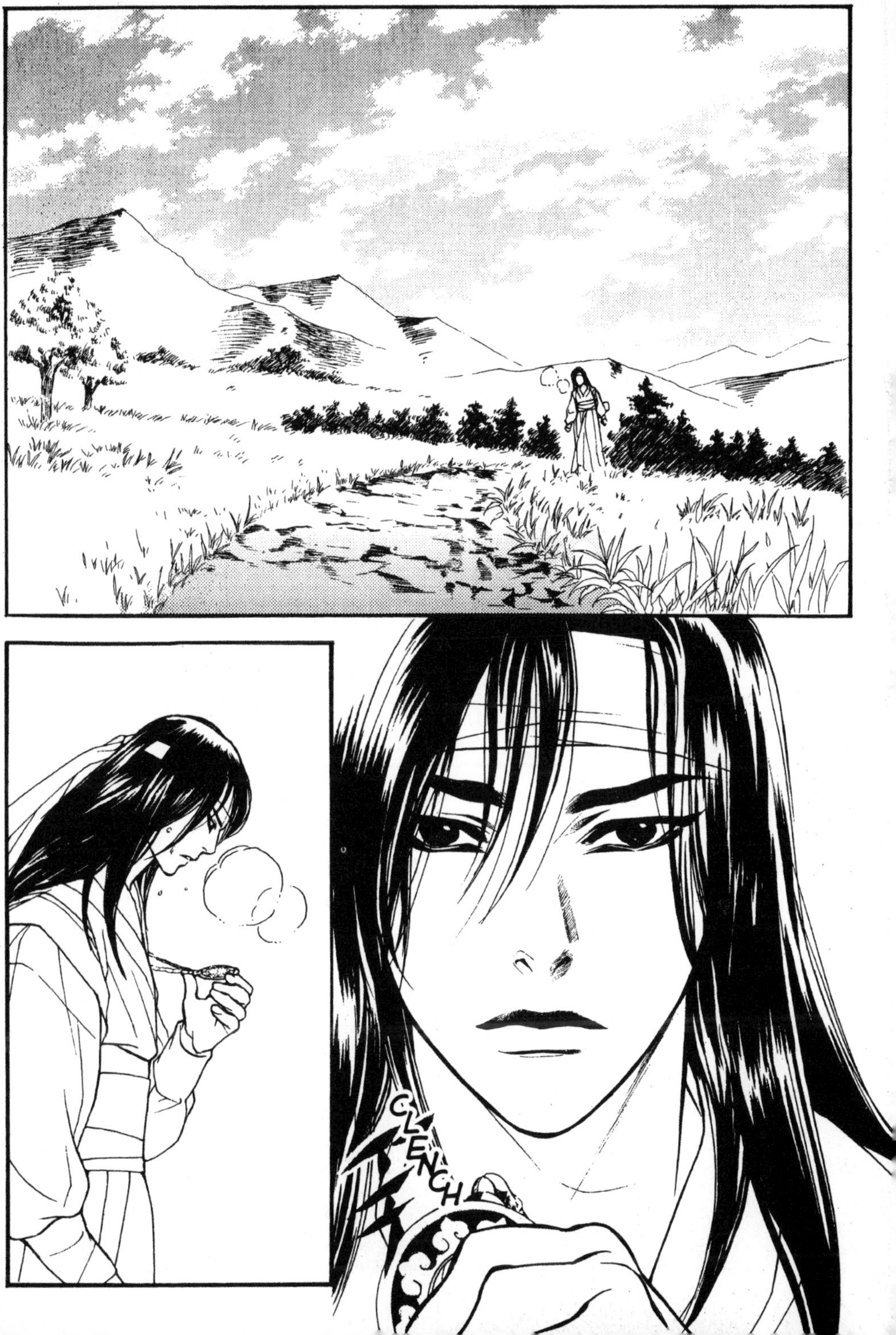
CLENCH

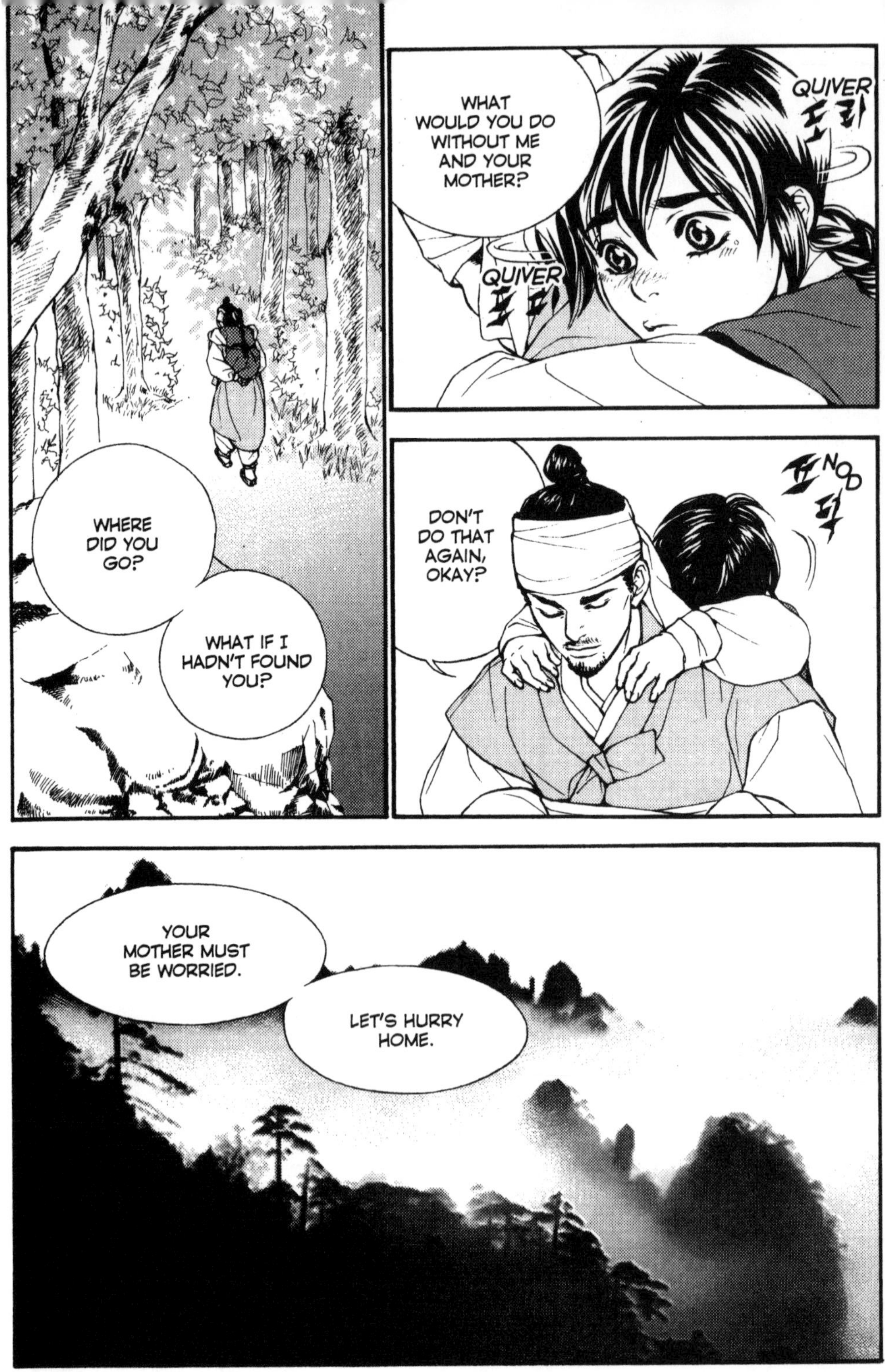
WHERE DID YOU GO?
WHAT IF I HADN'T FOUND YOU?
WHAT WOULD YOU DO WITHOUT ME AND YOUR MOTHER?
QUIVER
QUIVER
DON'T DO THAT AGAIN, OKAY?
NOD
YOUR MOTHER MUST BE WORRIED.
LET'S HURRY HOME.

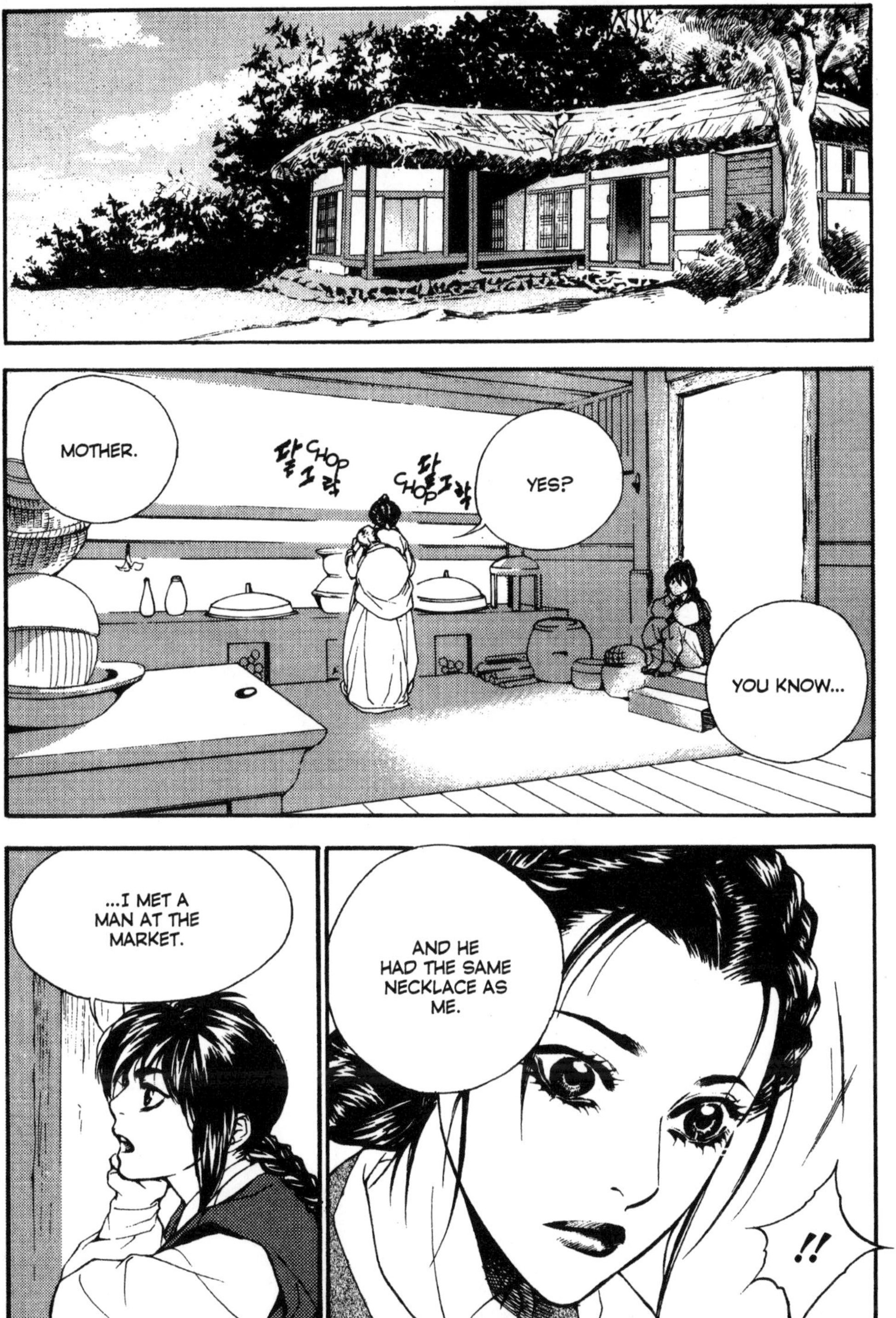
MOTHER.
CHOP
CHOP
YES?
YOU KNOW...
...I MET A MAN AT THE MARKET.
AND HE HAD THE SAME NECKLACE AS ME.
!!

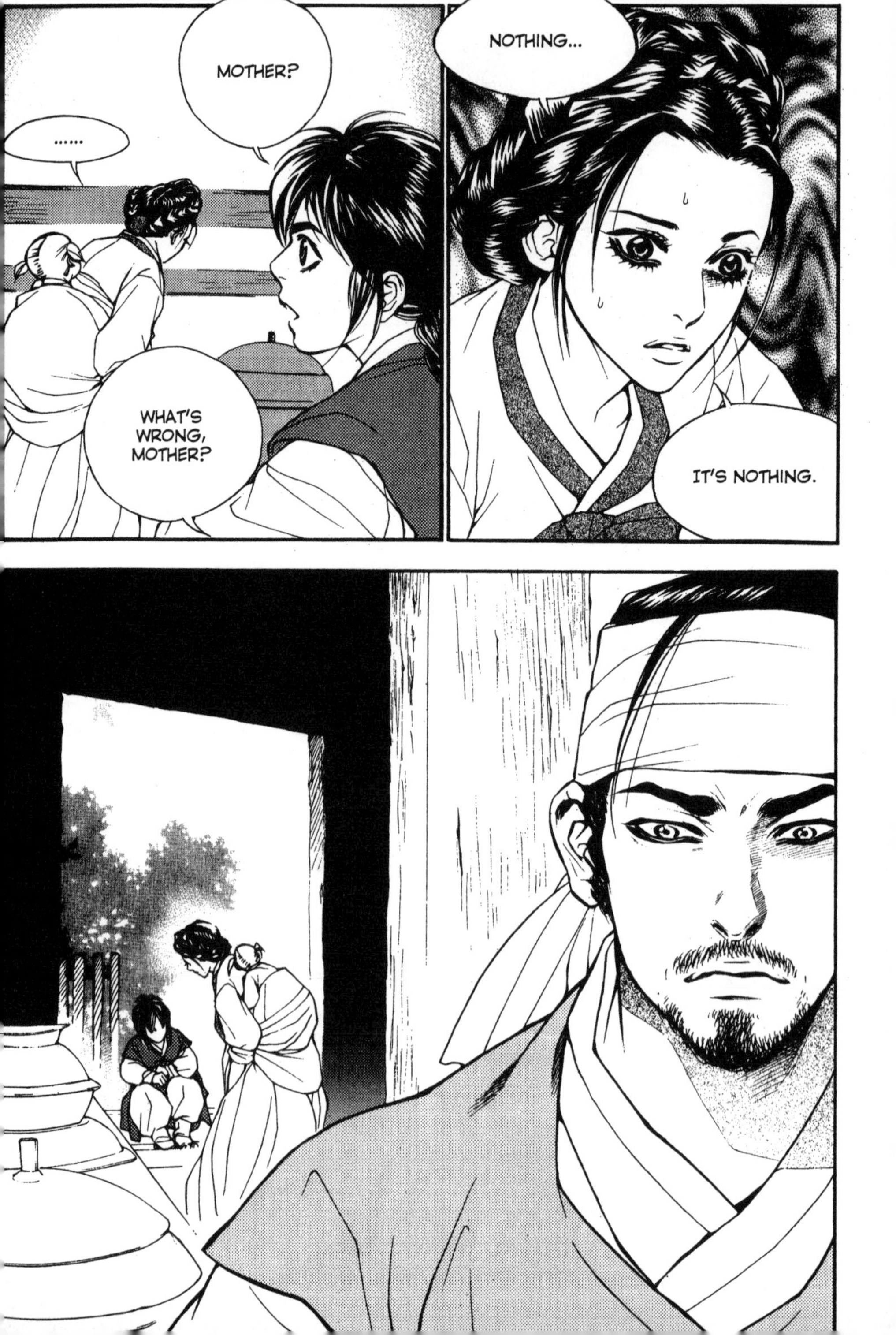
......
MOTHER?
WHAT'S WRONG, MOTHER?
NOTHING...
IT'S NOTHING.

NIGHT STORY 4

THE MOTHER AND THE WOODSMAN

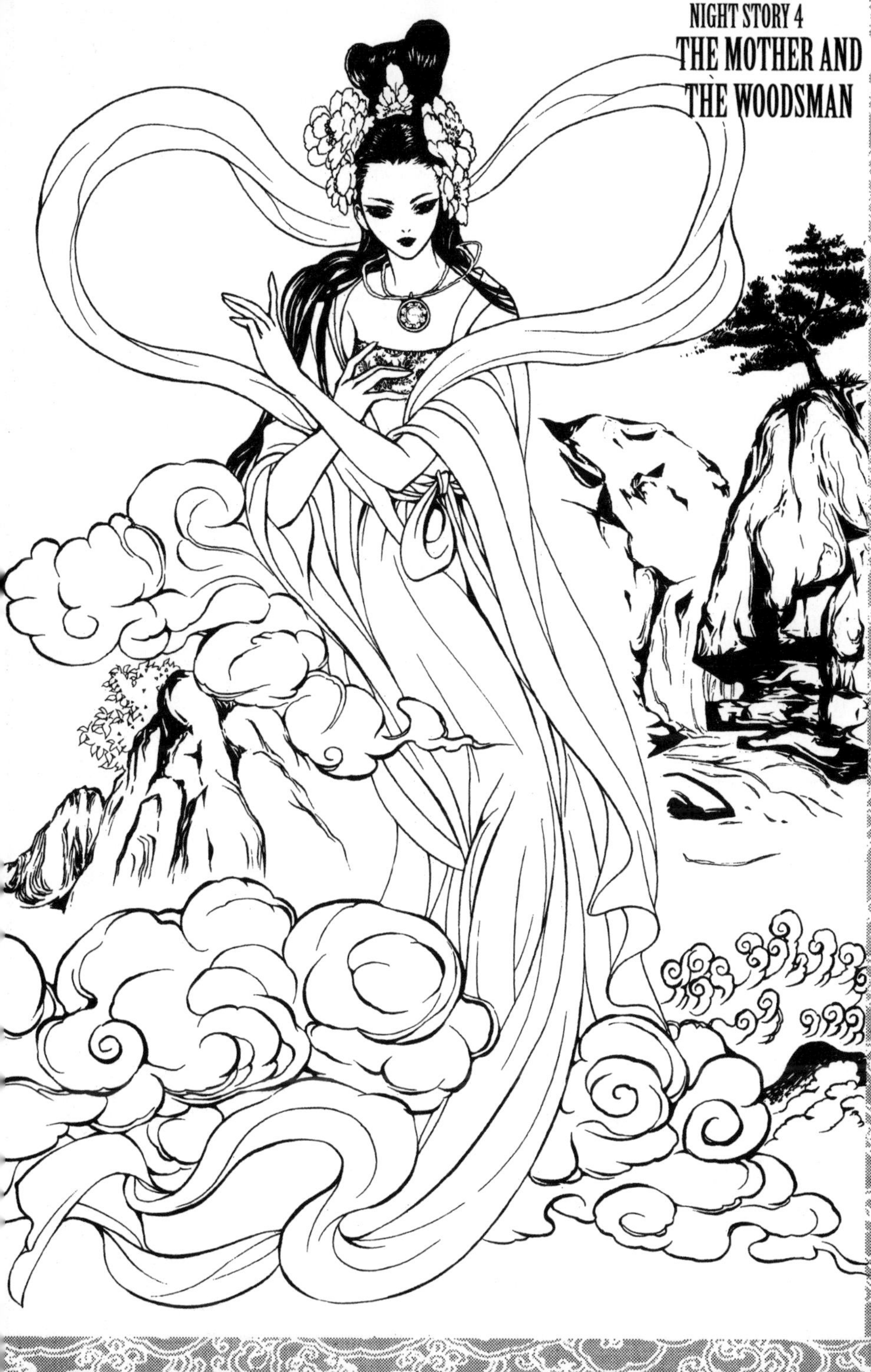

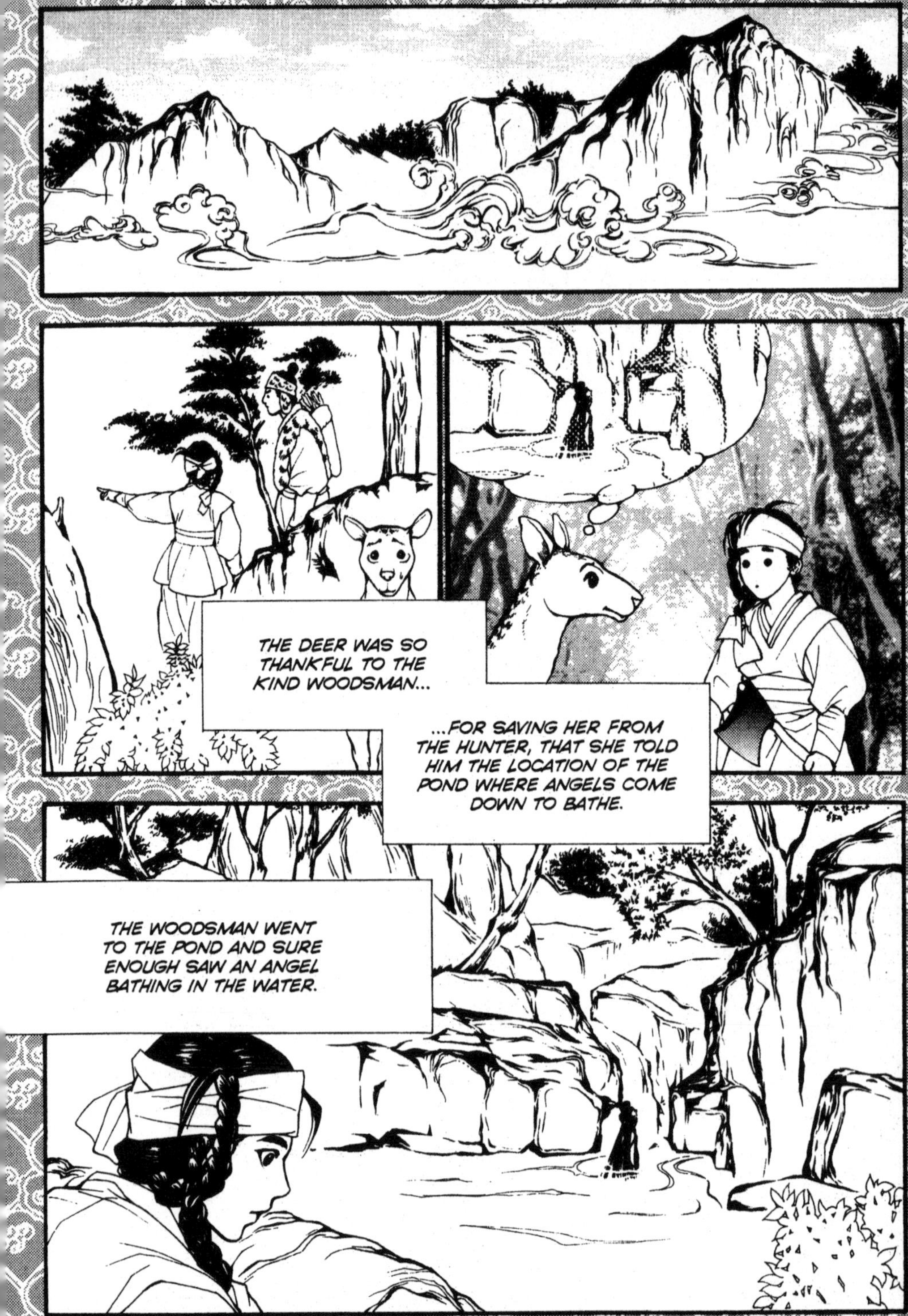
THE DEER WAS SO THANKFUL TO THE KIND WOODSMAN...
...FOR SAVING HER FROM THE HUNTER, THAT SHE TOLD HIM THE LOCATION OF THE POND WHERE ANGELS COME DOWN TO BATHE.
THE WOODSMAN WENT TO THE POND AND SURE ENOUGH SAW AN ANGEL BATHING IN THE WATER.

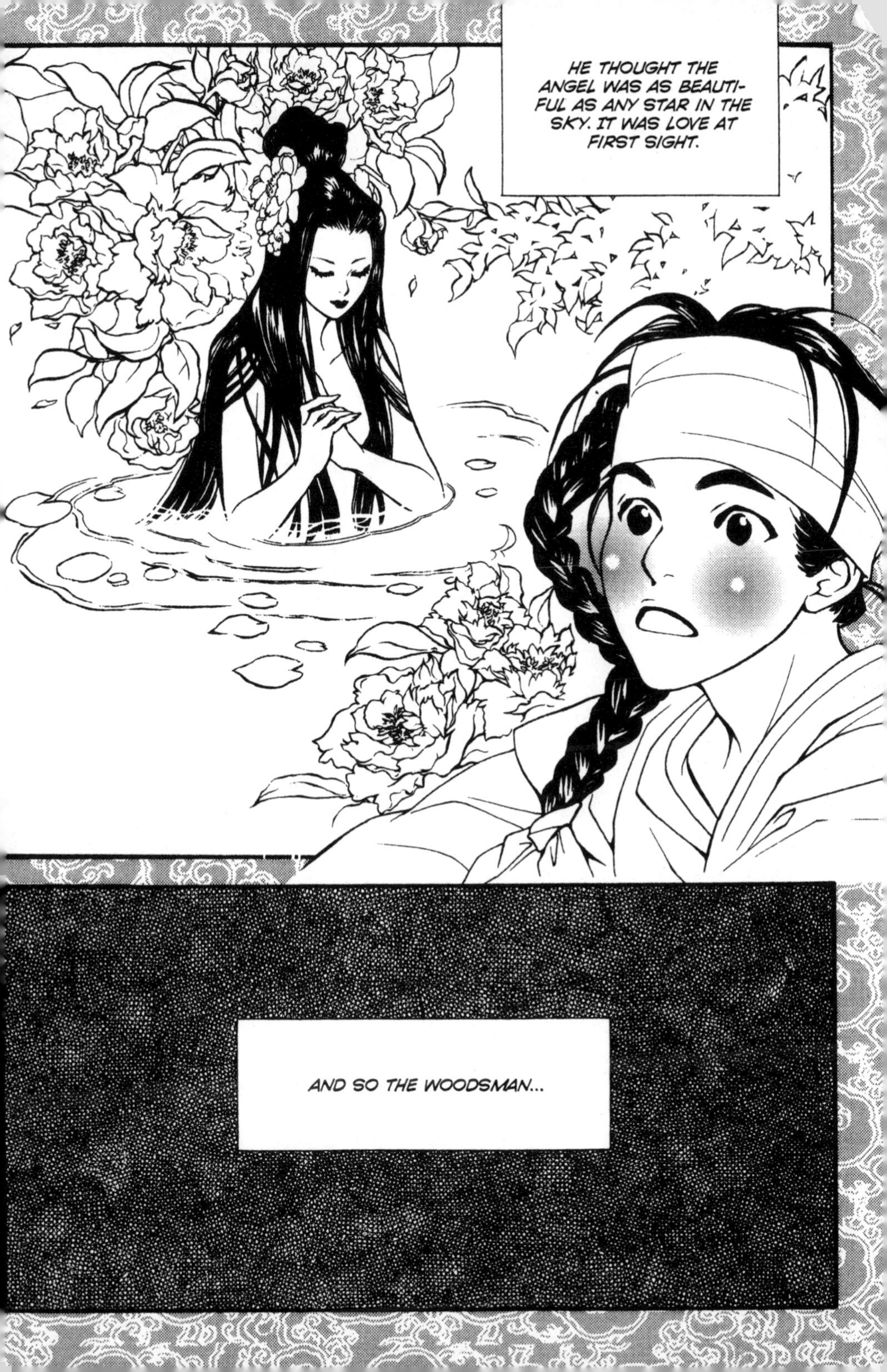
HE THOUGHT THE ANGEL WAS AS BEAUTI-FUL AS ANY STAR IN THE SKY. IT WAS LOVE AT FIRST SIGHT.
AND SO THE WOODSMAN...

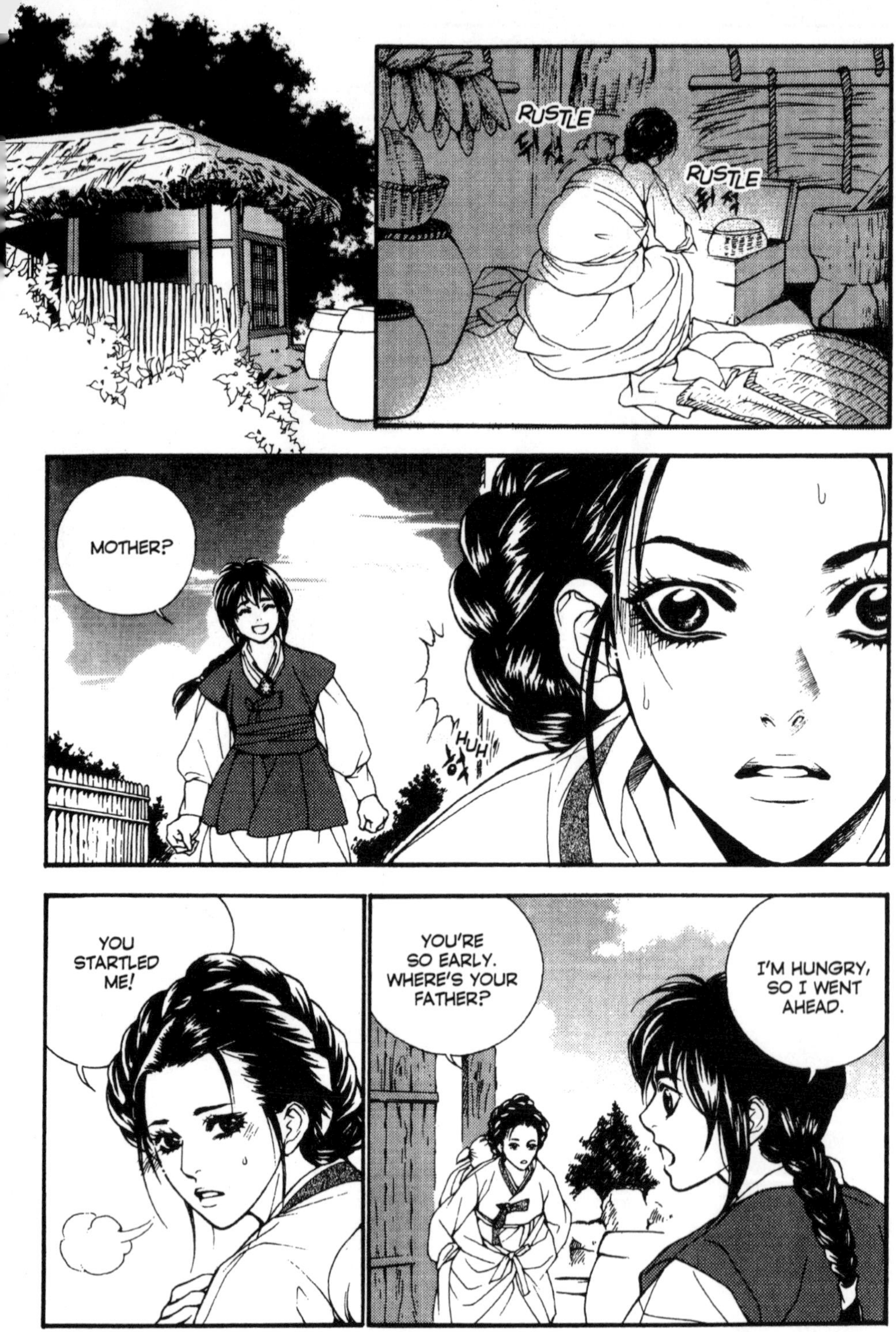
RUSTLE
RUSTLE
MOTHER?
HUH
YOU STARTLED ME!
YOU'RE SO EARLY. WHERE'S YOUR FATHER?
I'M HUNGRY, SO I WENT AHEAD.

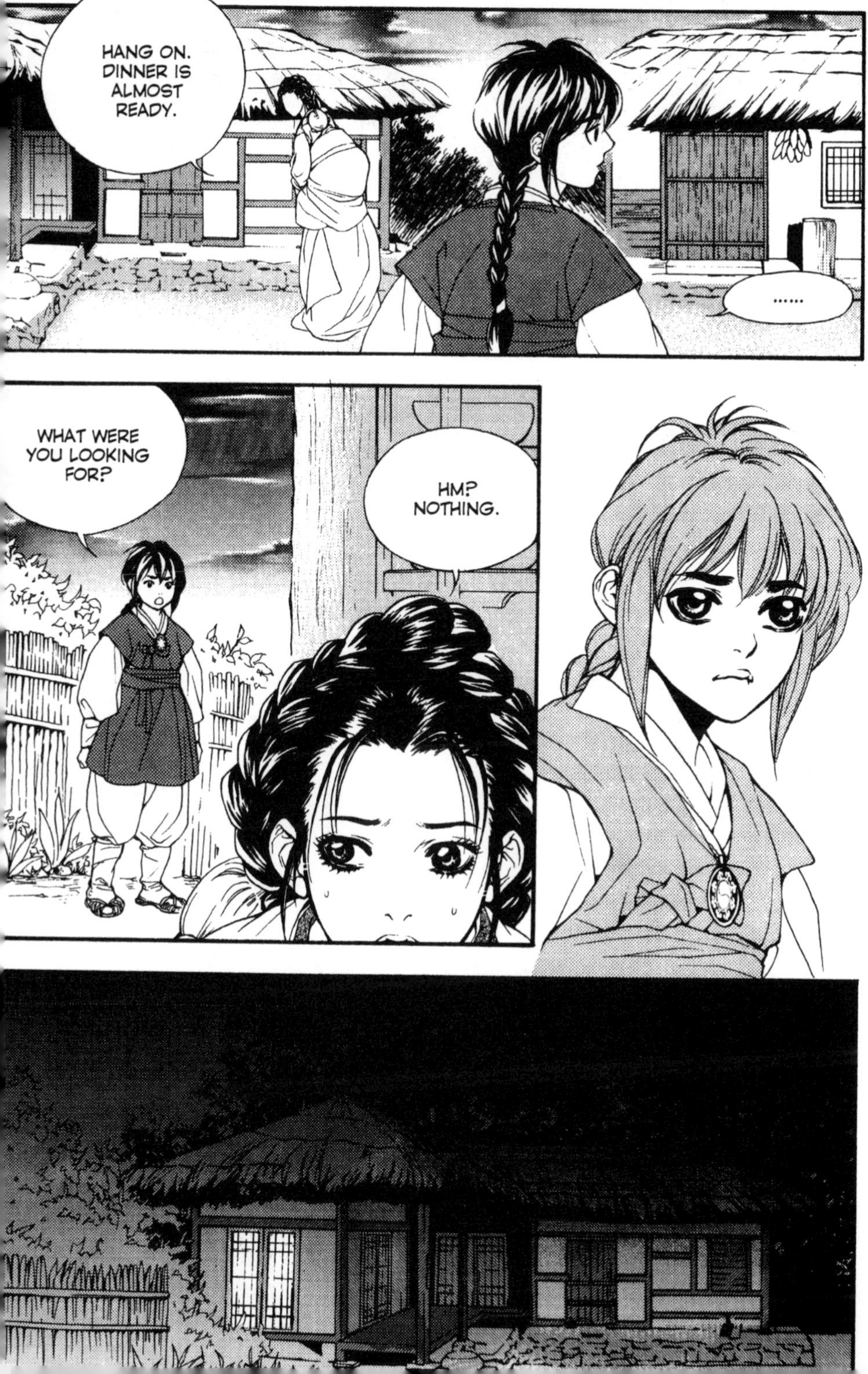
HANG ON. DINNER IS ALMOST READY.
......
WHAT WERE YOU LOOKING FOR?
HM? NOTHING.

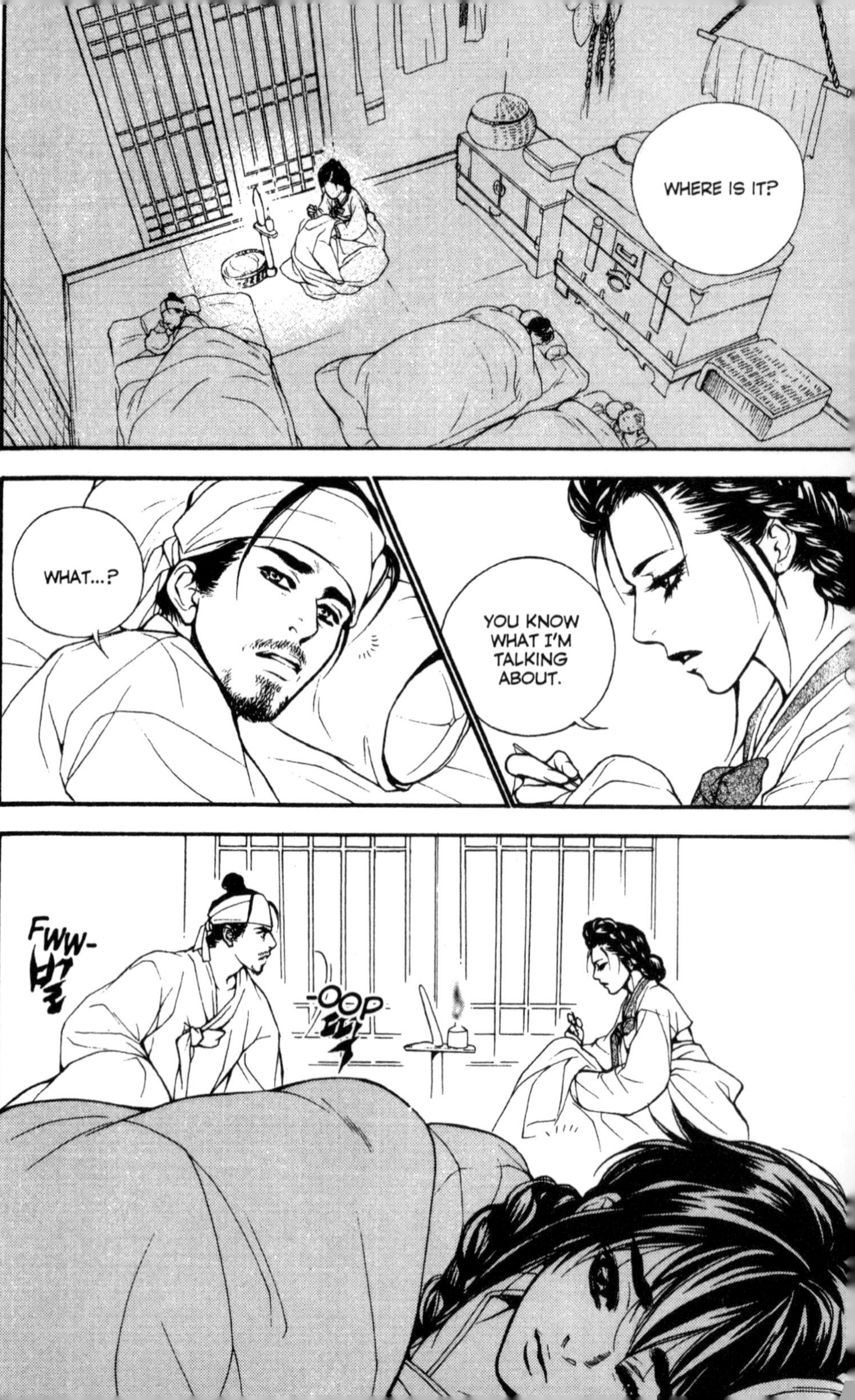
WHERE IS IT?
WHAT...?
YOU KNOW WHAT I'M TALKING ABOUT.
FWW-
-OOP

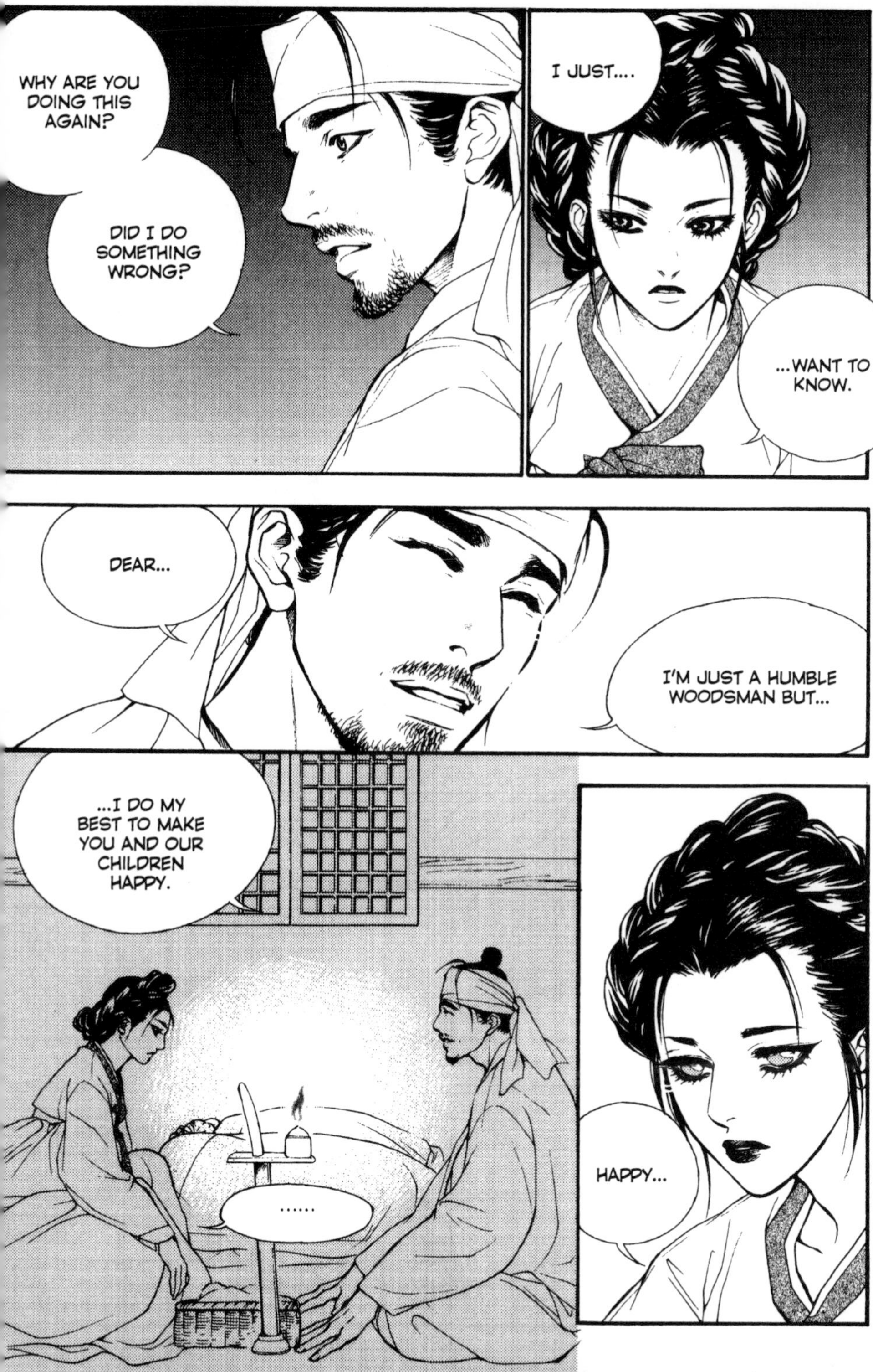
WHY ARE YOU DOING THIS AGAIN?
DID I DO SOMETHING WRONG?
I JUST....
...WANT TO KNOW.
DEAR...
I'M JUST A HUMBLE WOODSMAN BUT...
...I DO MY BEST TO MAKE YOU AND OUR CHILDREN HAPPY.
......
HAPPY...

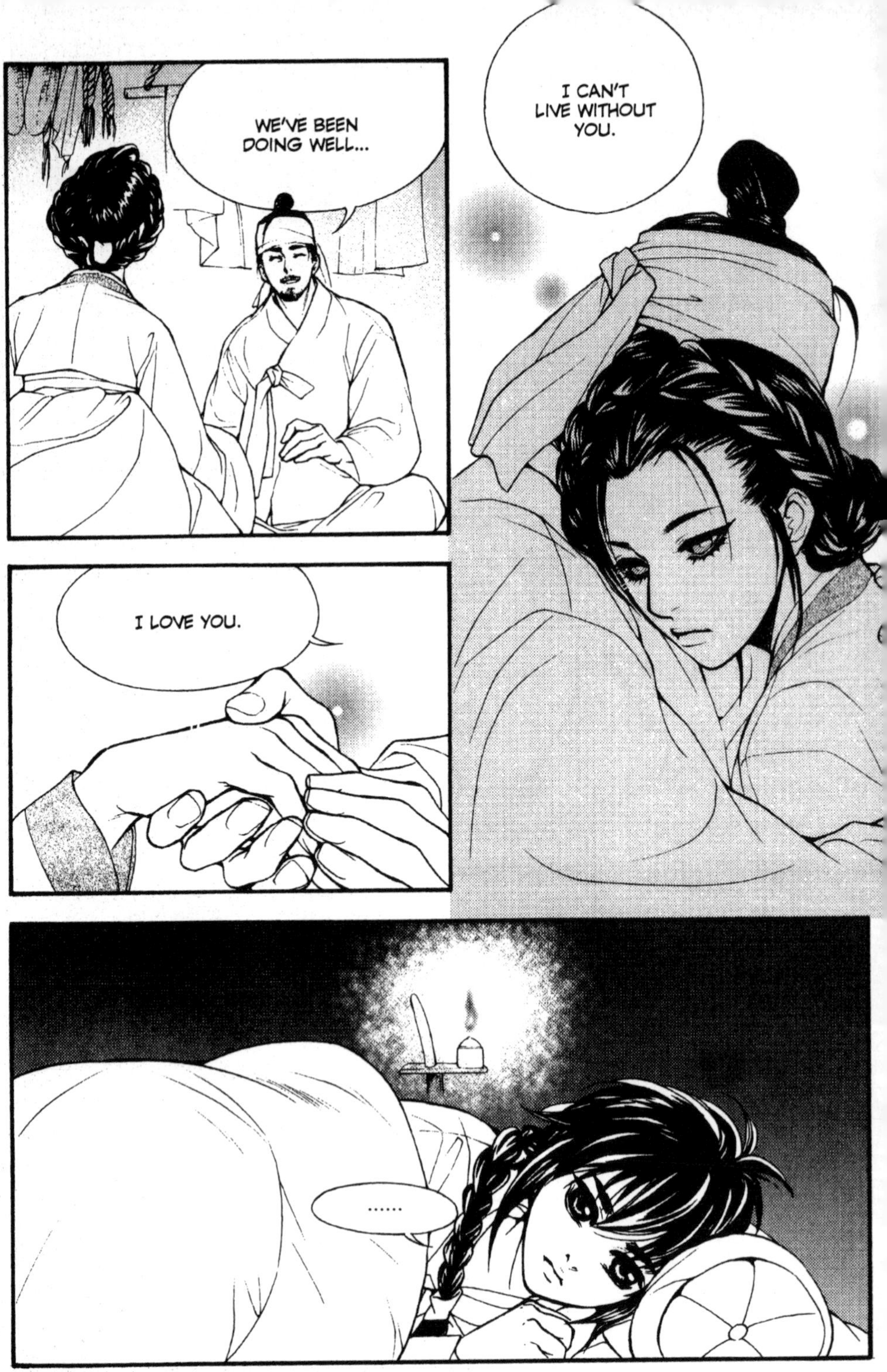
WE'VE BEEN DOING WELL...
I LOVE YOU.
I CAN'T LIVE WITHOUT YOU.
......

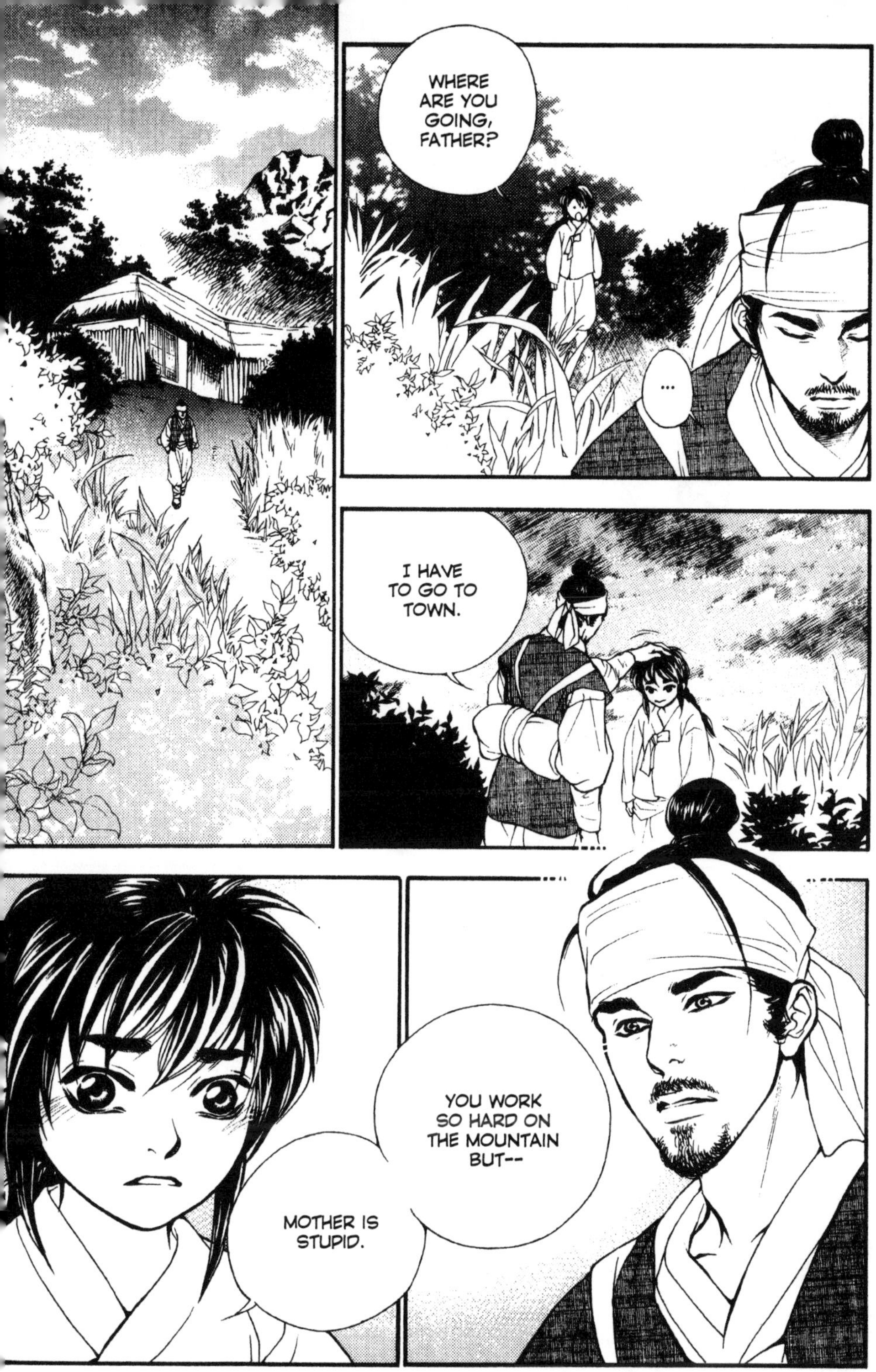
WHERE ARE YOU GOING, FATHER?
...
I HAVE TO GO TO TOWN.
MOTHER IS STUPID.
YOU WORK SO HARD ON THE MOUNTAIN BUT--

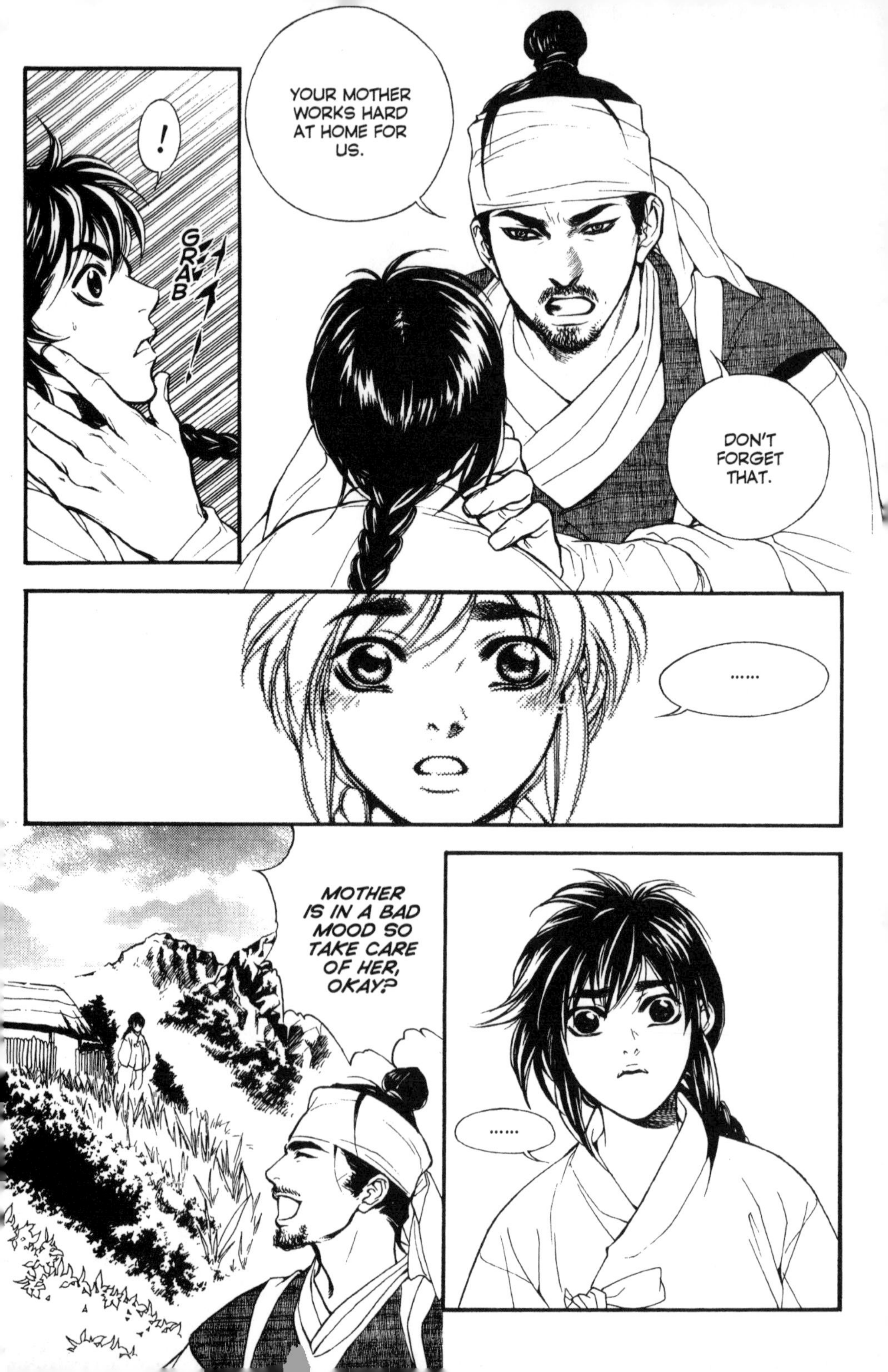
!
GRAB
YOUR MOTHER WORKS HARD AT HOME FOR US.
DON'T FORGET THAT.
......
MOTHER IS IN A BAD MOOD SO TAKE CARE OF HER, OKAY?
......

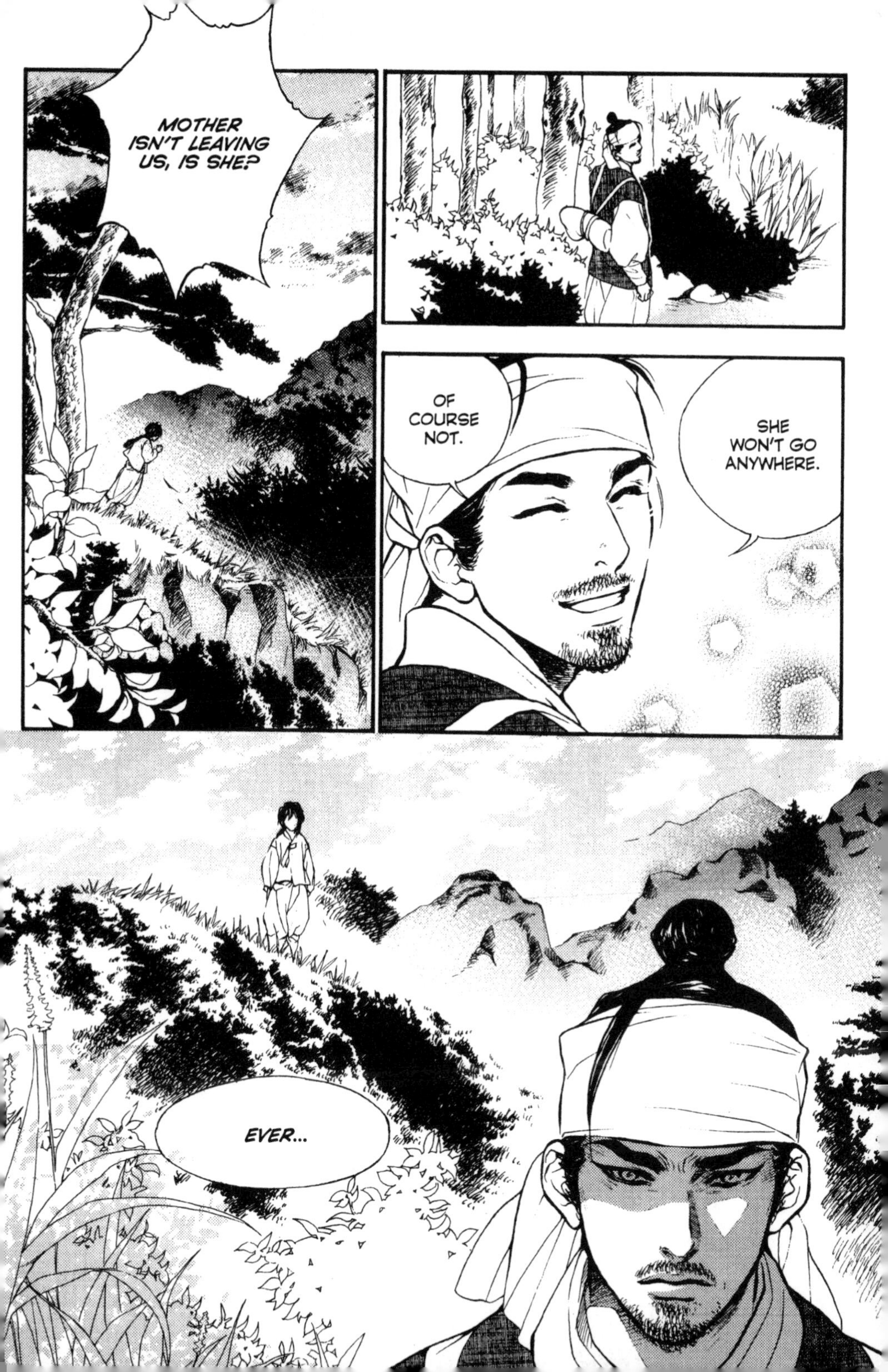
MOTHER ISN'T LEAVING US, IS SHE?
OF COURSE NOT.
SHE WON'T GO ANYWHERE.
EVER...

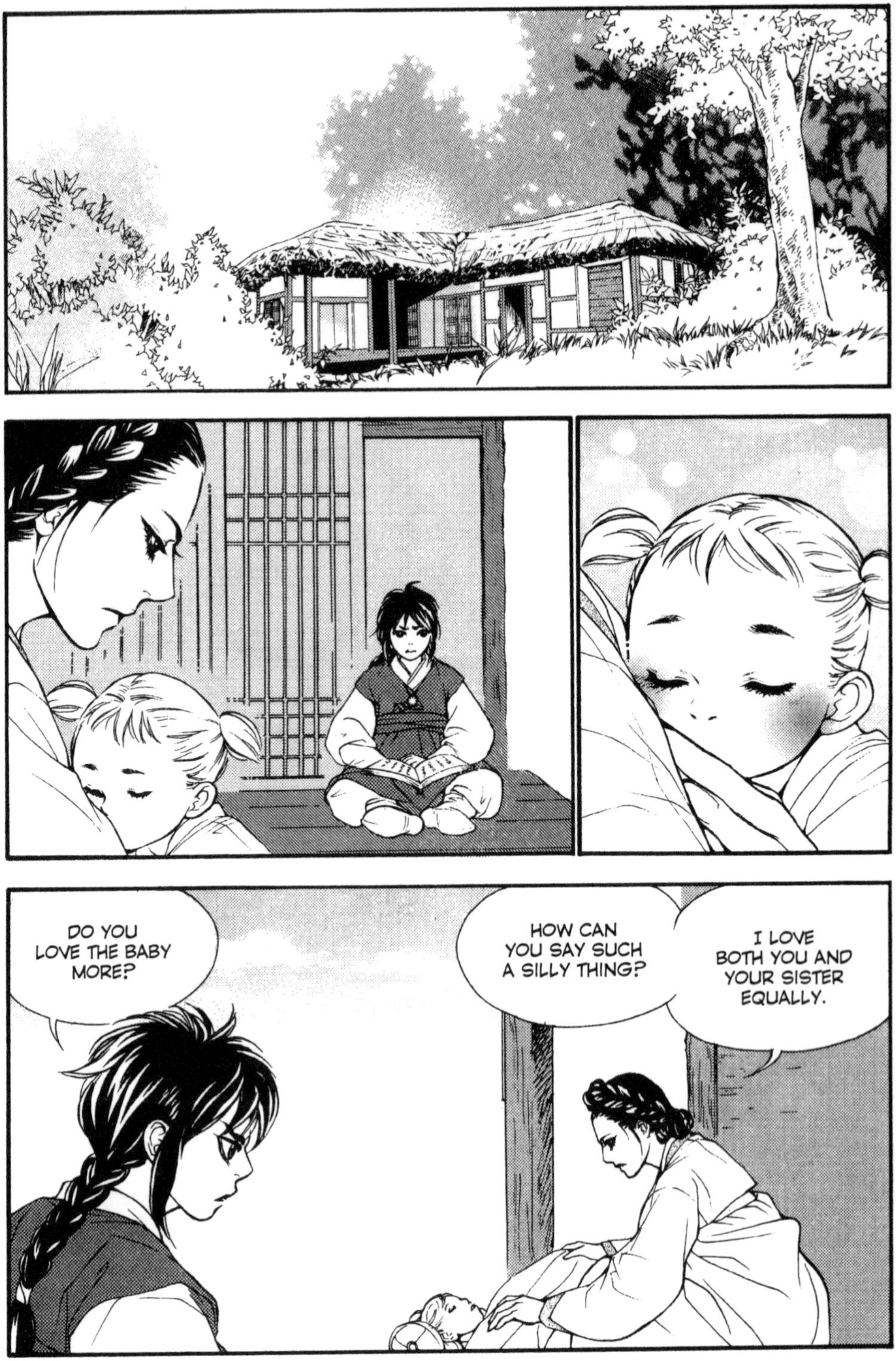
DO YOU LOVE THE BABY MORE?
HOW CAN YOU SAY SUCH A SILLY THING?
I LOVE BOTH YOU AND YOUR SISTER EQUALLY.

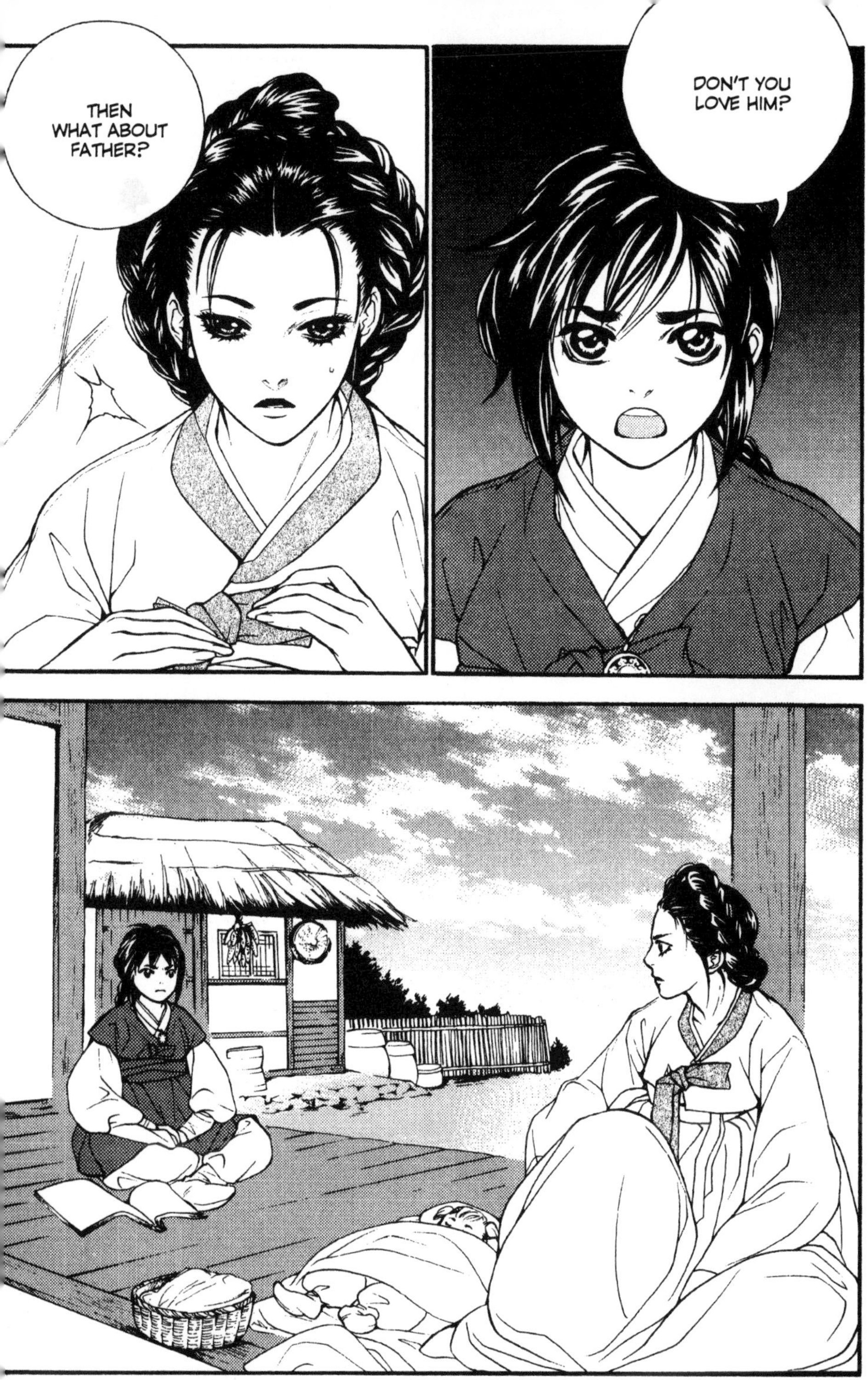
THEN WHAT ABOUT FATHER?
DON'T YOU LOVE HIM?

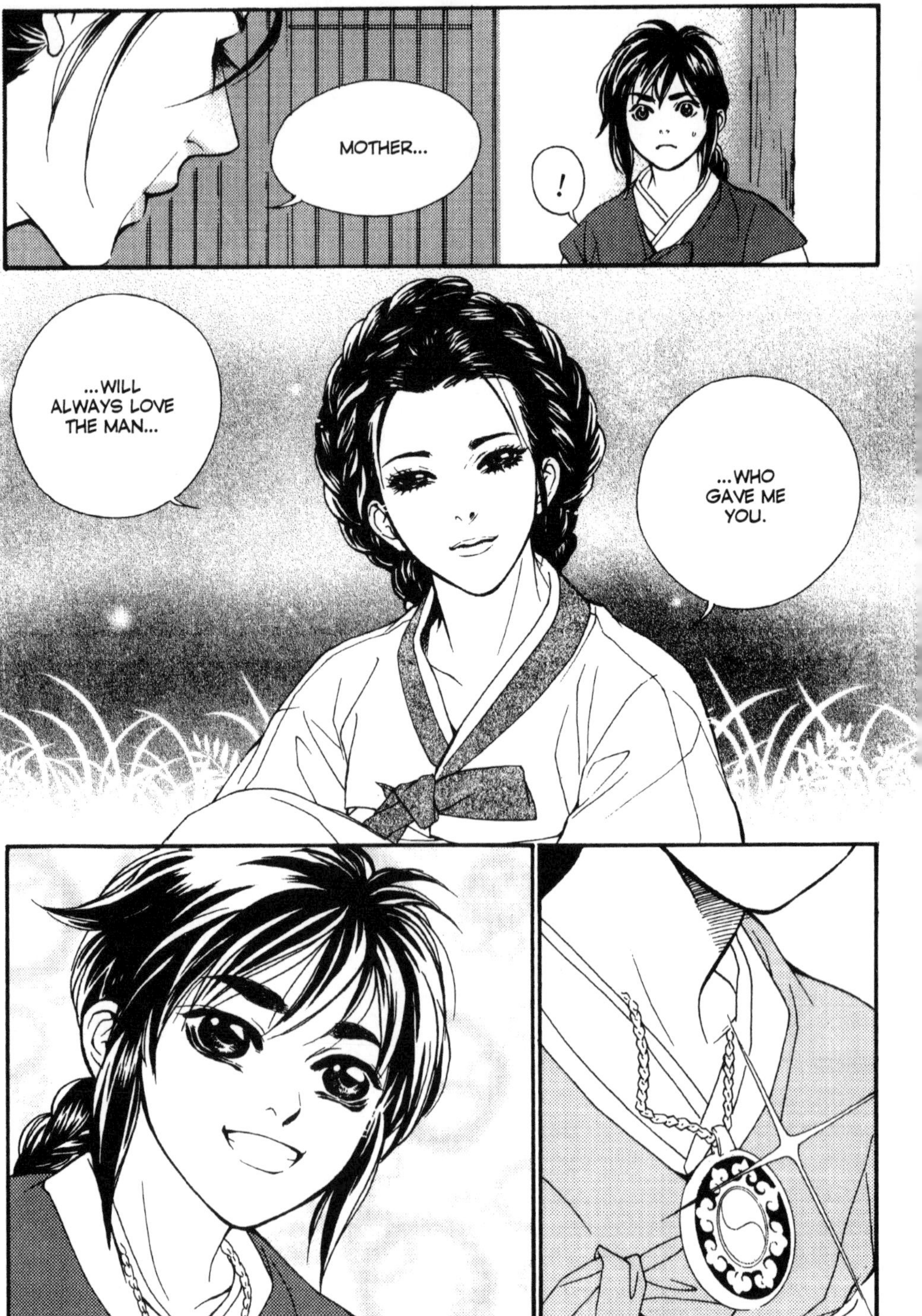
MOTHER...
!
...WILL ALWAYS LOVE THE MAN...
...WHO GAVE ME YOU.

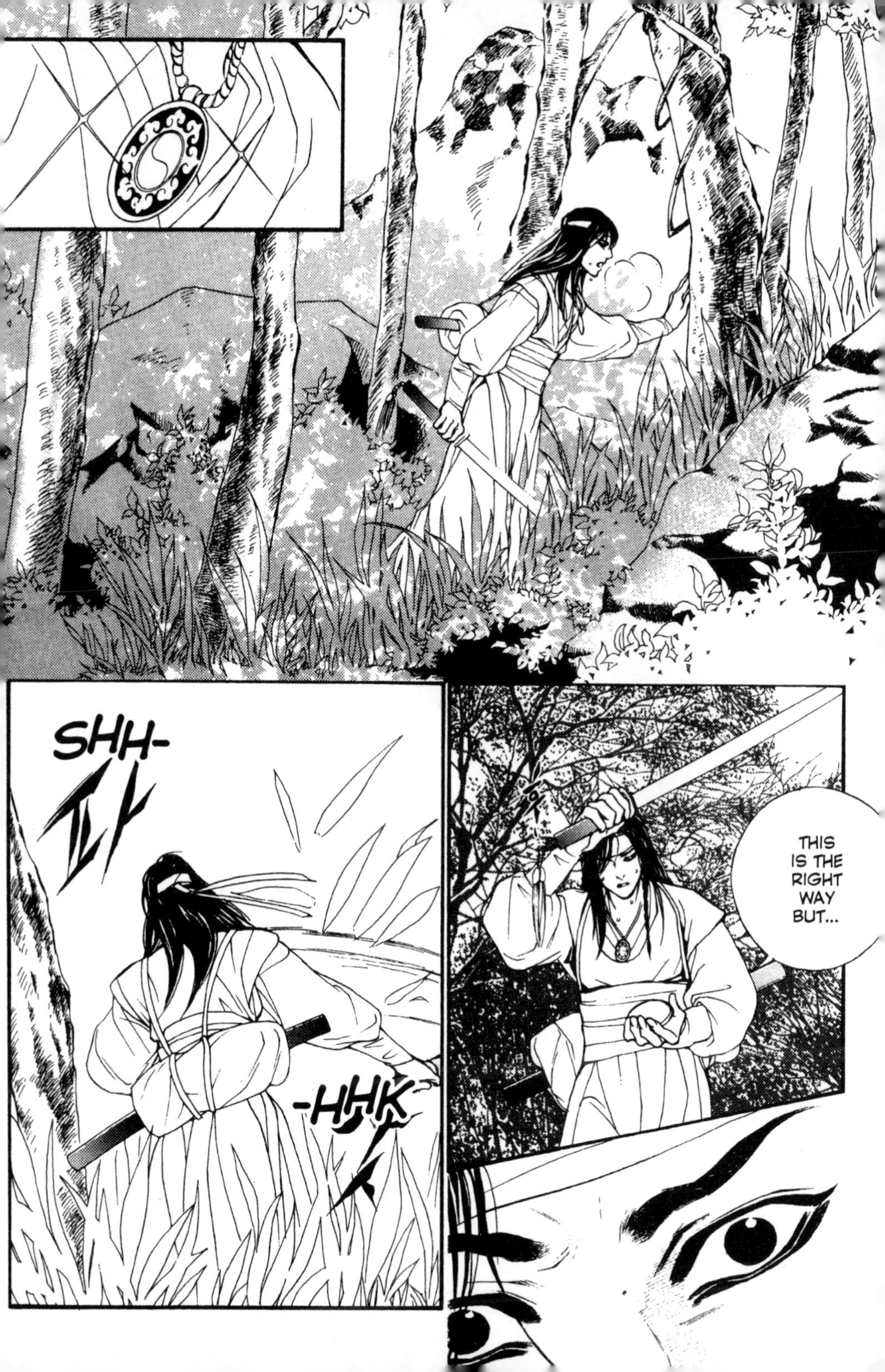
SHH-
-HHK
THIS IS THE RIGHT WAY BUT...

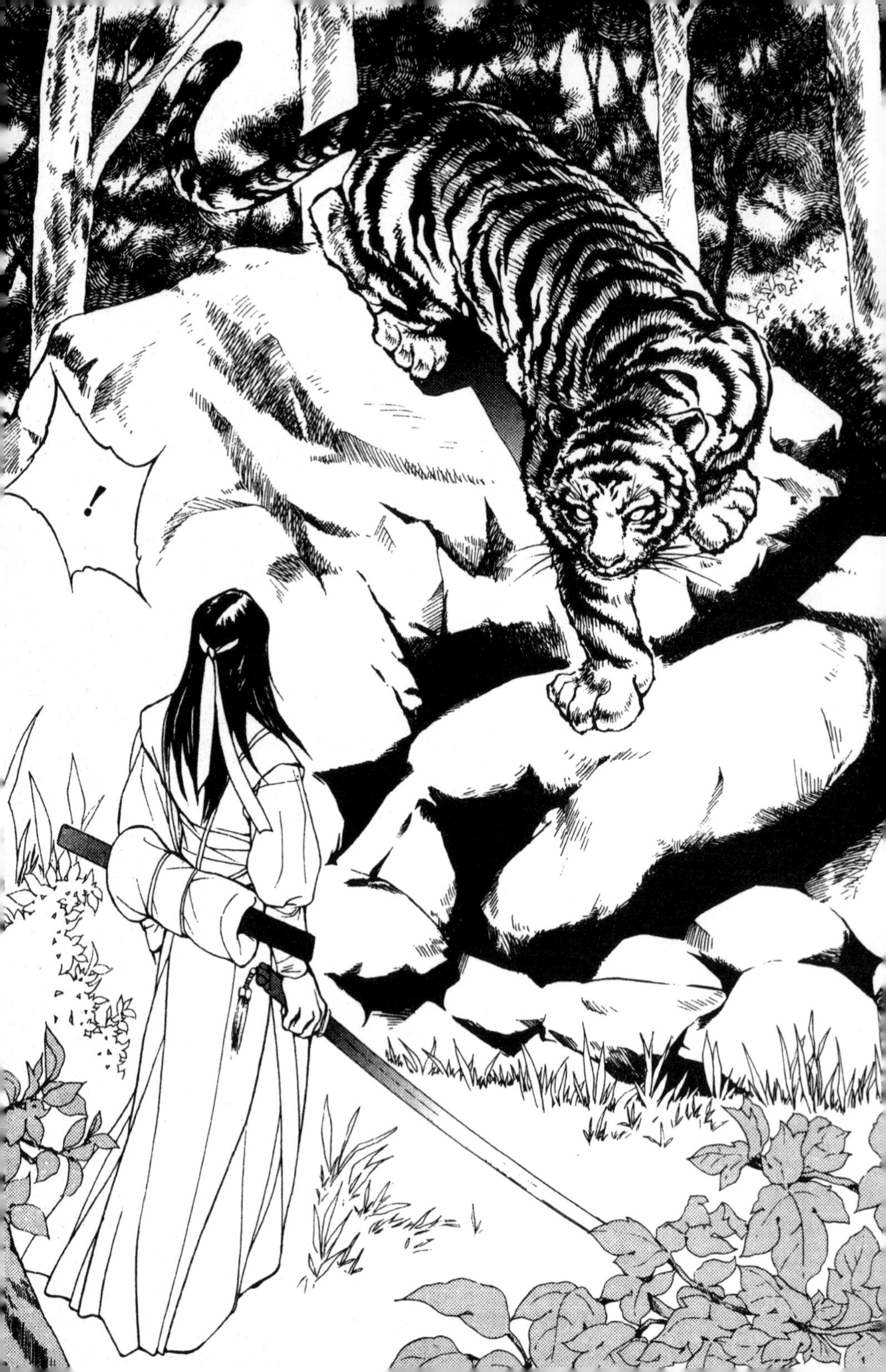
!

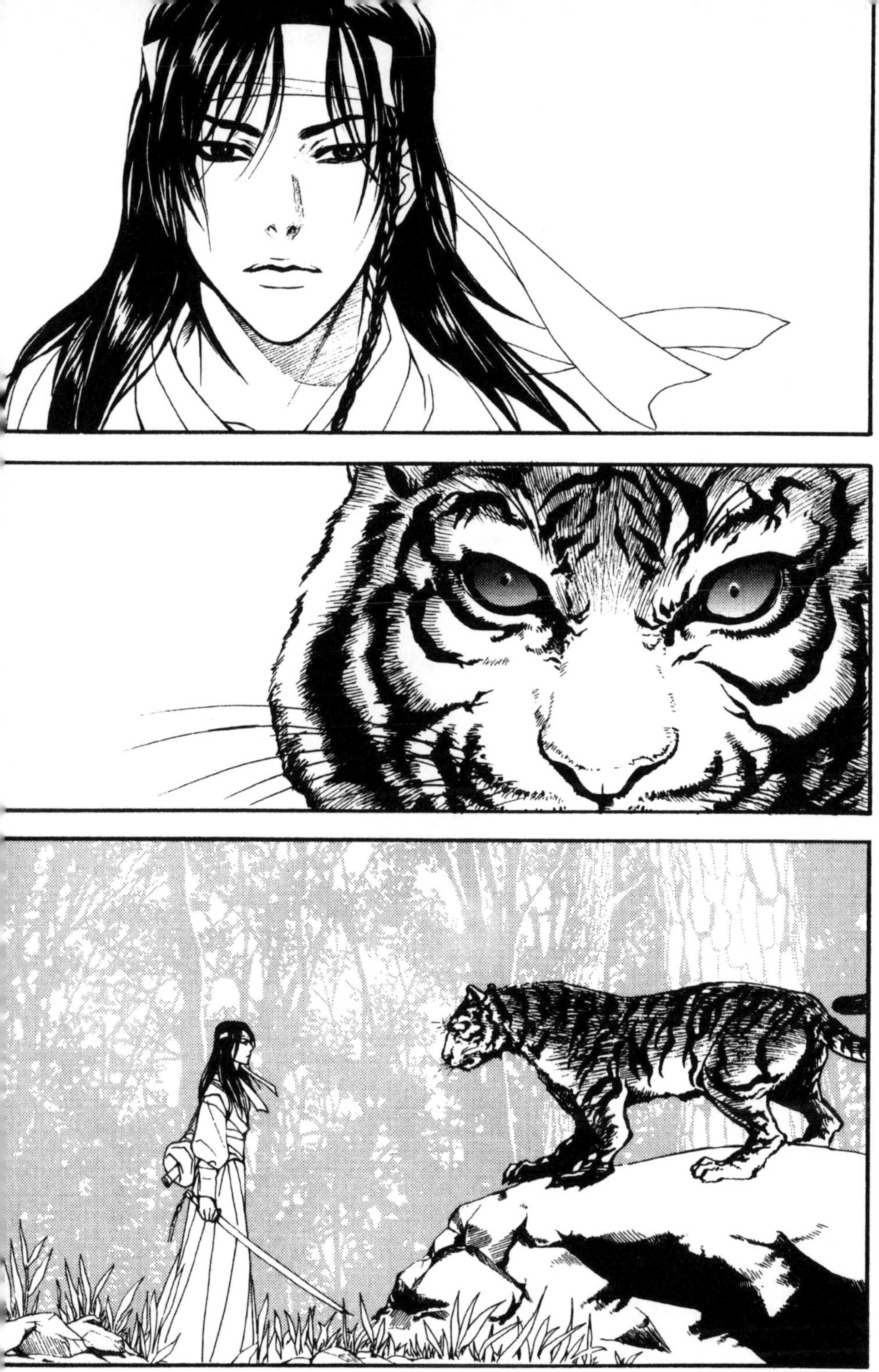

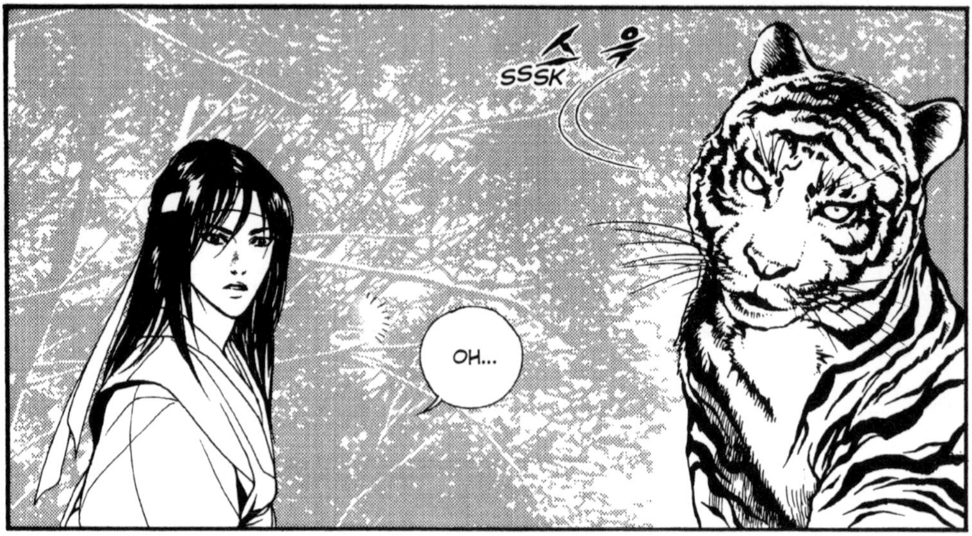
SSSK
OH...

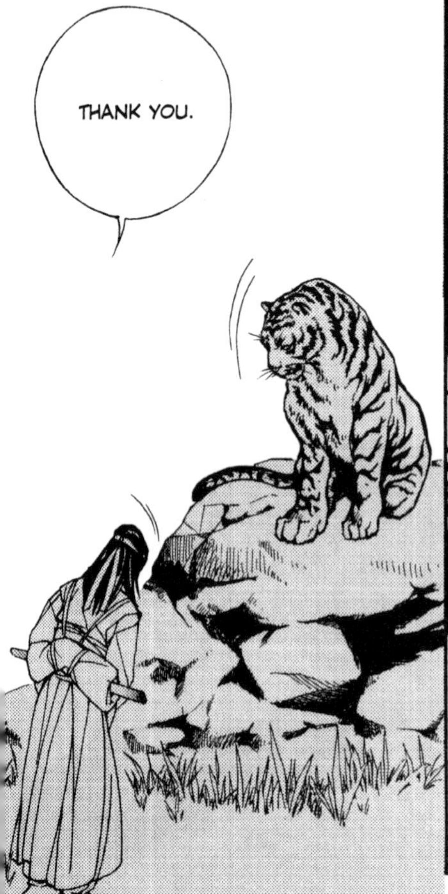
THANK YOU.

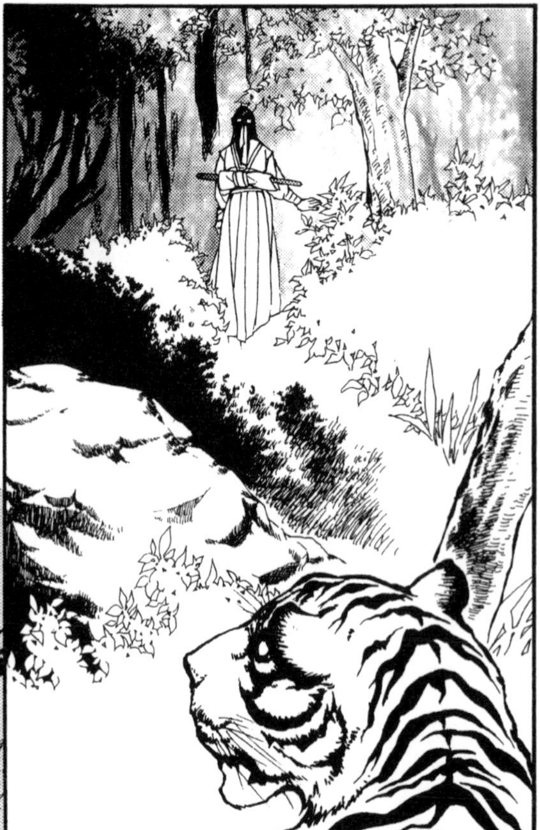

DO YOU KNOW A BOY ABOUT THIS HEIGHT? LIVES NEARBY?

SORRY...

EXCUSE ME...

THEN...HAVE YOU SEEN A WOMAN...

...ABOUT THIRTY YEARS OLD AND...

...VERY BEAUTIFUL?

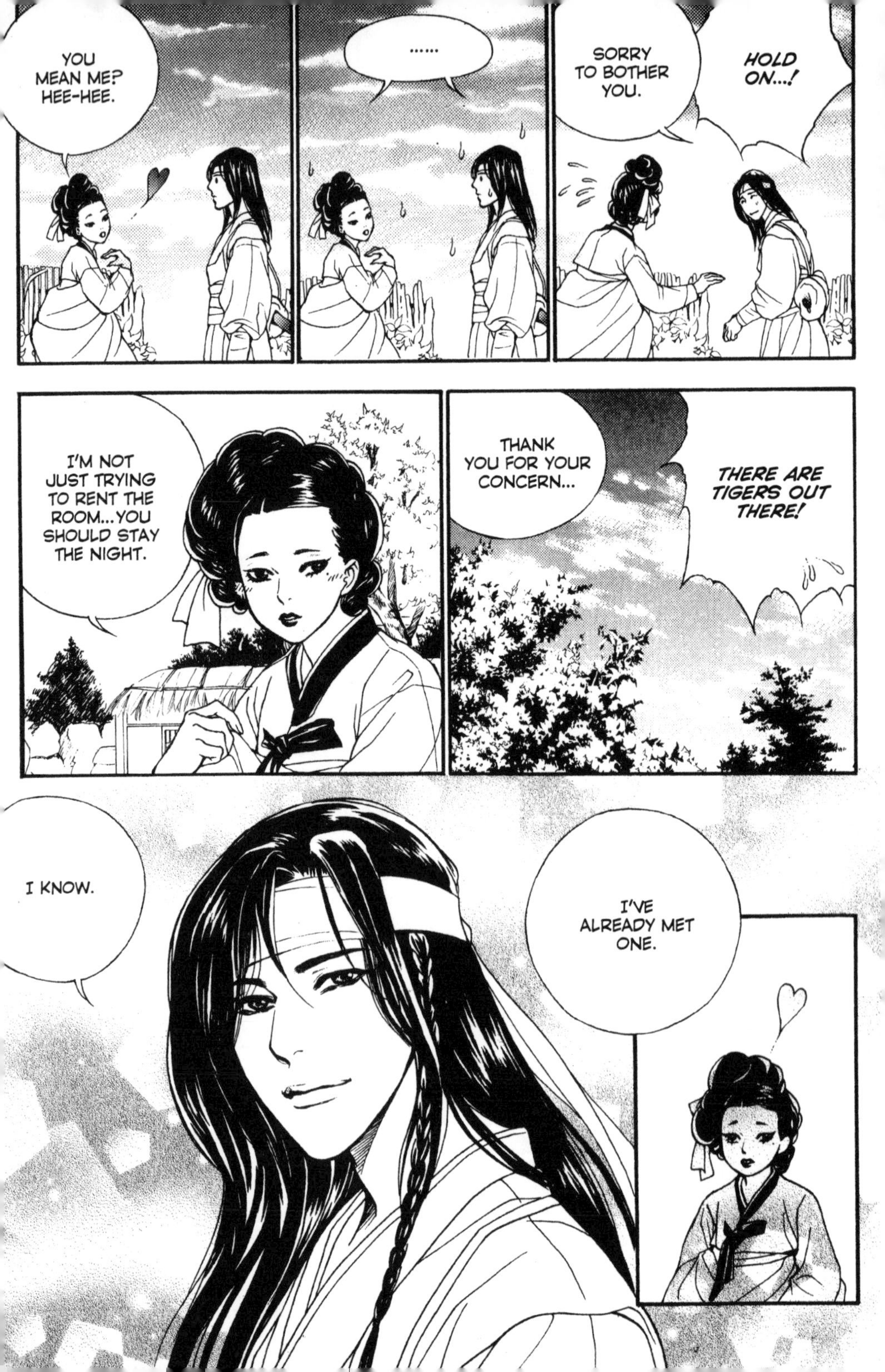
YOU MEAN ME? HEE-HEE.
......
SORRY TO BOTHER YOU.
HOLD ON...!
I'M NOT JUST TRYING TO RENT THE ROOM...YOU SHOULD STAY THE NIGHT.
THANK YOU FOR YOUR CONCERN...
THERE ARE TIGERS OUT THERE!
I KNOW.
I'VE ALREADY MET ONE.

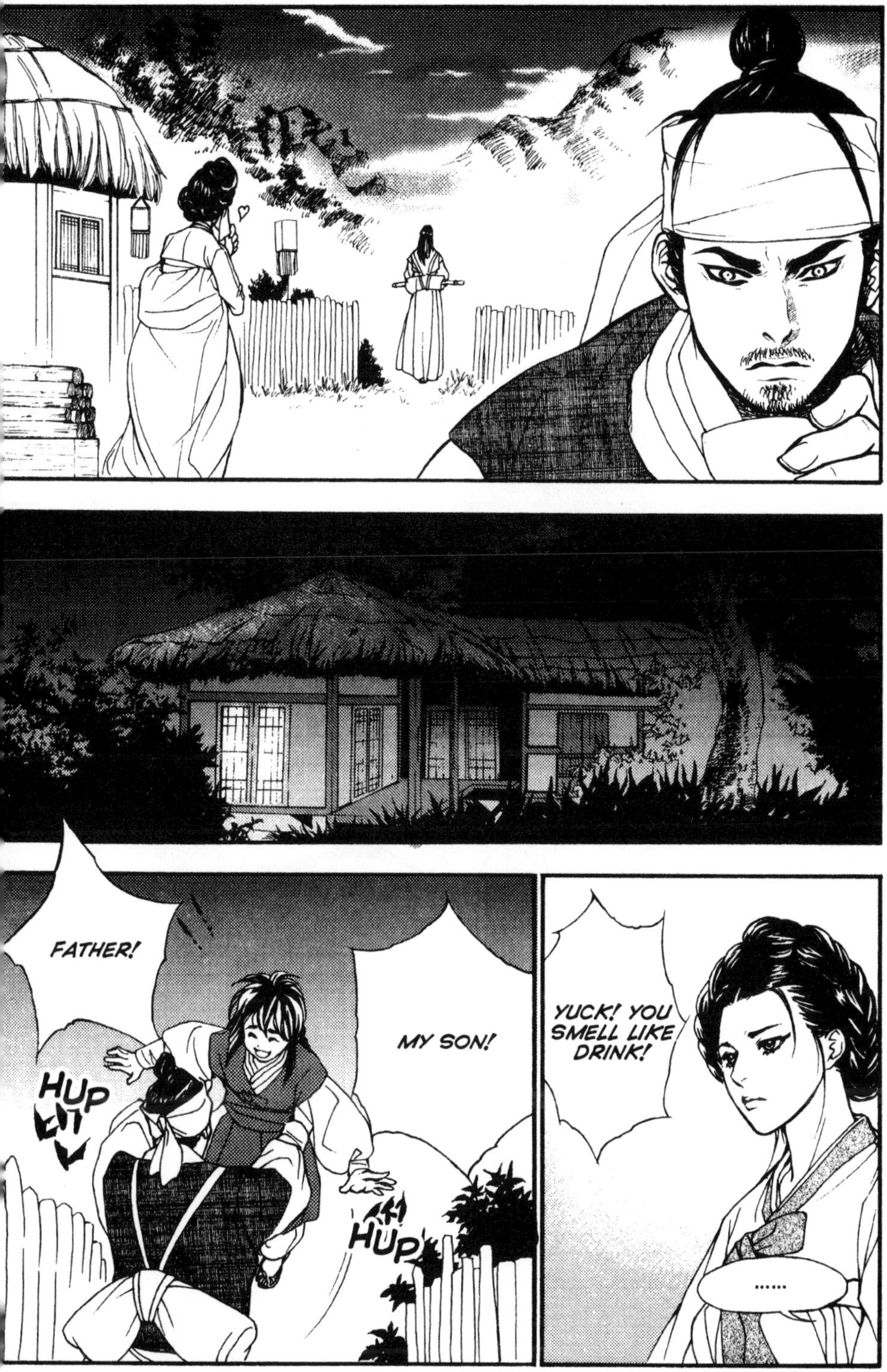
FATHER!
HUP
MY SON!
HUP
YUCK! YOU SMELL LIKE DRINK!
......

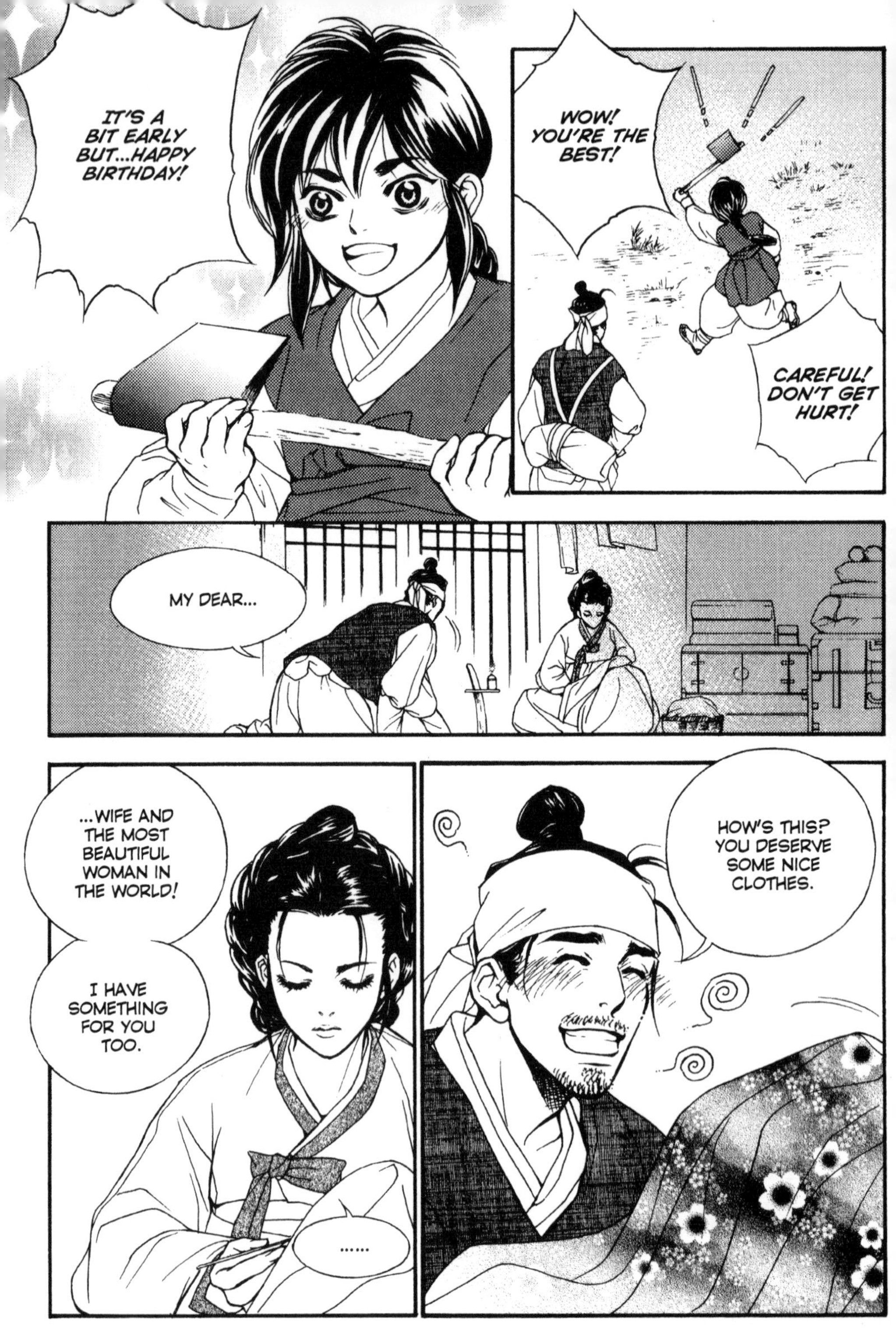
IT'S A BIT EARLY BUT...HAPPY BIRTHDAY!
WOW! YOU'RE THE BEST!
CAREFUL! DON'T GET HURT!
MY DEAR...
...WIFE AND THE MOST BEAUTIFUL WOMAN IN THE WORLD!
I HAVE SOMETHING FOR YOU TOO.
......
HOW'S THIS? YOU DESERVE SOME NICE CLOTHES.

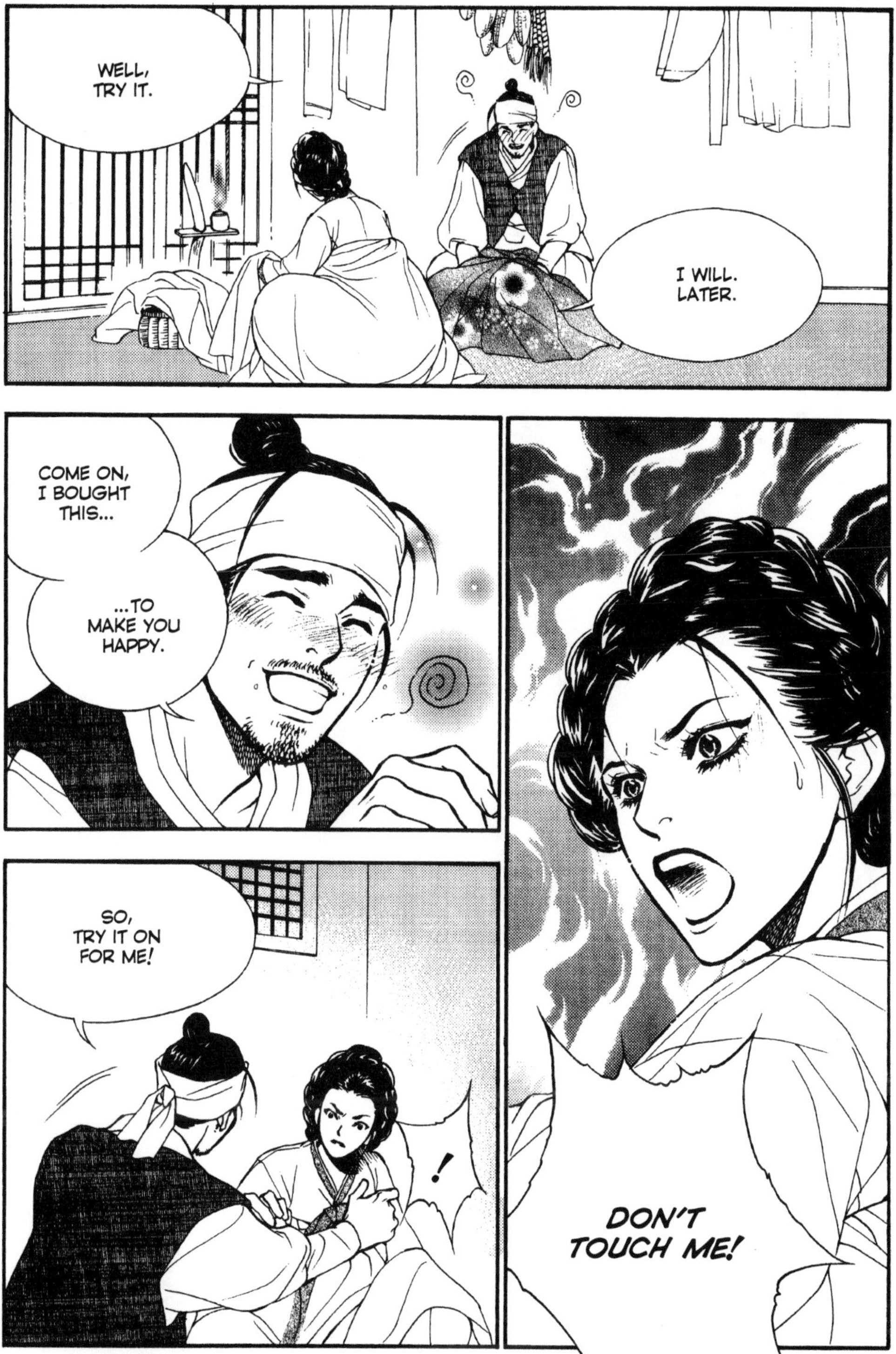
WELL, TRY IT.
I WILL. LATER.
COME ON, I BOUGHT THIS...
...TO MAKE YOU HAPPY.
SO, TRY IT ON FOR ME!
!
DON'T TOUCH ME!

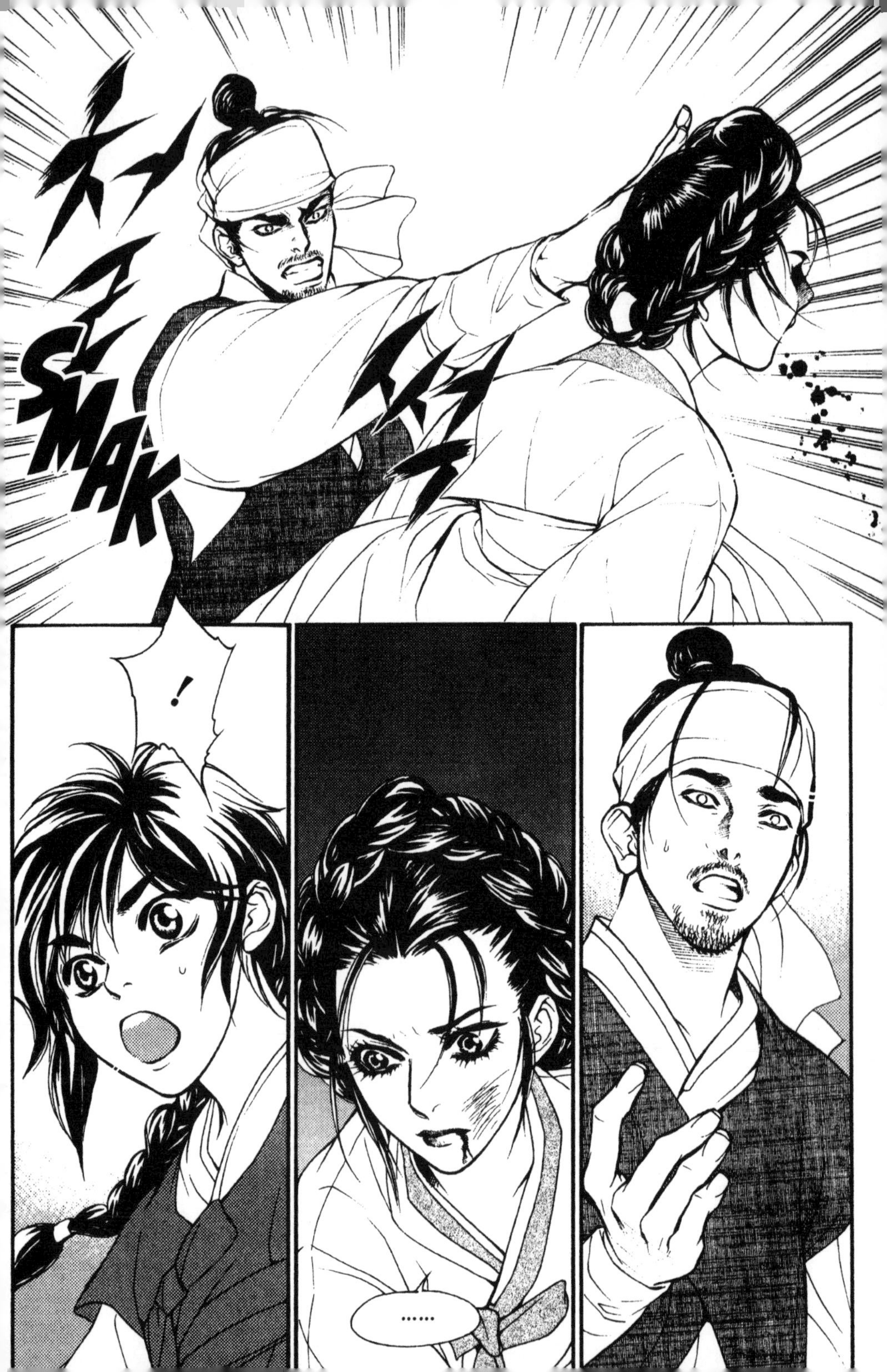
SMAK
!
……

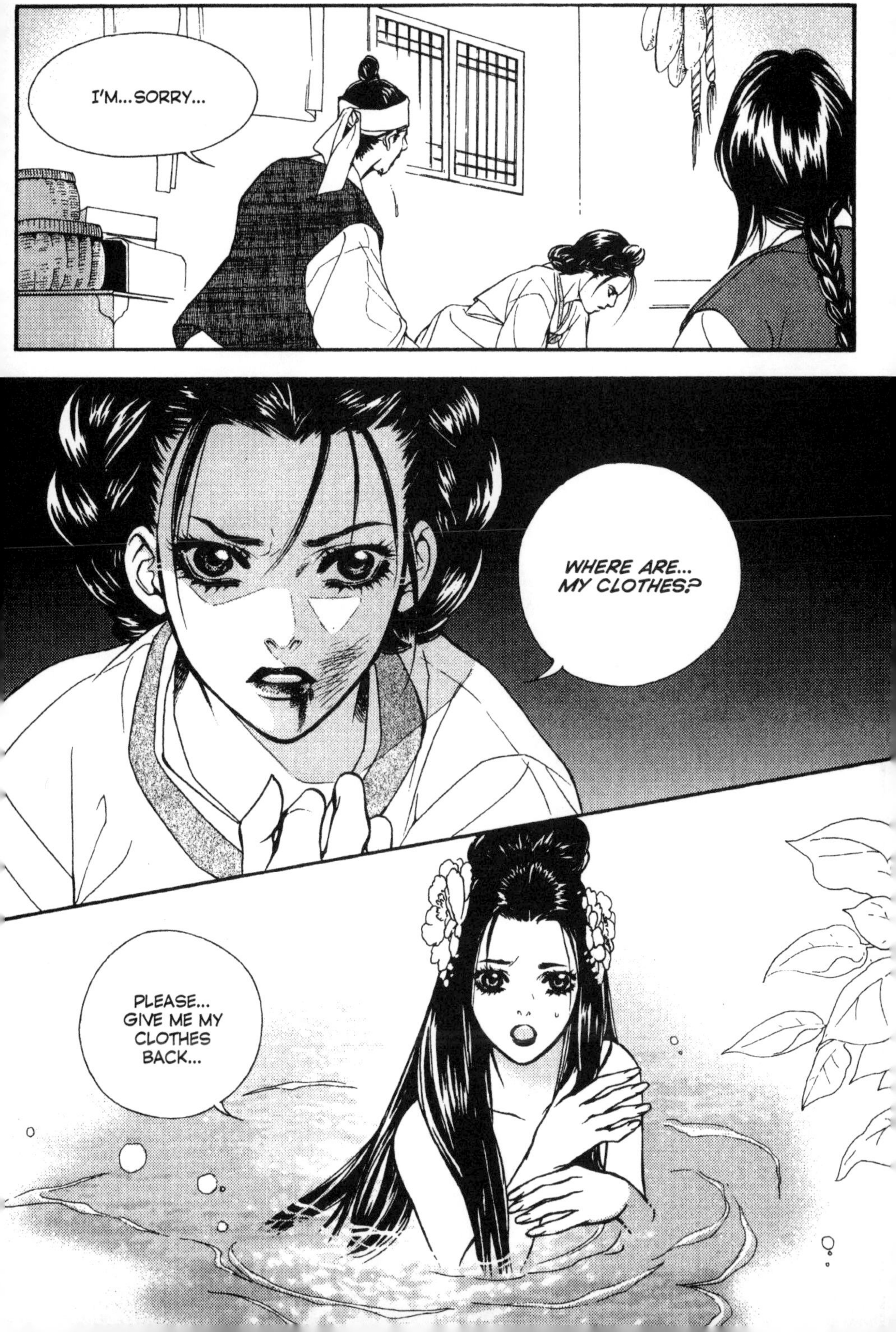
I'M...SORRY...
WHERE ARE... MY CLOTHES?
PLEASE... GIVE ME MY CLOTHES BACK...

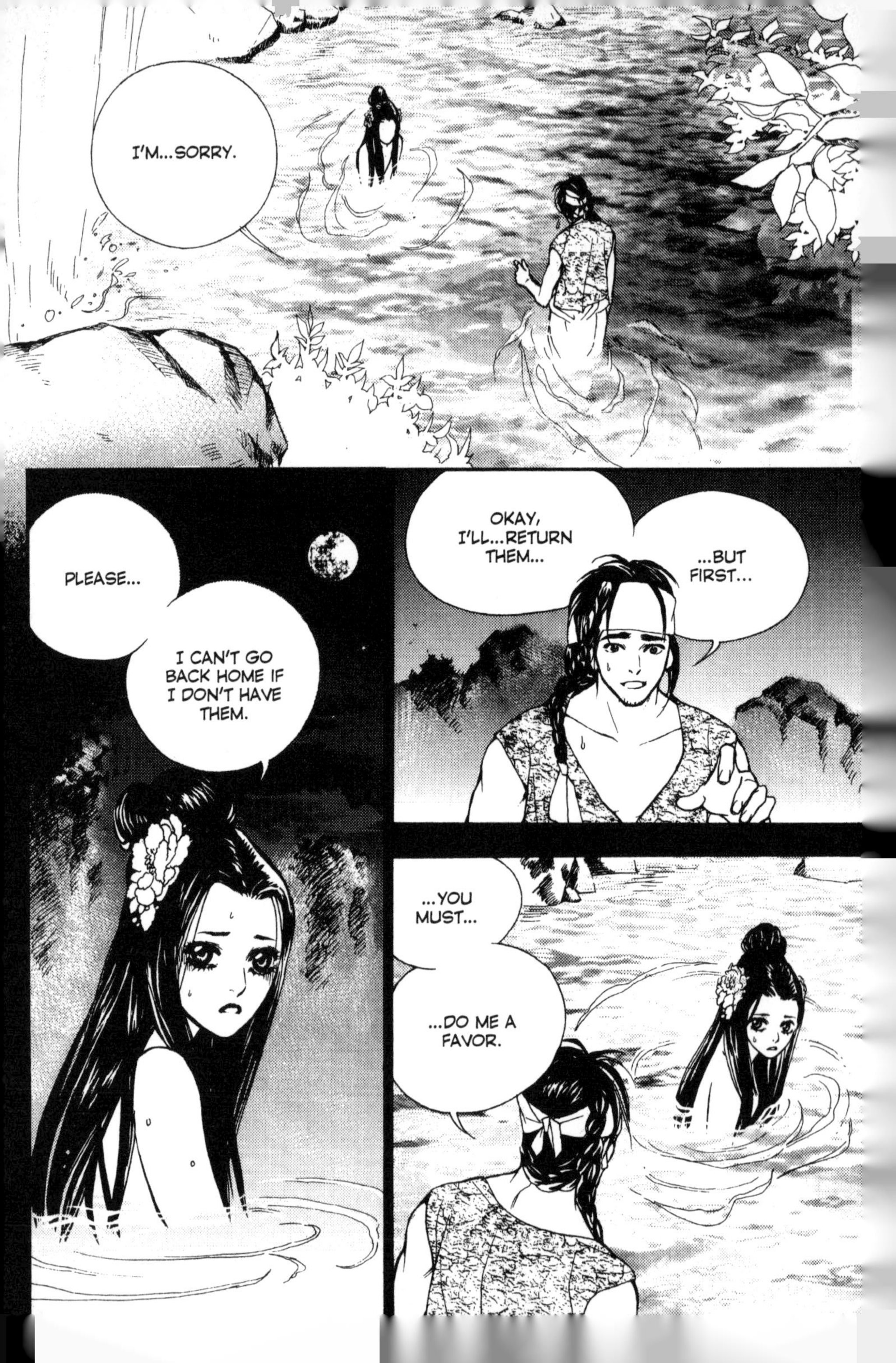
I'M...SORRY.
PLEASE...
I CAN'T GO BACK HOME IF I DON'T HAVE THEM.
OKAY, I'LL...RETURN THEM...
...BUT FIRST...
...YOU MUST...
...DO ME A FAVOR.

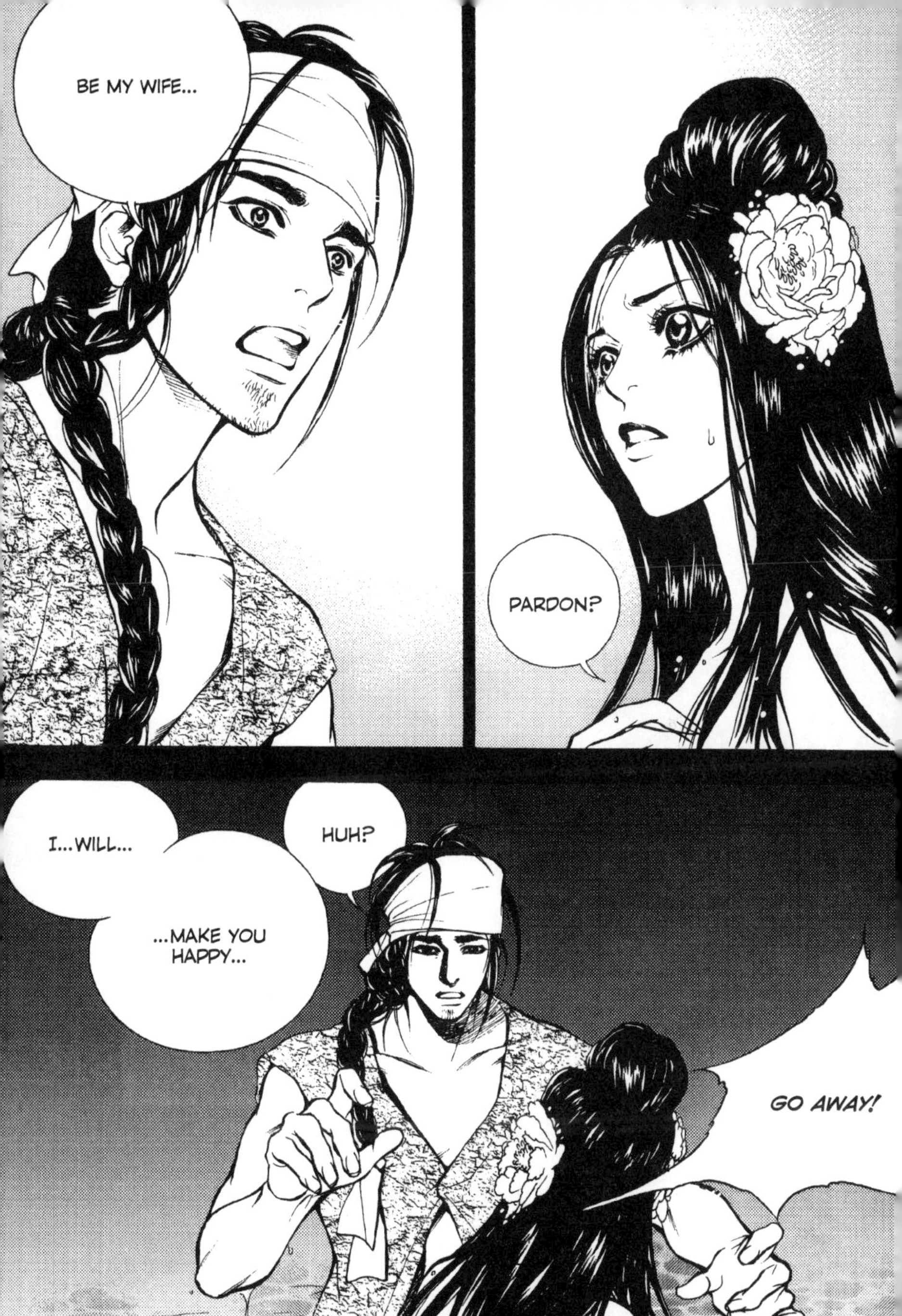
BE MY WIFE...
PARDON?
I...WILL...
HUH?
...MAKE YOU HAPPY...
GO AWAY!

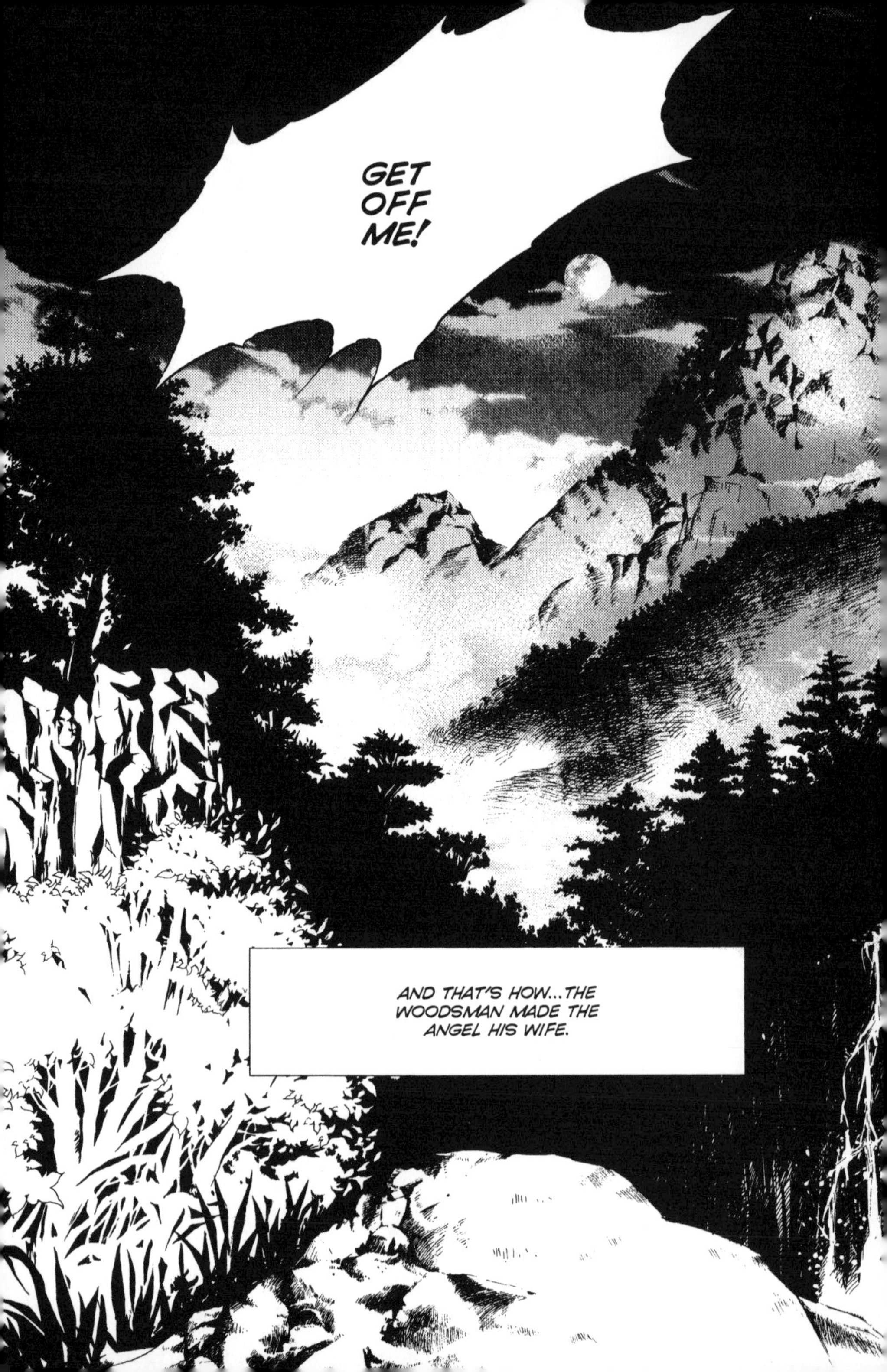
GET OFF ME!
AND THAT'S HOW...THE WOODSMAN MADE THE ANGEL HIS WIFE.

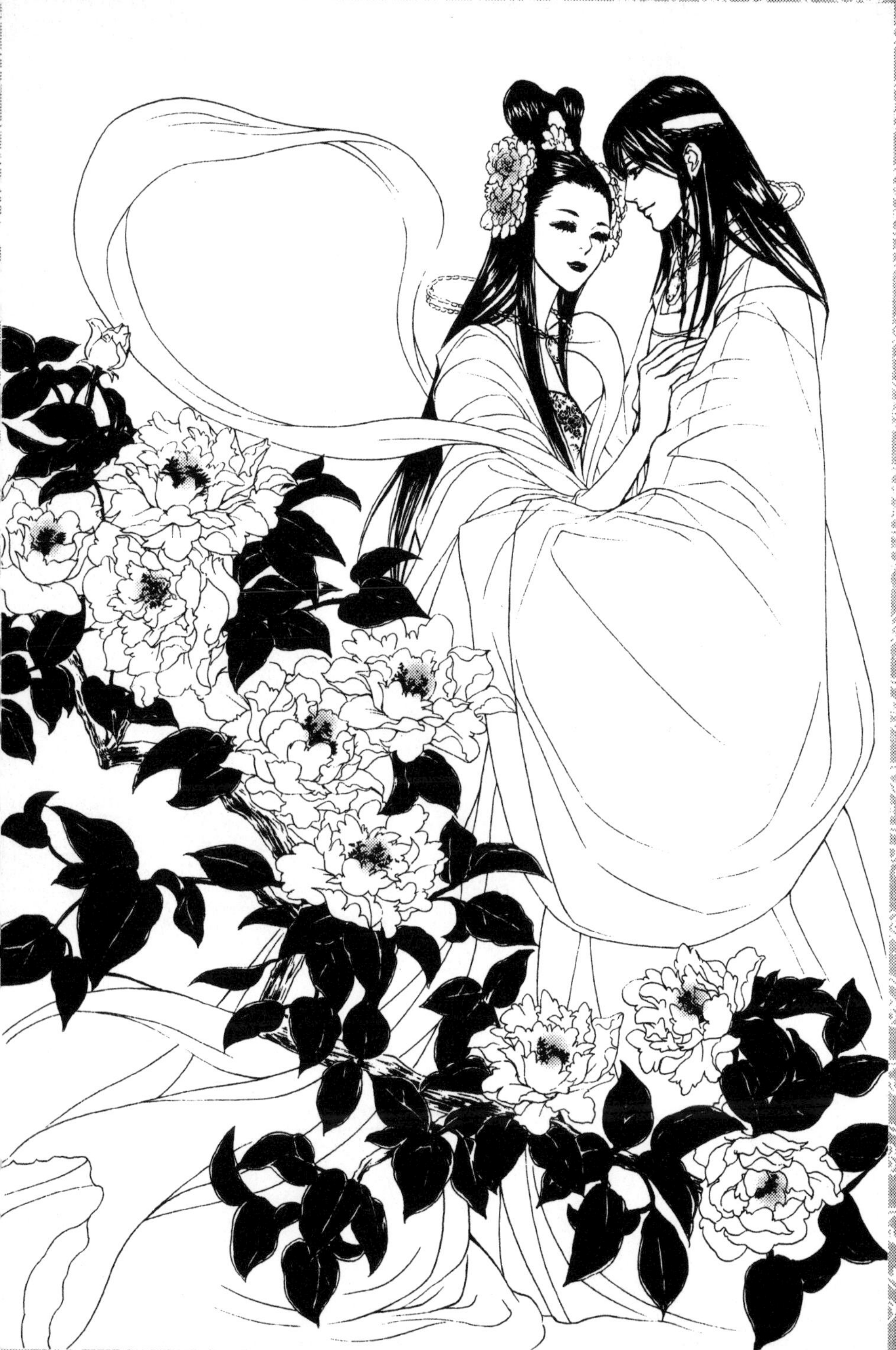

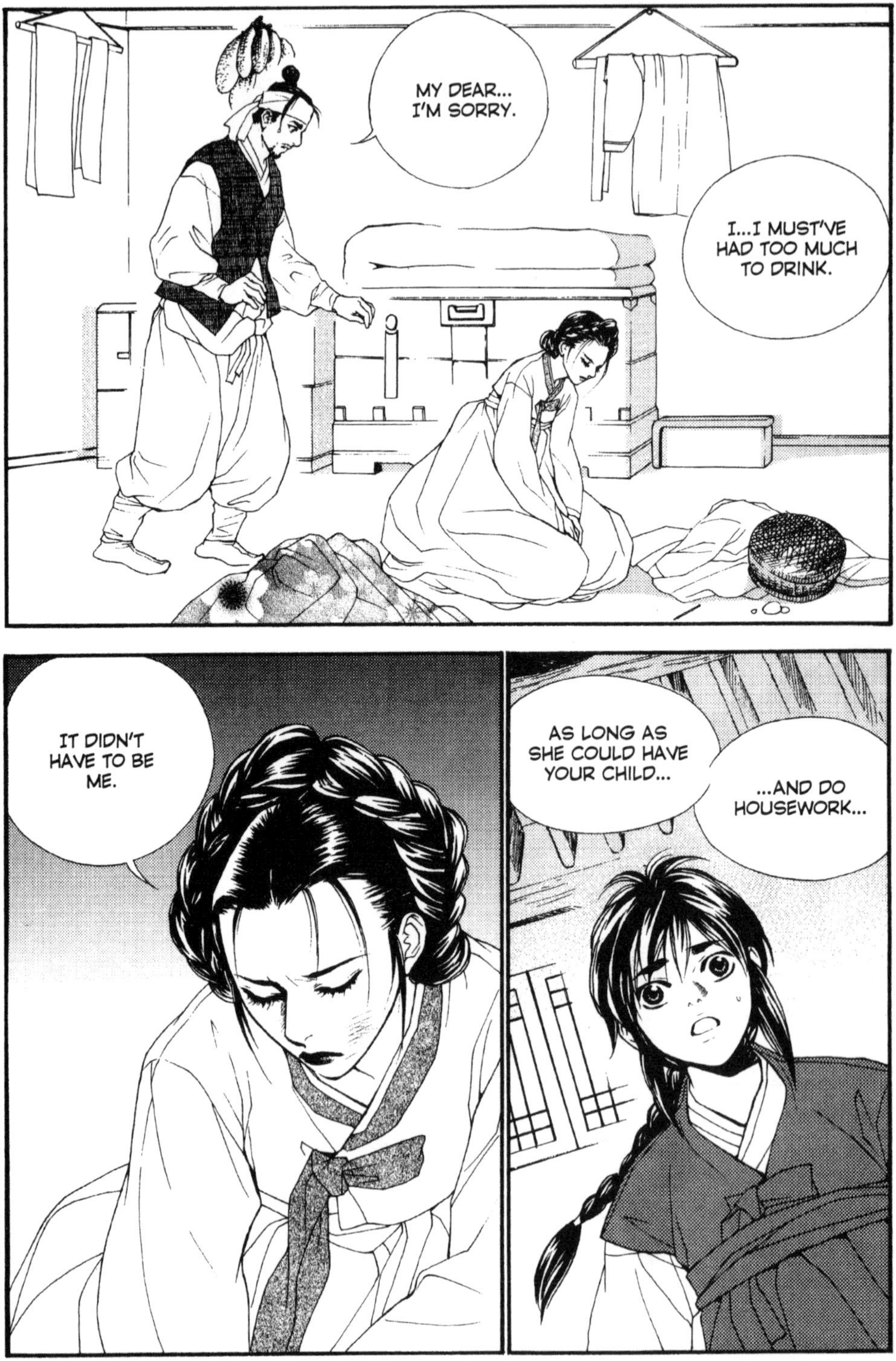
MY DEAR... I'M SORRY.
I...I MUST'VE HAD TOO MUCH TO DRINK.
IT DIDN'T HAVE TO BE ME.
AS LONG AS SHE COULD HAVE YOUR CHILD...
...AND DO HOUSEWORK...

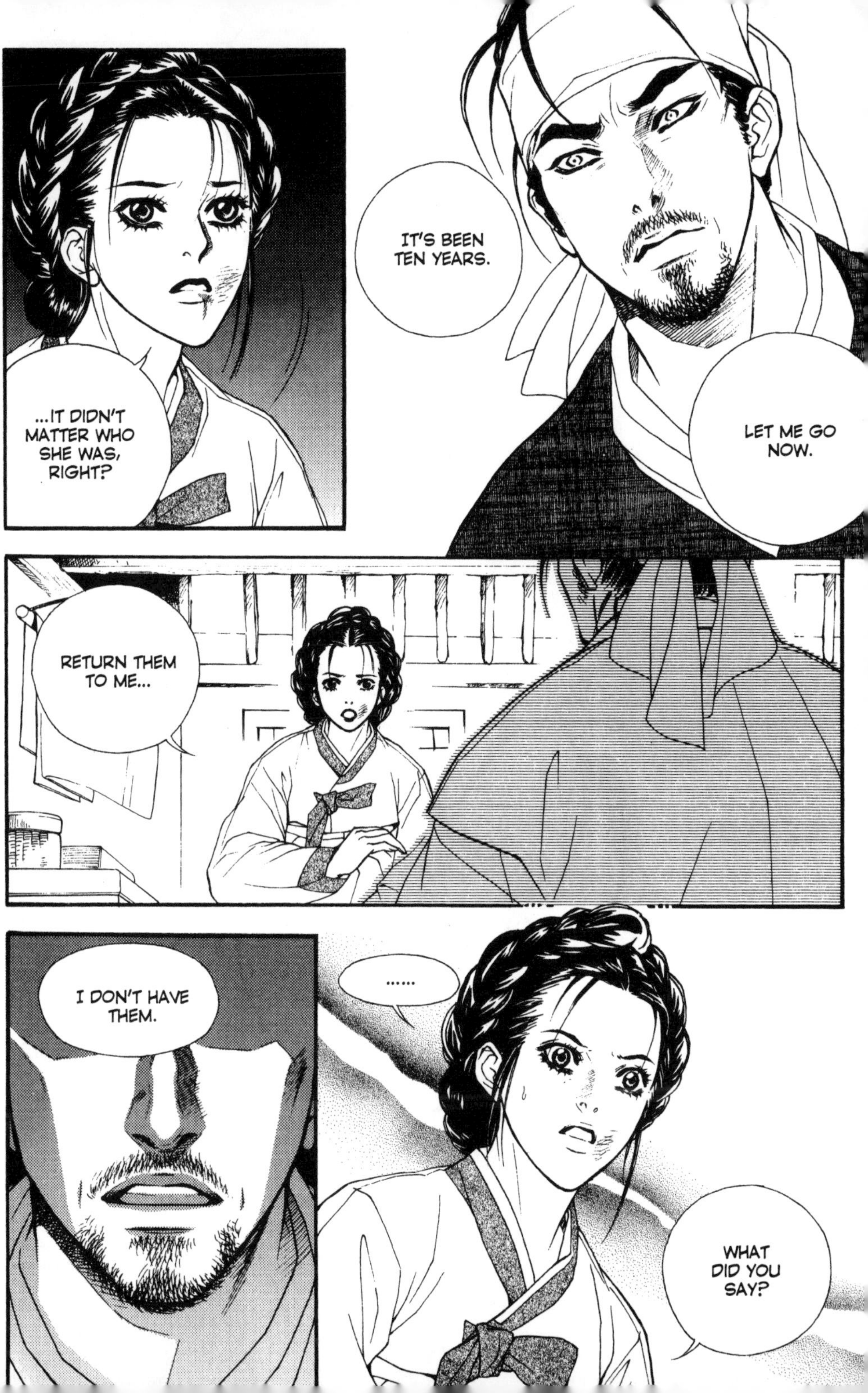
...IT DIDN'T MATTER WHO SHE WAS, RIGHT?
IT'S BEEN TEN YEARS.
LET ME GO NOW.
RETURN THEM TO ME...
I DON'T HAVE THEM.
......
WHAT DID YOU SAY?

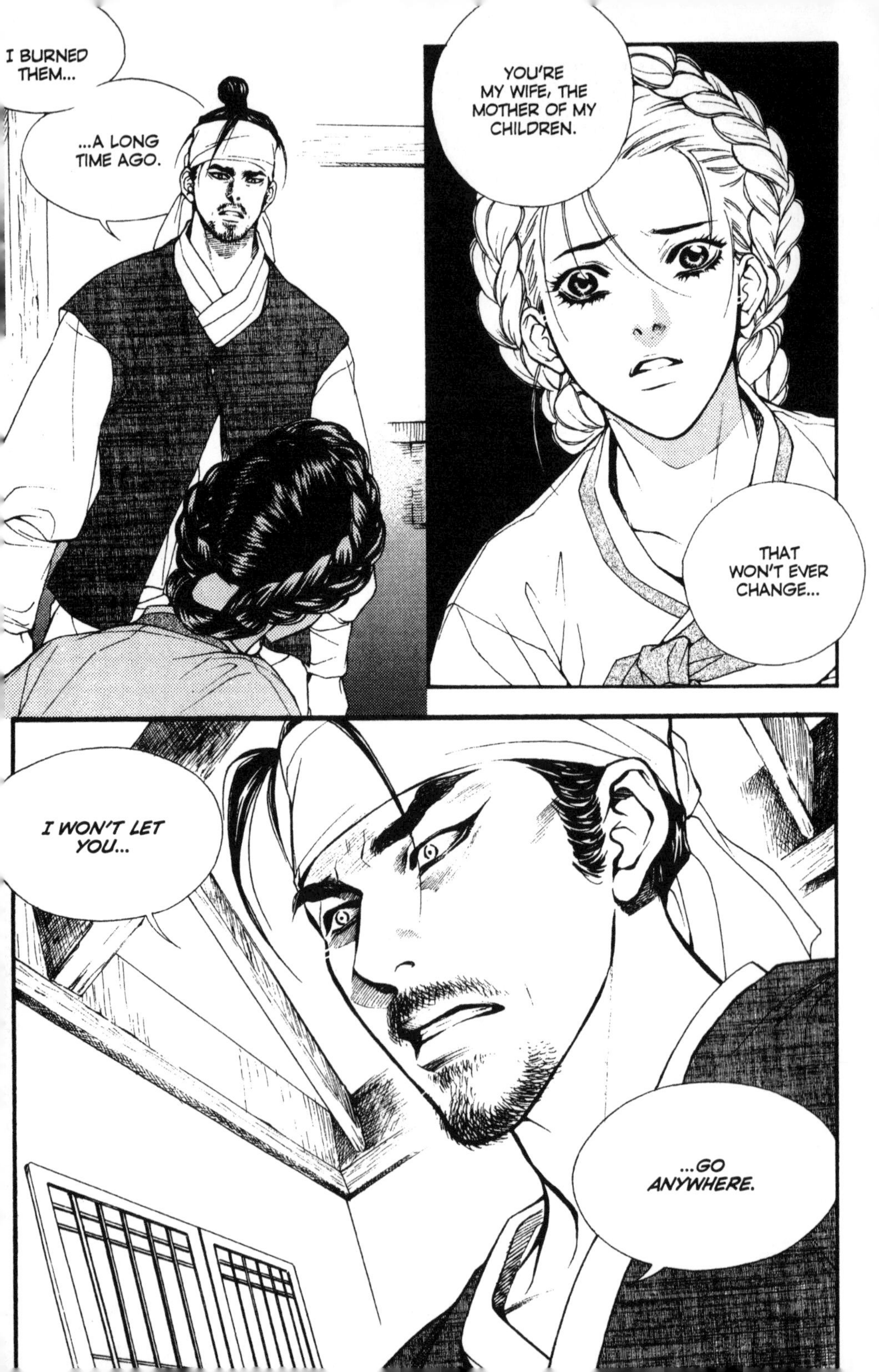
I BURNED THEM...
...A LONG TIME AGO.
YOU'RE MY WIFE, THE MOTHER OF MY CHILDREN.
THAT WON'T EVER CHANGE...
I WON'T LET YOU...
...GO ANYWHERE.

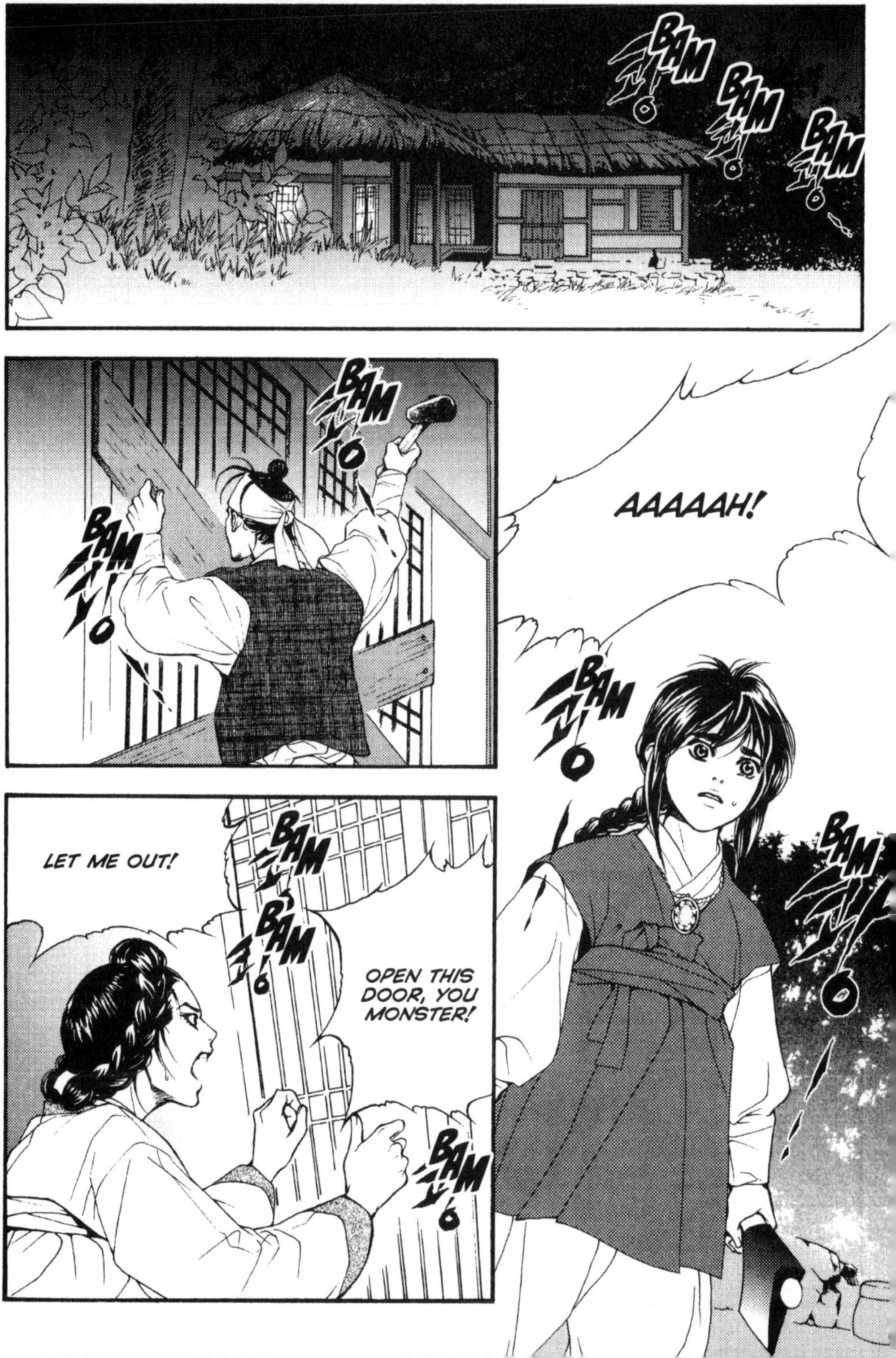
BAM
BAM
BAM
BAM
BAM
LET ME OUT!
BAM
BAM
OPEN THIS DOOR, YOU MONSTER!
BAM
AAAAAH!
BAM
BAM

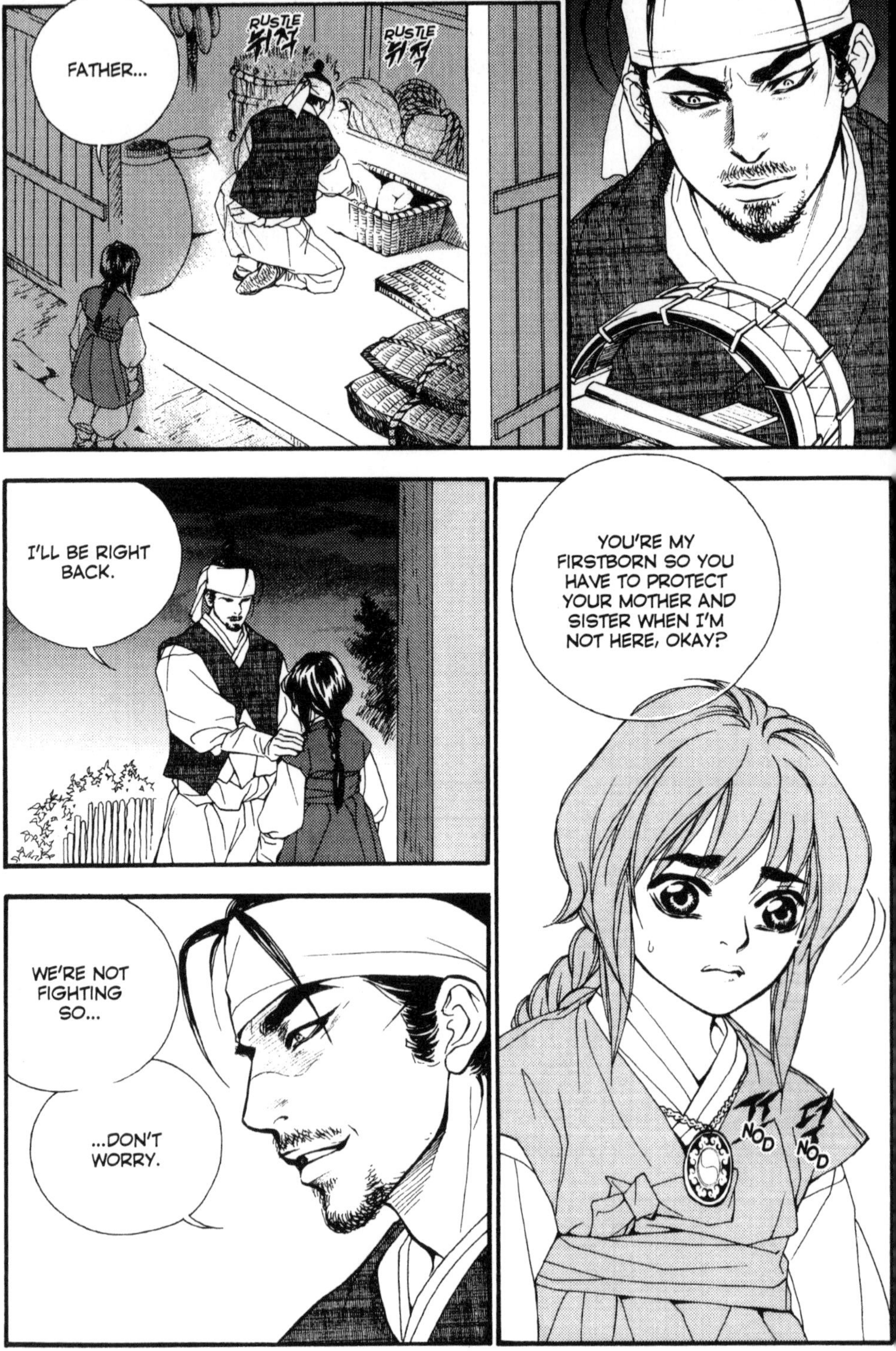
FATHER...
RUSTLE
뒤적
RUSTLE
뒤적
I'LL BE RIGHT BACK.
WE'RE NOT FIGHTING SO...
...DON'T WORRY.
YOU'RE MY FIRSTBORN SO YOU HAVE TO PROTECT YOUR MOTHER AND SISTER WHEN I'M NOT HERE, OKAY?
NOD
NOD

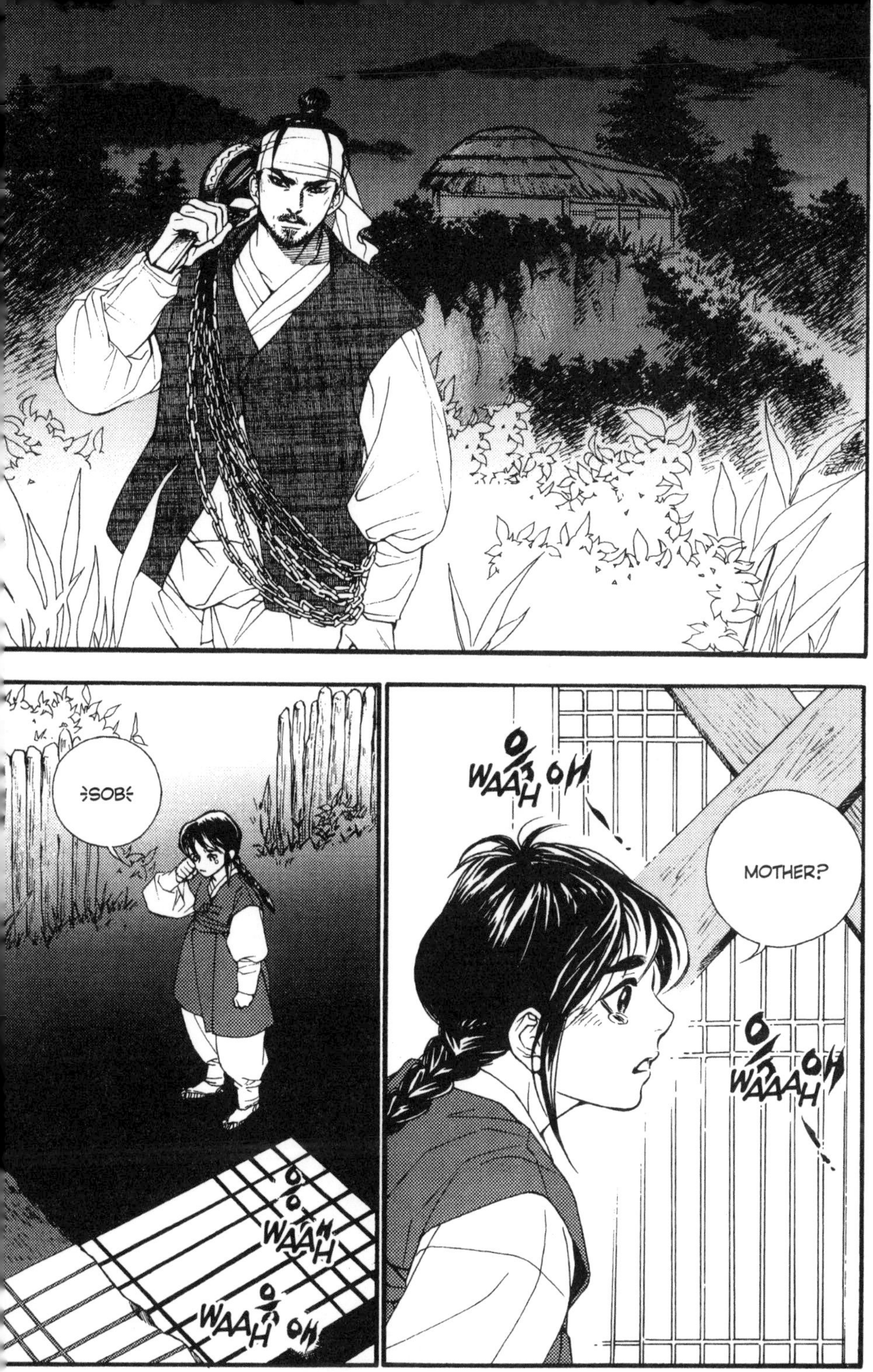
SOB
WAAH
WAAH OH
WAAH OH
MOTHER?
WAAAH OH

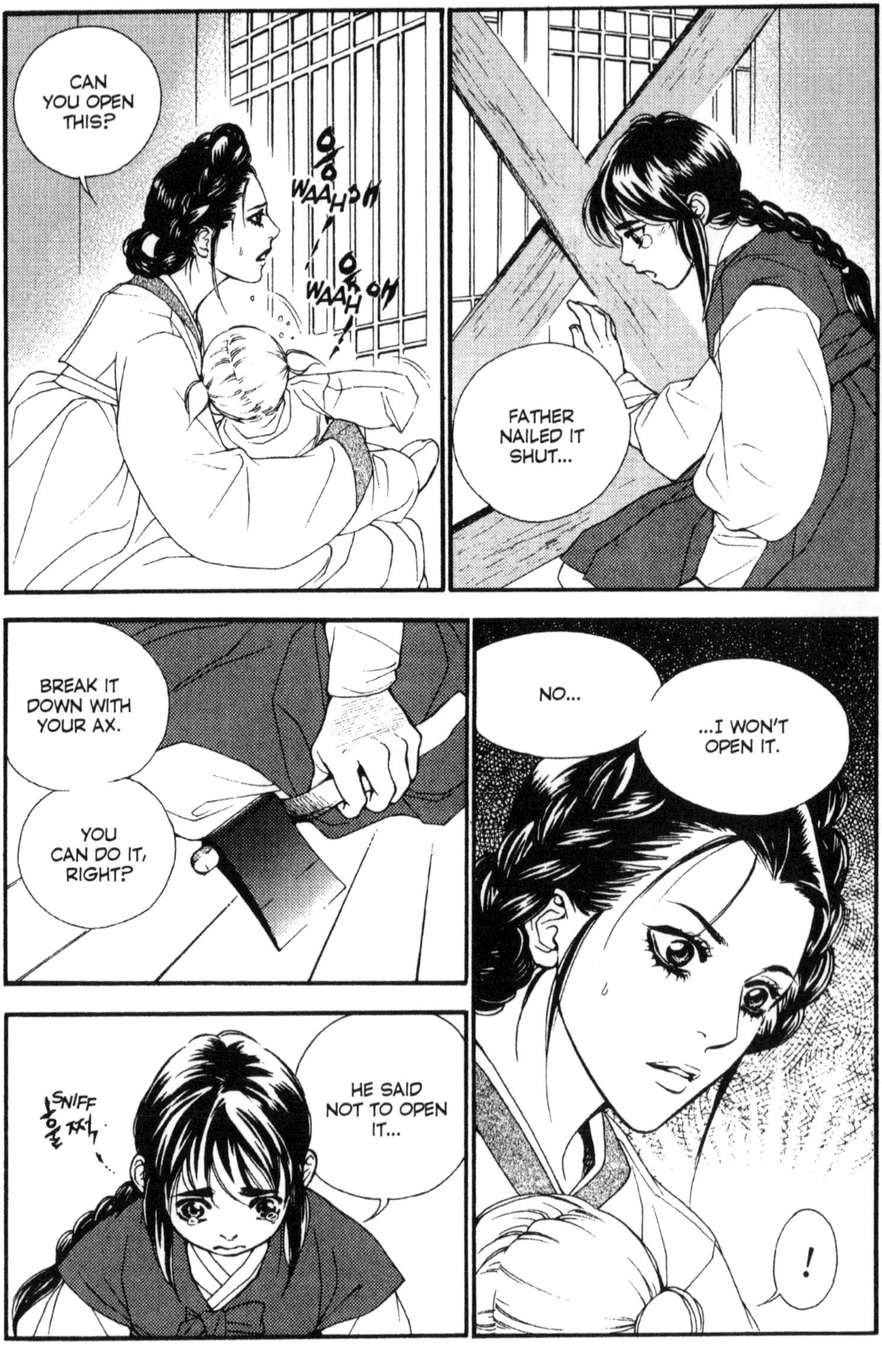
CAN YOU OPEN THIS?
WAAH
WAAH
FATHER NAILED IT SHUT...
BREAK IT DOWN WITH YOUR AX.
YOU CAN DO IT, RIGHT?
SNIFF
HE SAID NOT TO OPEN IT...
NO...
...I WON'T OPEN IT.
!

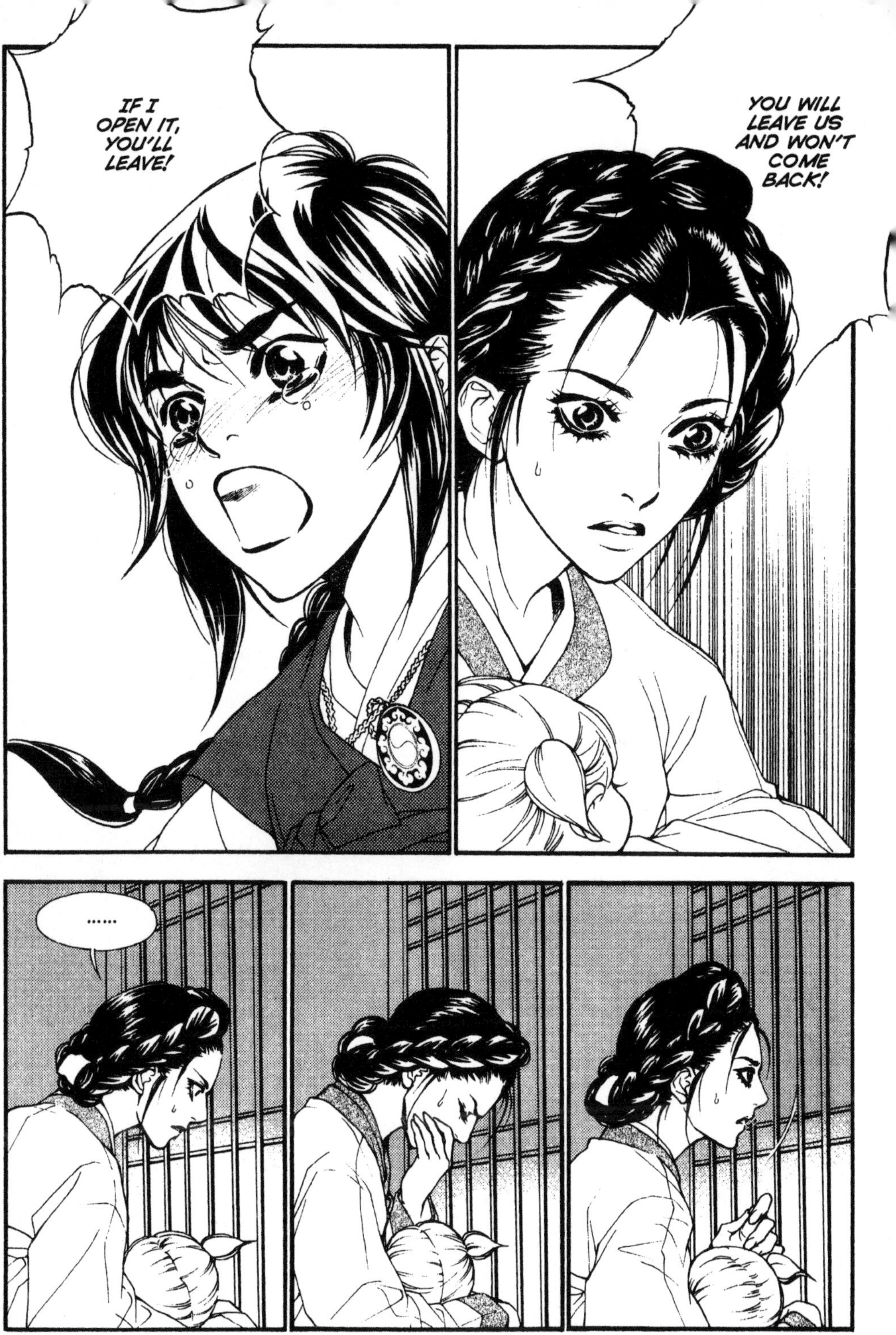
IF I OPEN IT, YOU'LL LEAVE!
YOU WILL LEAVE US AND WON'T COME BACK!
......

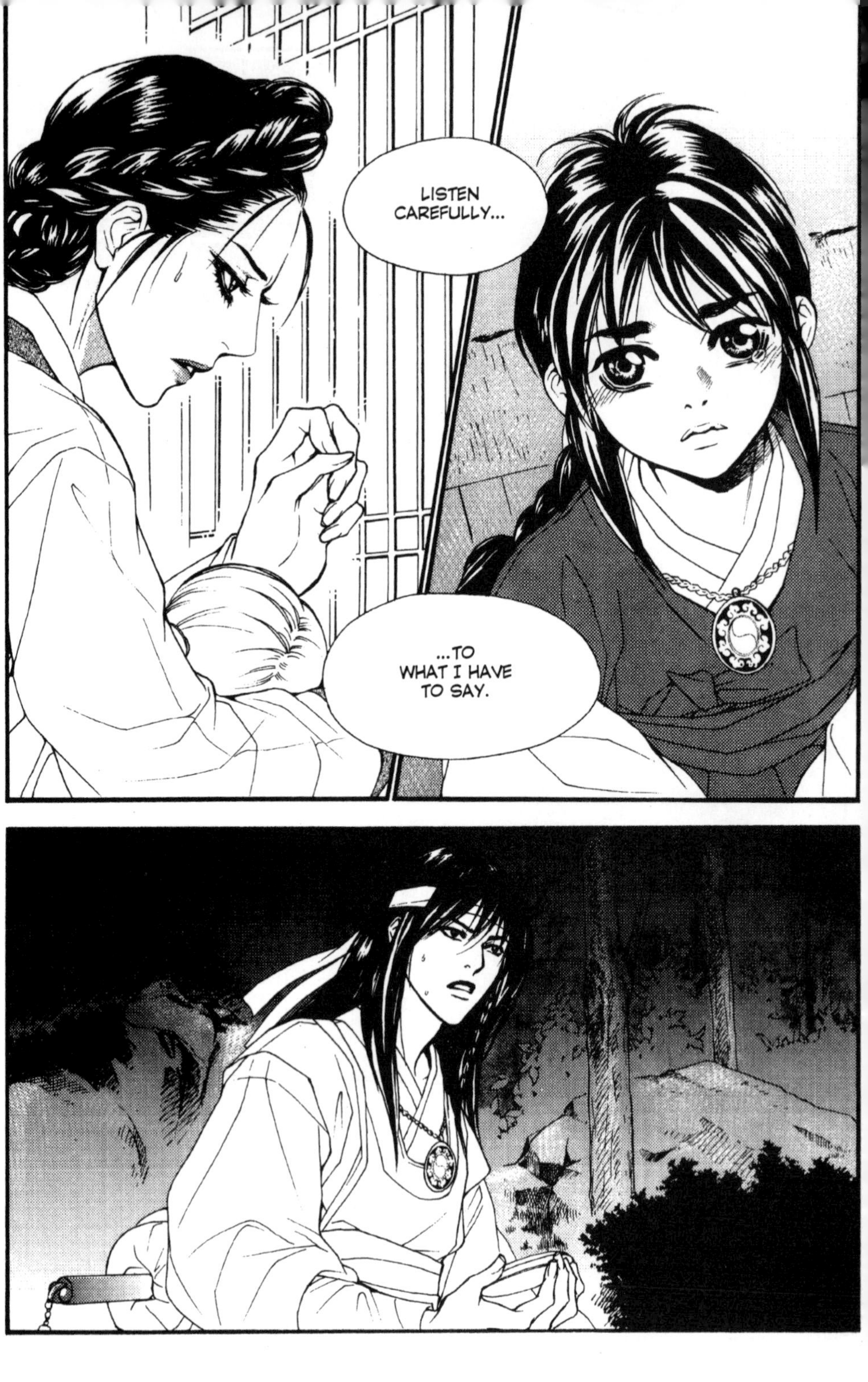
LISTEN CAREFULLY...
...TO WHAT I HAVE TO SAY.

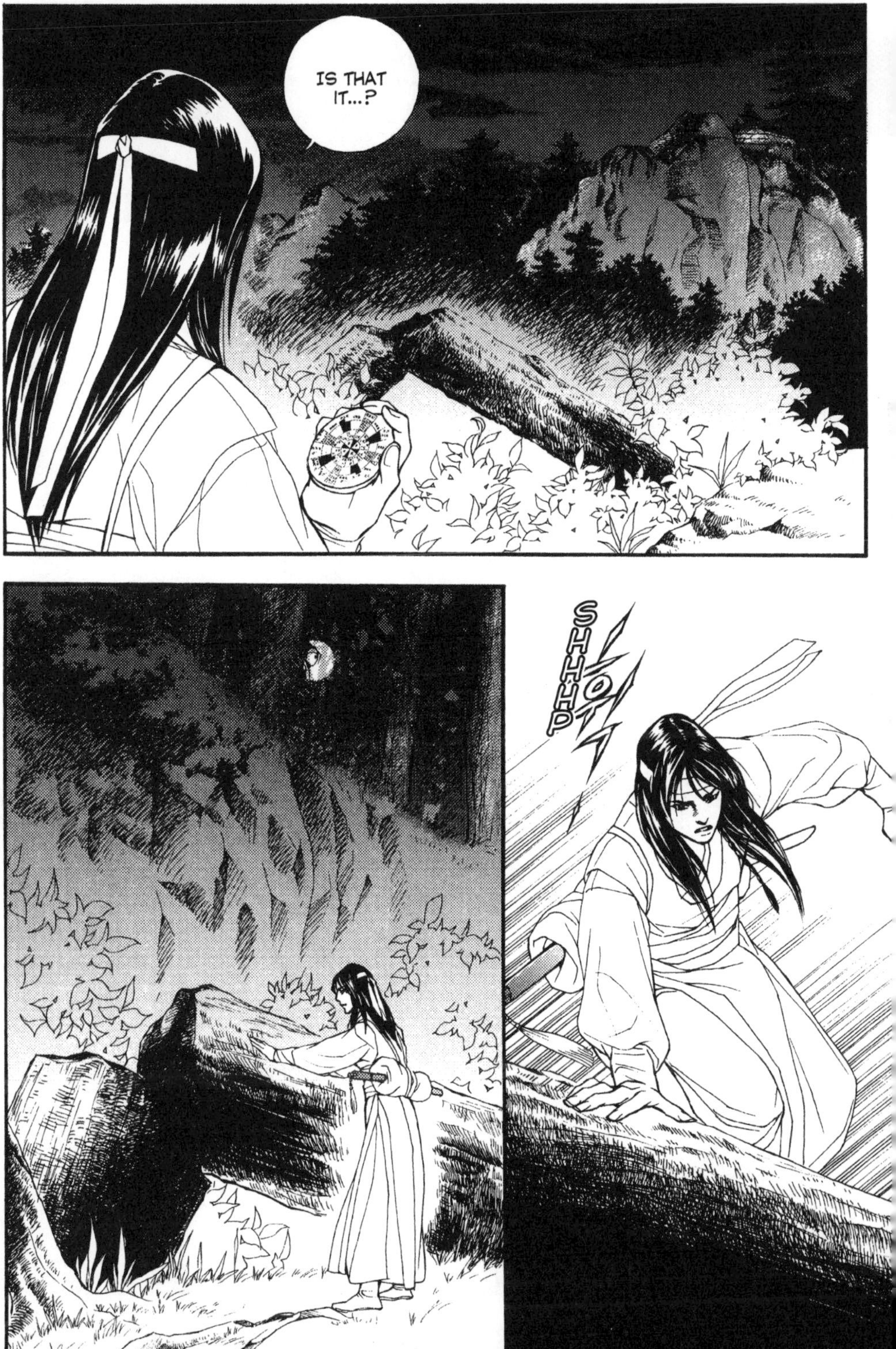
IS THAT IT...?
SHHHP

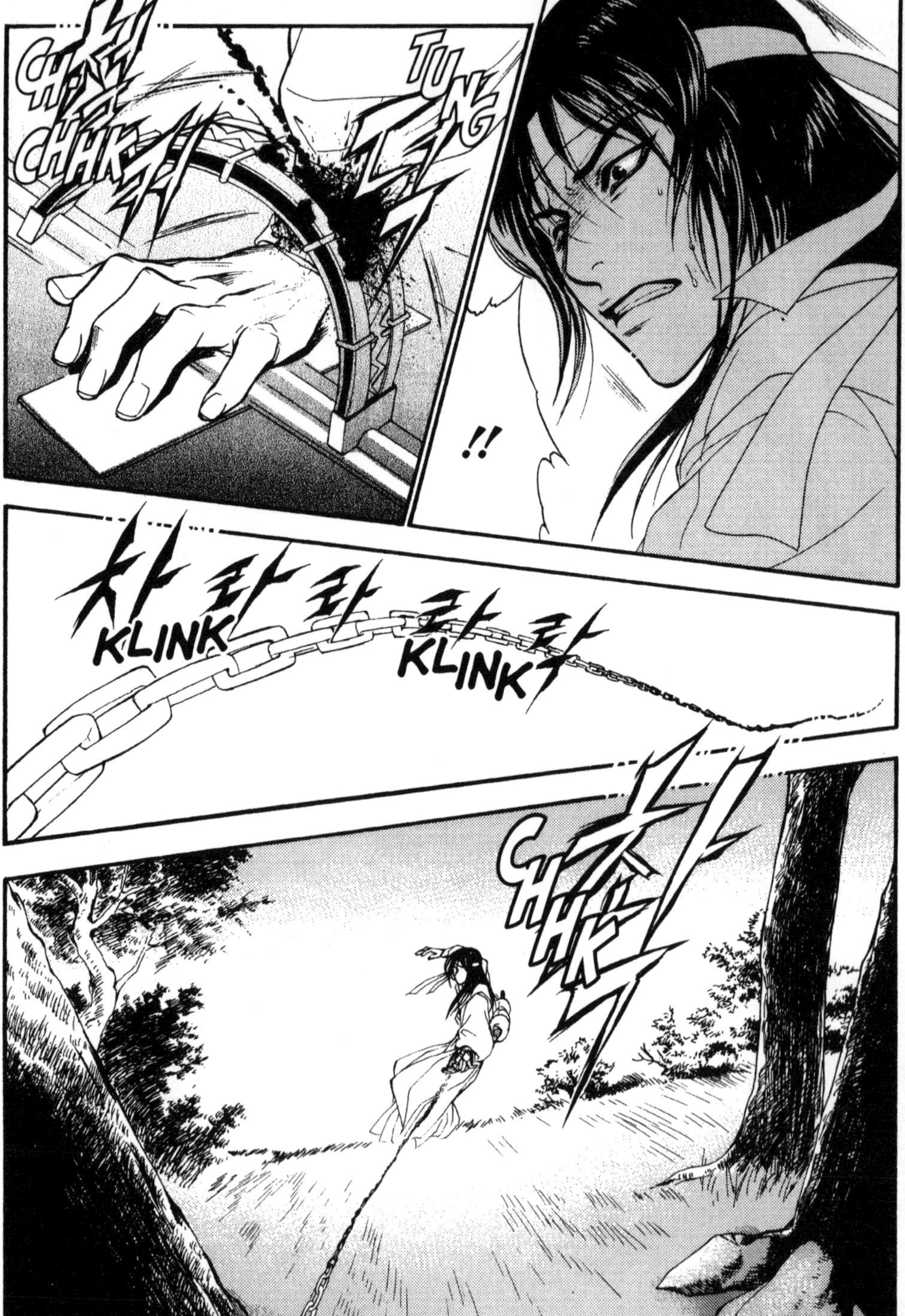
CHHR
TUNG
!!
KLINK
KLINK
CHHK

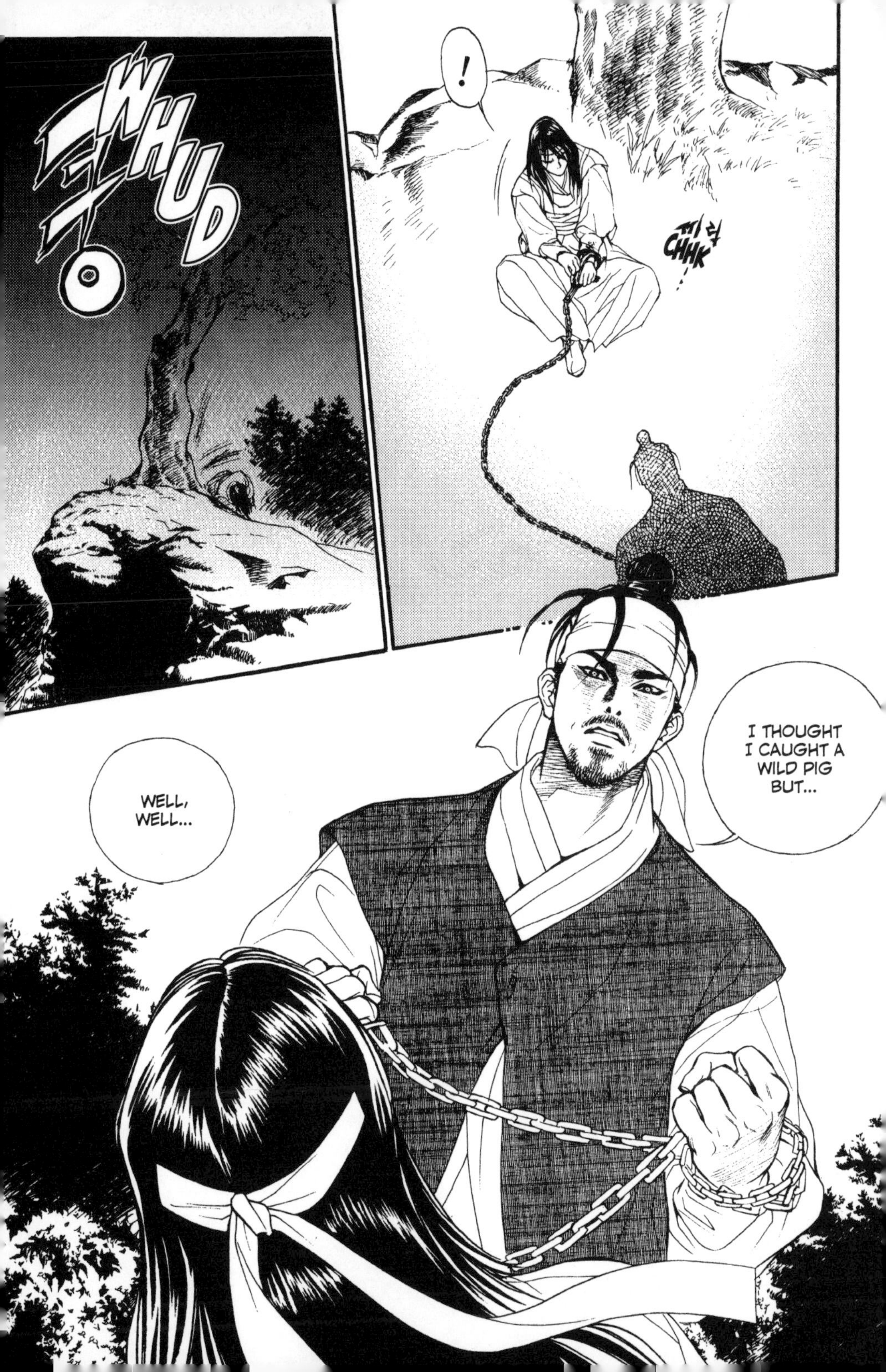

!
WHUD
CHHK
I THOUGHT I CAUGHT A WILD PIG BUT...
WELL, WELL...

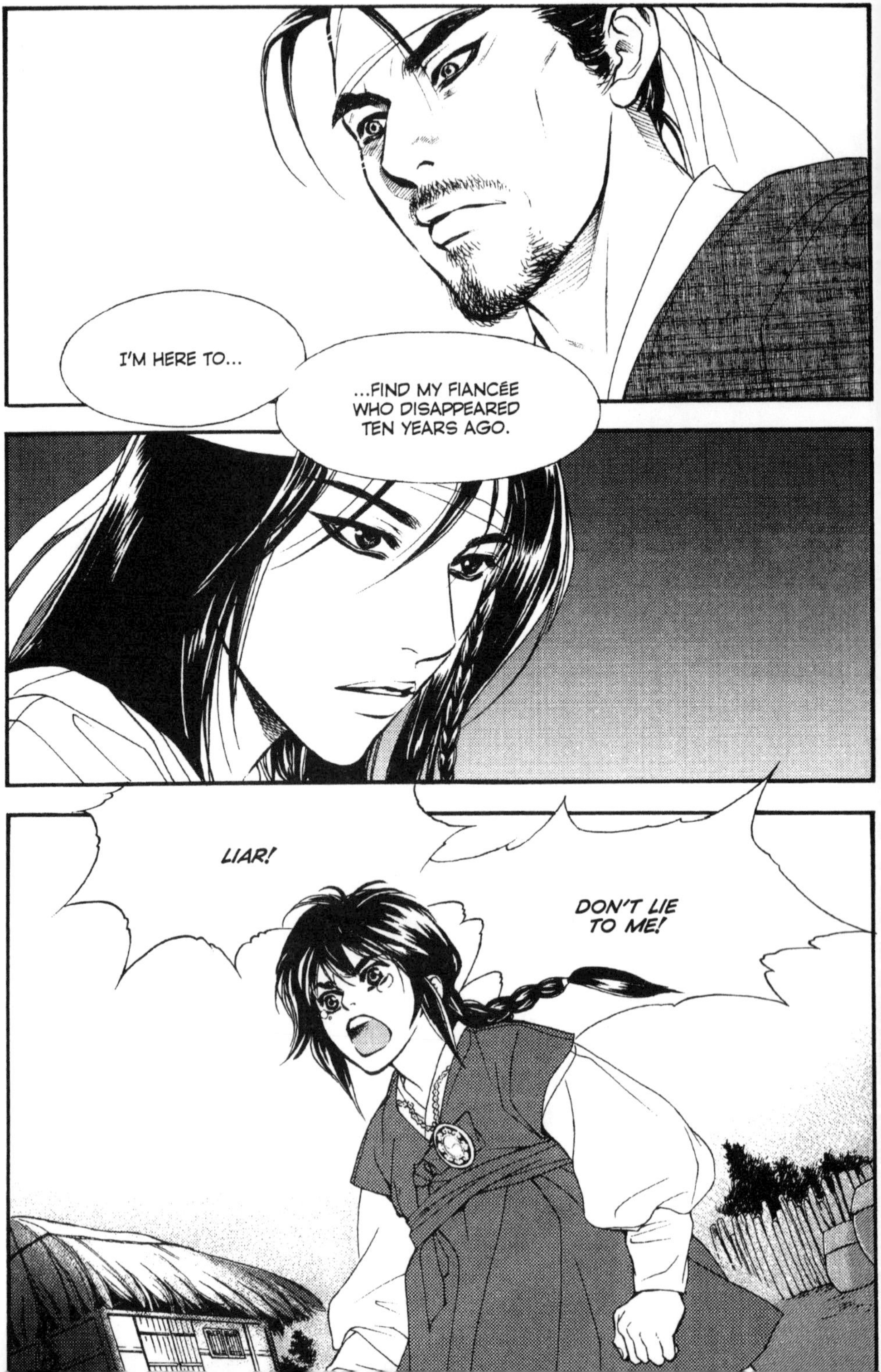
I'M HERE TO...
...FIND MY FIANCÉE WHO DISAPPEARED TEN YEARS AGO.
LIAR!
DON'T LIE TO ME!

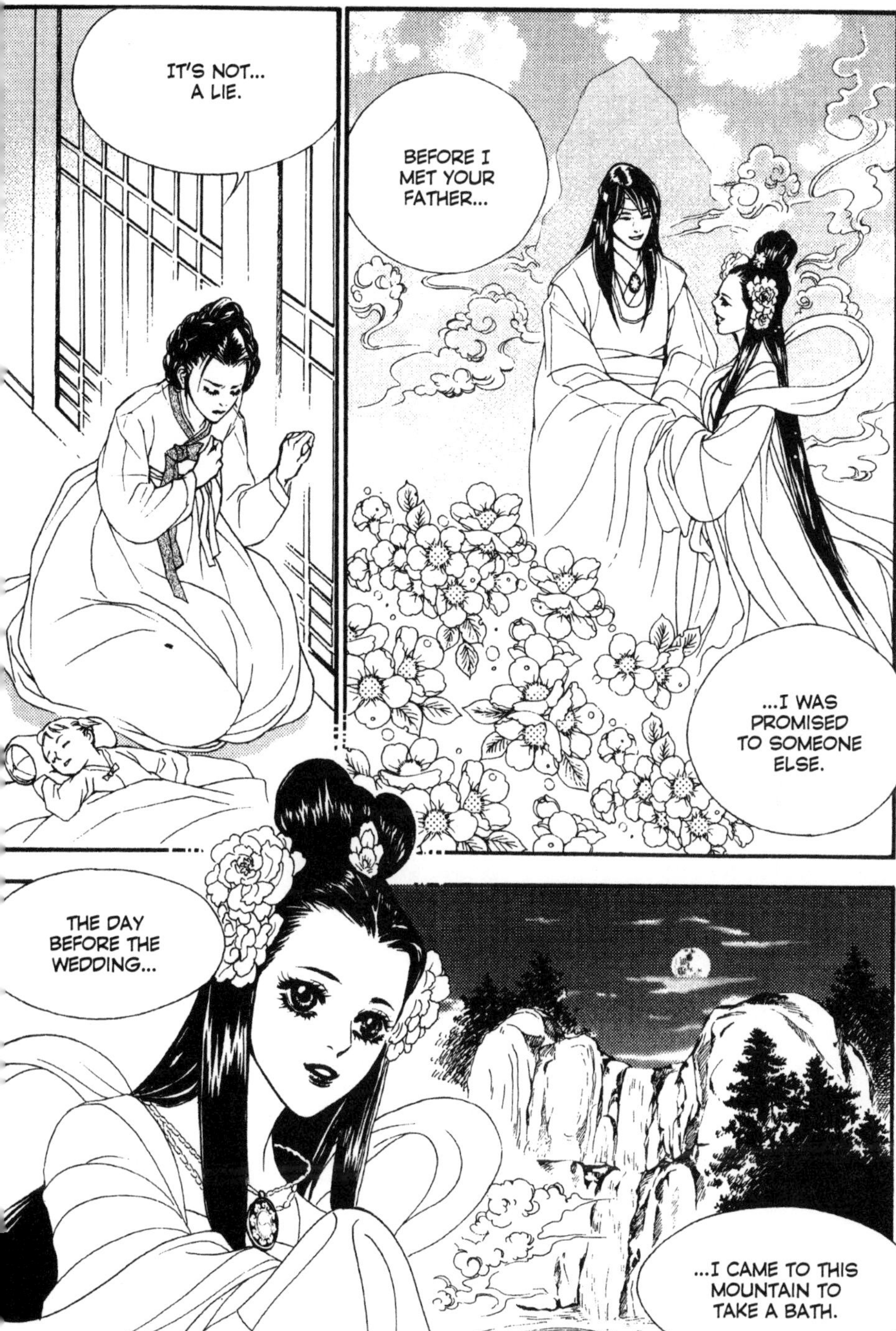
IT'S NOT... A LIE.
BEFORE I MET YOUR FATHER...
...I WAS PROMISED TO SOMEONE ELSE.
THE DAY BEFORE THE WEDDING...
...I CAME TO THIS MOUNTAIN TO TAKE A BATH.

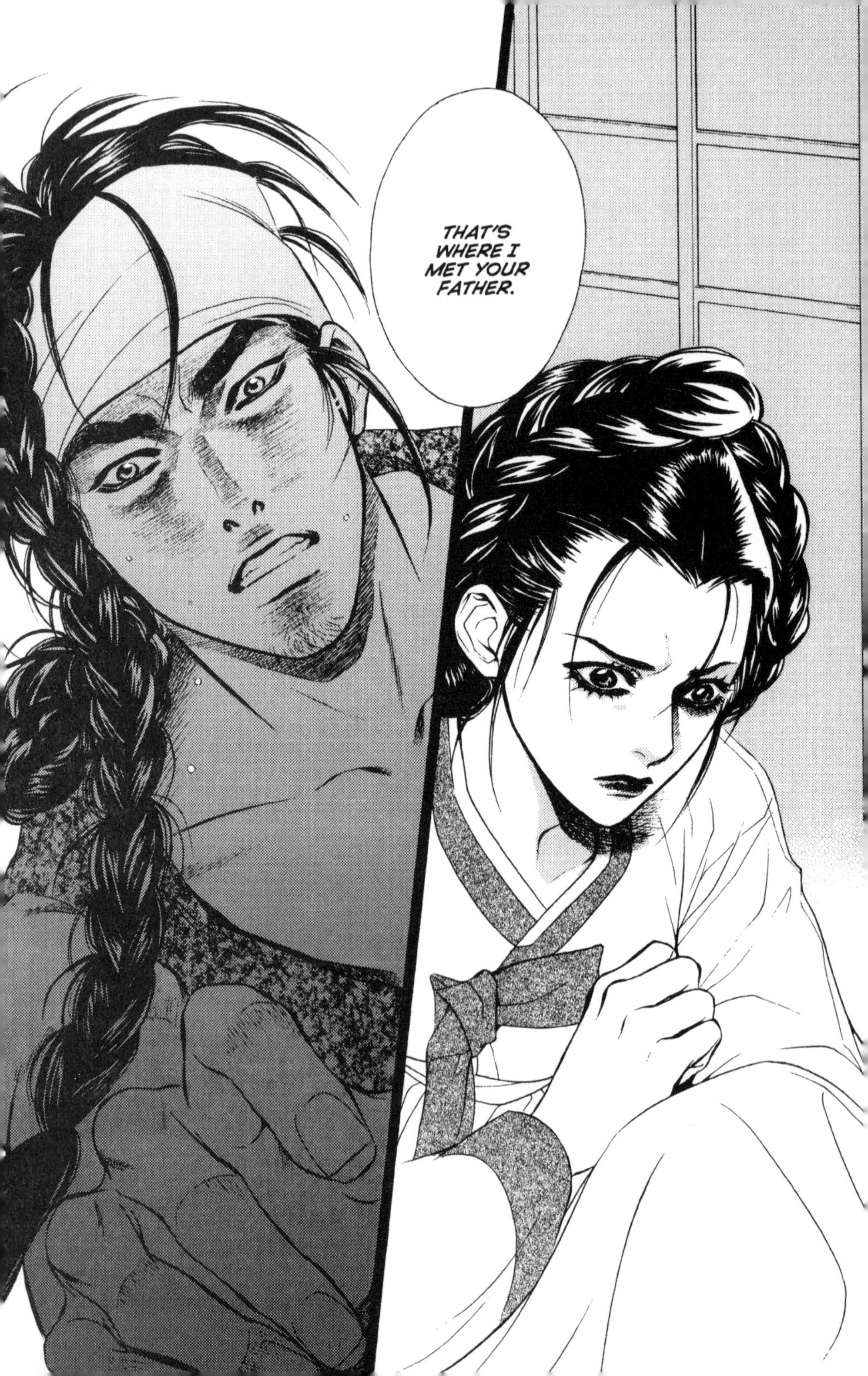
THAT'S WHERE I MET YOUR FATHER.

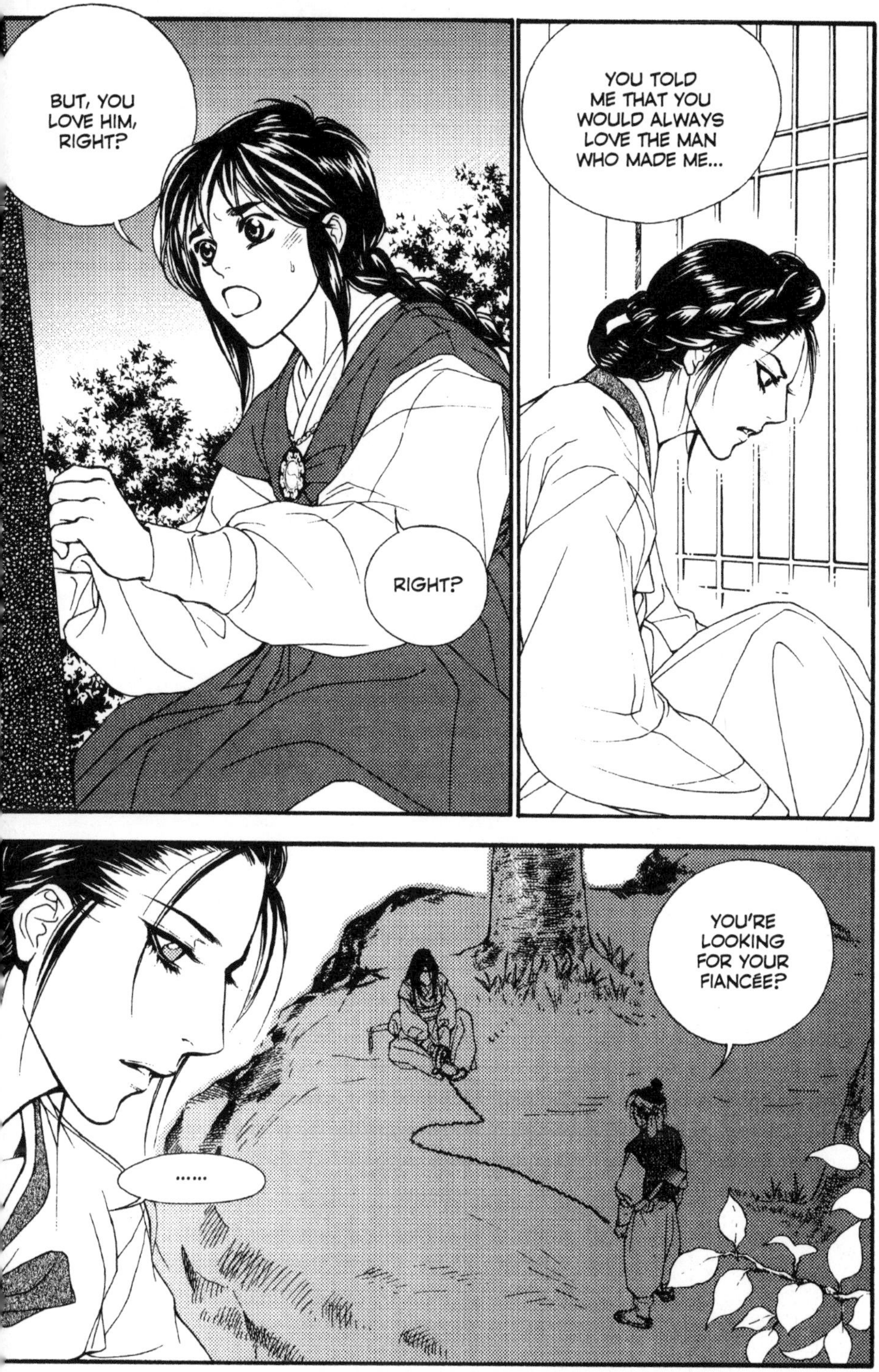
BUT, YOU LOVE HIM, RIGHT?
RIGHT?
YOU TOLD ME THAT YOU WOULD ALWAYS LOVE THE MAN WHO MADE ME...
......
YOU'RE LOOKING FOR YOUR FIANCÉE?

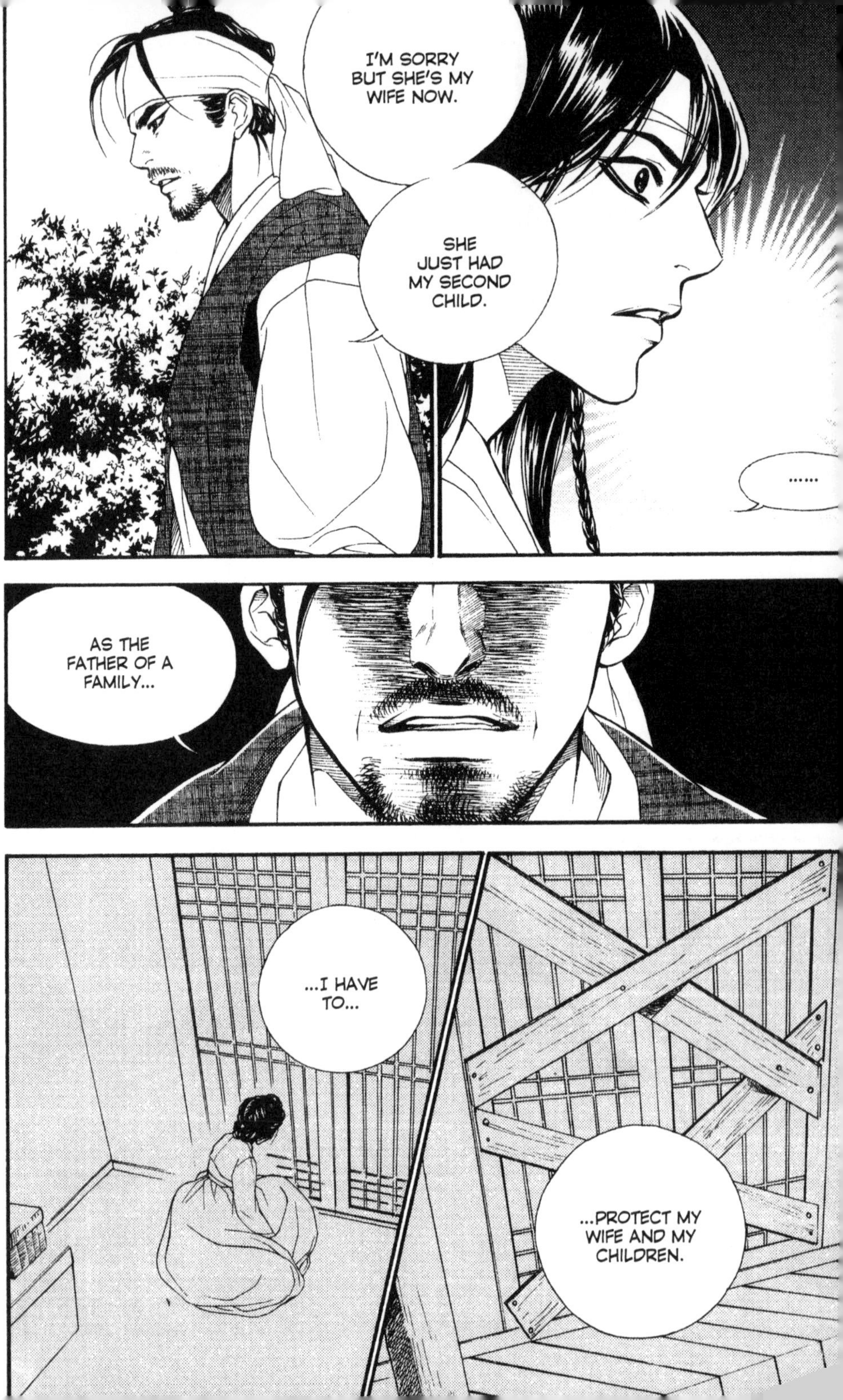
I'M SORRY BUT SHE'S MY WIFE NOW.
SHE JUST HAD MY SECOND CHILD.
......
AS THE FATHER OF A FAMILY...
...I HAVE TO...
...PROTECT MY WIFE AND MY CHILDREN.

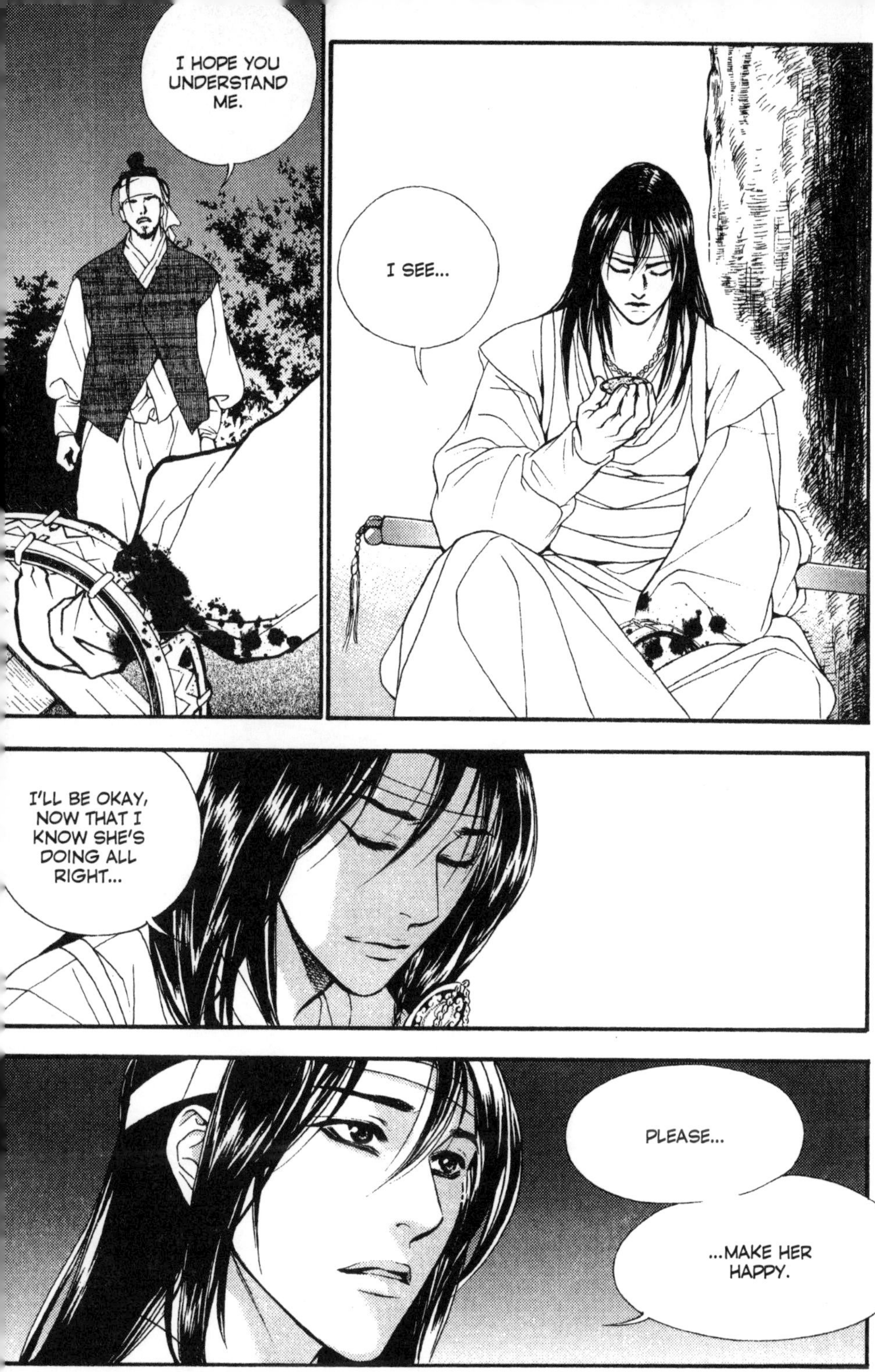
I HOPE YOU UNDERSTAND ME.
I SEE...
I'LL BE OKAY, NOW THAT I KNOW SHE'S DOING ALL RIGHT...
PLEASE...
...MAKE HER HAPPY.

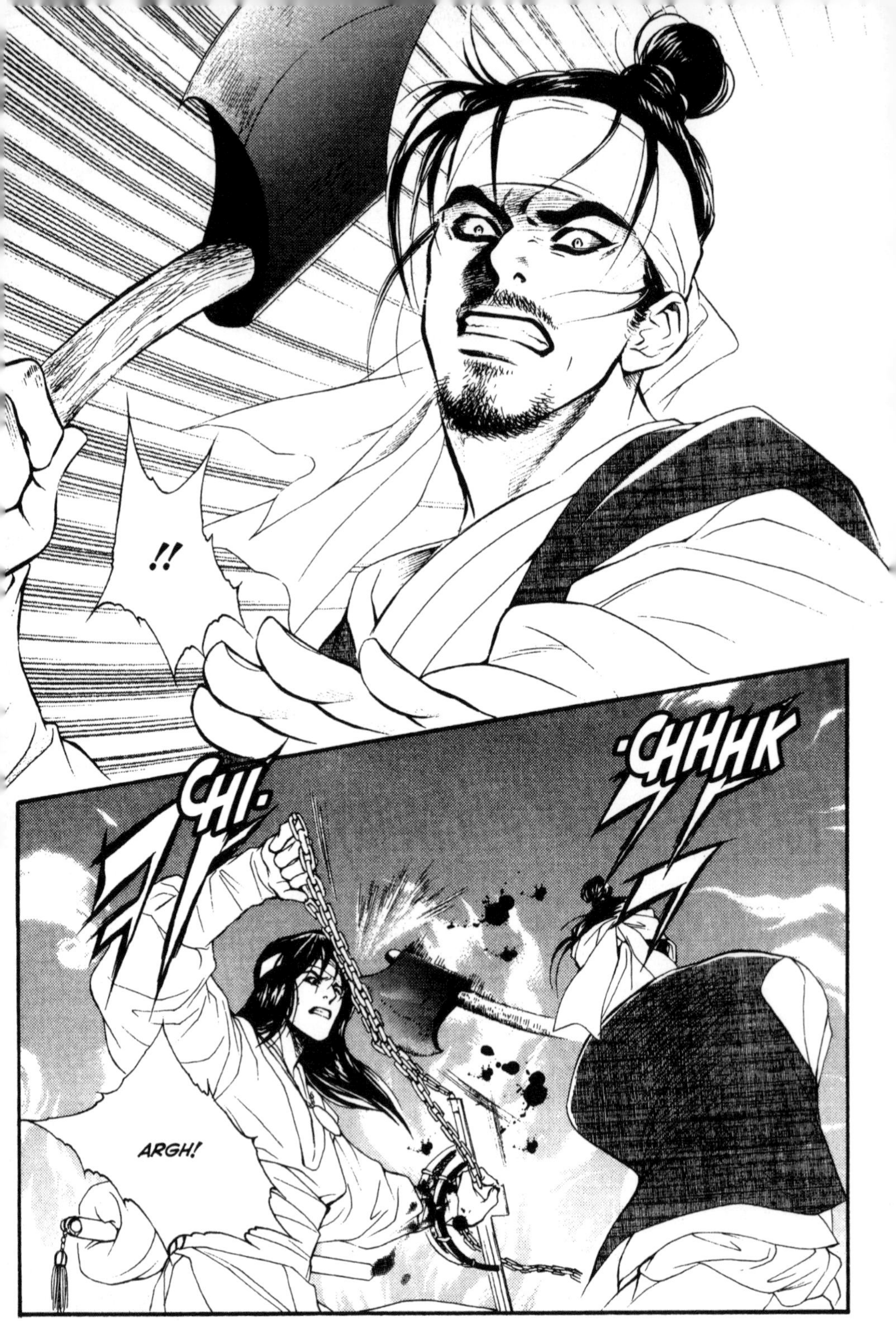
!!
CHI-
-CHHHK
ARGH!

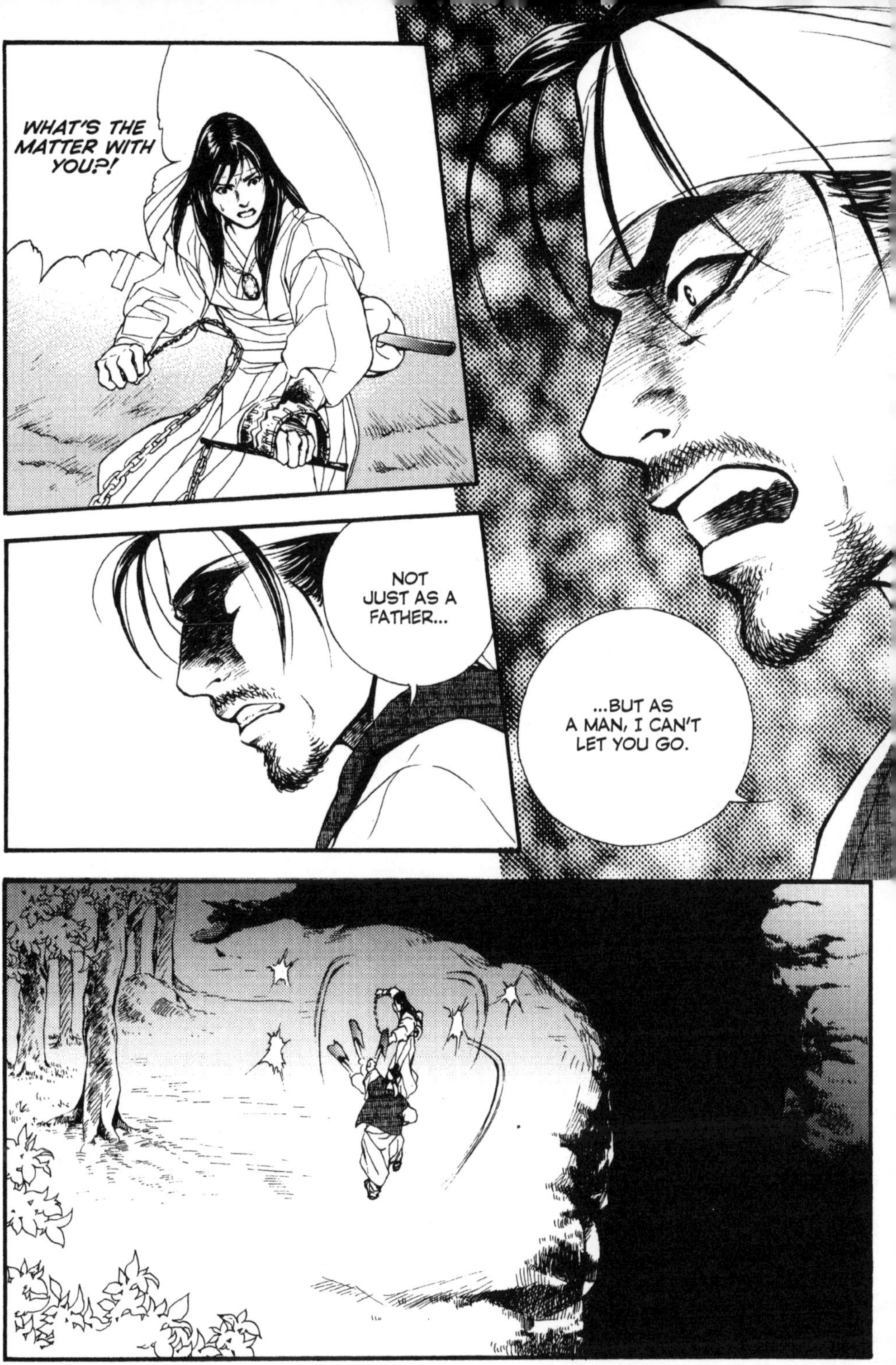
WHAT'S THE MATTER WITH YOU?!
NOT JUST AS A FATHER...
...BUT AS A MAN, I CAN'T LET YOU GO.

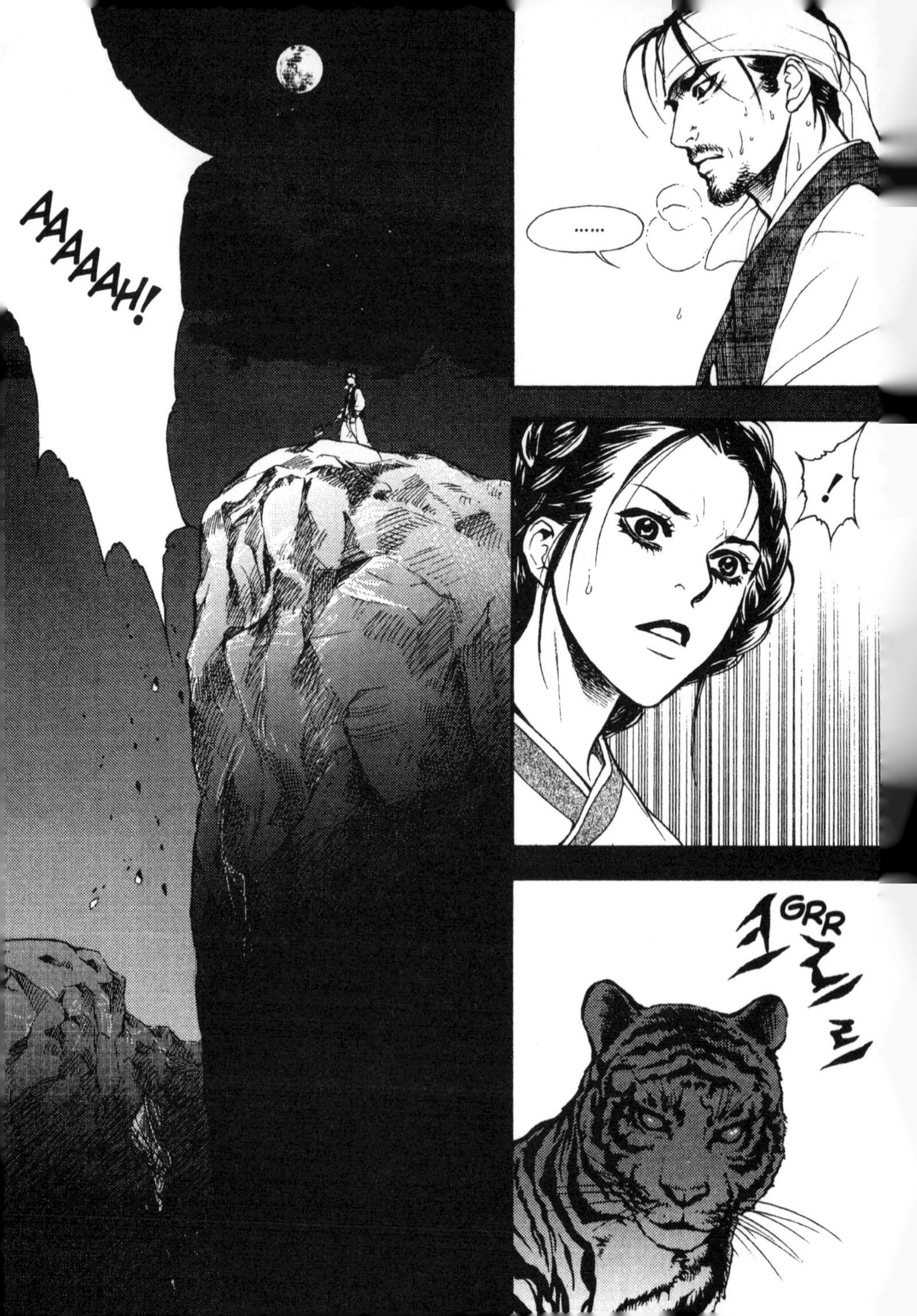
AAAAAH!
......
!
GRR

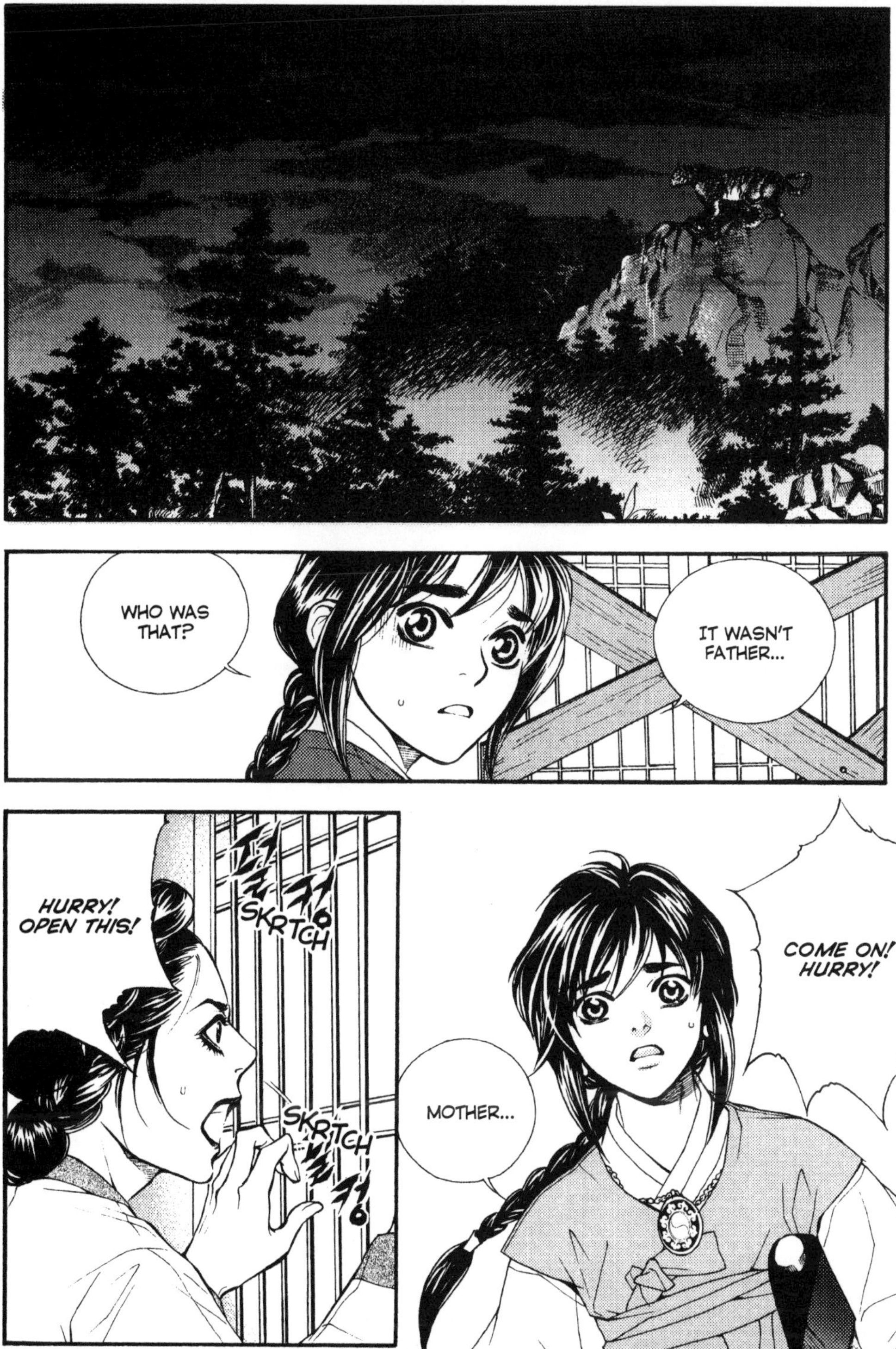
WHO WAS THAT?
IT WASN'T FATHER...
HURRY! OPEN THIS!
SKRTCH
SKRTCH
COME ON! HURRY!
MOTHER...

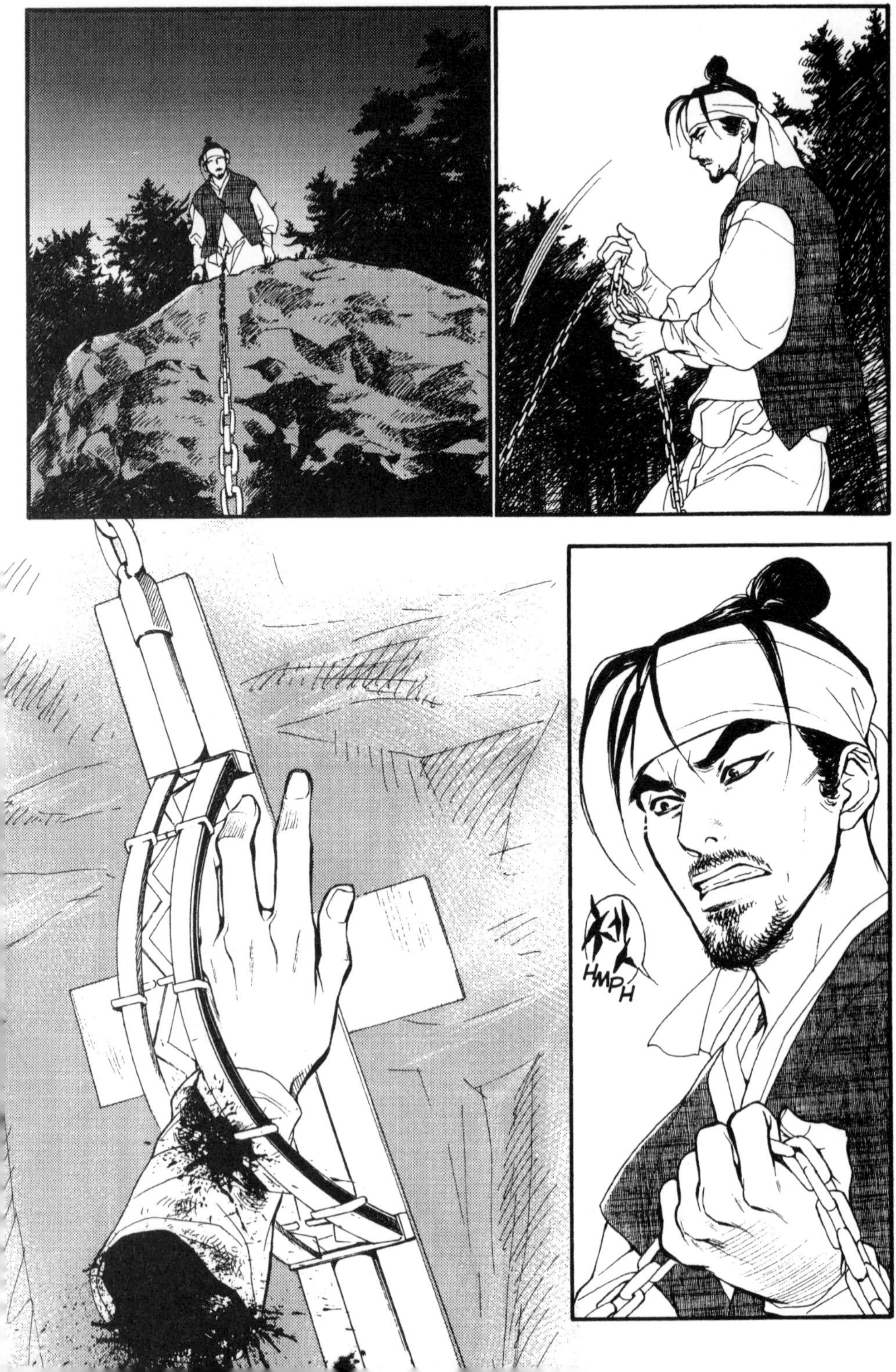
HMPH

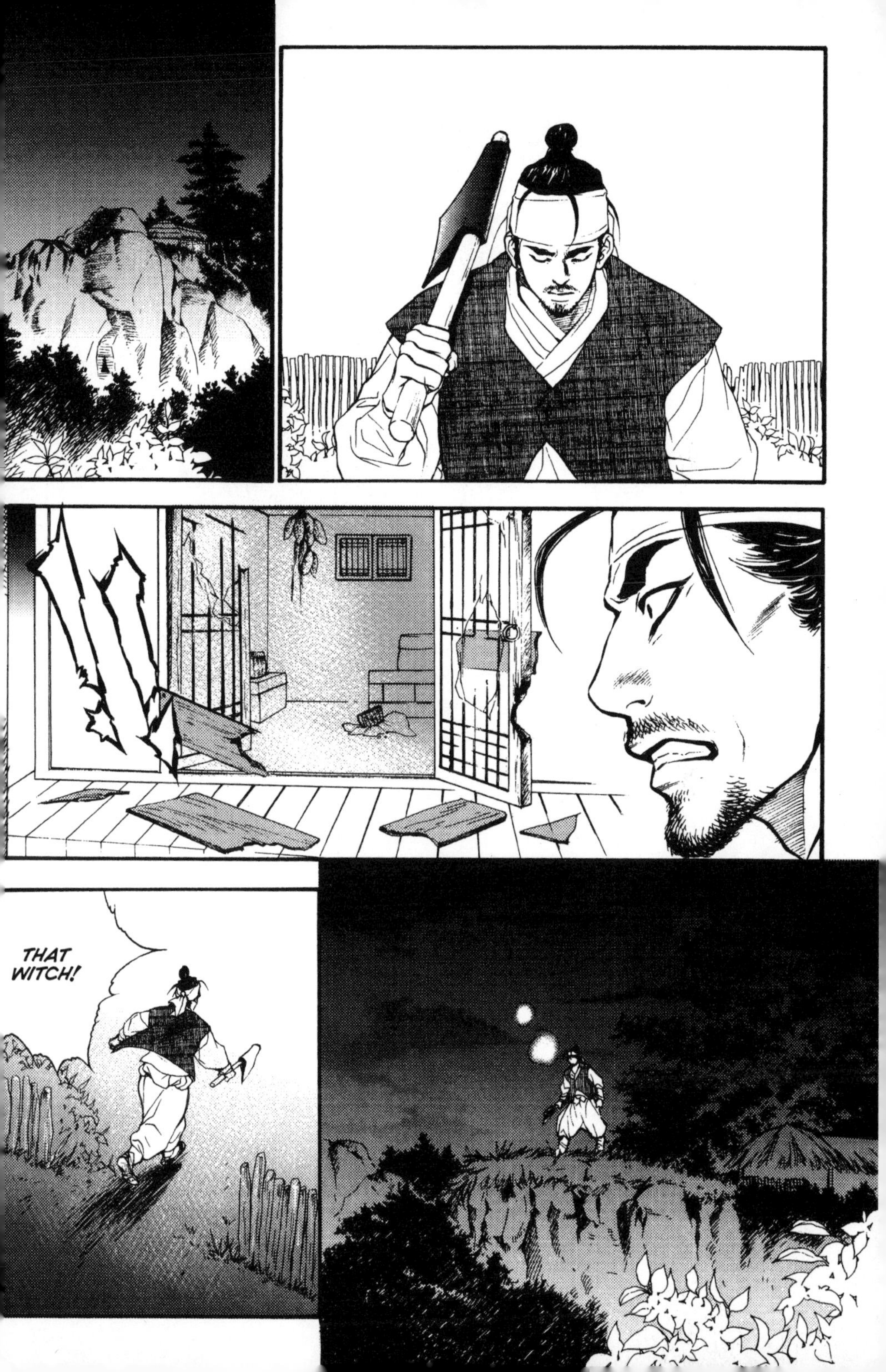
THAT WITCH!

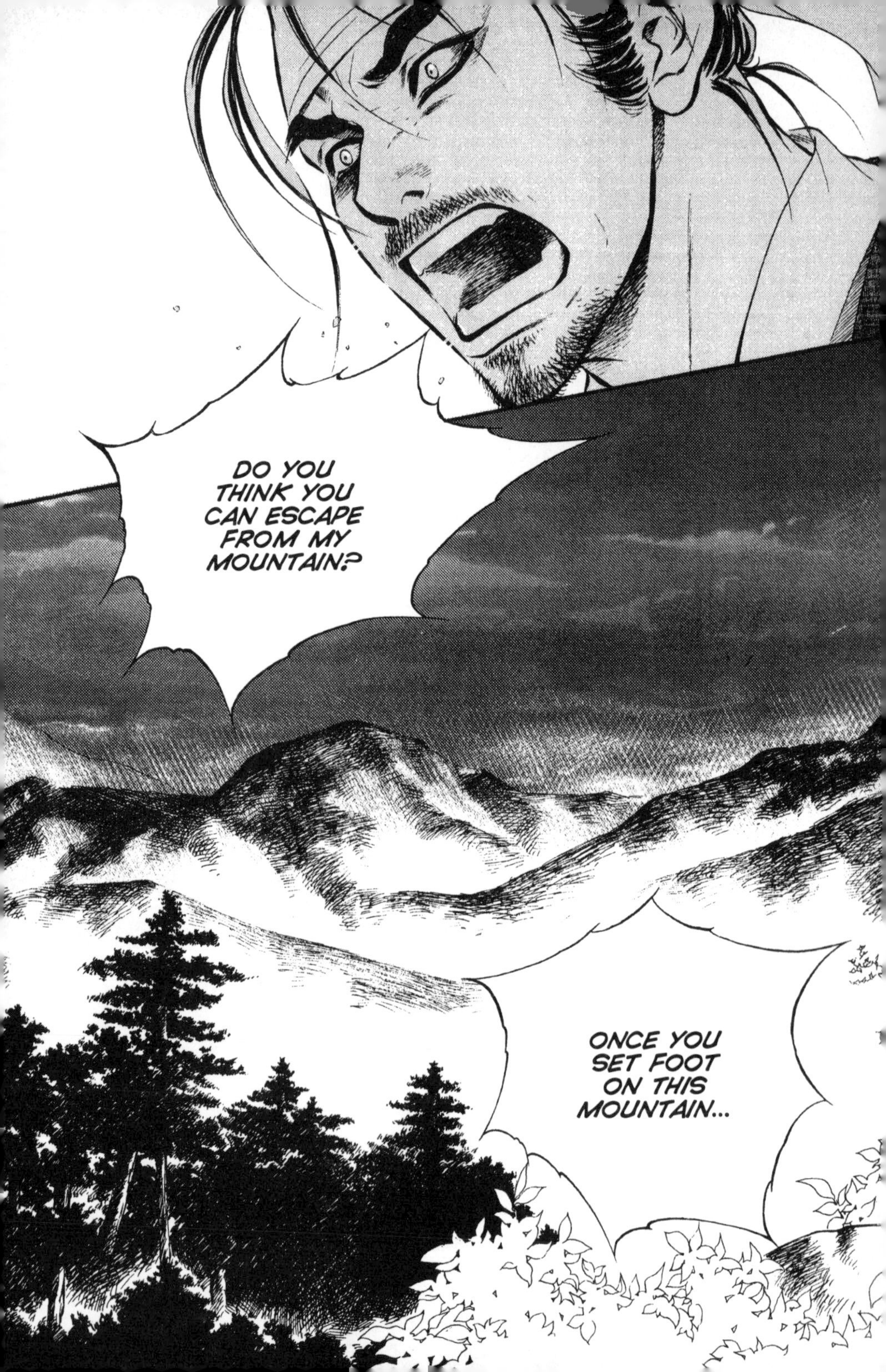
DO YOU THINK YOU CAN ESCAPE FROM MY MOUNTAIN?
ONCE YOU SET FOOT ON THIS MOUNTAIN...

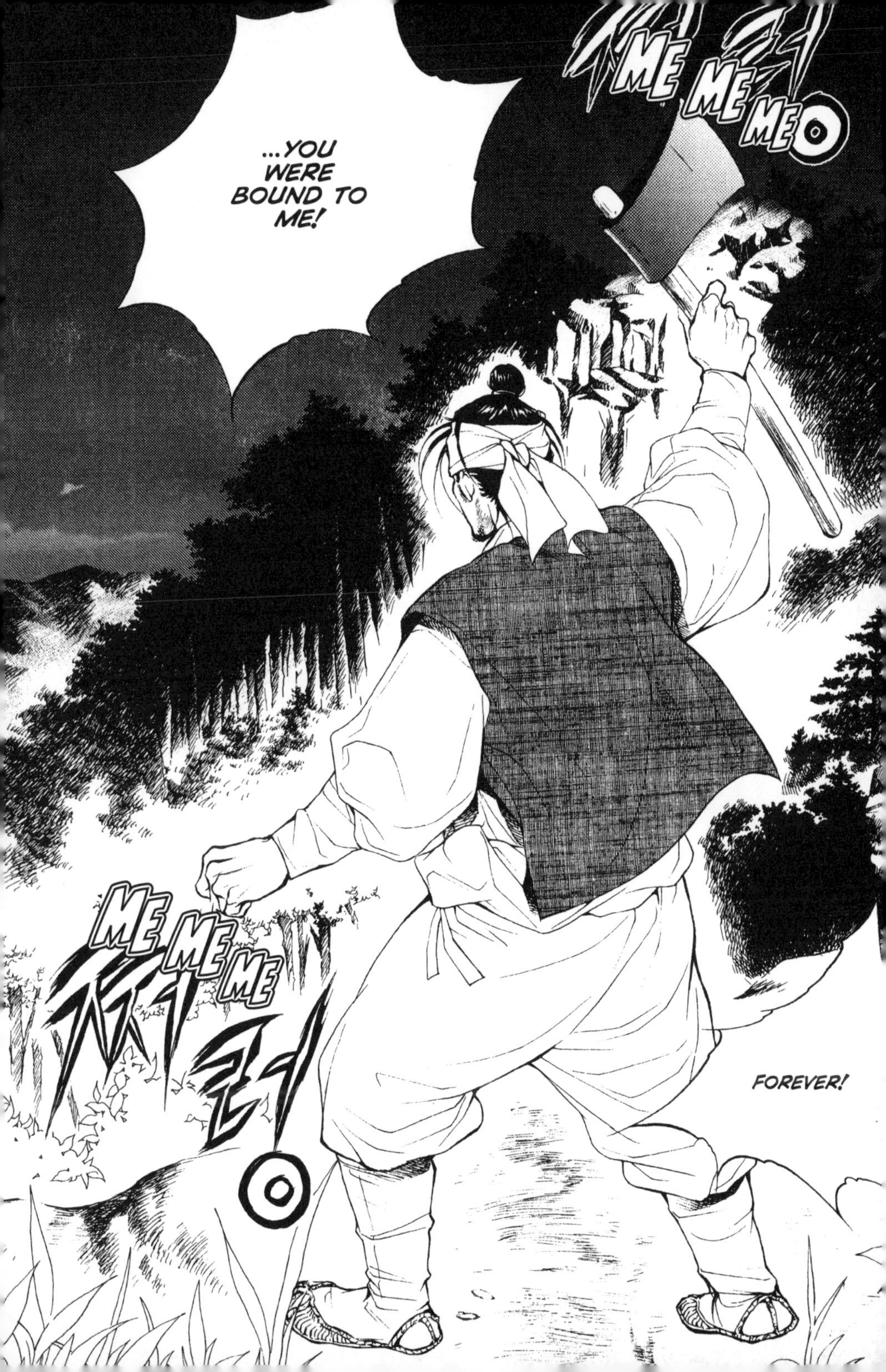
...YOU WERE BOUND TO ME!
ME ME ME
ME ME ME
FOREVER!

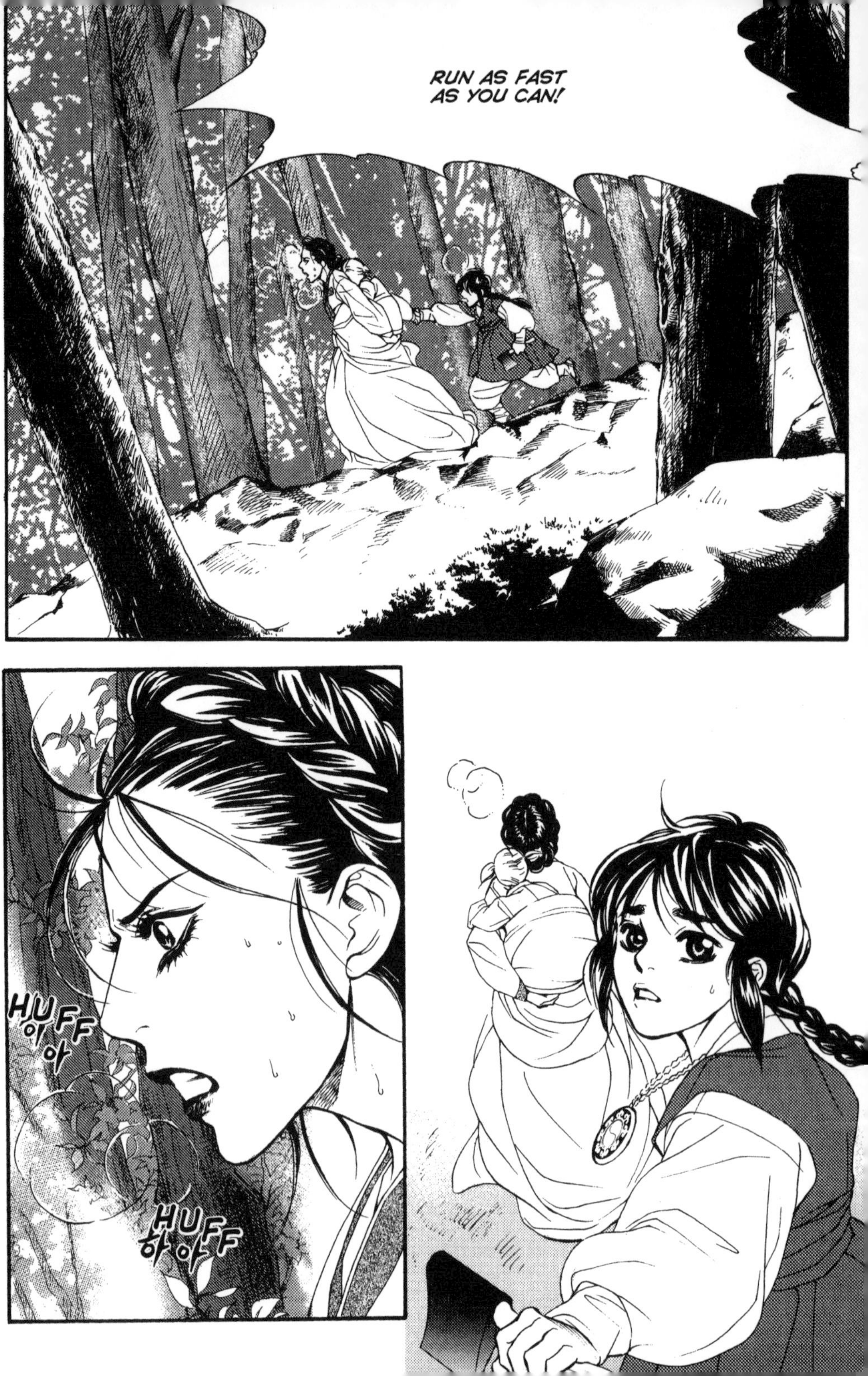
RUN AS FAST AS YOU CAN!
HUFF 하아
HUFF 하아

One thousand
and one nights

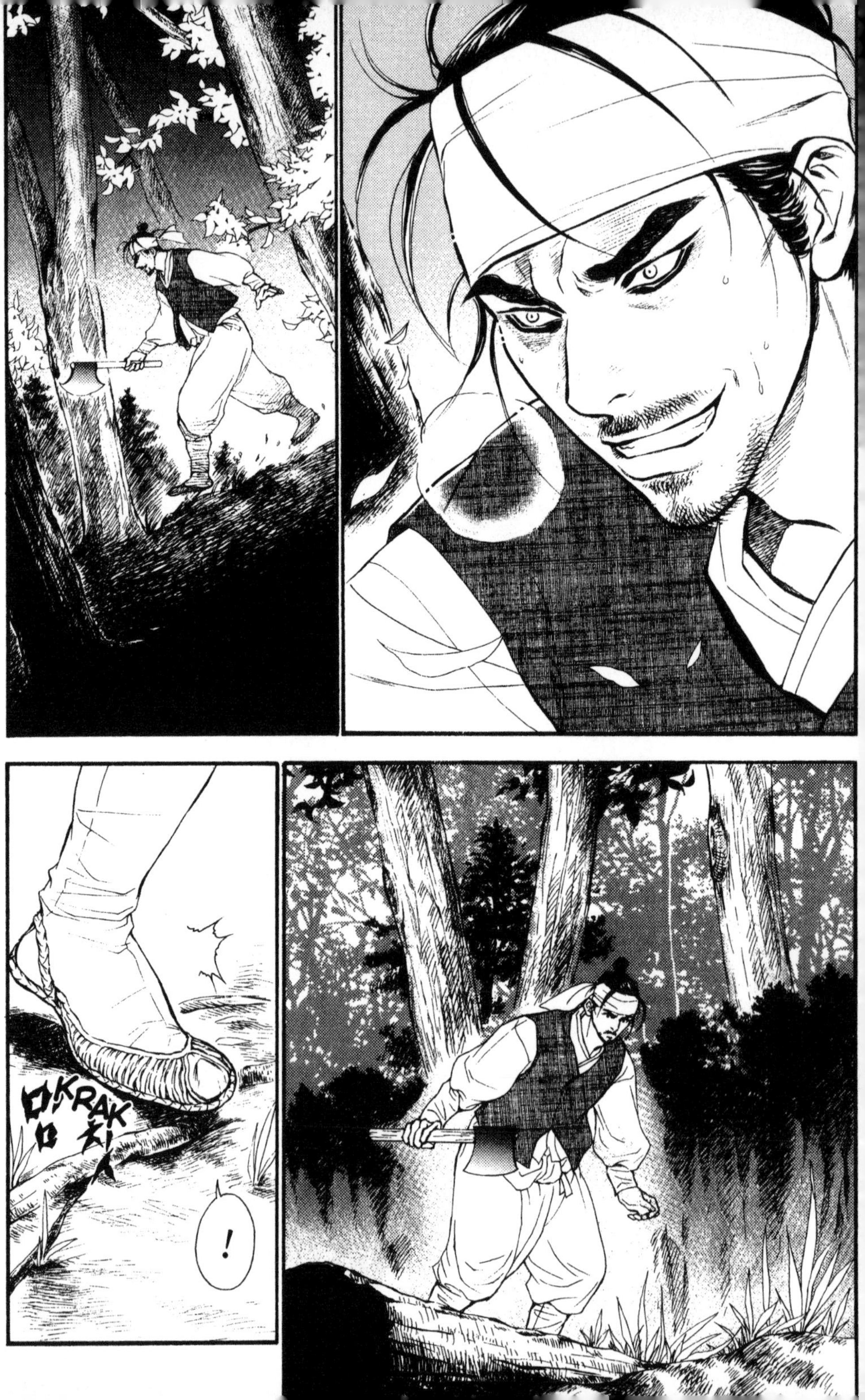
KRAK
!

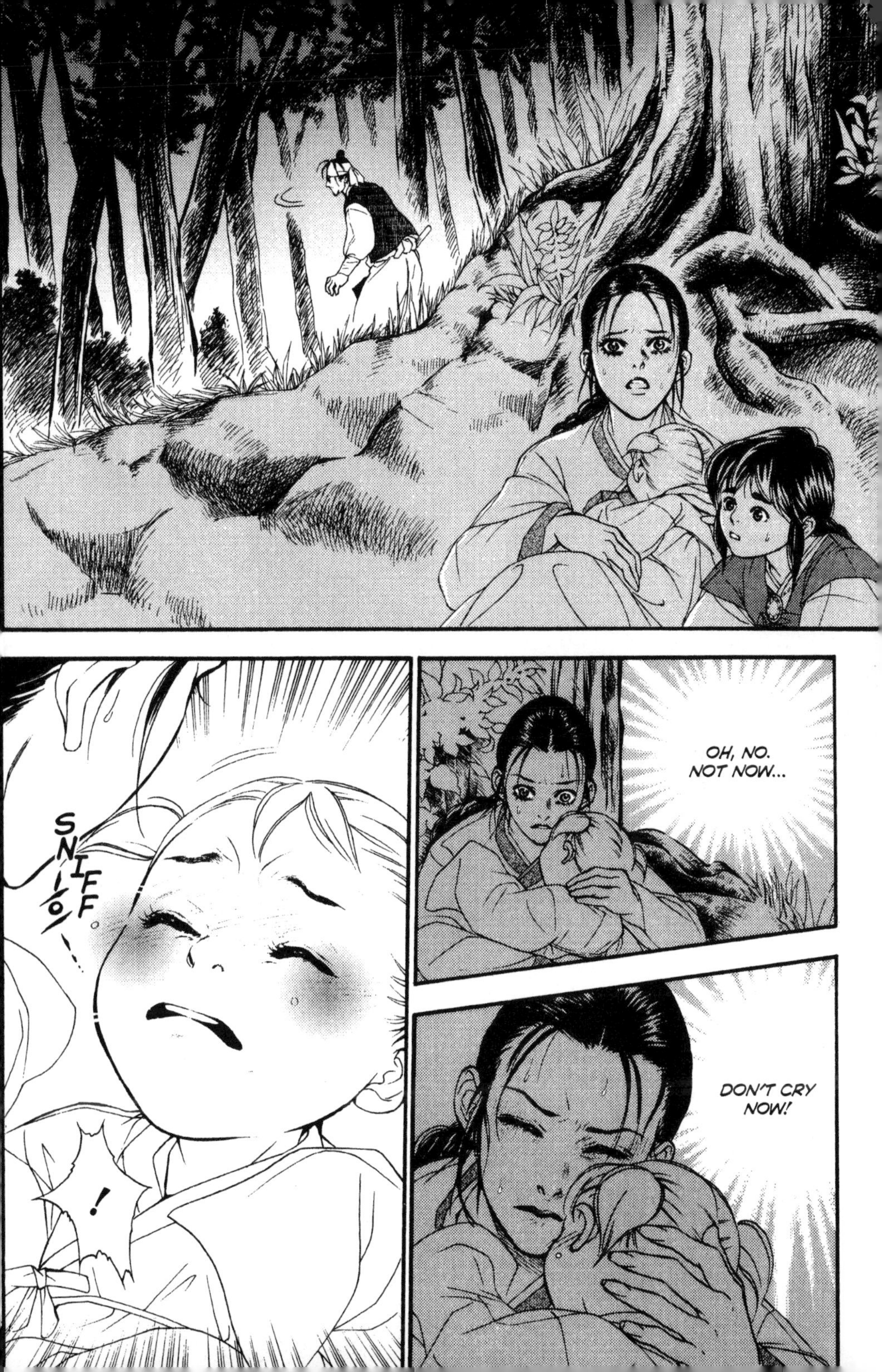
SNIFF
OH, NO.
NOT NOW...
DON'T CRY
NOW!

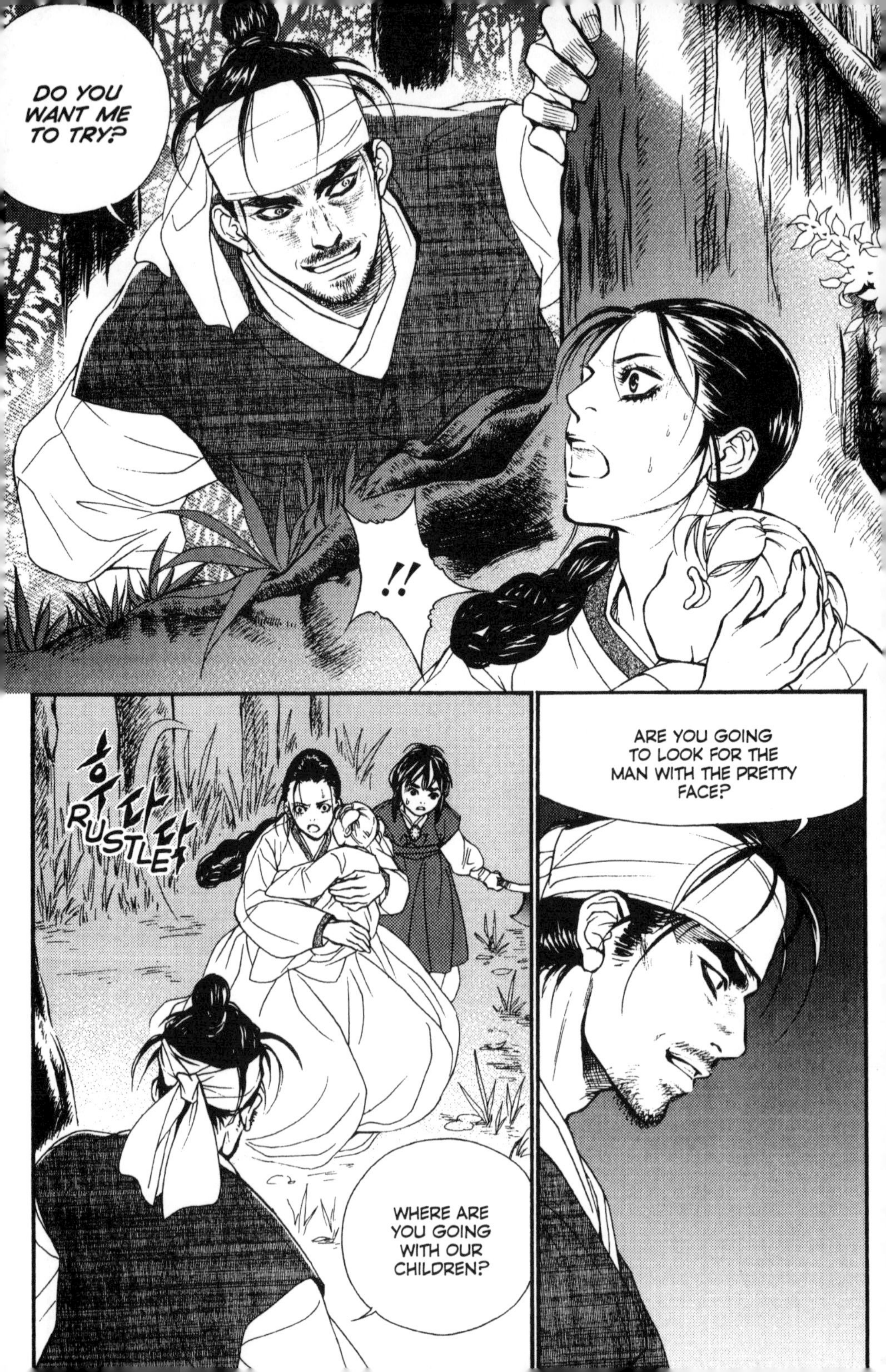
DO YOU WANT ME TO TRY?
!!
RUSTLE
WHERE ARE YOU GOING WITH OUR CHILDREN?
ARE YOU GOING TO LOOK FOR THE MAN WITH THE PRETTY FACE?

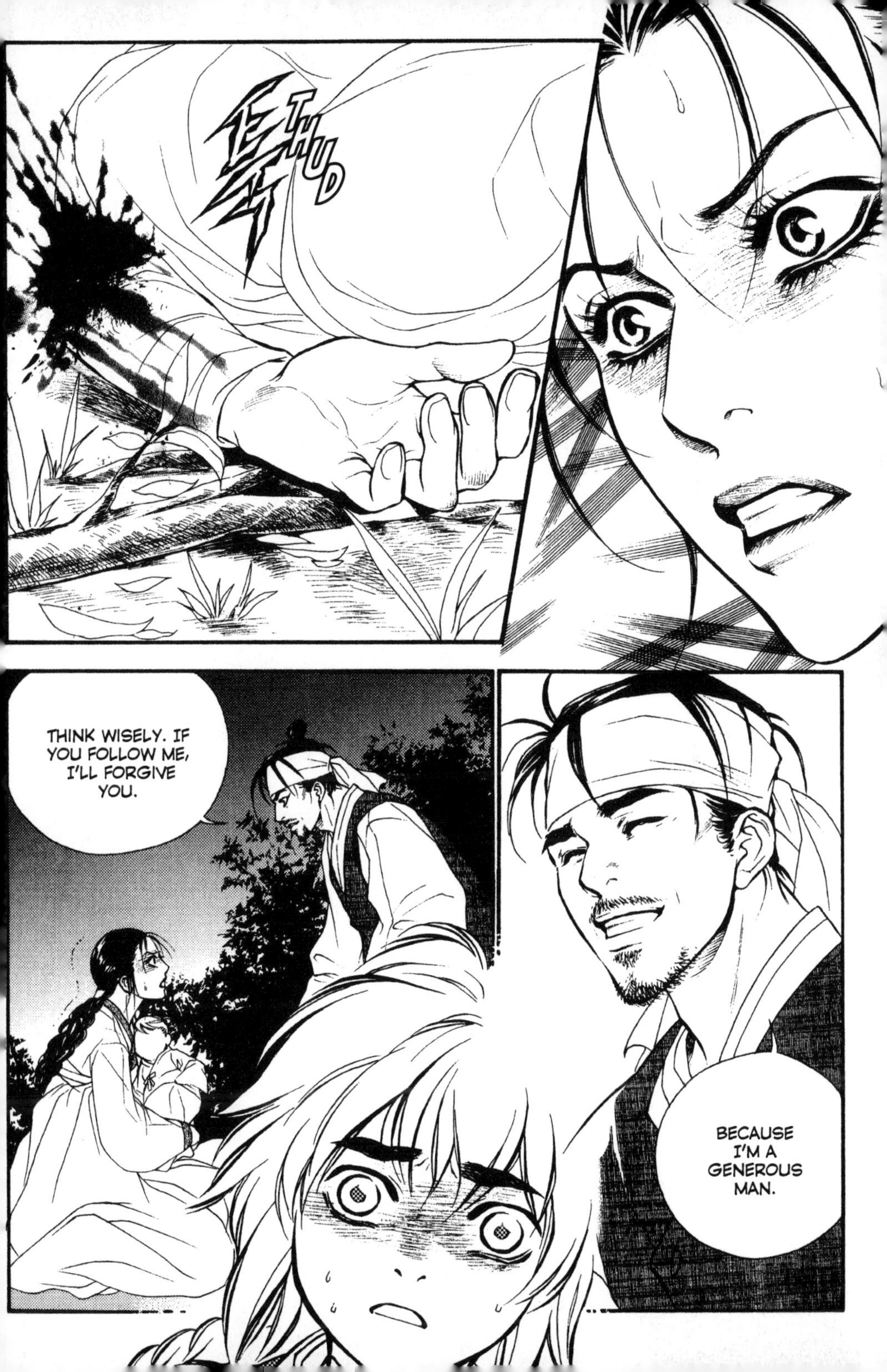
THUD
THINK WISELY. IF YOU FOLLOW ME, I'LL FORGIVE YOU.
BECAUSE I'M A GENEROUS MAN.

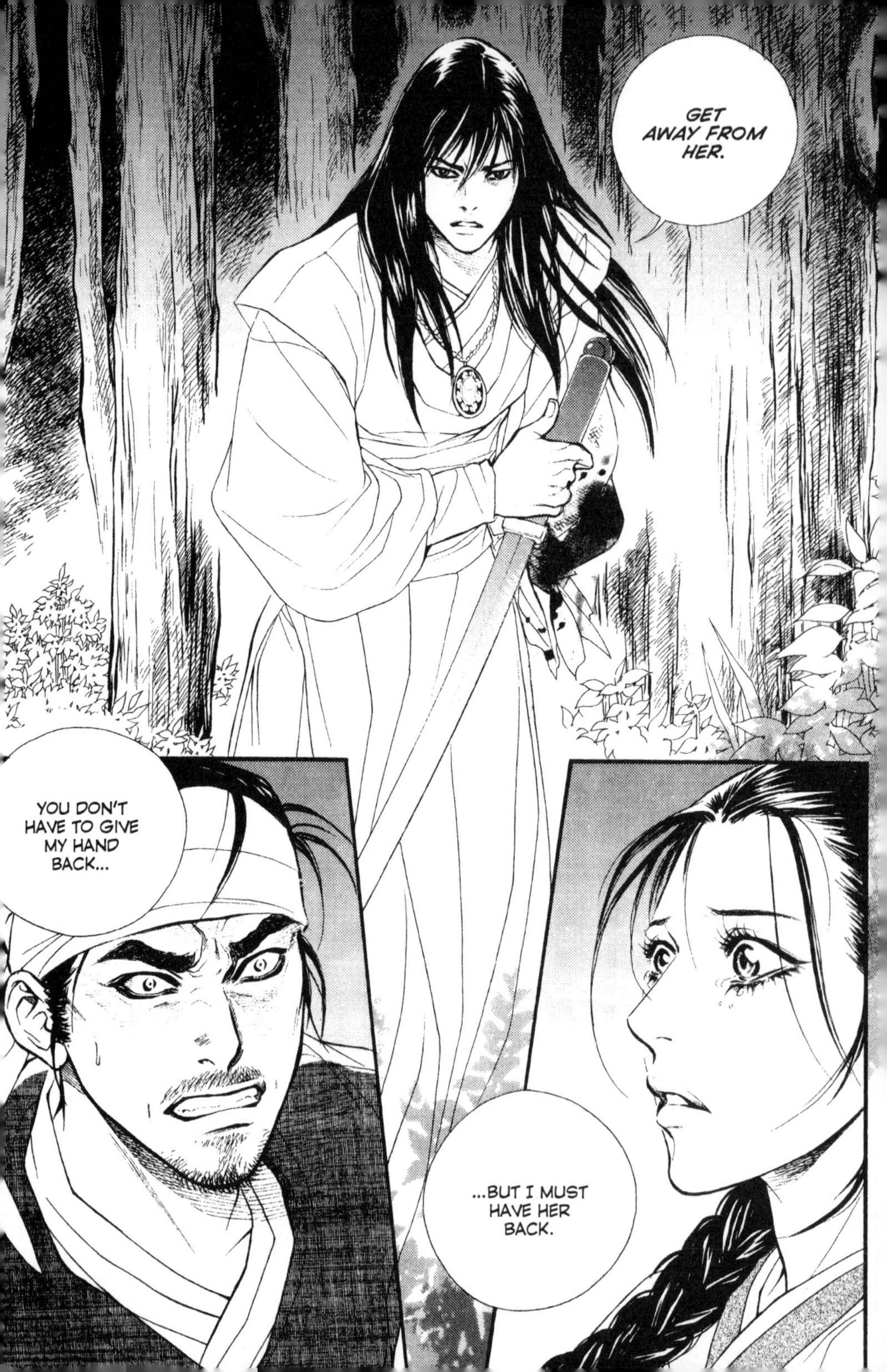
GET AWAY FROM HER.
YOU DON'T HAVE TO GIVE MY HAND BACK...
...BUT I MUST HAVE HER BACK.

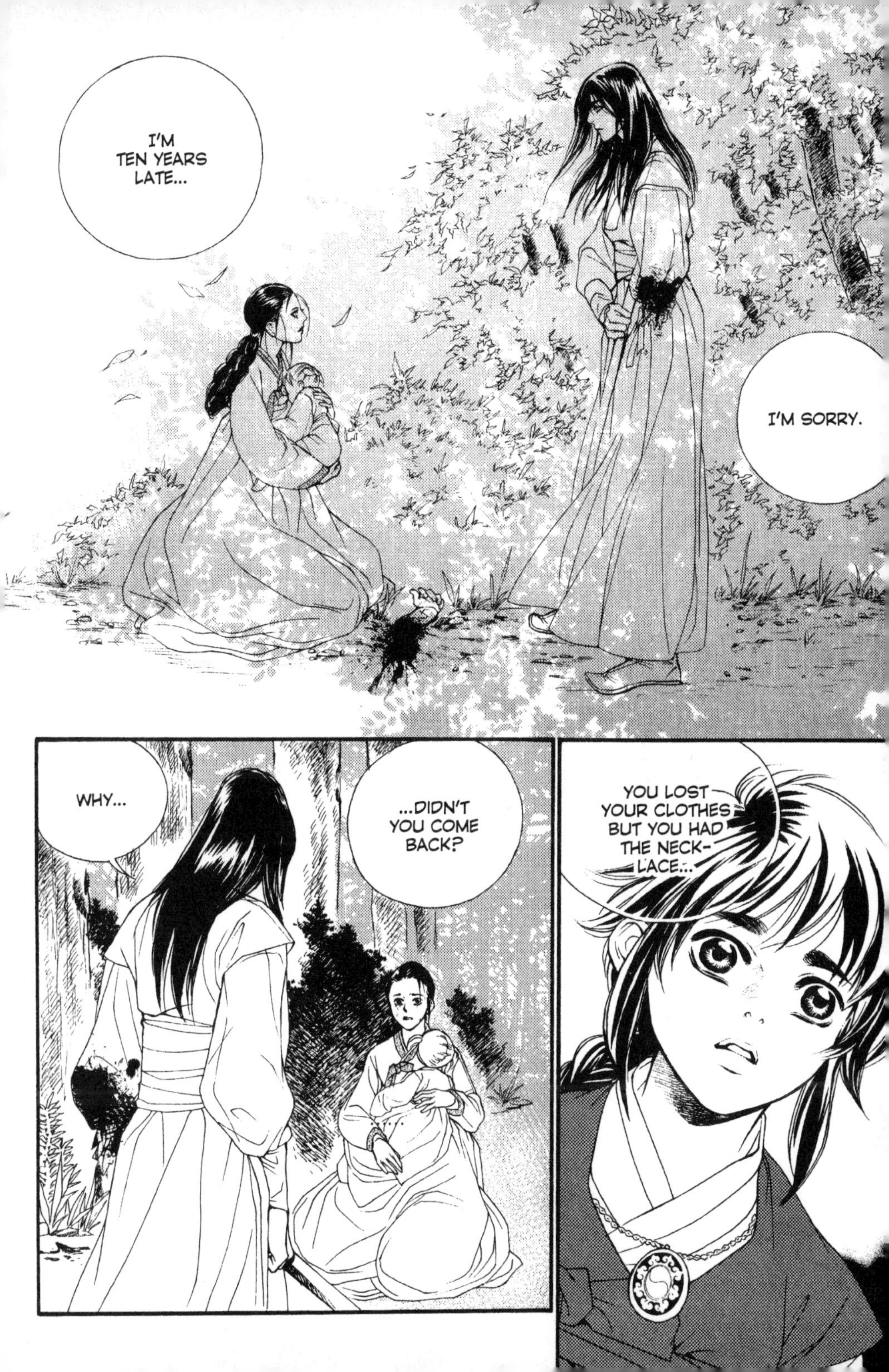
I'M TEN YEARS LATE...
I'M SORRY.
WHY...
...DIDN'T YOU COME BACK?
YOU LOST YOUR CLOTHES BUT YOU HAD THE NECK-LACE...

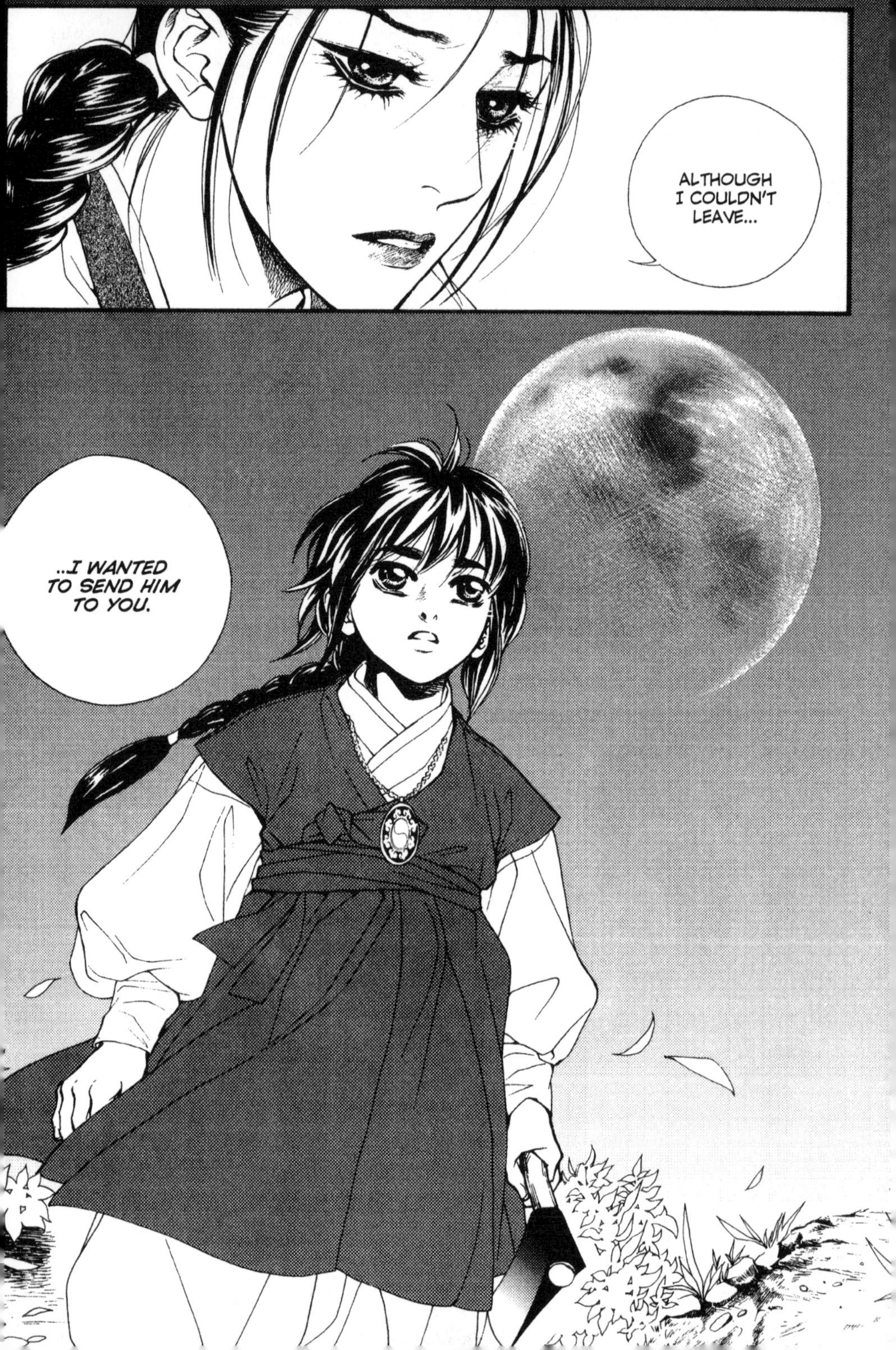
ALTHOUGH I COULDN'T LEAVE...
...I WANTED TO SEND HIM TO YOU.

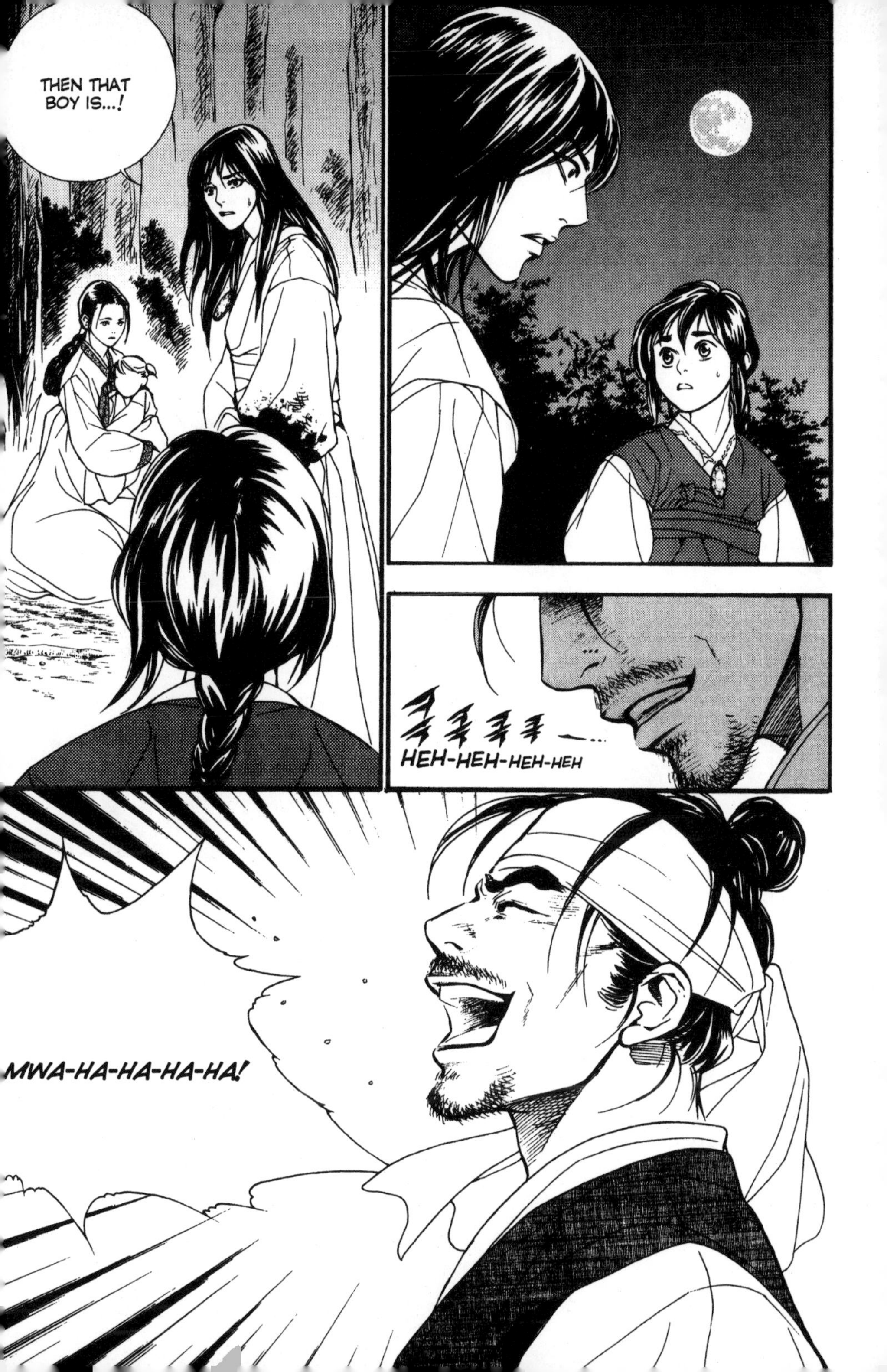
THEN THAT BOY IS...!
HEH-HEH-HEH-HEH
MWA-HA-HA-HA-HA!

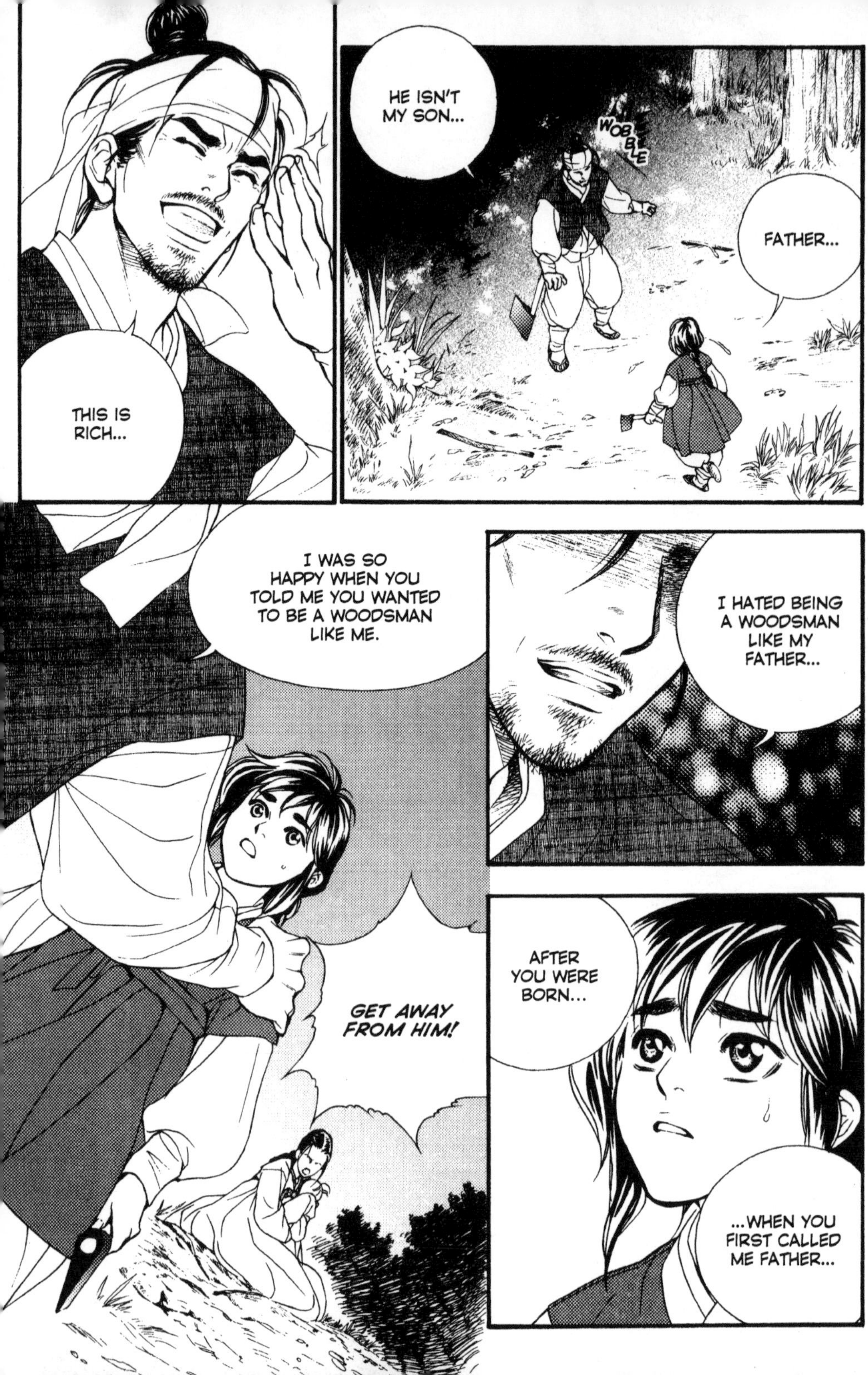
THIS IS RICH...
HE ISN'T MY SON...
WOBBLE
FATHER...
I WAS SO HAPPY WHEN YOU TOLD ME YOU WANTED TO BE A WOODSMAN LIKE ME.
GET AWAY FROM HIM!
I HATED BEING A WOODSMAN LIKE MY FATHER...
AFTER YOU WERE BORN...
...WHEN YOU FIRST CALLED ME FATHER...

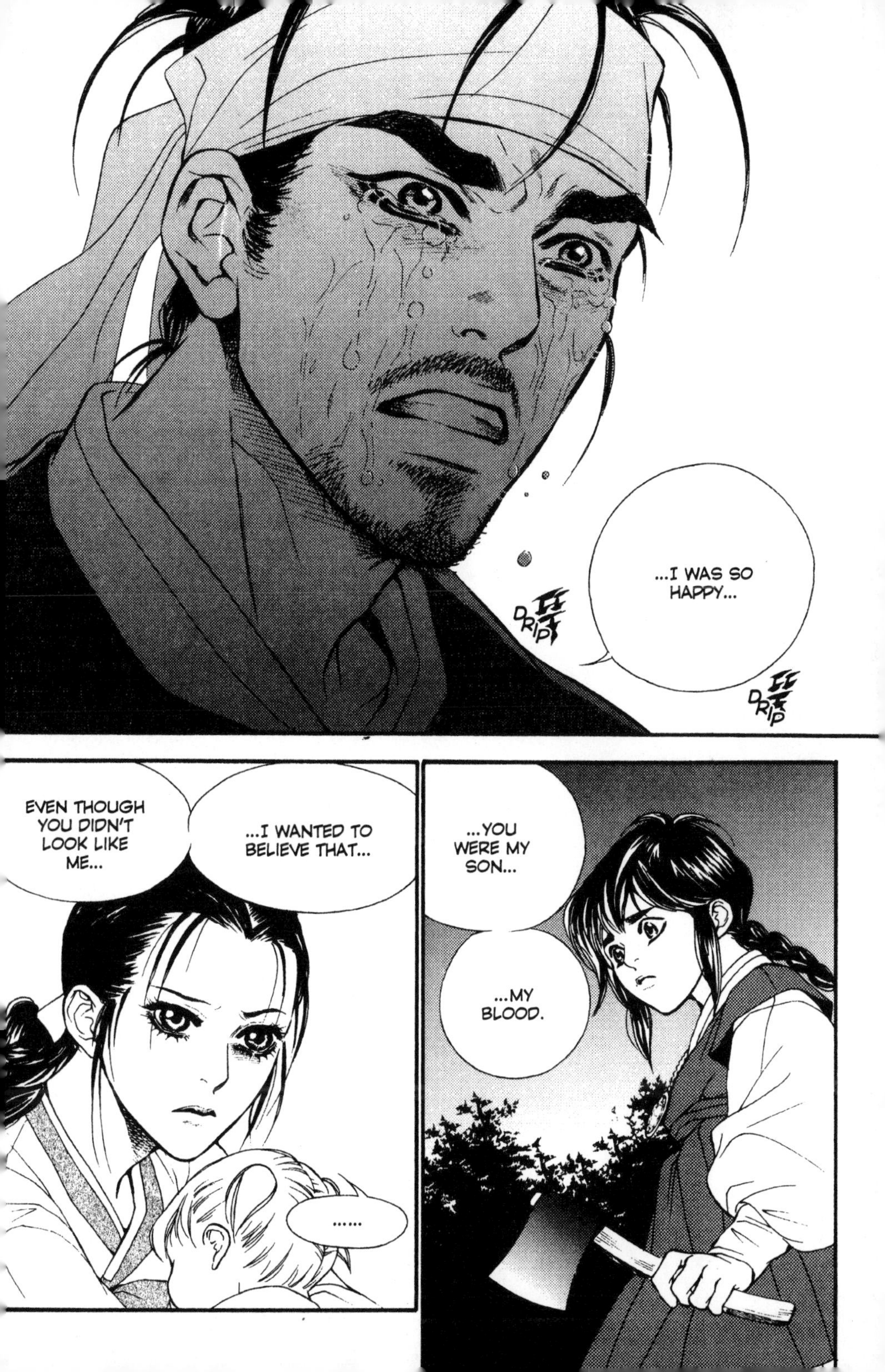

...I WAS SO HAPPY...
DRIP
DRIP
EVEN THOUGH YOU DIDN'T LOOK LIKE ME...
...I WANTED TO BELIEVE THAT...
......
...YOU WERE MY SON...
...MY BLOOD.

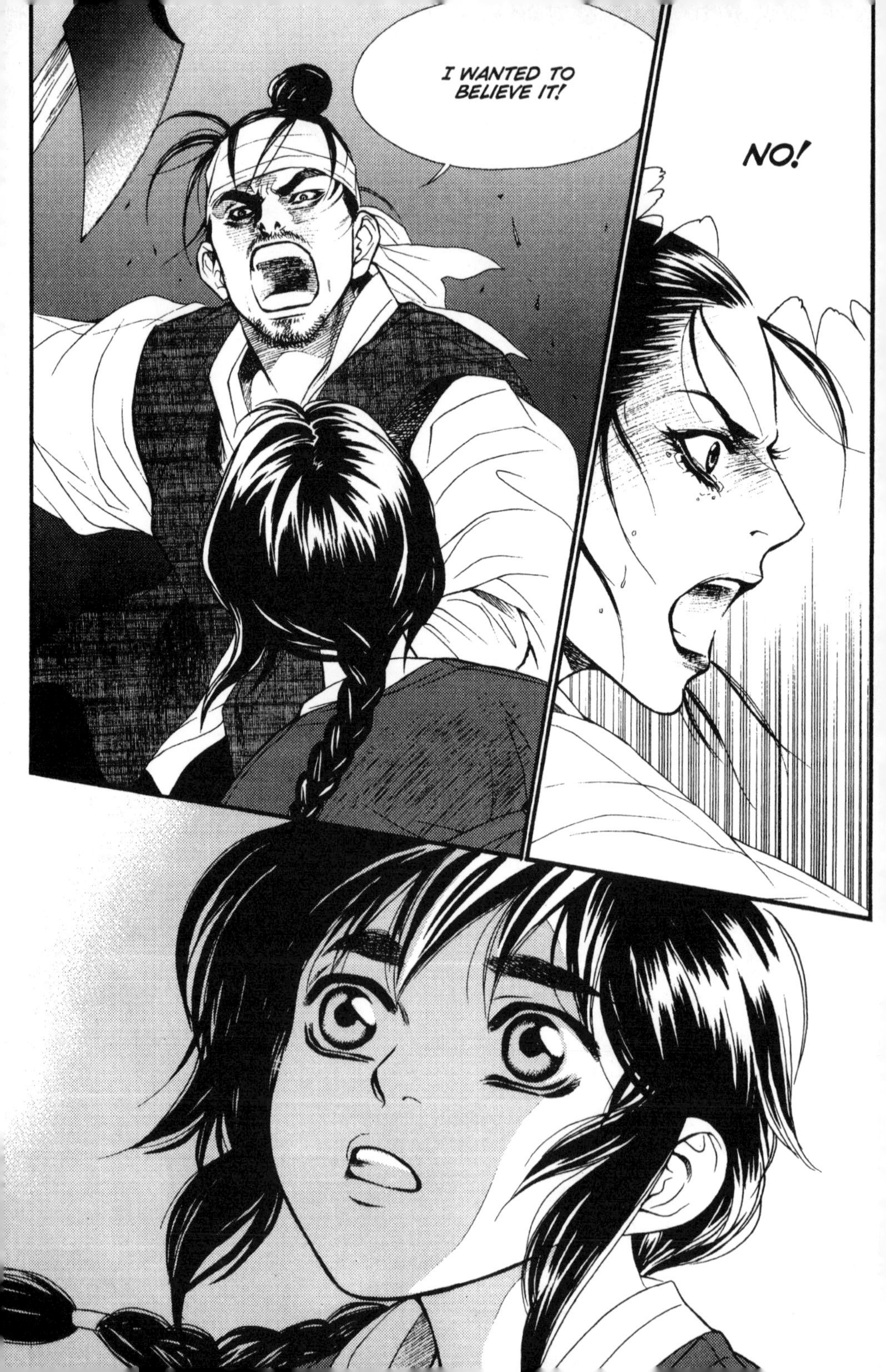
I WANTED TO BELIEVE IT!
NO!

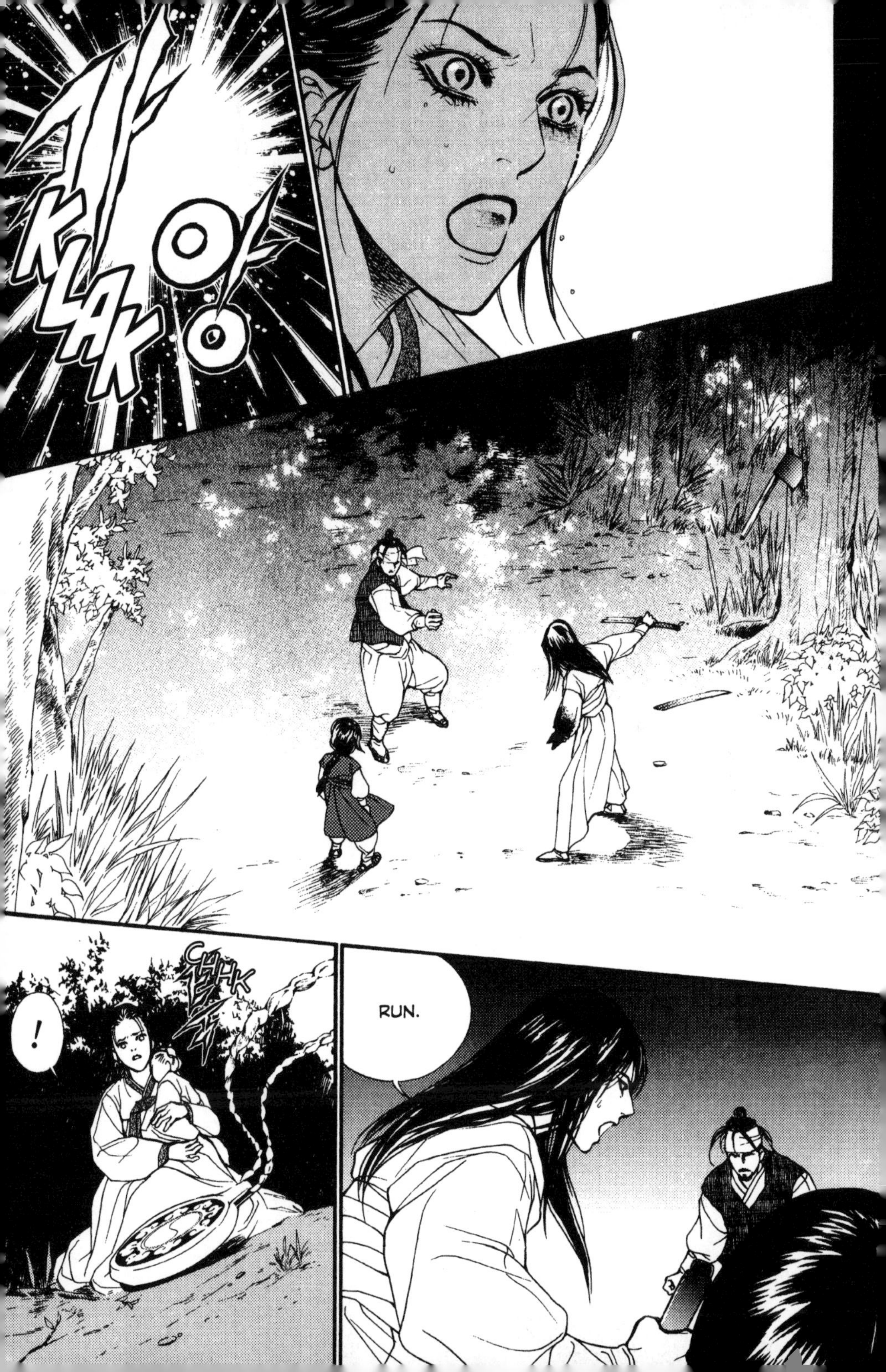
KLAK
!
CHHK
RUN.

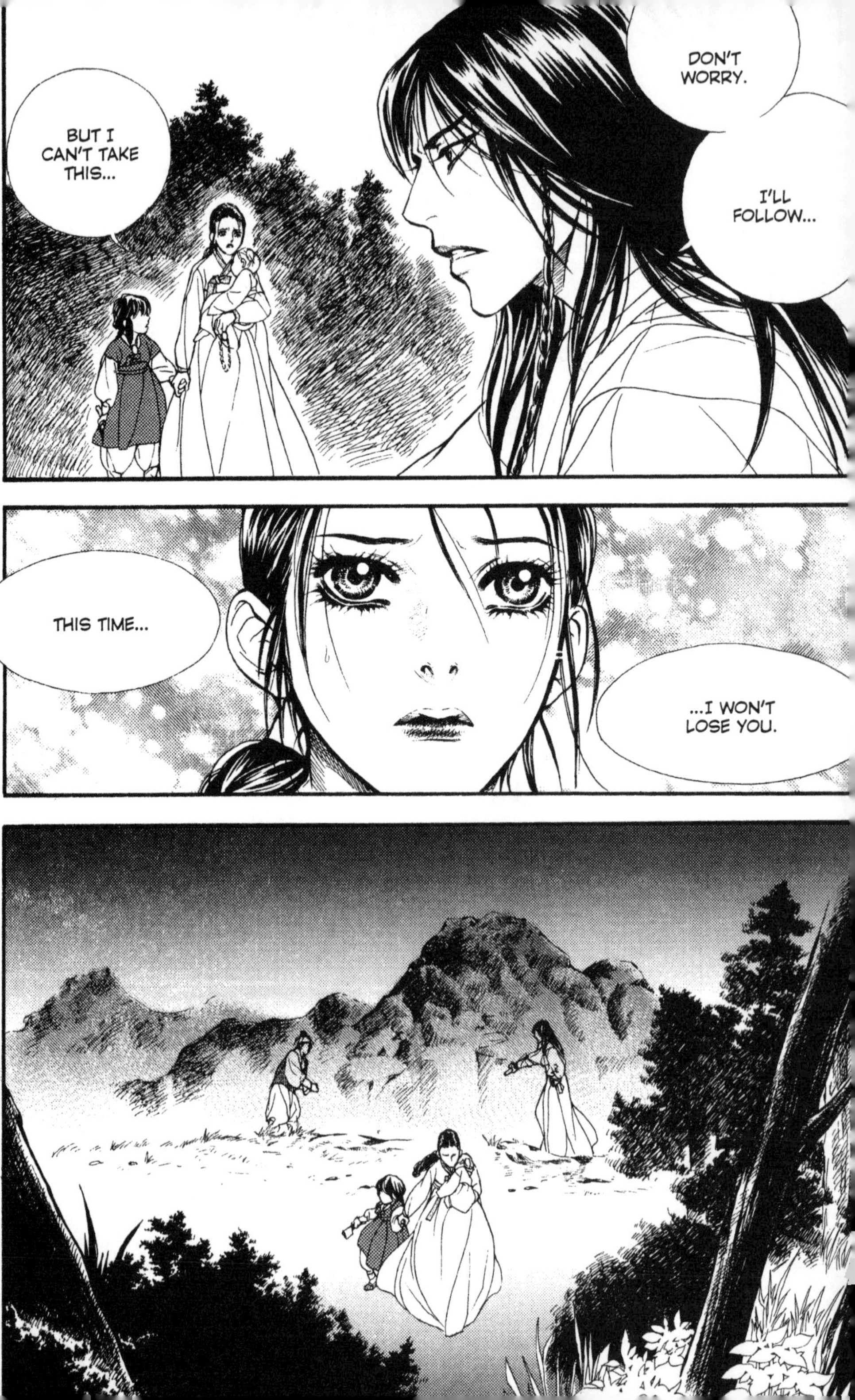
BUT I CAN'T TAKE THIS...
DON'T WORRY.
I'LL FOLLOW...
THIS TIME...
...I WON'T LOSE YOU.

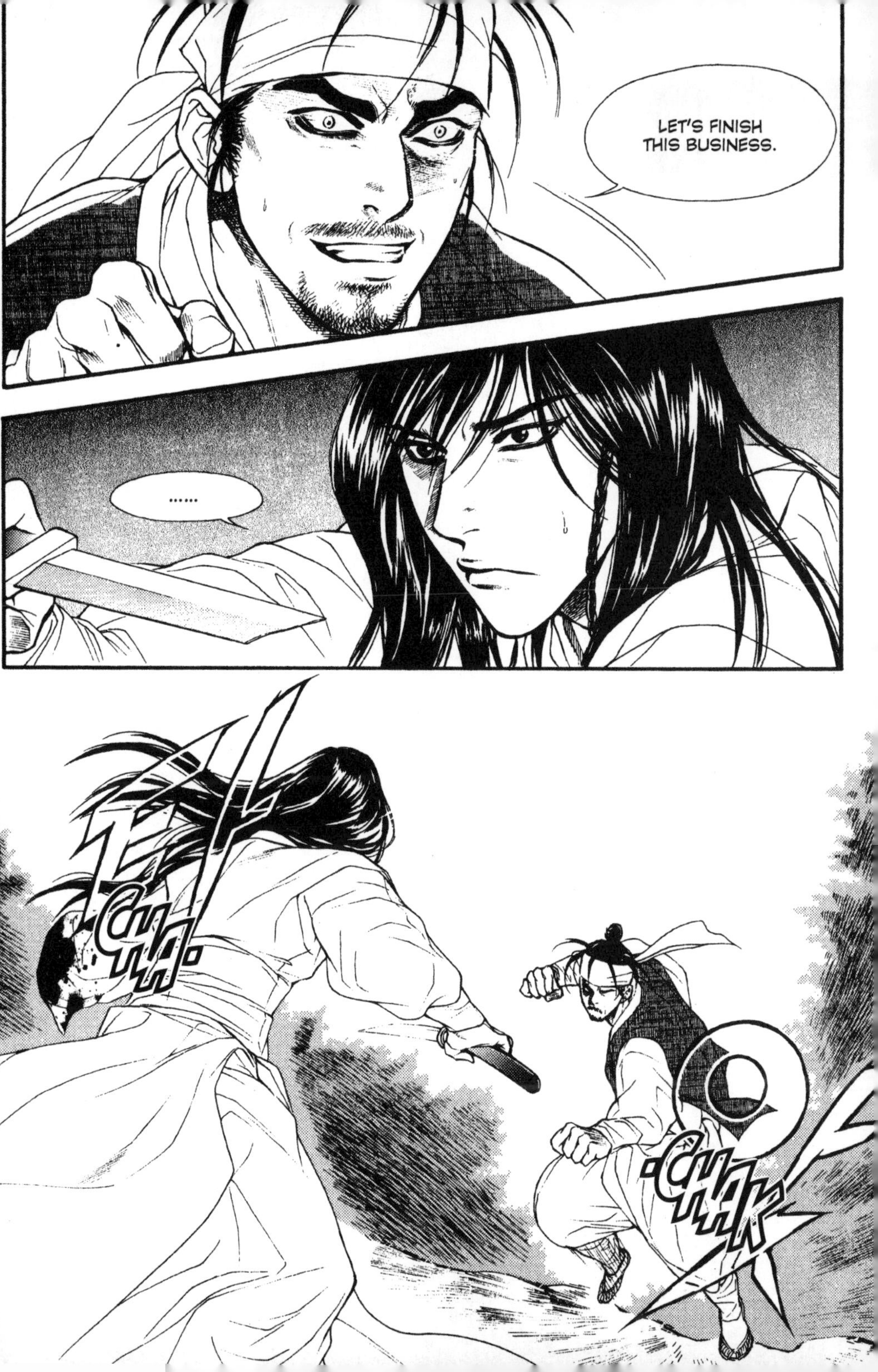
LET'S FINISH THIS BUSINESS.
......
CHA
CHAK

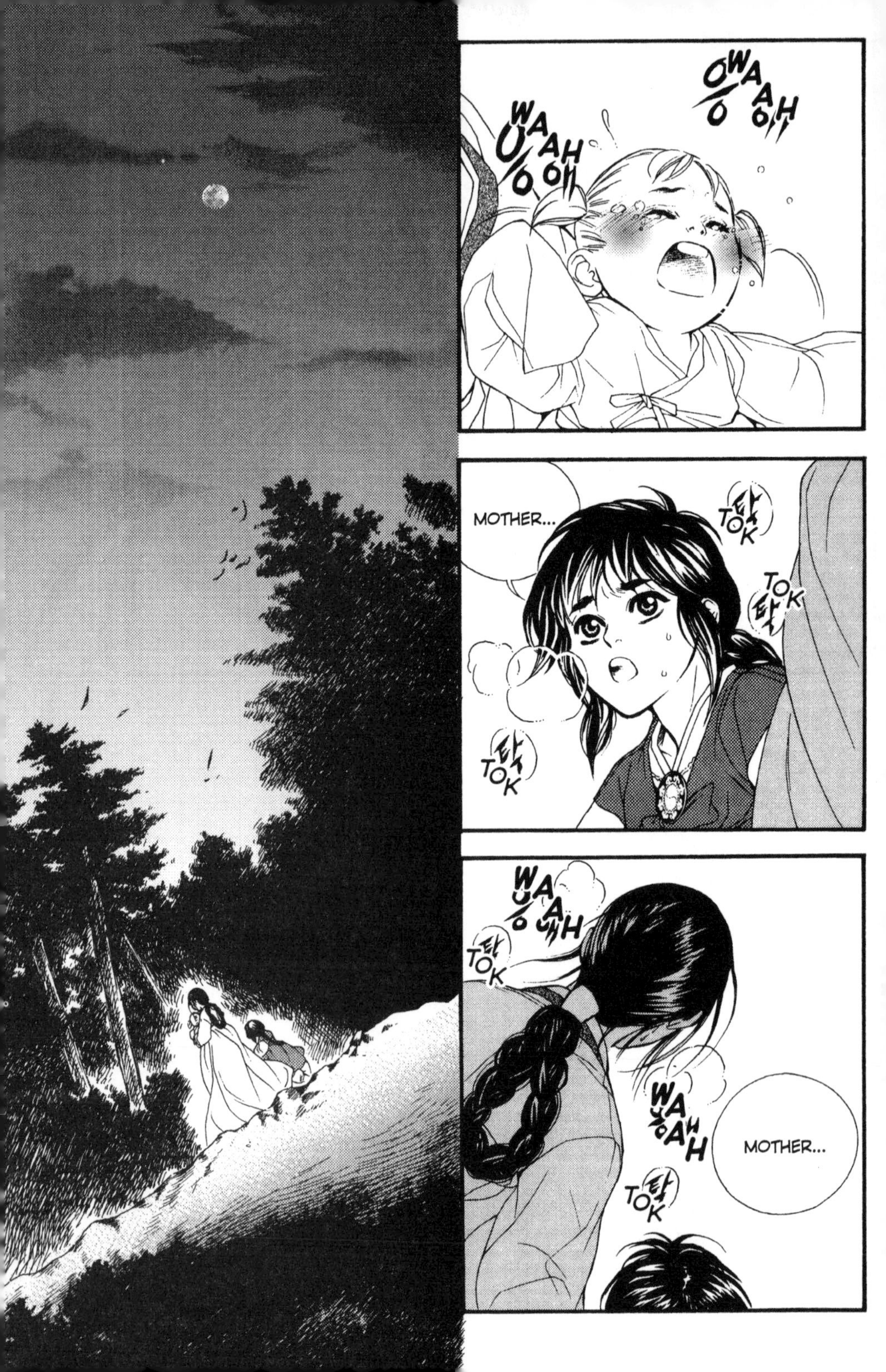
WAAH
OWAAH
MOTHER...
탁 TOK
TOK 탁
탁 TOK
WAAH
탁 TOK
WAAH
MOTHER...
TOK 탁

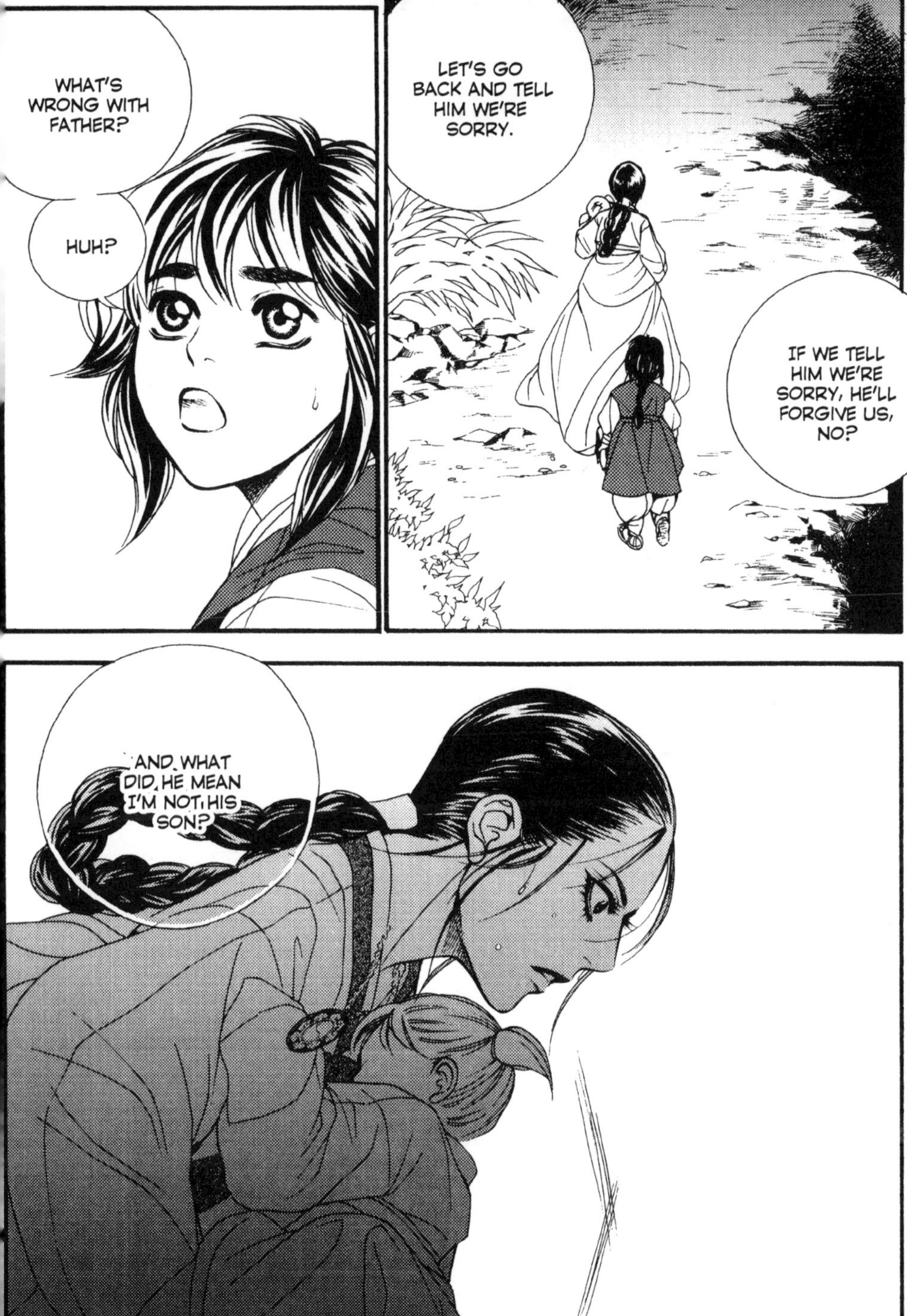
WHAT'S WRONG WITH FATHER?
HUH?
LET'S GO BACK AND TELL HIM WE'RE SORRY.
IF WE TELL HIM WE'RE SORRY, HE'LL FORGIVE US, NO?
AND WHAT DID HE MEAN I'M NOT HIS SON?

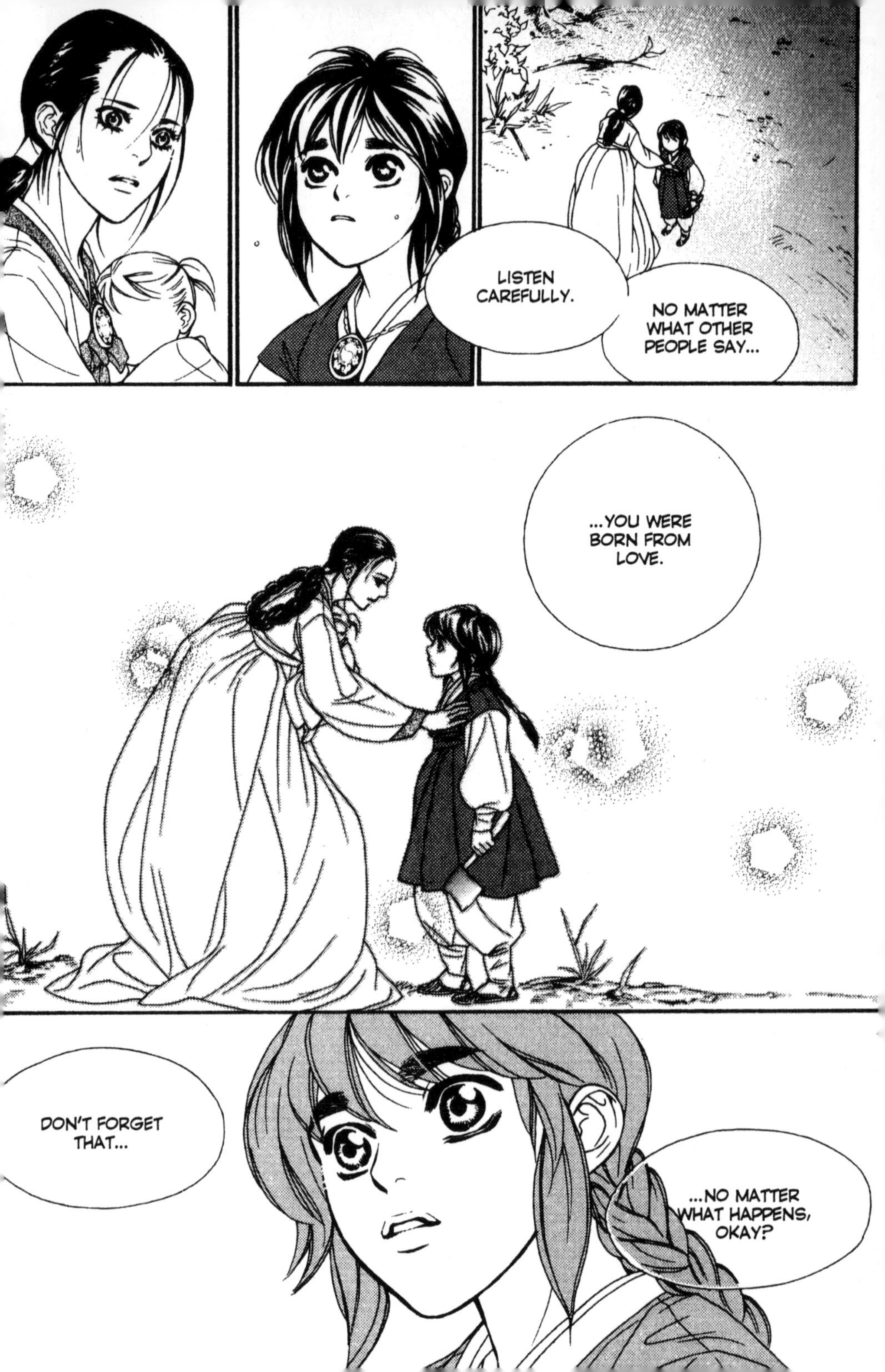
LISTEN CAREFULLY.
NO MATTER WHAT OTHER PEOPLE SAY...
...YOU WERE BORN FROM LOVE.
DON'T FORGET THAT...
...NO MATTER WHAT HAPPENS, OKAY?

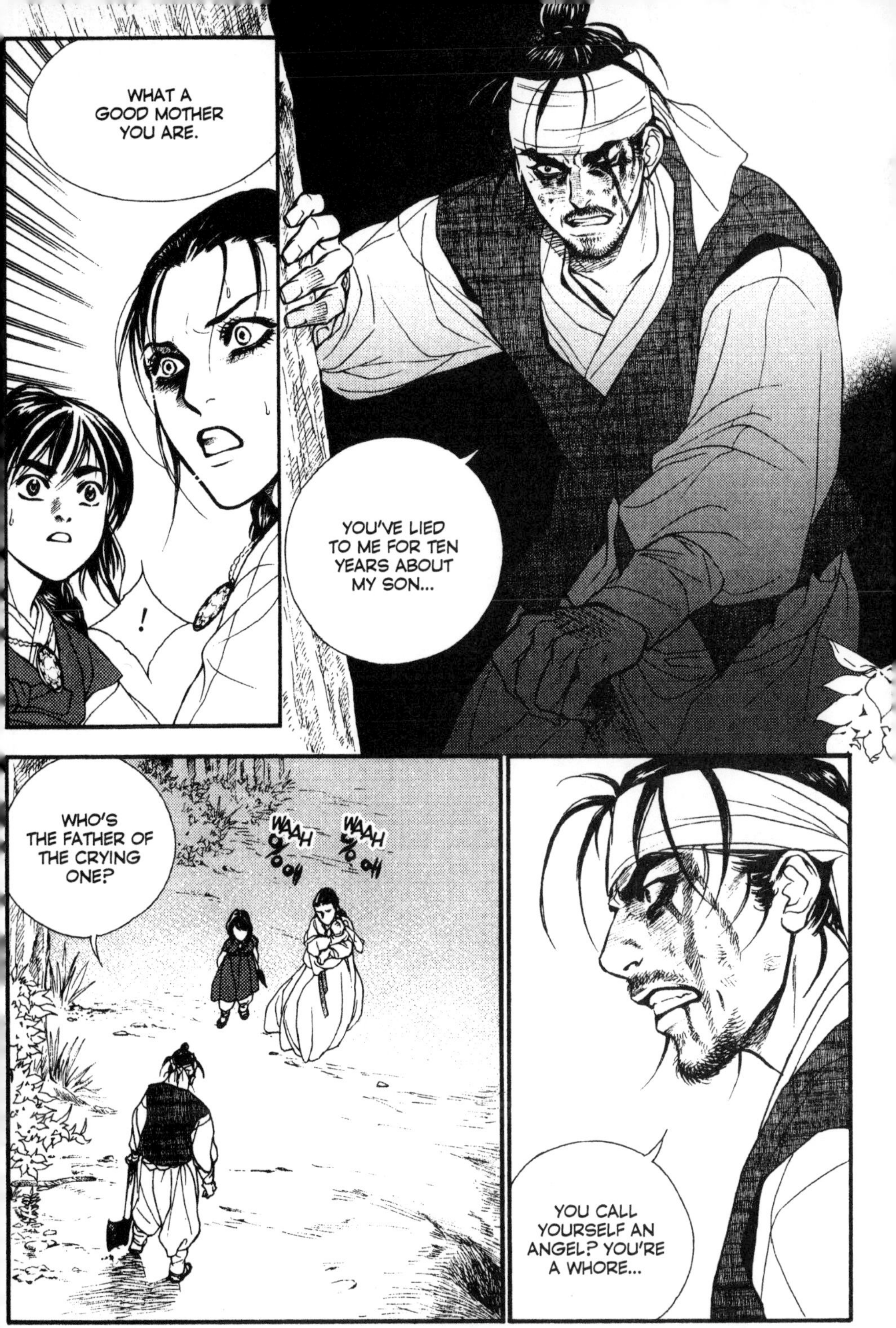
WHAT A GOOD MOTHER YOU ARE.
!
YOU'VE LIED TO ME FOR TEN YEARS ABOUT MY SON...
WHO'S THE FATHER OF THE CRYING ONE?
WAAH
WAAH
YOU CALL YOURSELF AN ANGEL? YOU'RE A WHORE...

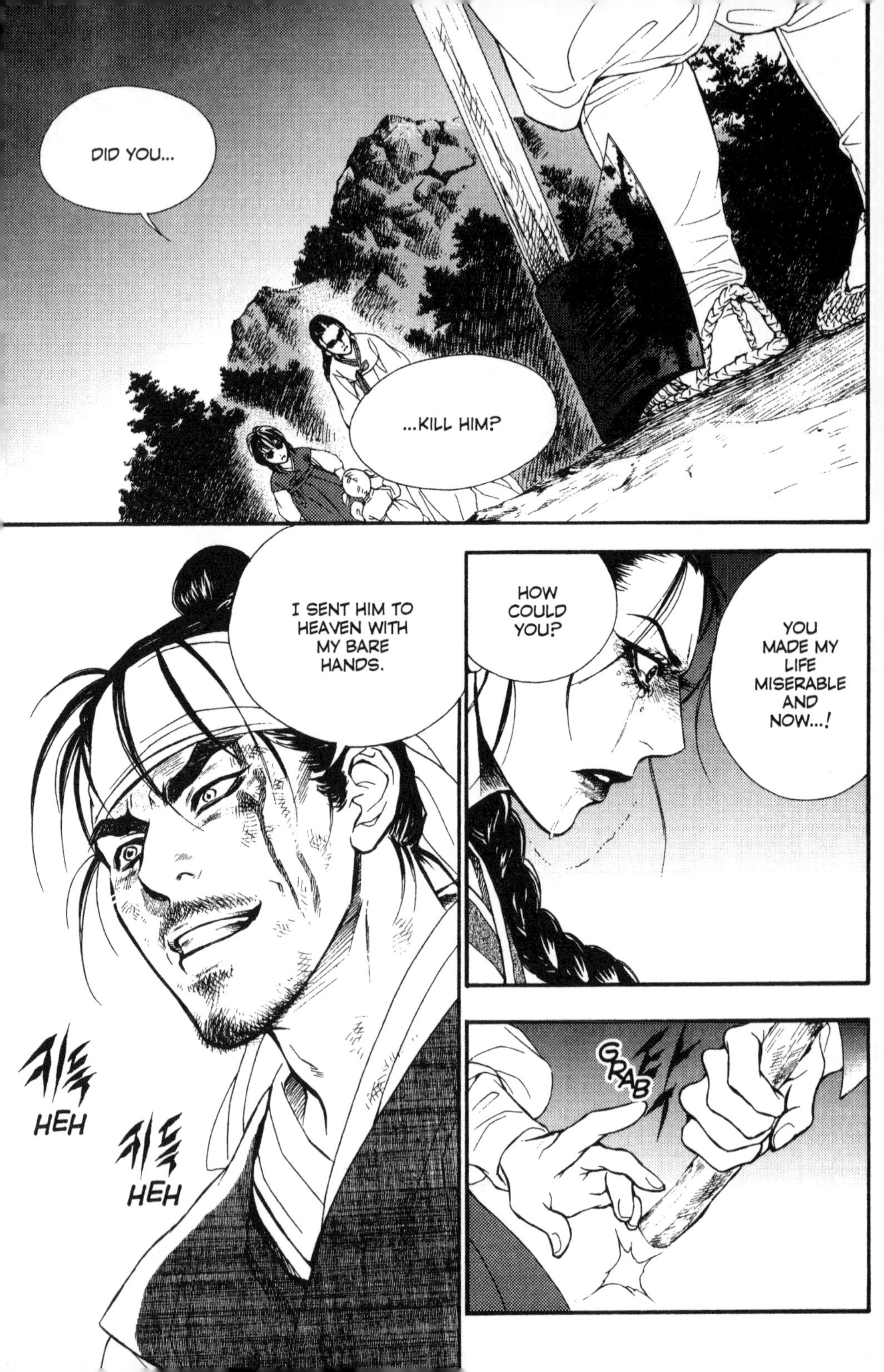
DID YOU...
...KILL HIM?
I SENT HIM TO HEAVEN WITH MY BARE HANDS.
키득
HEH
키득
HEH
HOW COULD YOU?
YOU MADE MY LIFE MISERABLE AND NOW...!
GRAB

MURDERER!

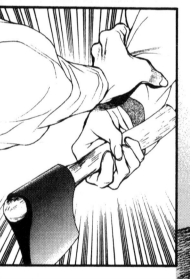

URK!

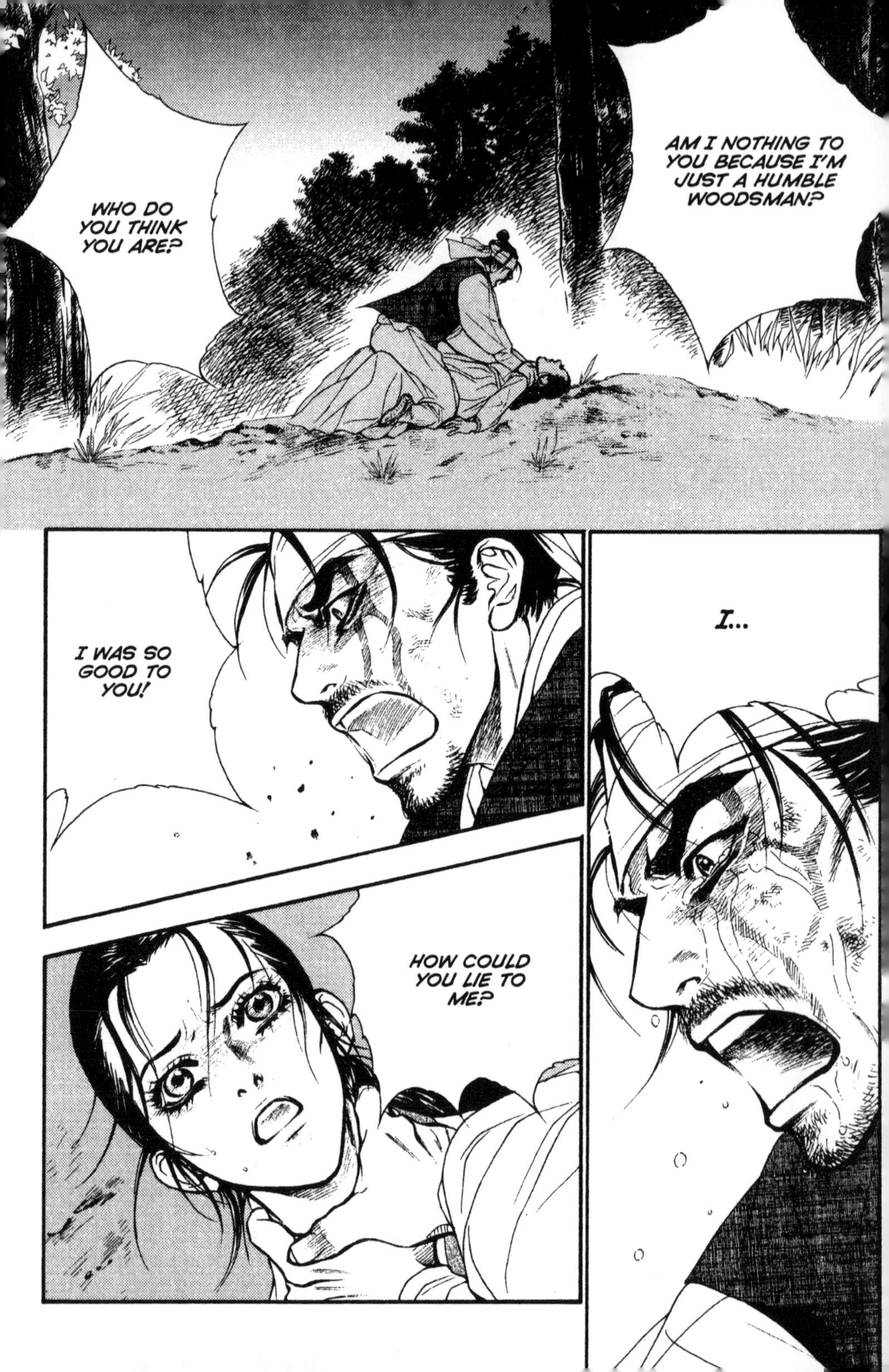
WHO DO YOU THINK YOU ARE?
AM I NOTHING TO YOU BECAUSE I'M JUST A HUMBLE WOODSMAN?
I WAS SO GOOD TO YOU!
I...
HOW COULD YOU LIE TO ME?

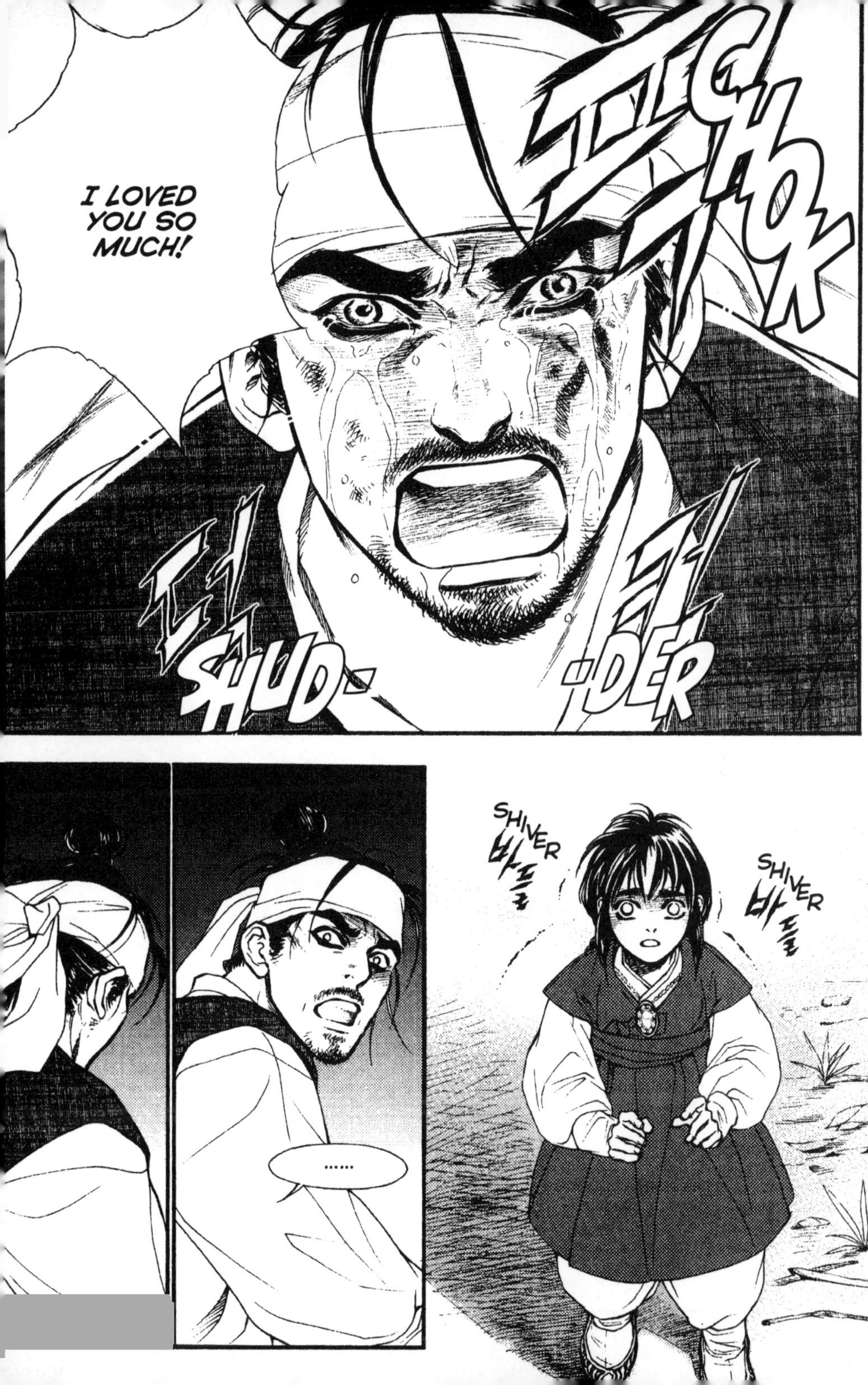
I LOVED YOU SO MUCH!
CHOK
SHUD-
-DER
......
SHIVER
SHIVER

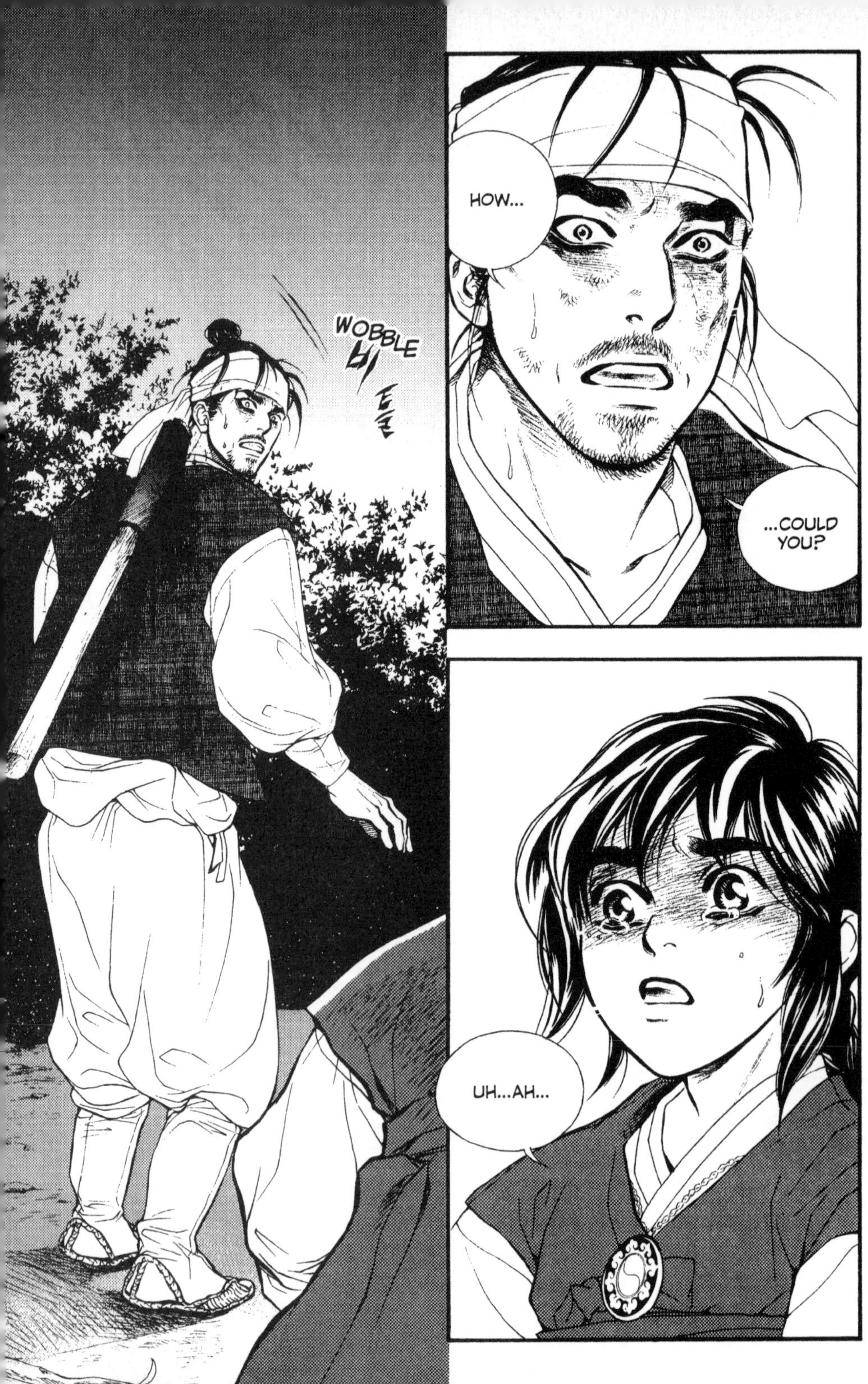
WOBBLE
HOW...
...COULD YOU?
UH...AH...

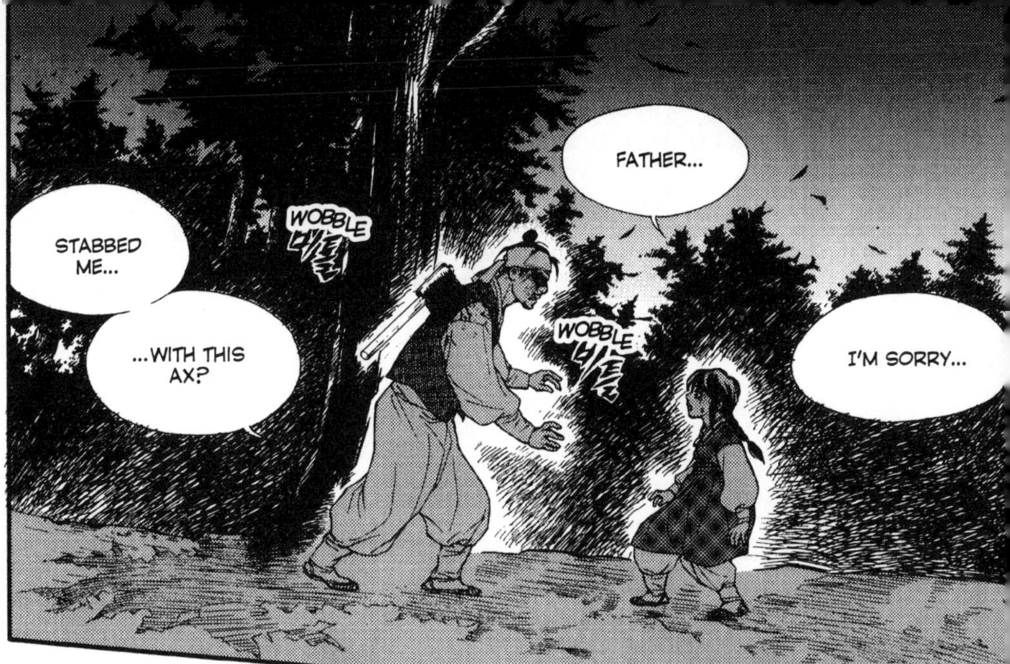
STABBED ME...
...WITH THIS AX?
WOBBLE
비틀
FATHER...
WOBBLE
비틀
I'M SORRY...
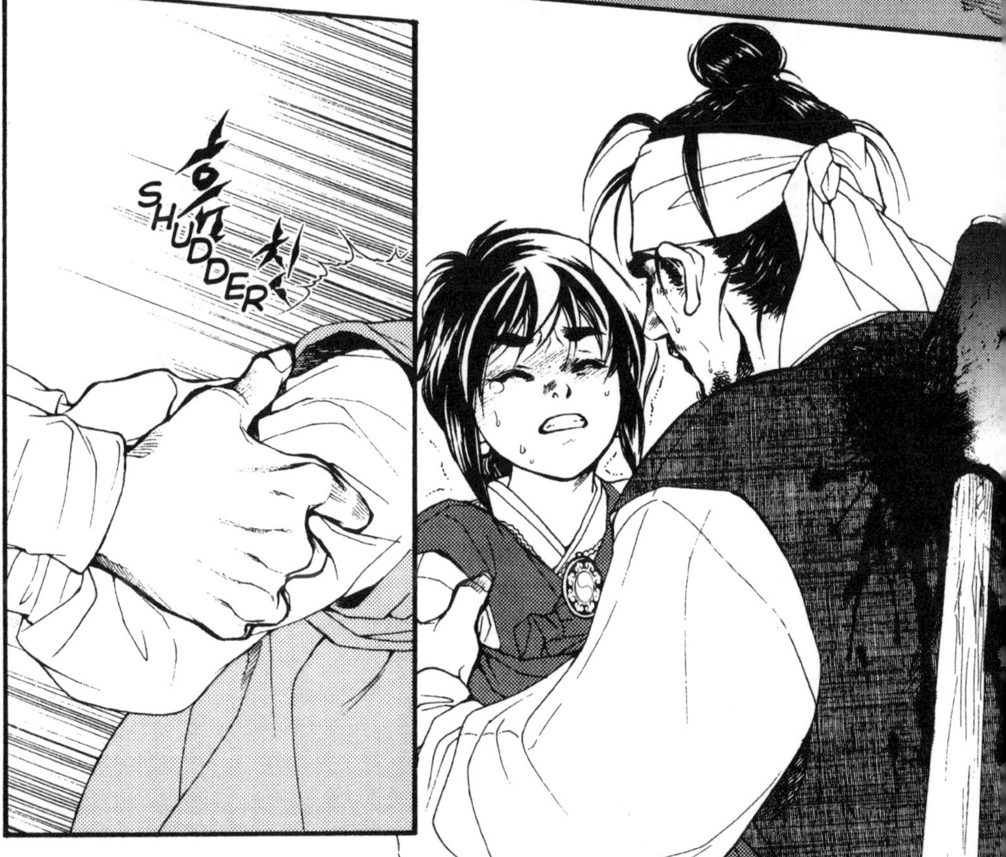
SHUDDER

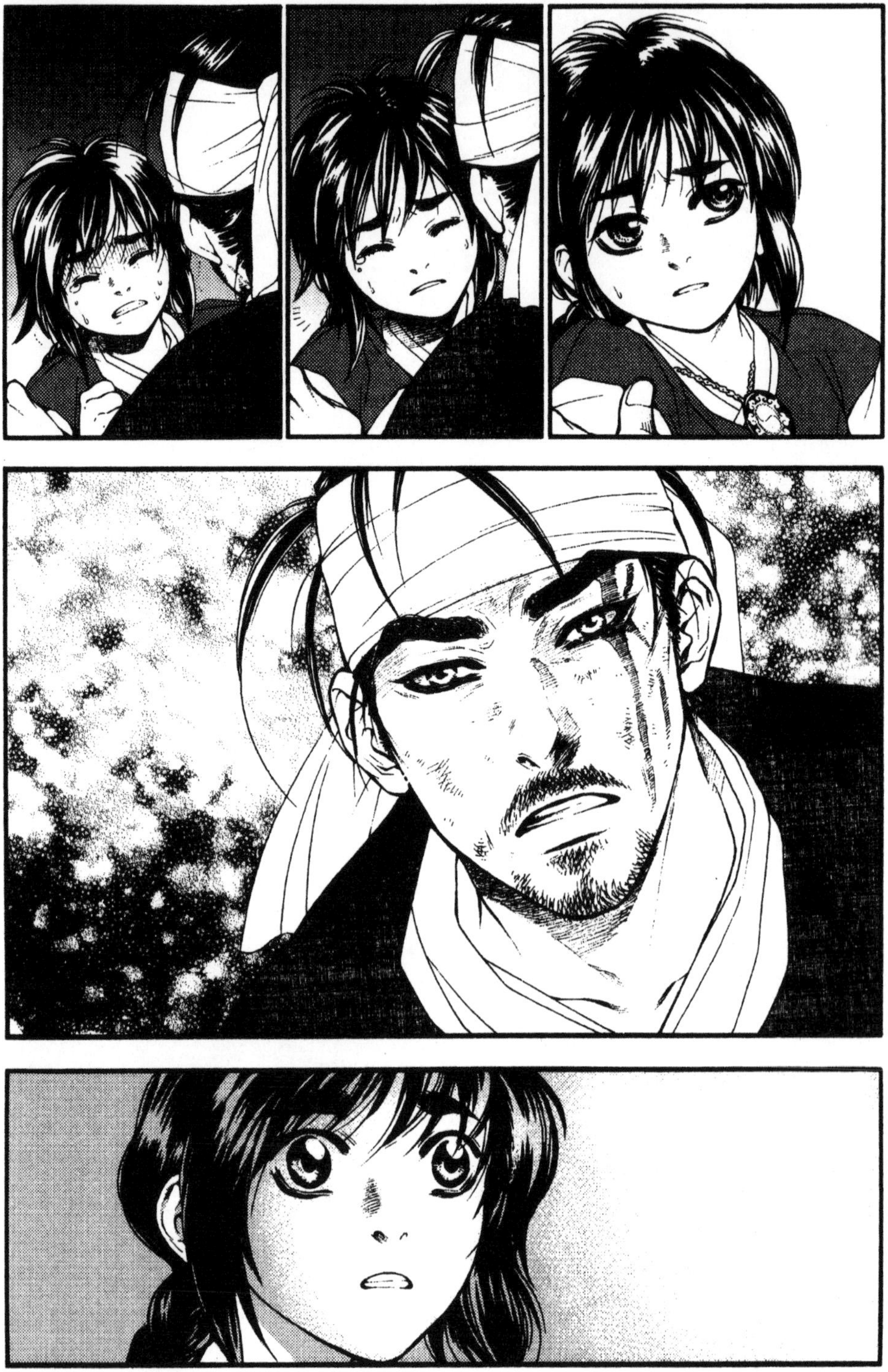

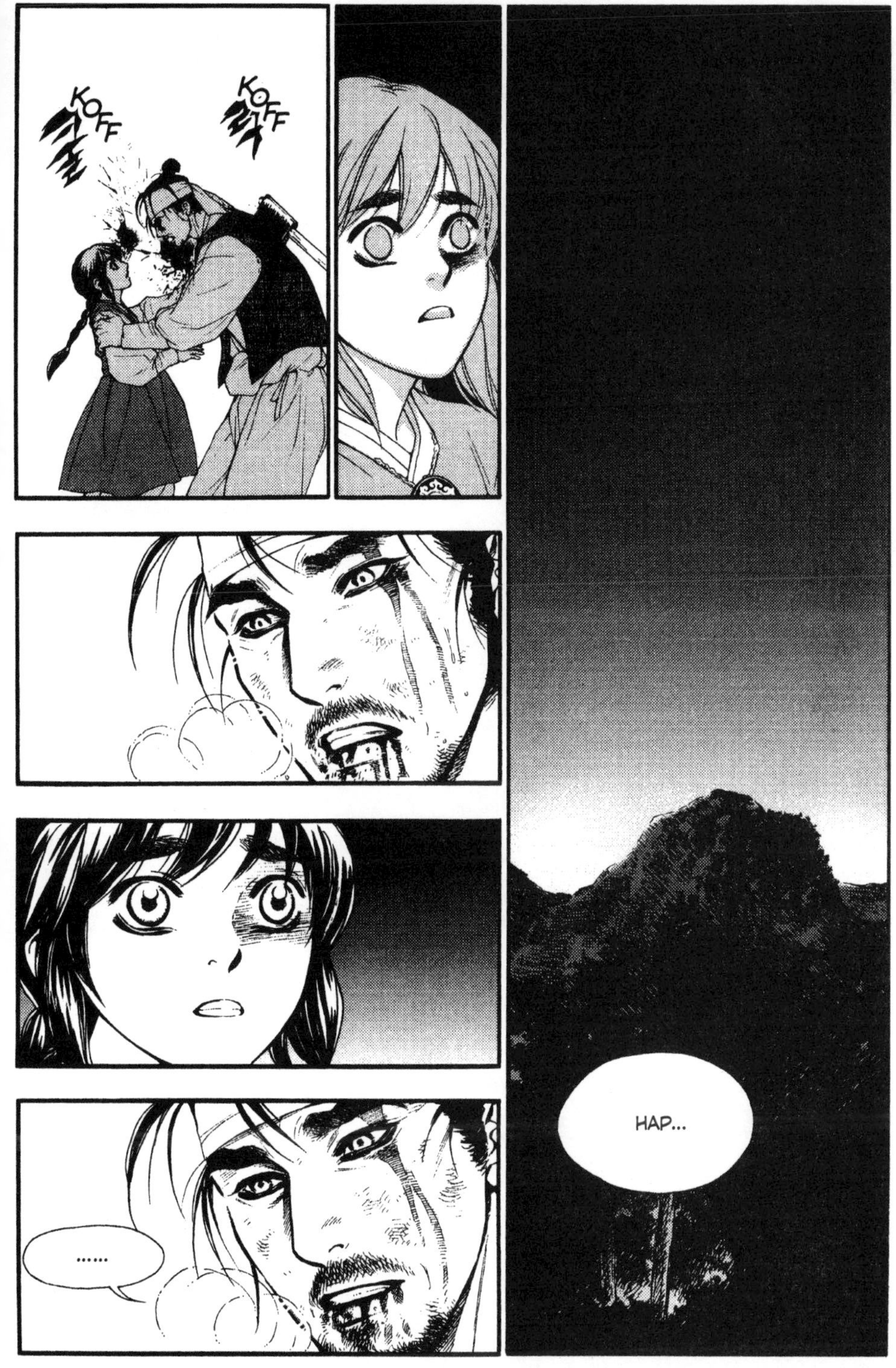
KOFF
KOFF
......
HAP...

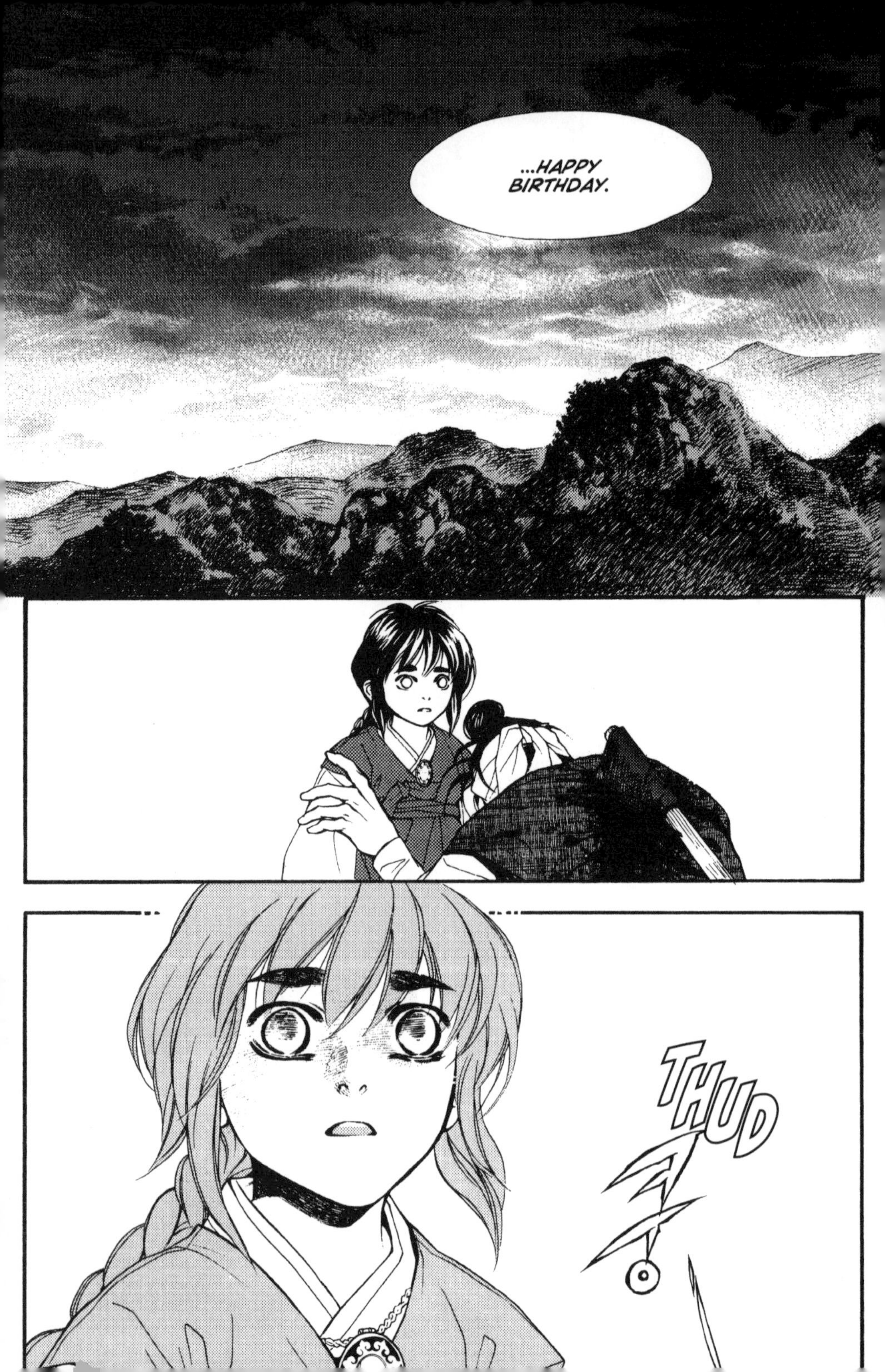
...HAPPY BIRTHDAY.
THUD

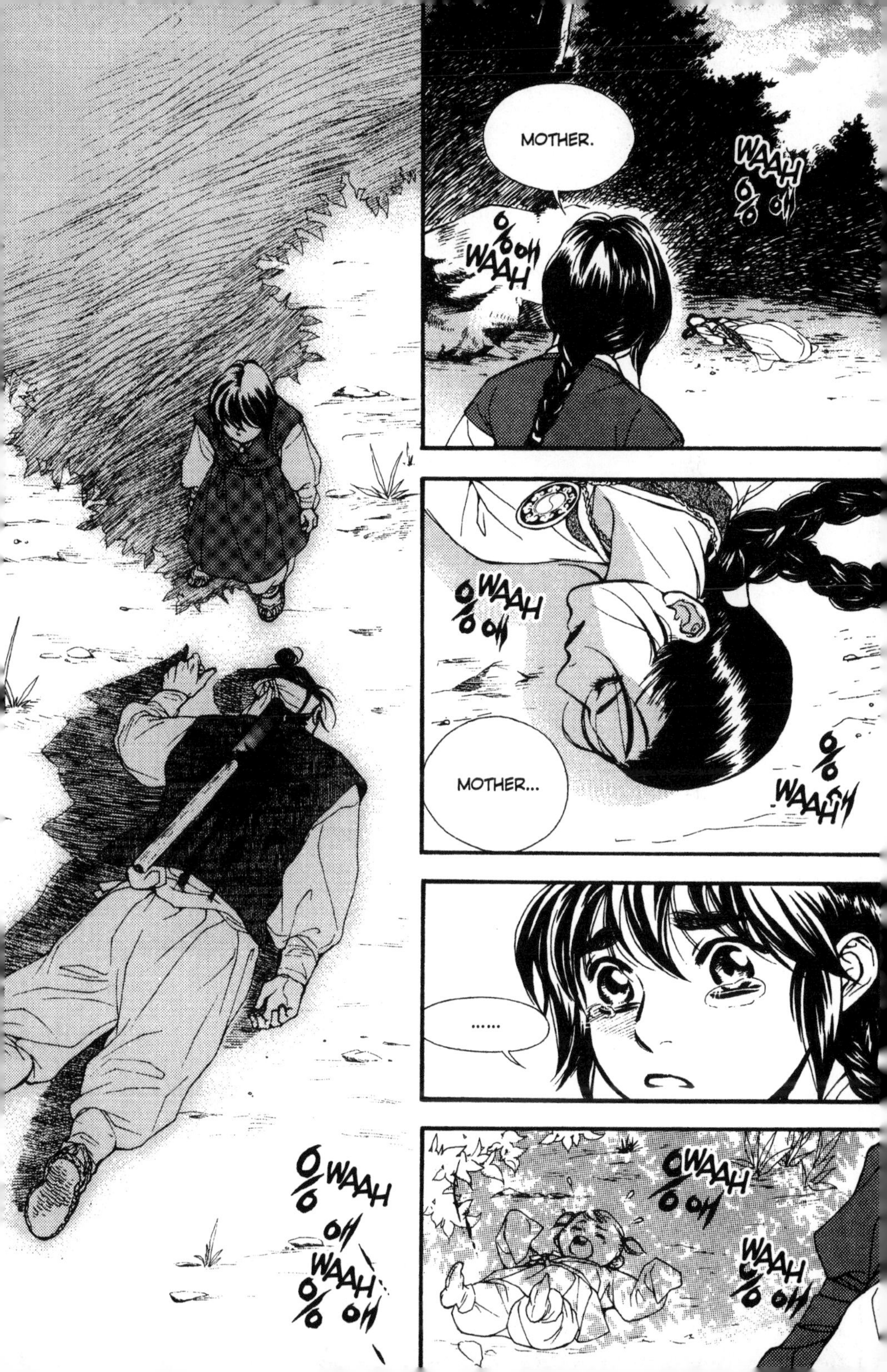
WAAH 응 애
WAAH 응 애
MOTHER.
WAAH 응 애
응 애 WAAH
WAAH 응 애
MOTHER...
응 애 WAAH
......
WAAH 응 애
WAAH 응 애

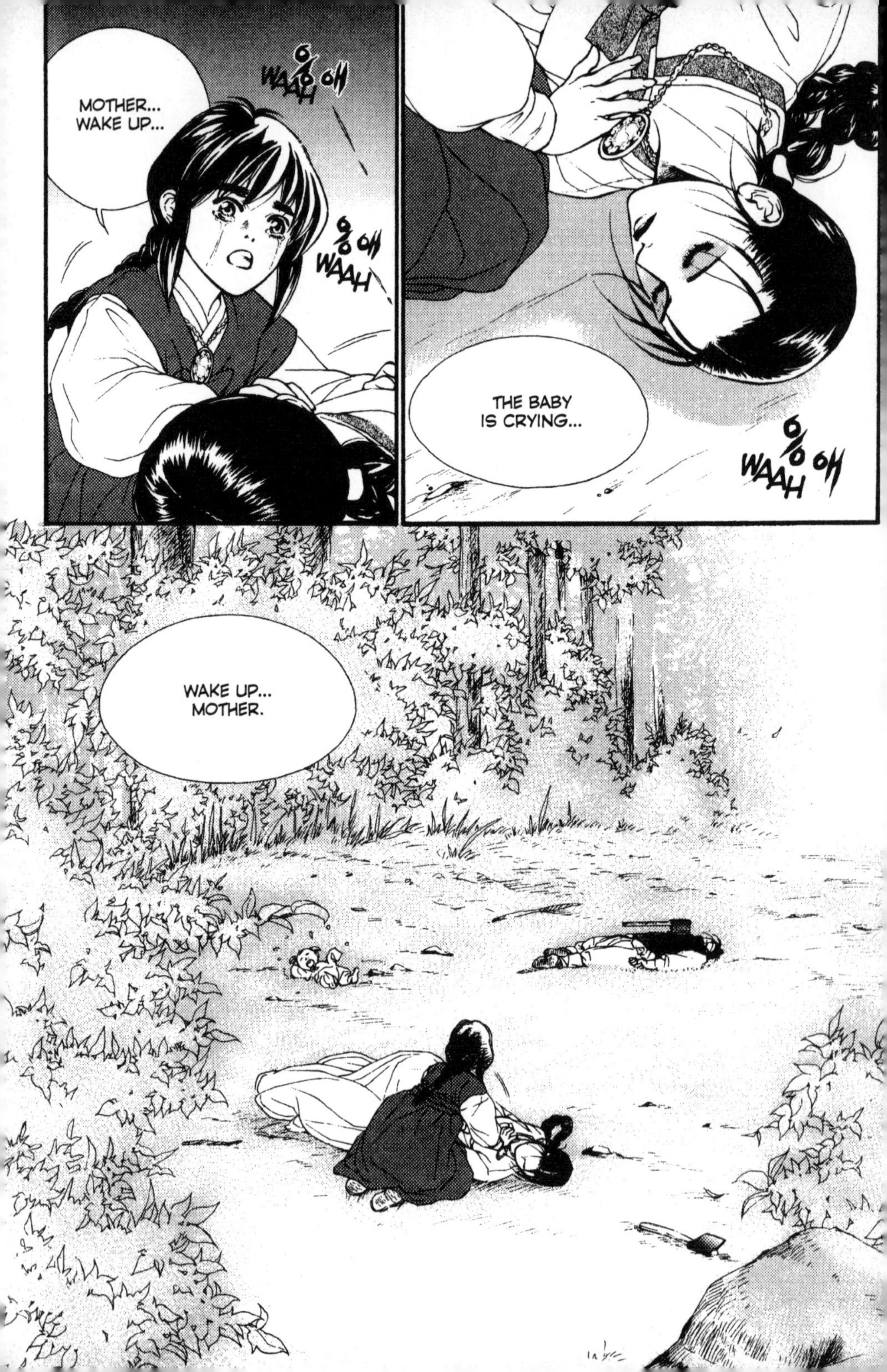
MOTHER... WAKE UP...
응애
WAAH
응애
WAAH
THE BABY IS CRYING...
응애
WAAH
WAKE UP... MOTHER.

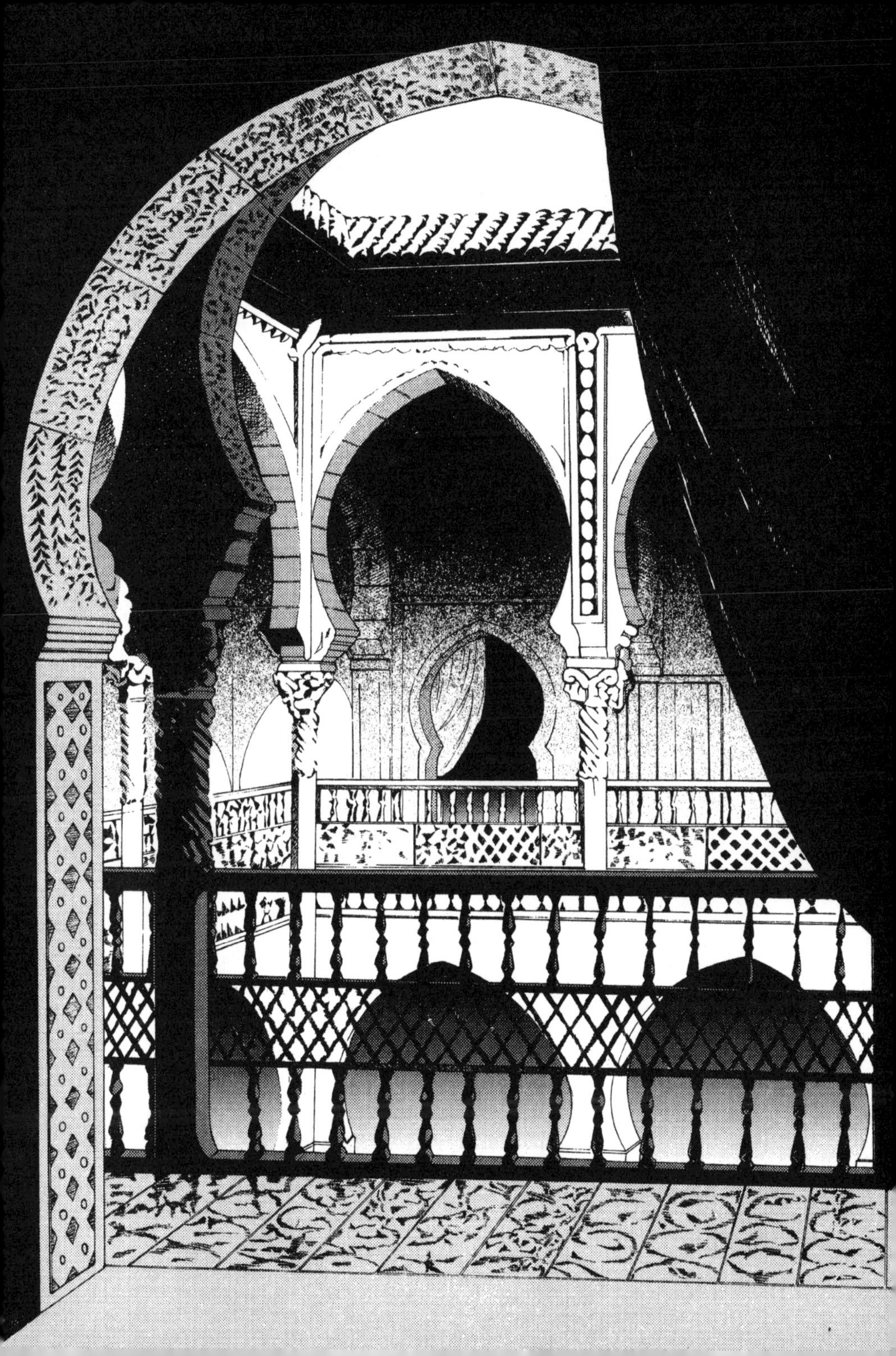

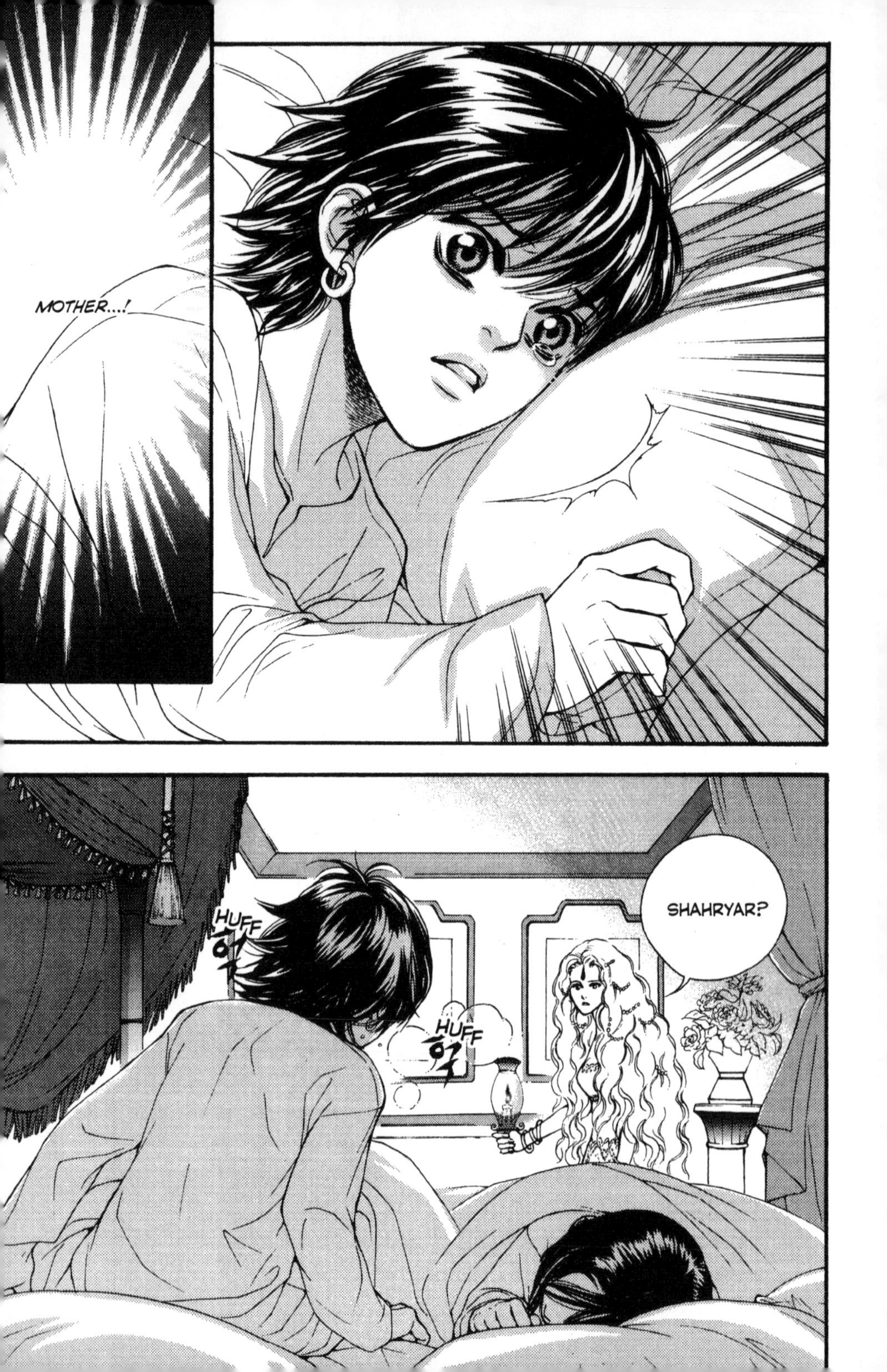
MOTHER...!
HUFF
HUFF
SHAHRYAR?

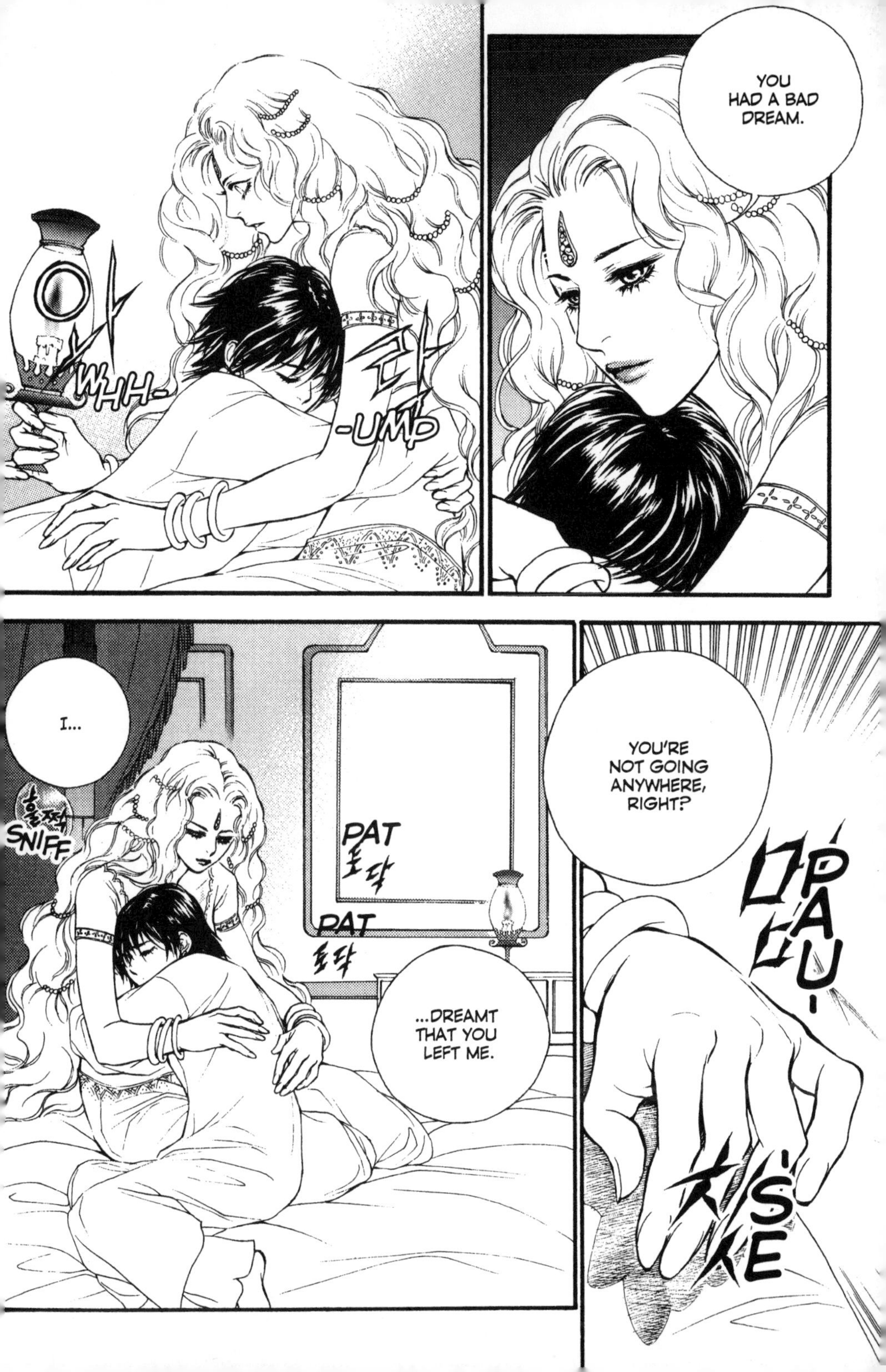
WHH-
-UMP
YOU HAD A BAD DREAM.
I...
훌쩍
SNIFF
PAT
토닥
PAT
토닥
...DREAMT THAT YOU LEFT ME.
YOU'RE NOT GOING ANYWHERE, RIGHT?
PAU-
SE

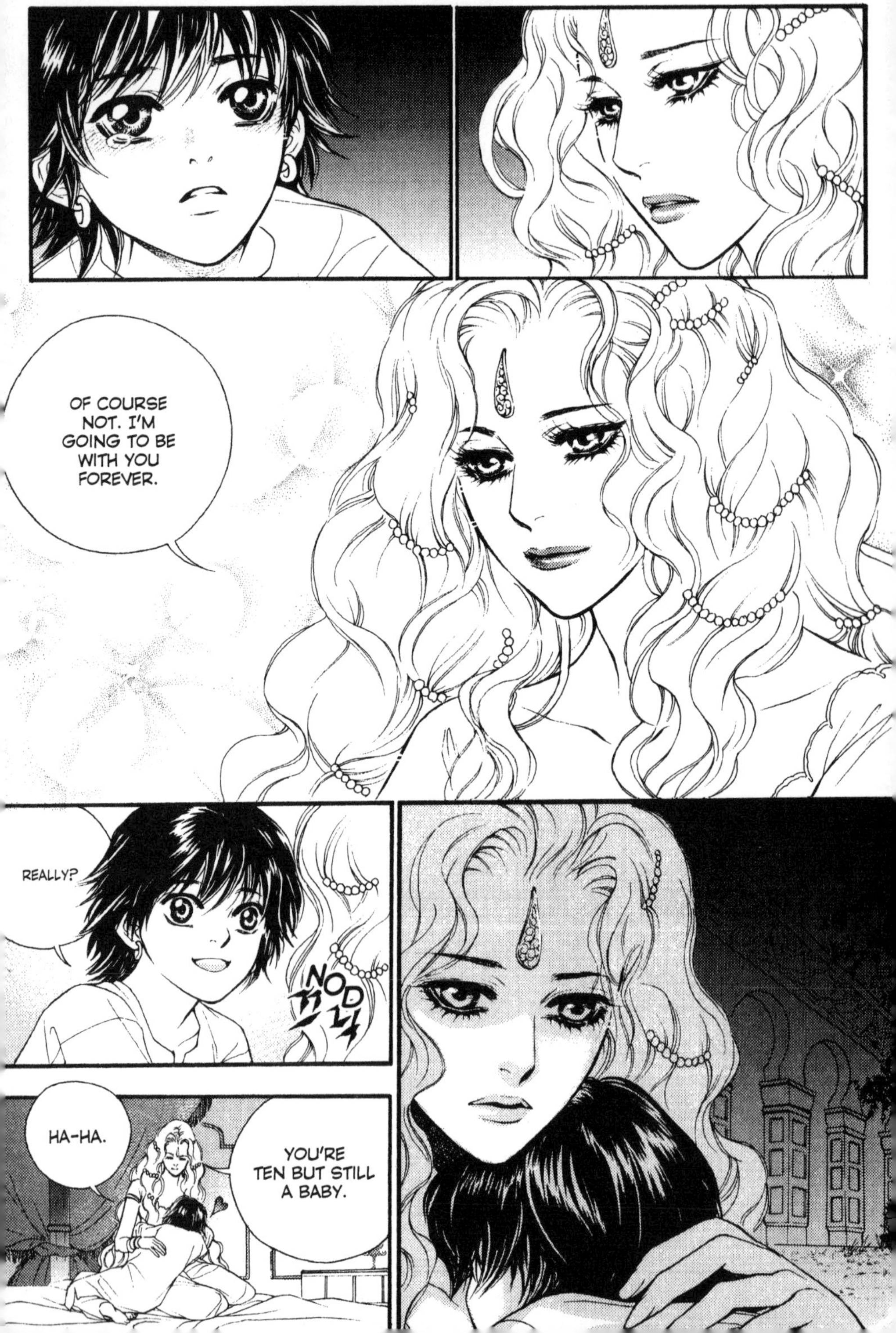
OF COURSE NOT. I'M GOING TO BE WITH YOU FOREVER.
REALLY?
NOD
HA-HA.
YOU'RE TEN BUT STILL A BABY.

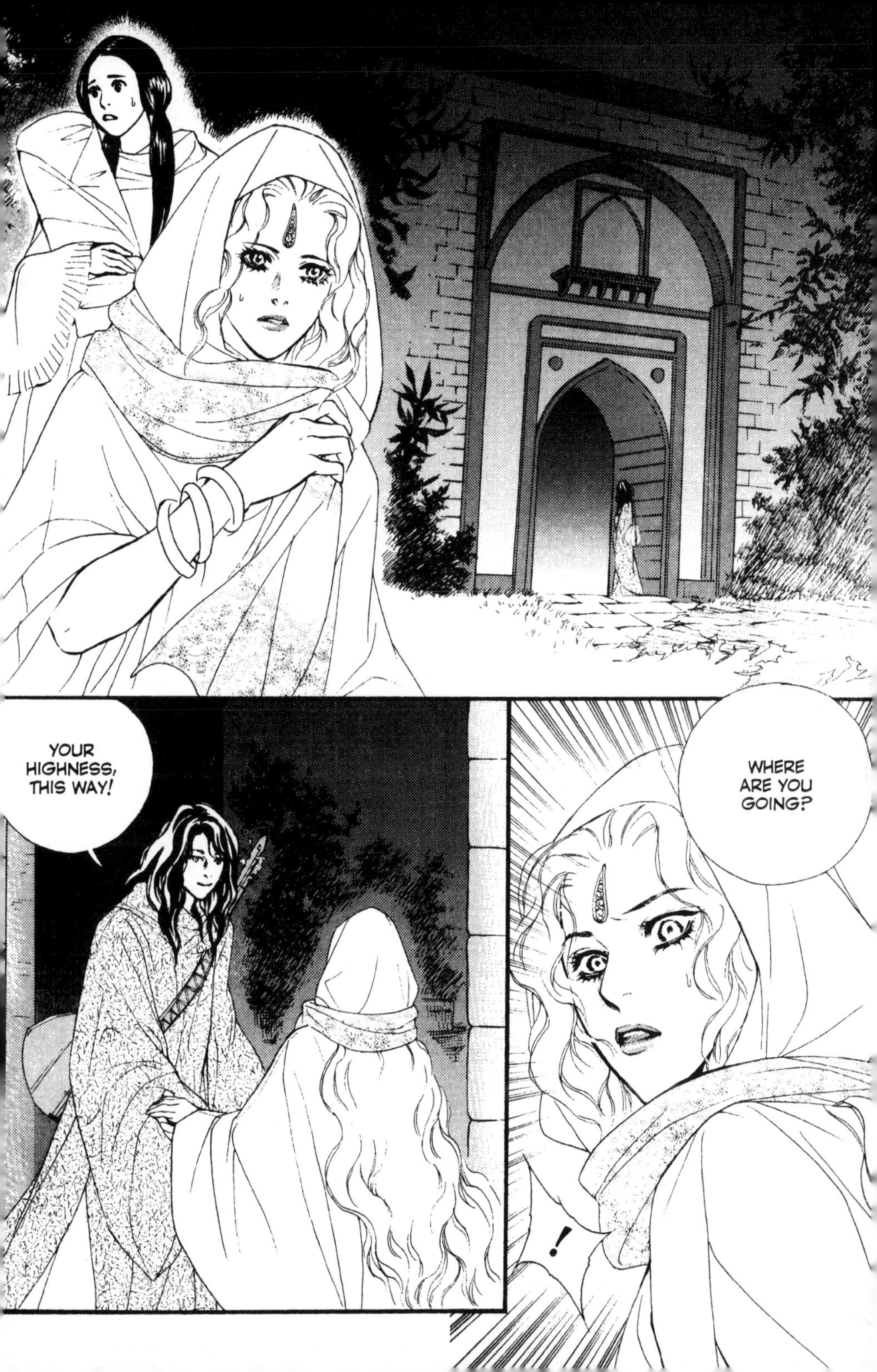
YOUR HIGHNESS, THIS WAY!
WHERE ARE YOU GOING?
!

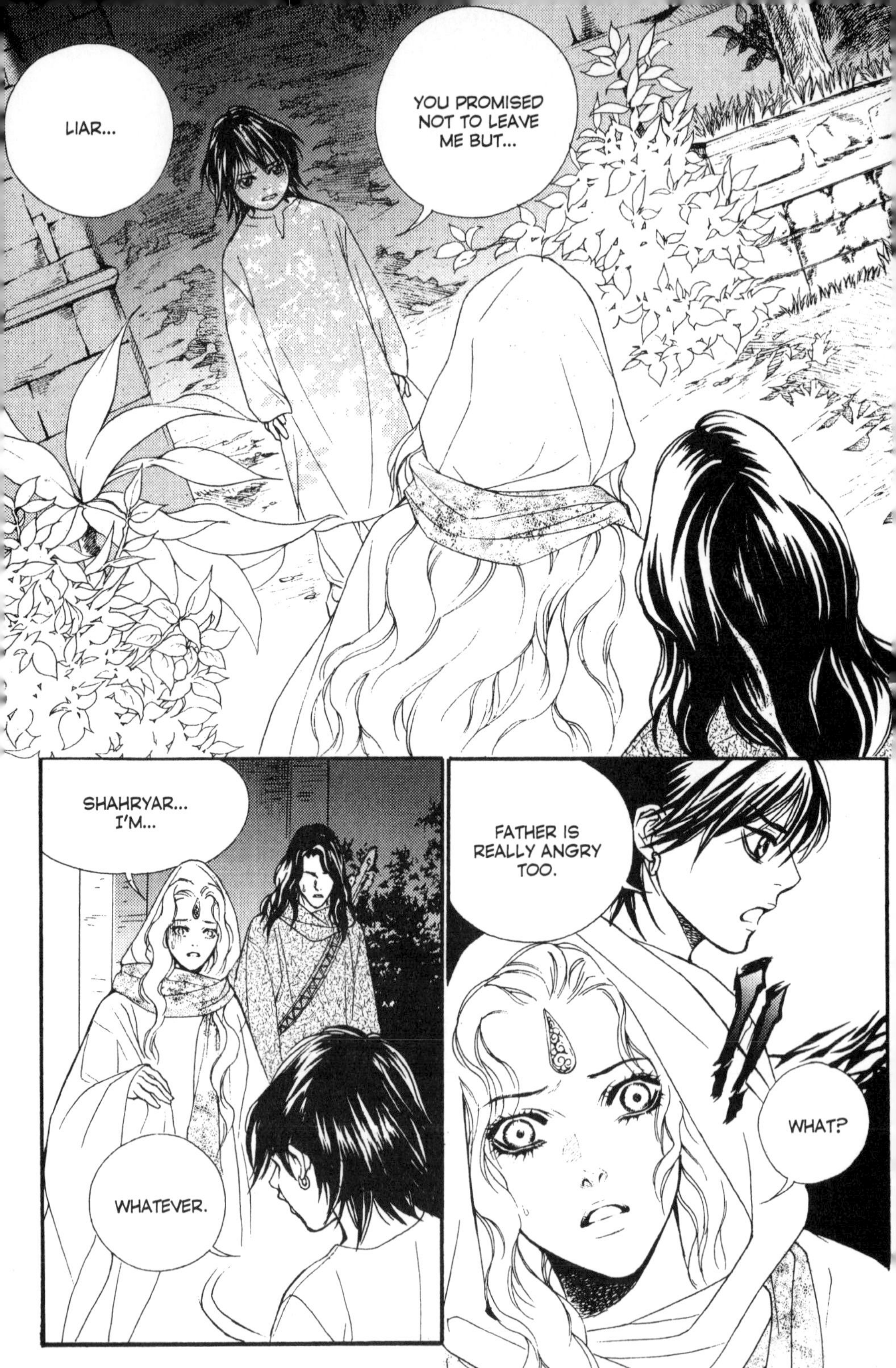
LIAR...
YOU PROMISED NOT TO LEAVE ME BUT...
SHAHRYAR... I'M...
WHATEVER.
FATHER IS REALLY ANGRY TOO.
WHAT?

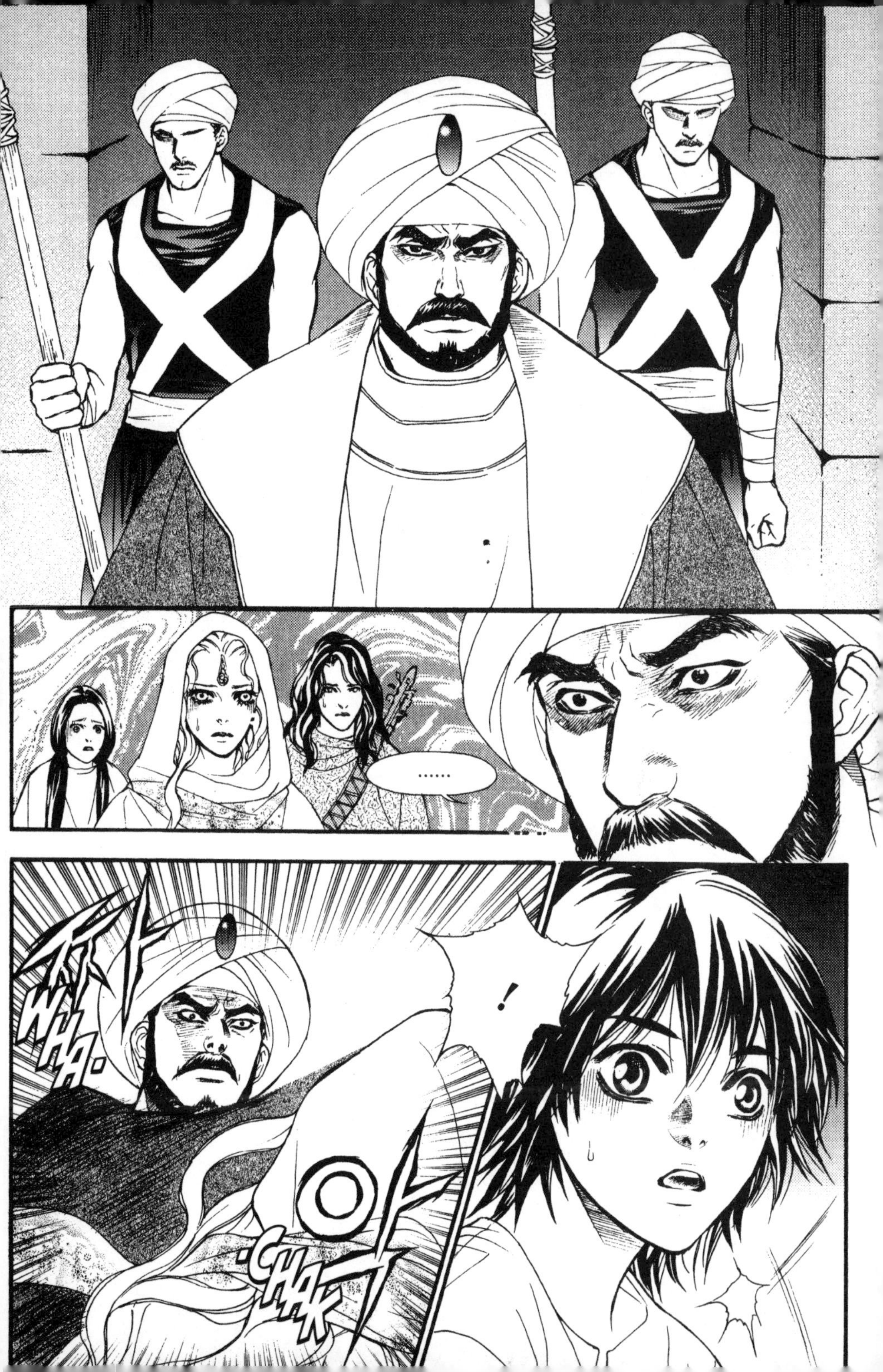

......
WHA-
!
CHAK

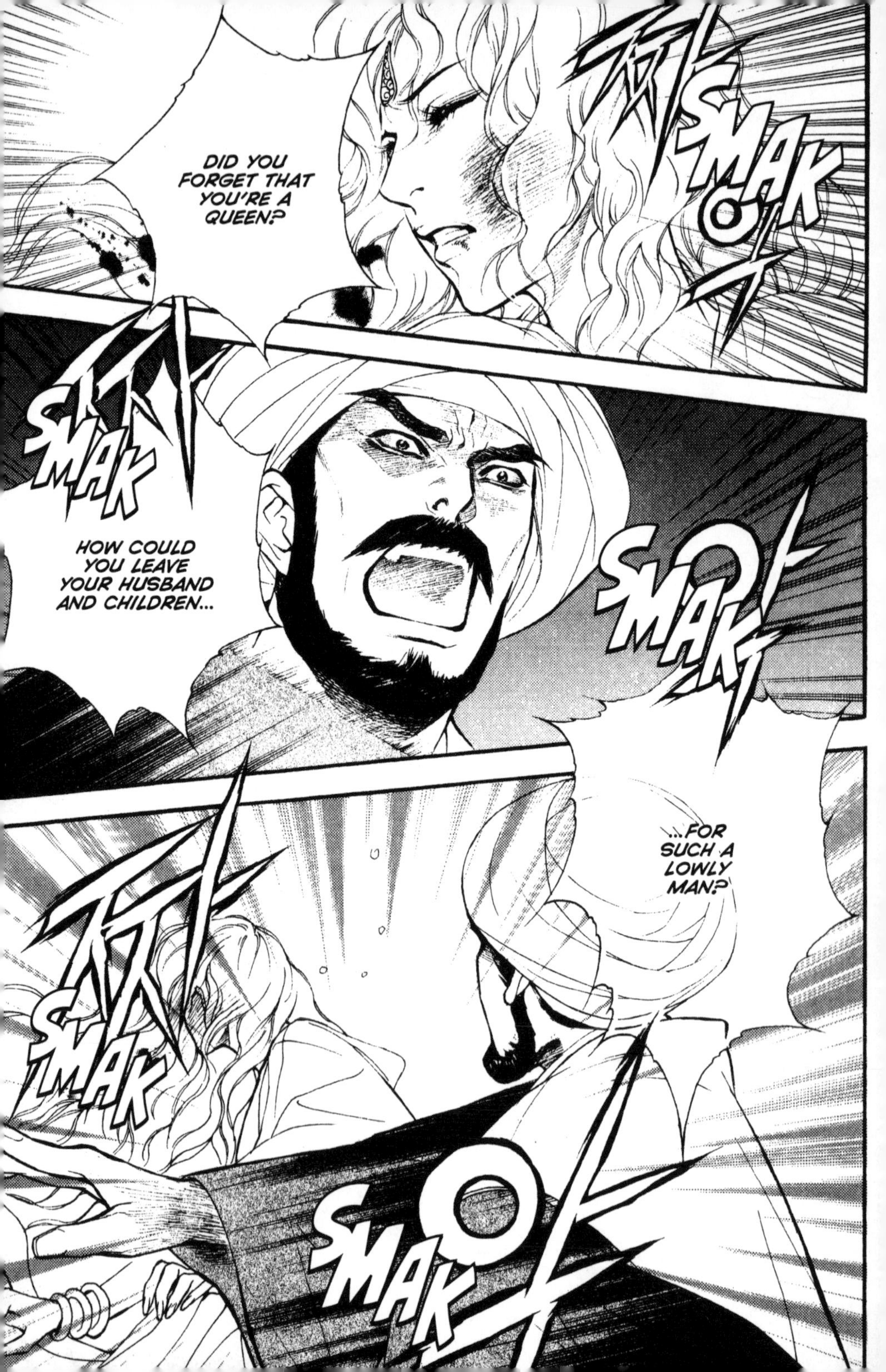
DID YOU FORGET THAT YOU'RE A QUEEN?
SMAK
SMAK
HOW COULD YOU LEAVE YOUR HUSBAND AND CHILDREN...
SMAK
SMAK
...FOR SUCH A LOWLY MAN?
SMAK

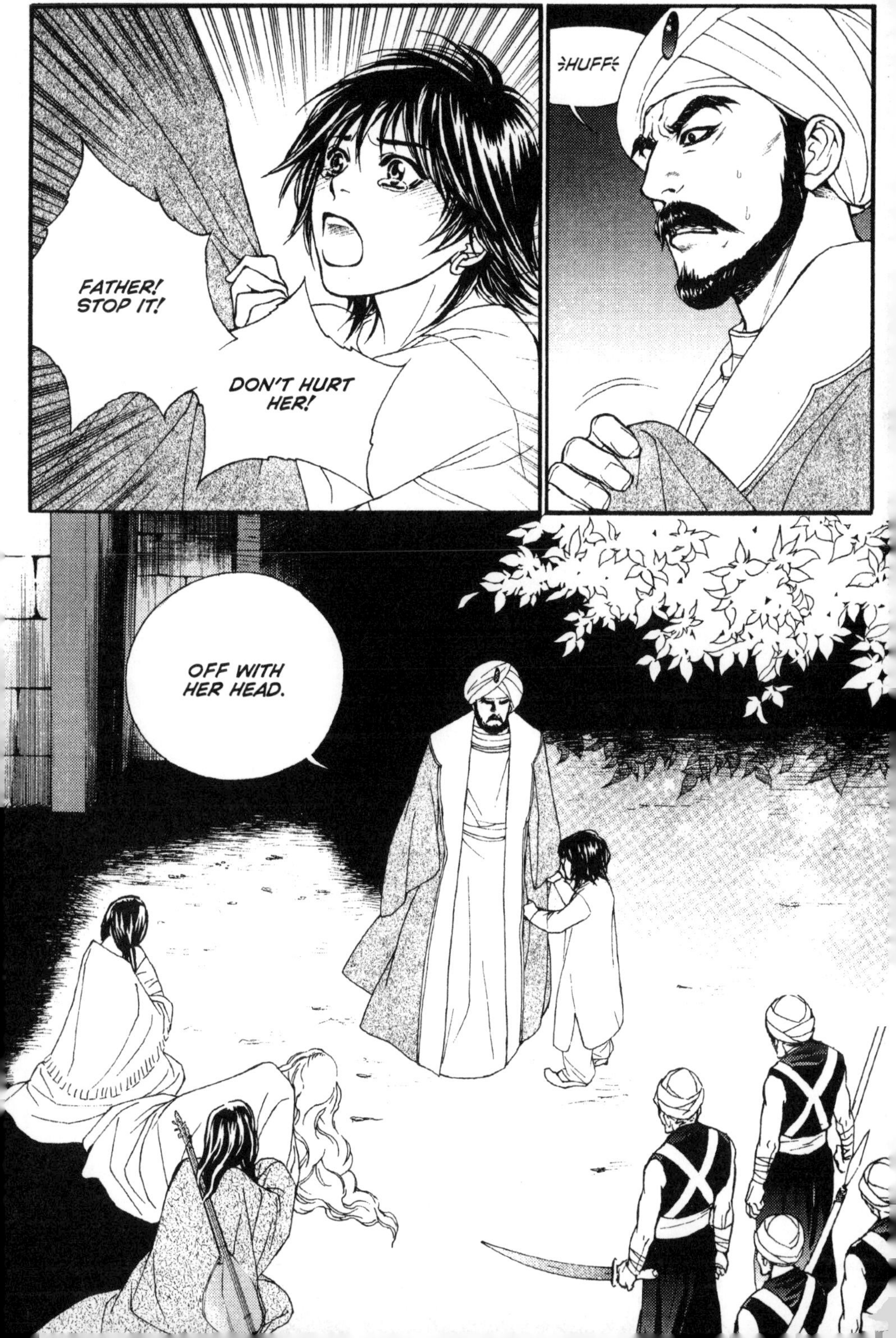
FATHER! STOP IT!
DON'T HURT HER!
HUFF
OFF WITH HER HEAD.

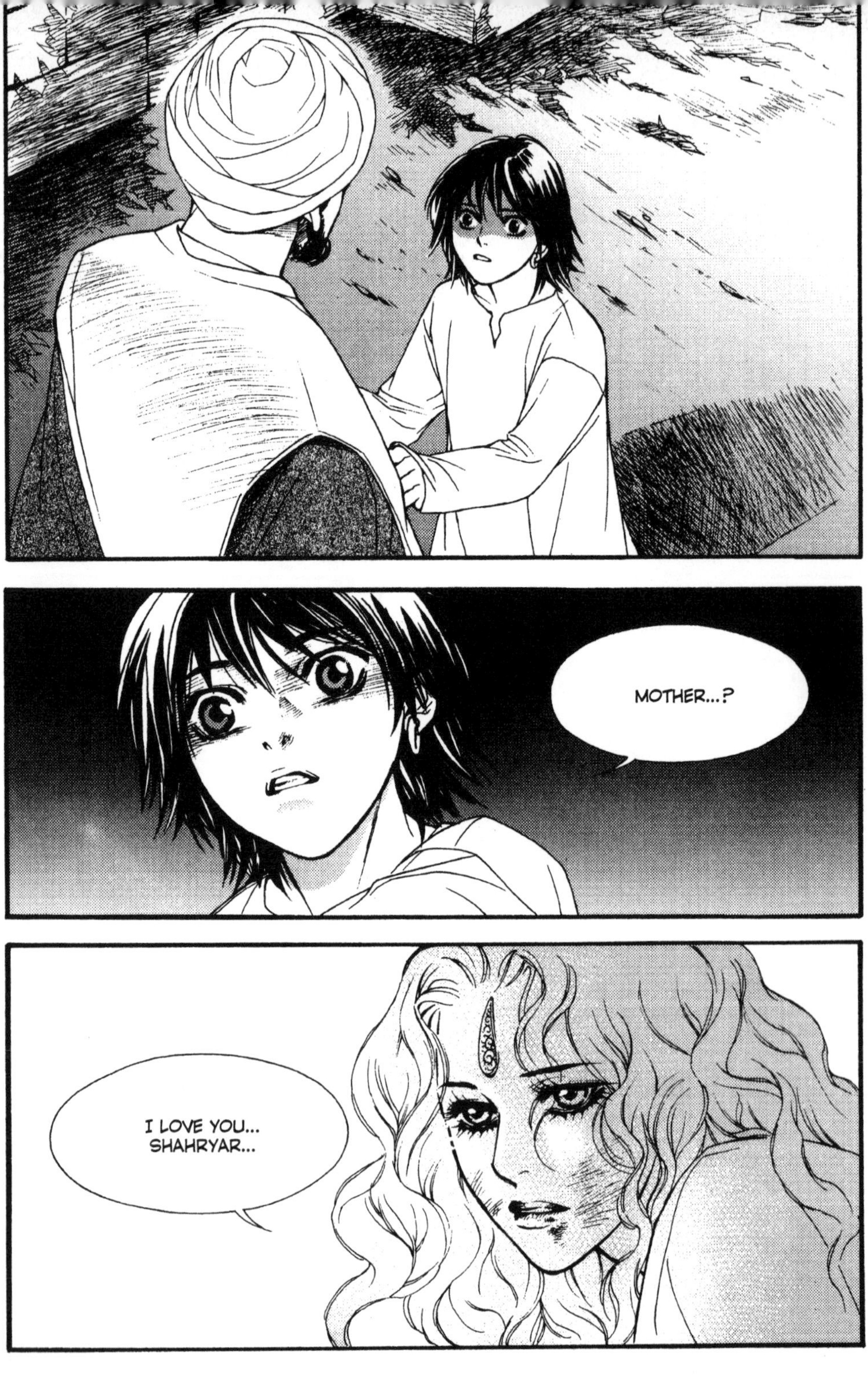
MOTHER...?
I LOVE YOU... SHAHRYAR...

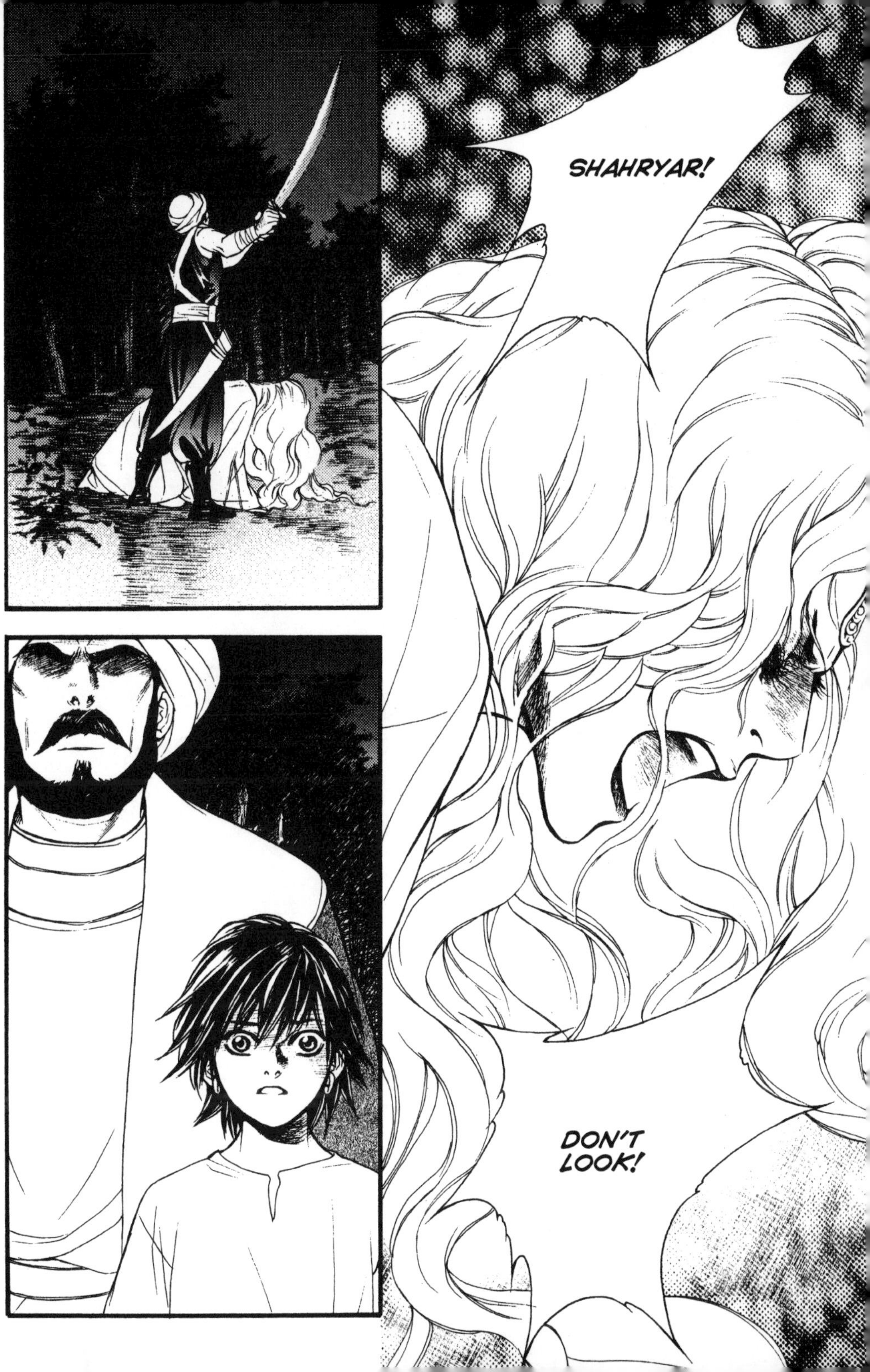
SHAHRYAR!
DON'T LOOK!

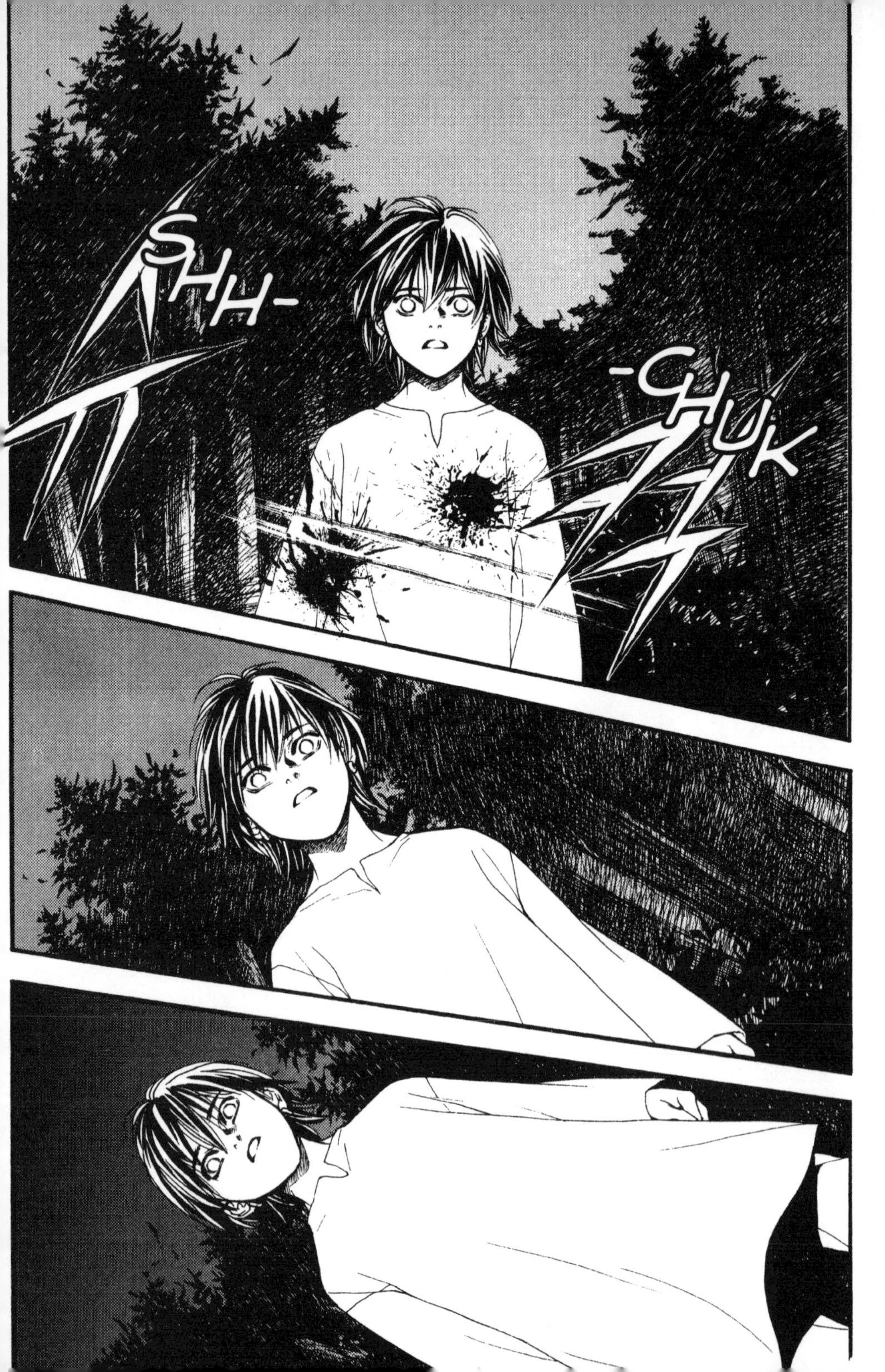
SHH-
-CHUK

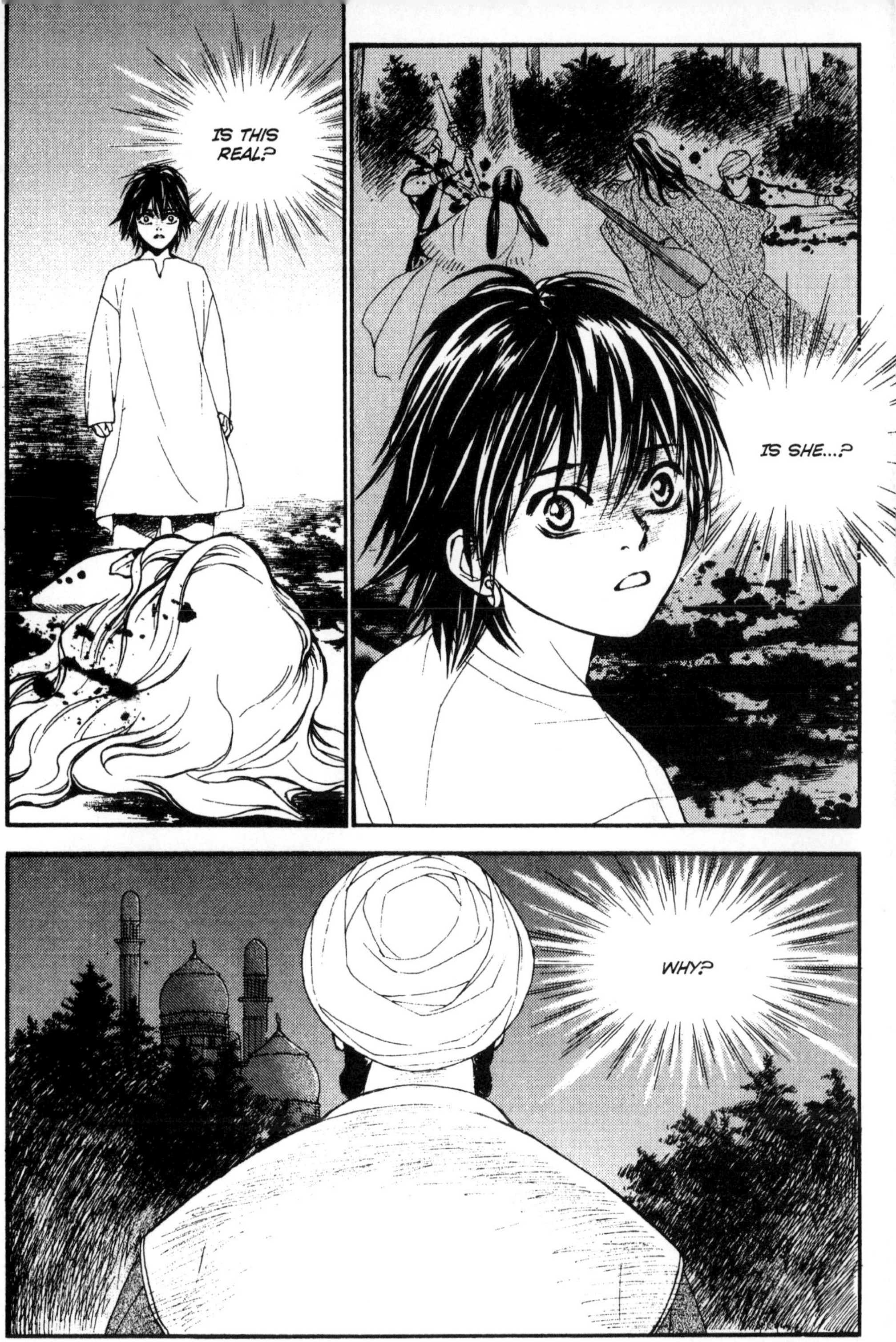
IS THIS REAL?
IS SHE...?
WHY?

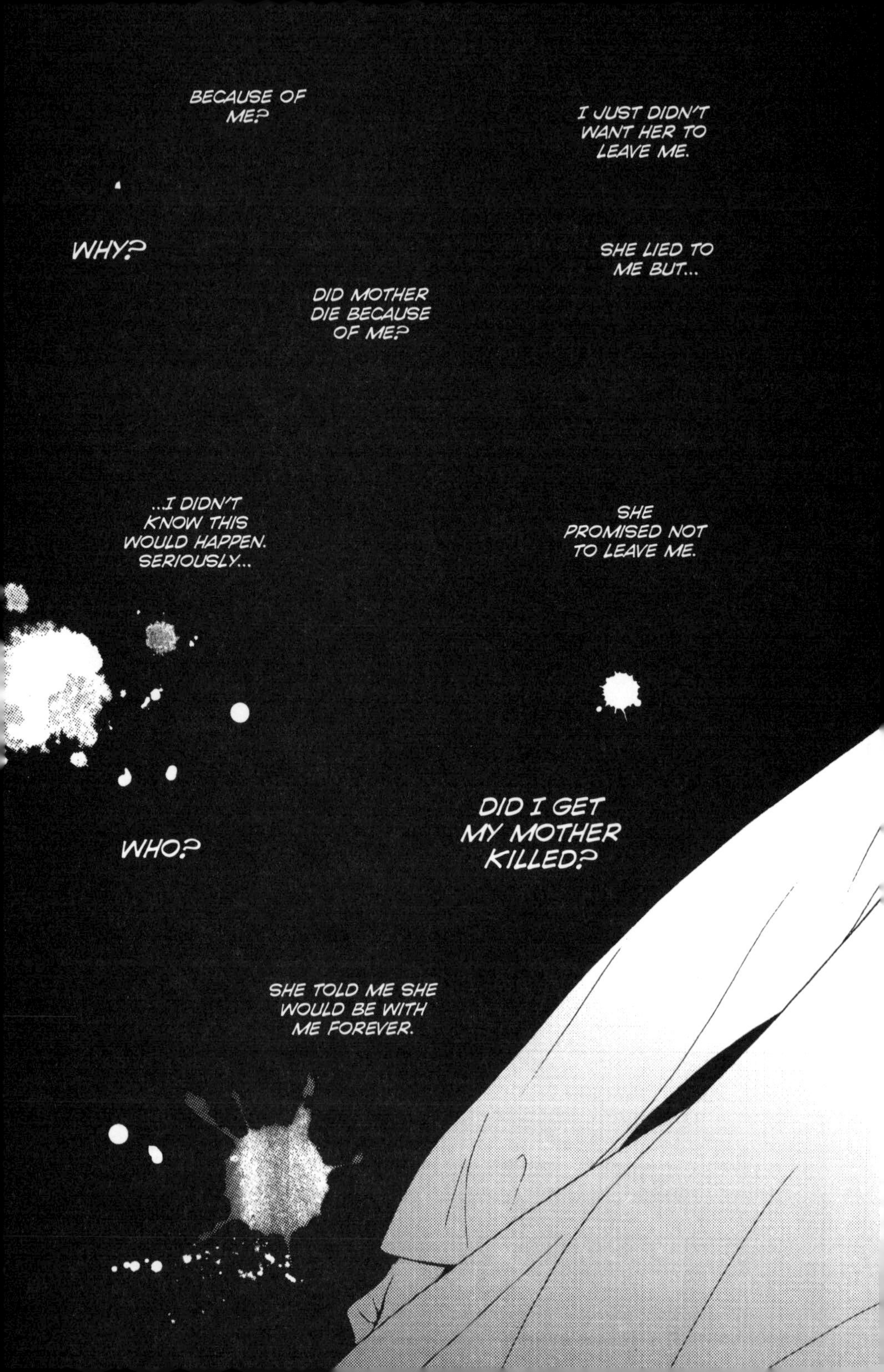
BECAUSE OF ME?
I JUST DIDN'T WANT HER TO LEAVE ME.
WHY?
SHE LIED TO ME BUT...
DID MOTHER DIE BECAUSE OF ME?
...I DIDN'T KNOW THIS WOULD HAPPEN. SERIOUSLY...
SHE PROMISED NOT TO LEAVE ME.
DID I GET MY MOTHER KILLED?
WHO?
SHE TOLD ME SHE WOULD BE WITH ME FOREVER.

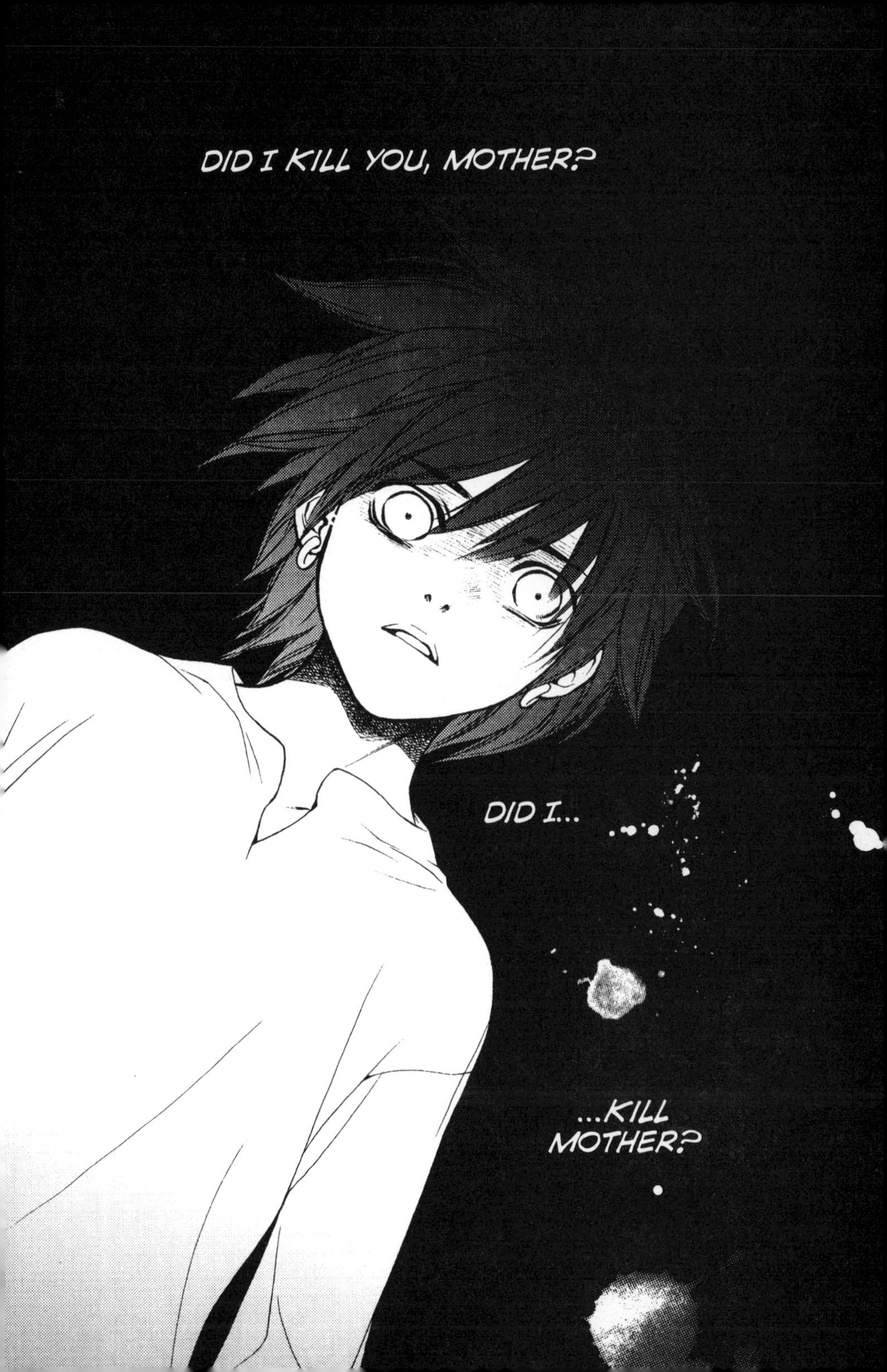
DID I KILL YOU, MOTHER?
DID I...
...KILL MOTHER?

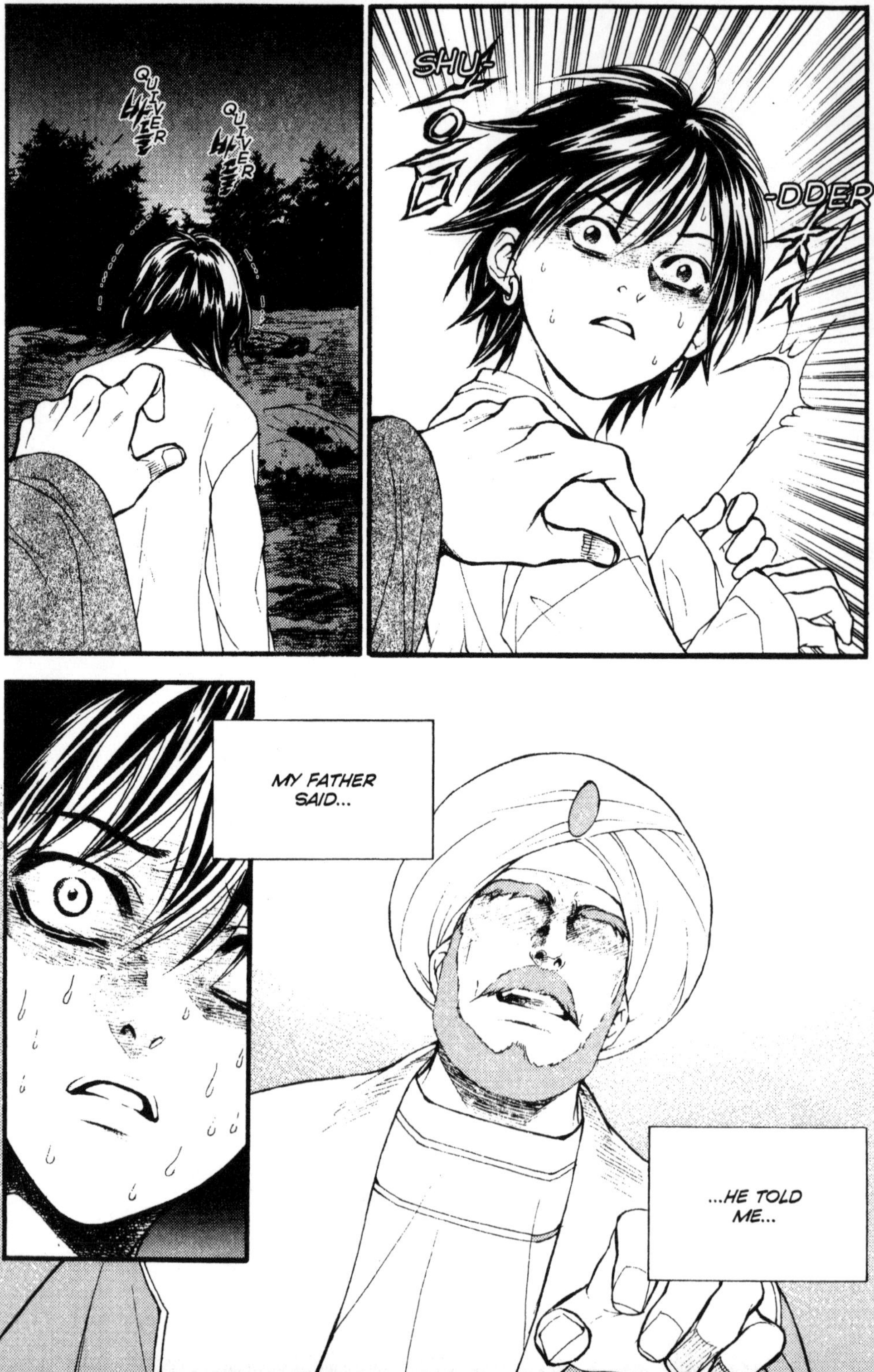
QUIVER
QUIVER
SHU-
-DDER
MY FATHER SAID...
...HE TOLD ME...

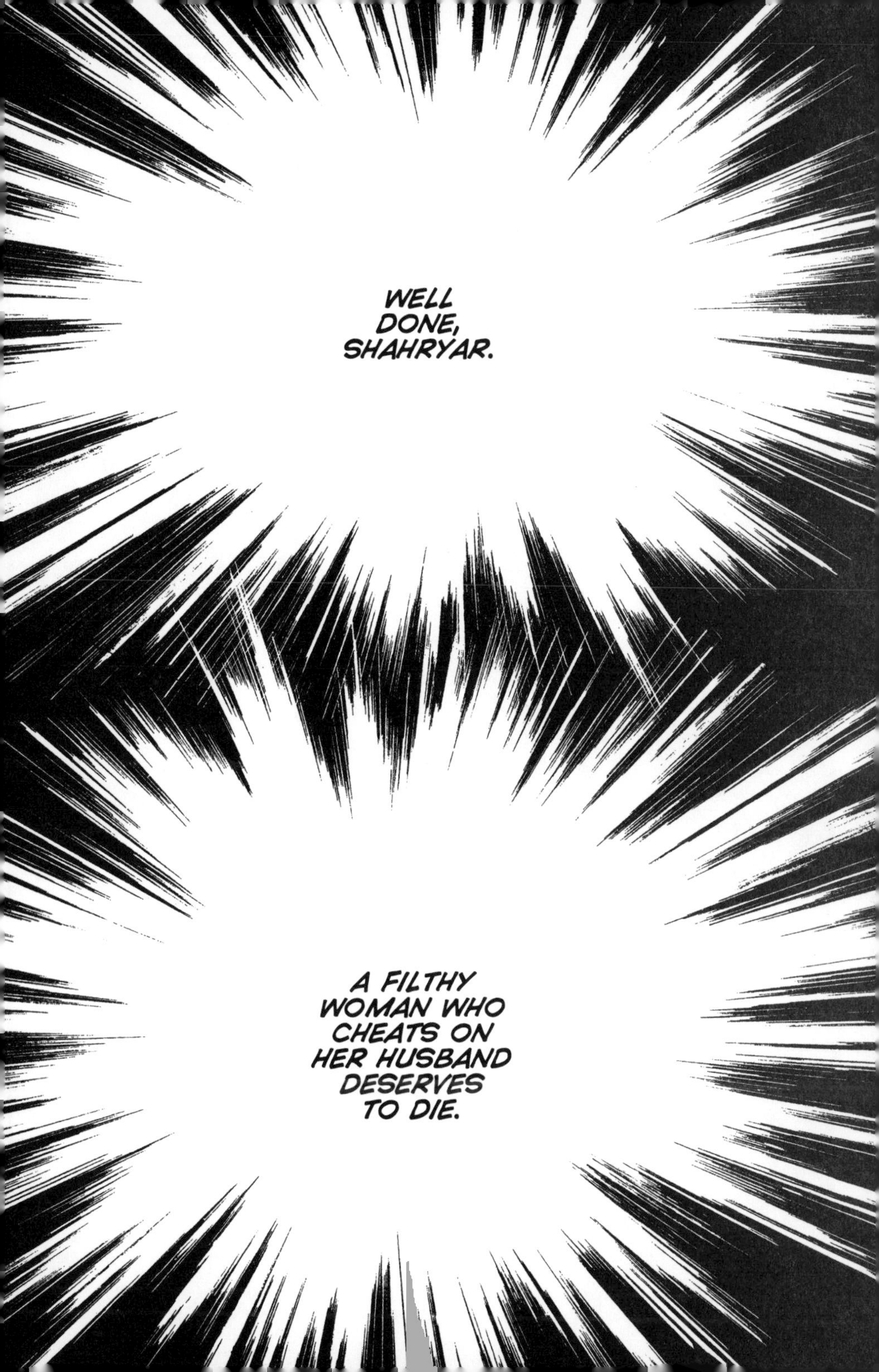
WELL DONE, SHAHRYAR.
A FILTHY WOMAN WHO CHEATS ON HER HUSBAND DESERVES TO DIE.

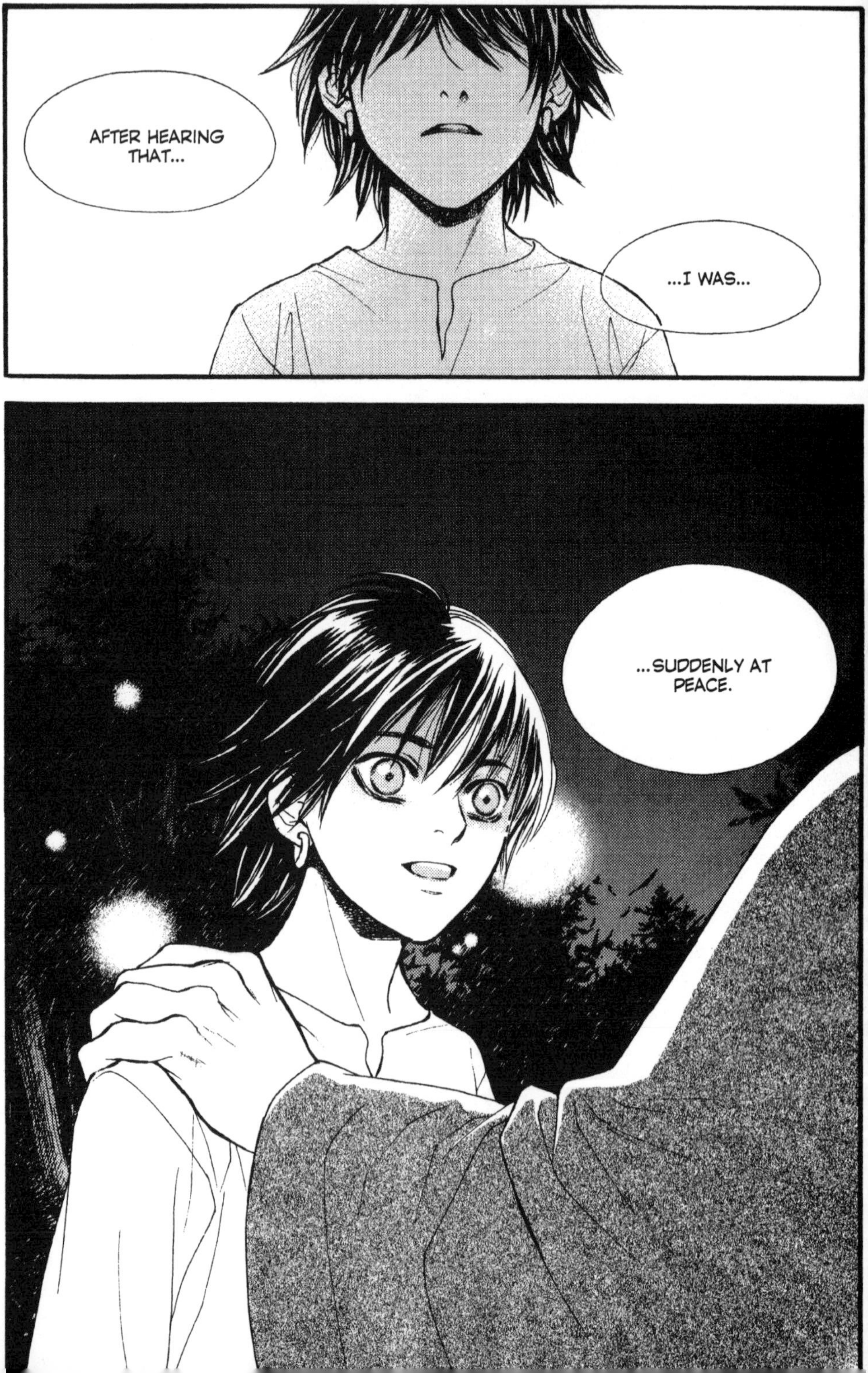
AFTER HEARING THAT...
...I WAS...
...SUDDENLY AT PEACE.

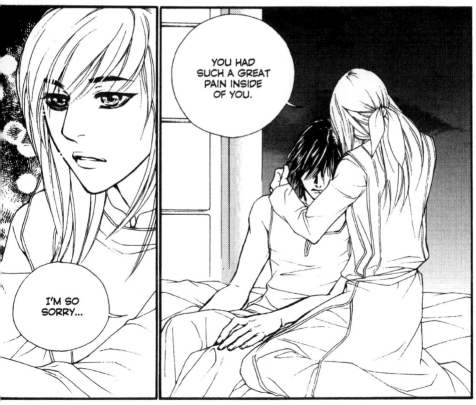

YOU HAD SUCH A GREAT PAIN INSIDE OF YOU.

I'M SO SORRY...

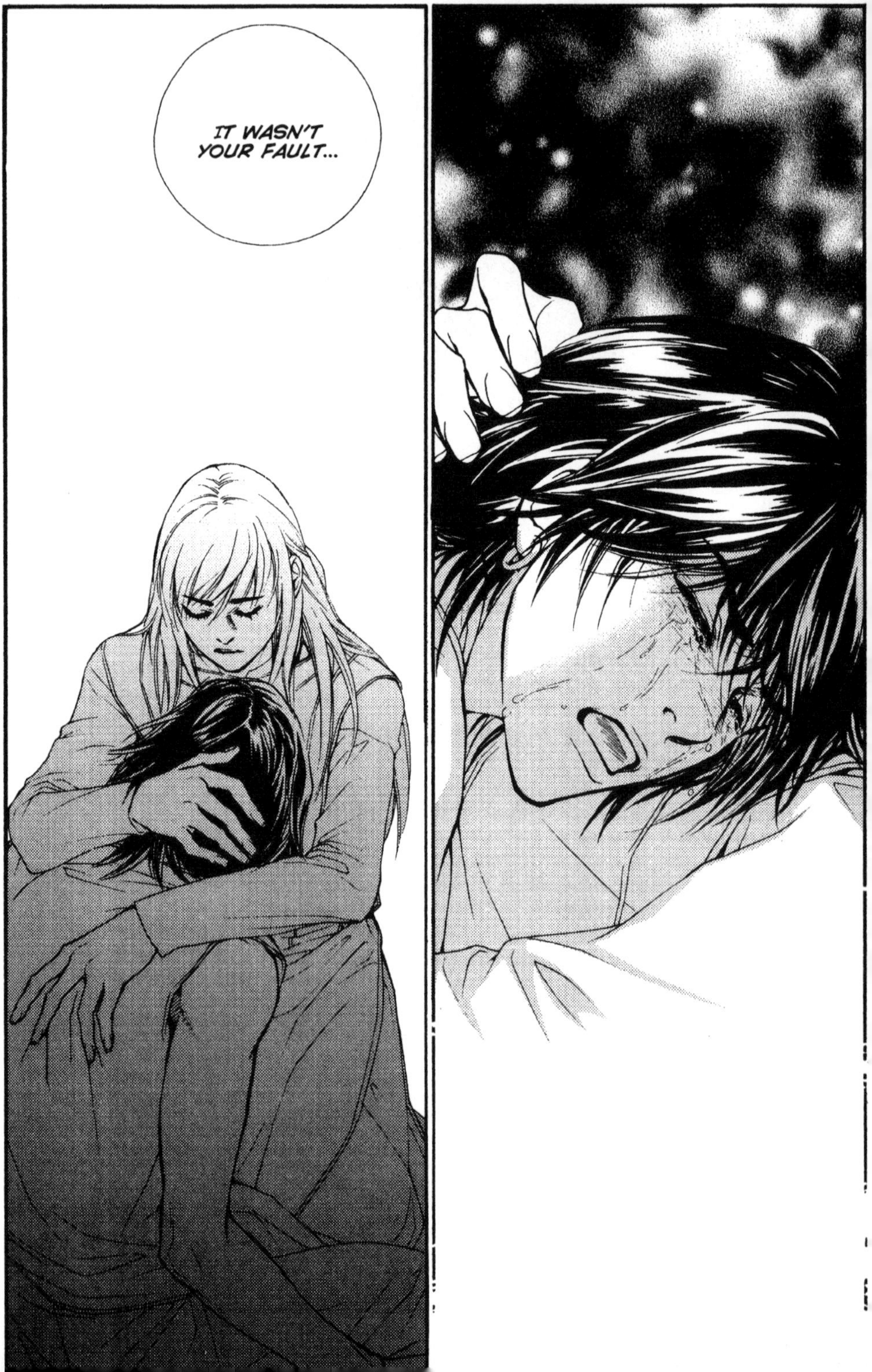
IT WASN'T YOUR FAULT...

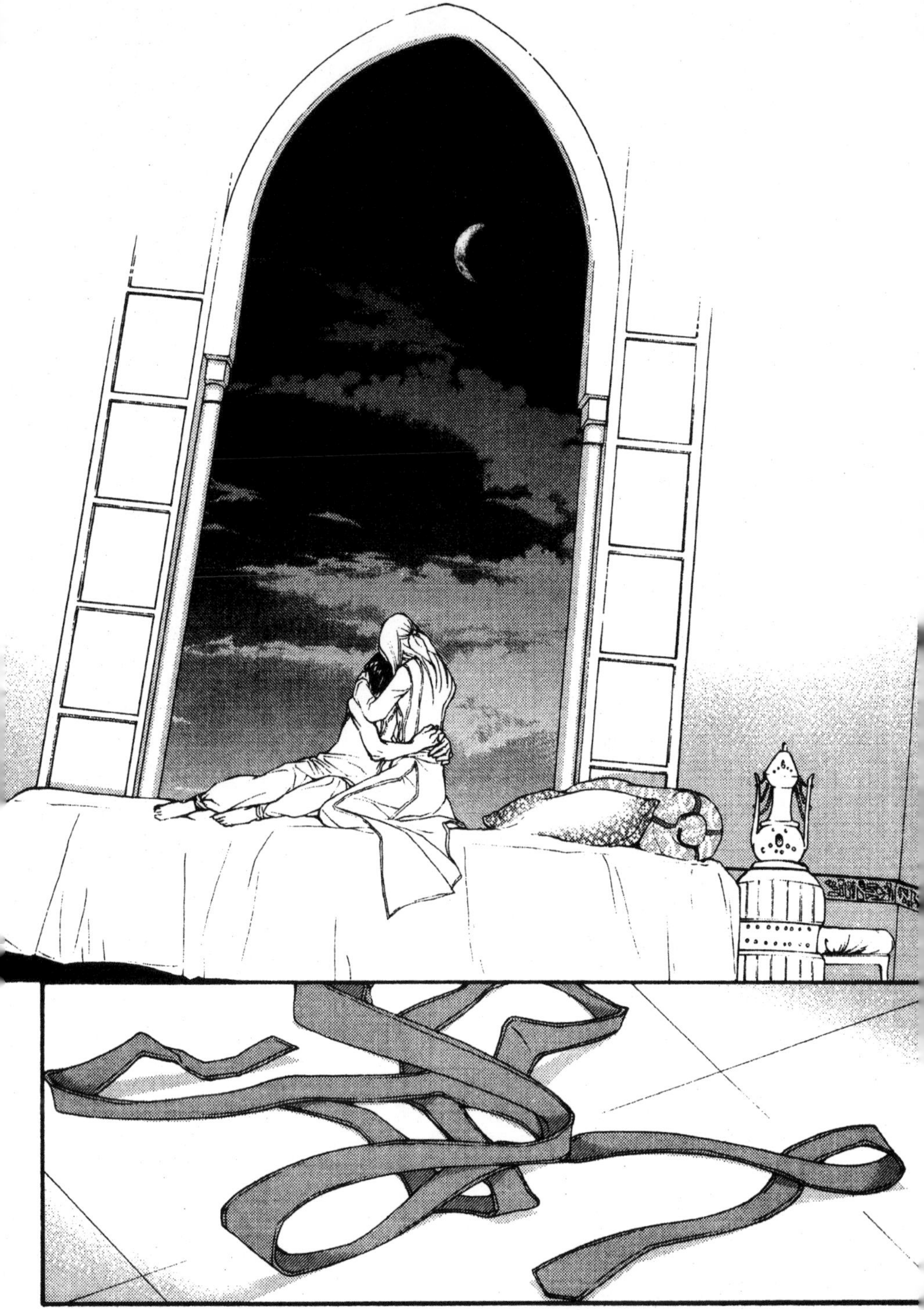

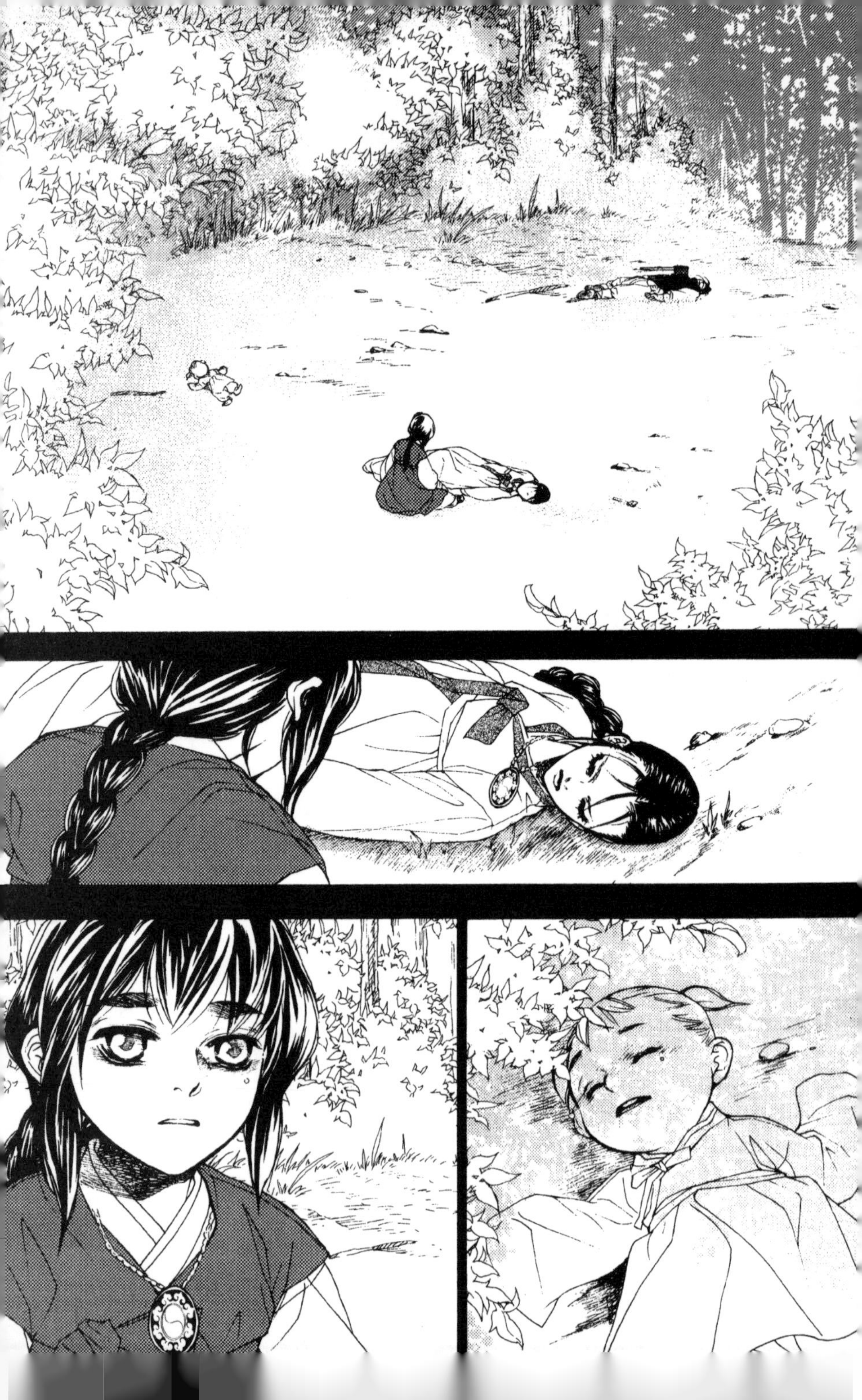

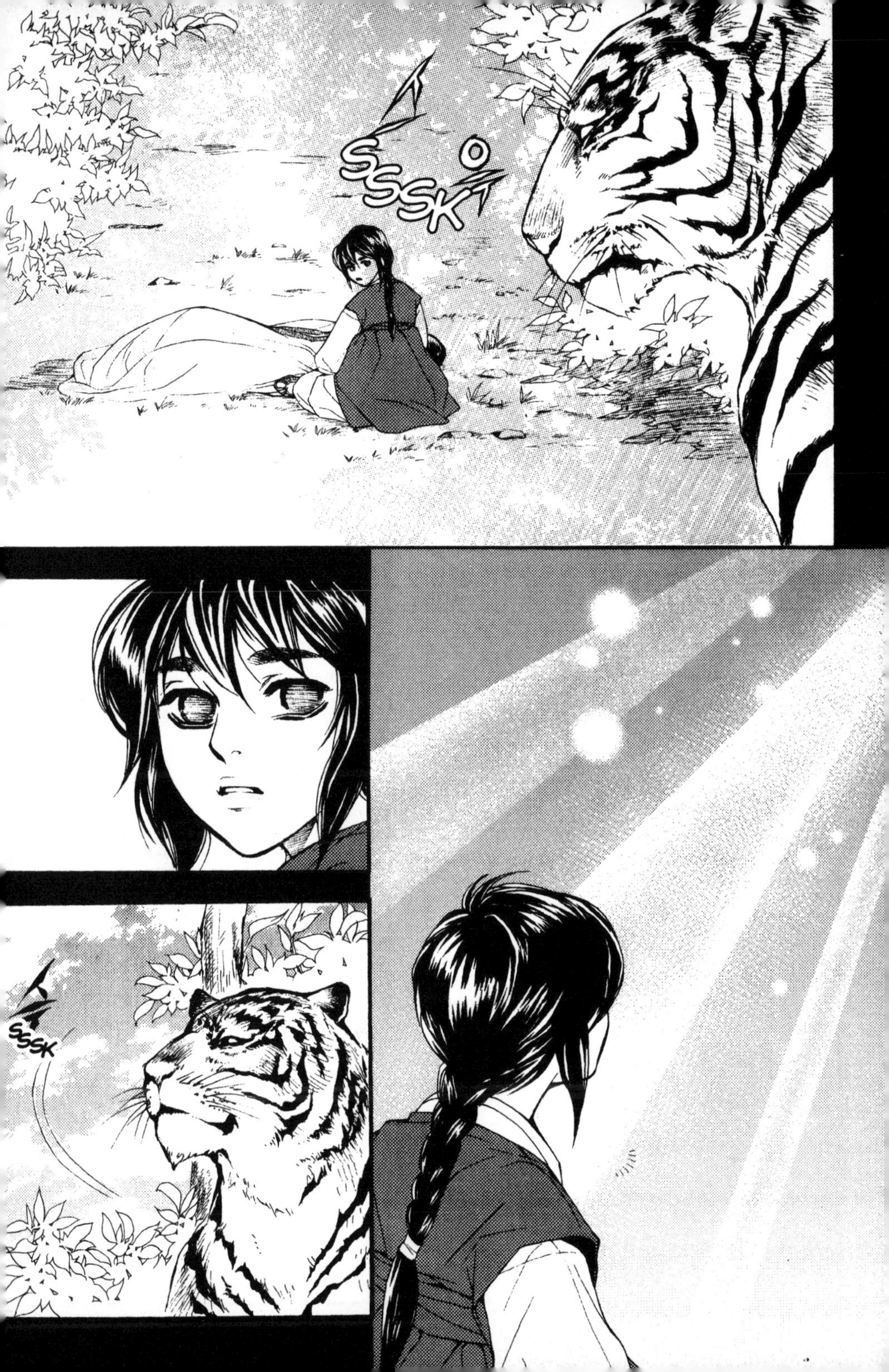
SSSK
SSSK

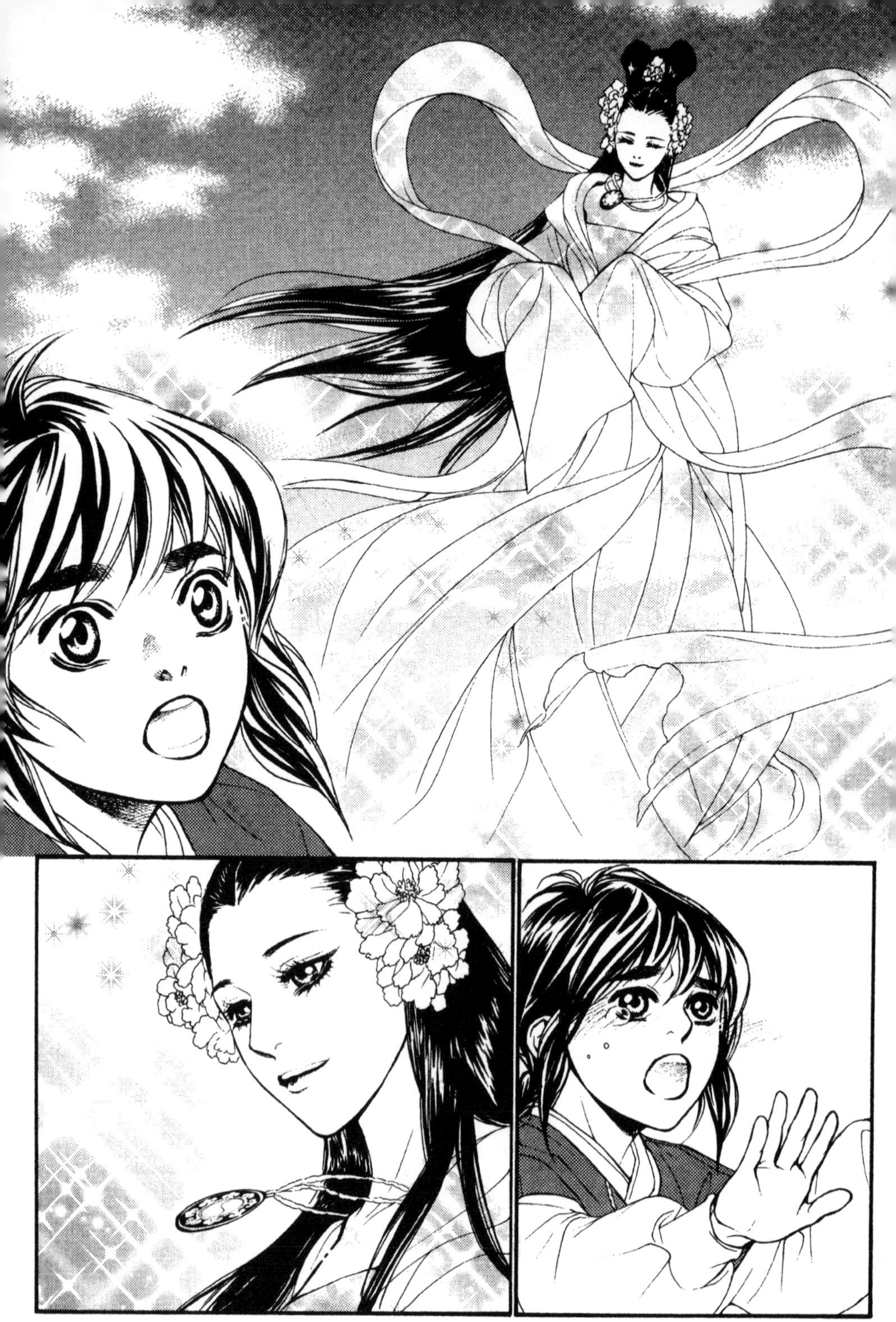

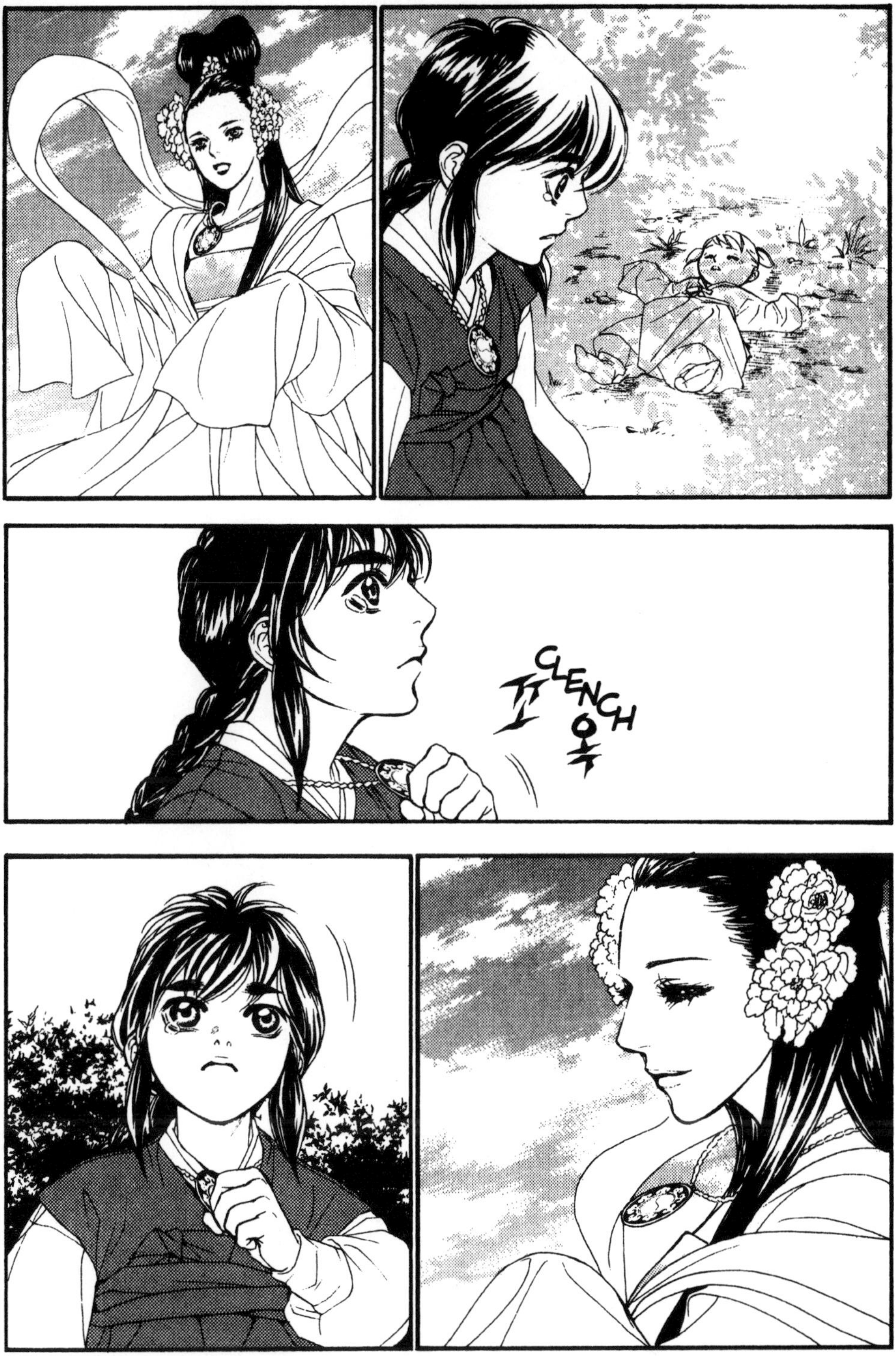
꼬옥
CLENCH

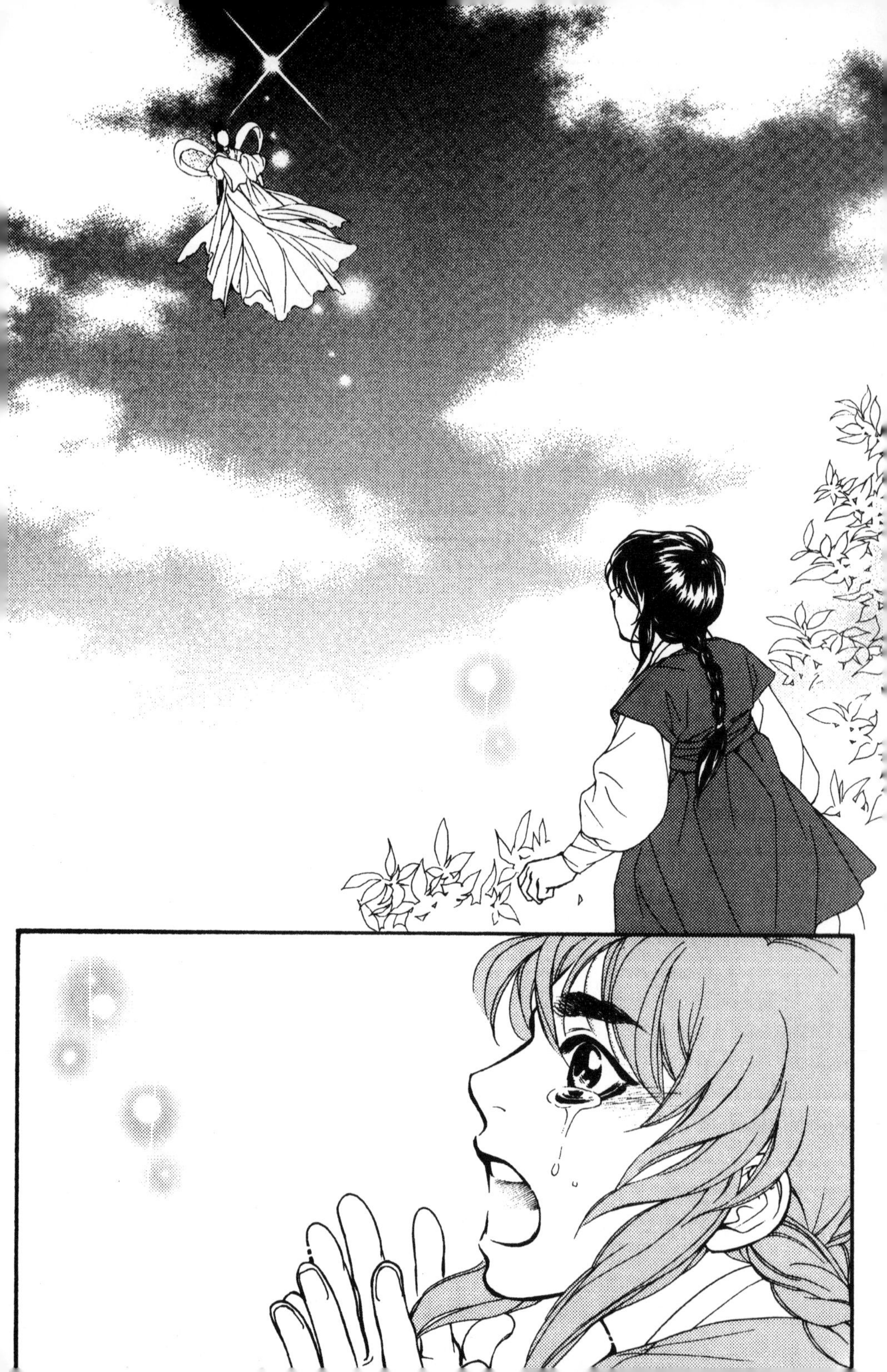

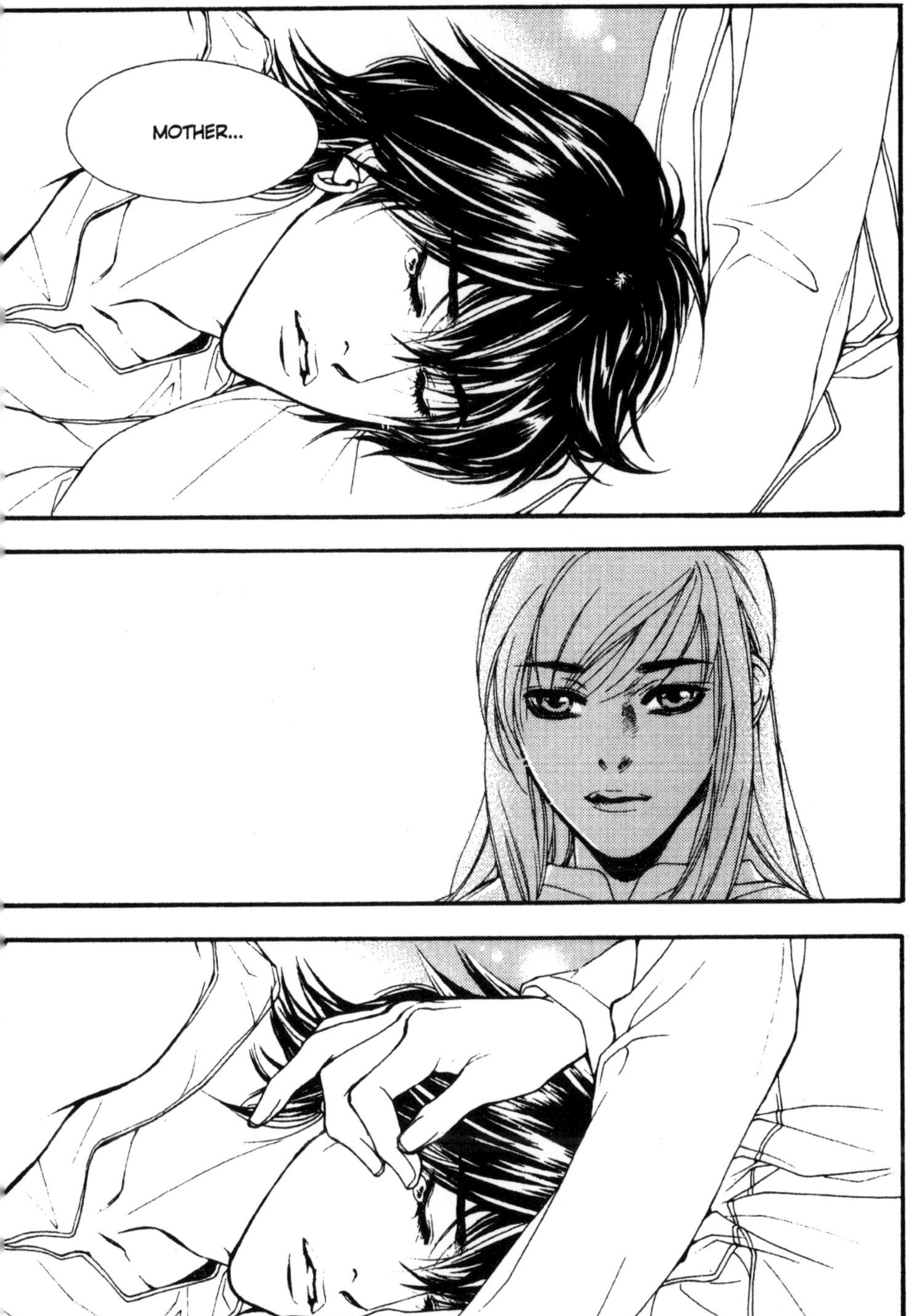
MOTHER...

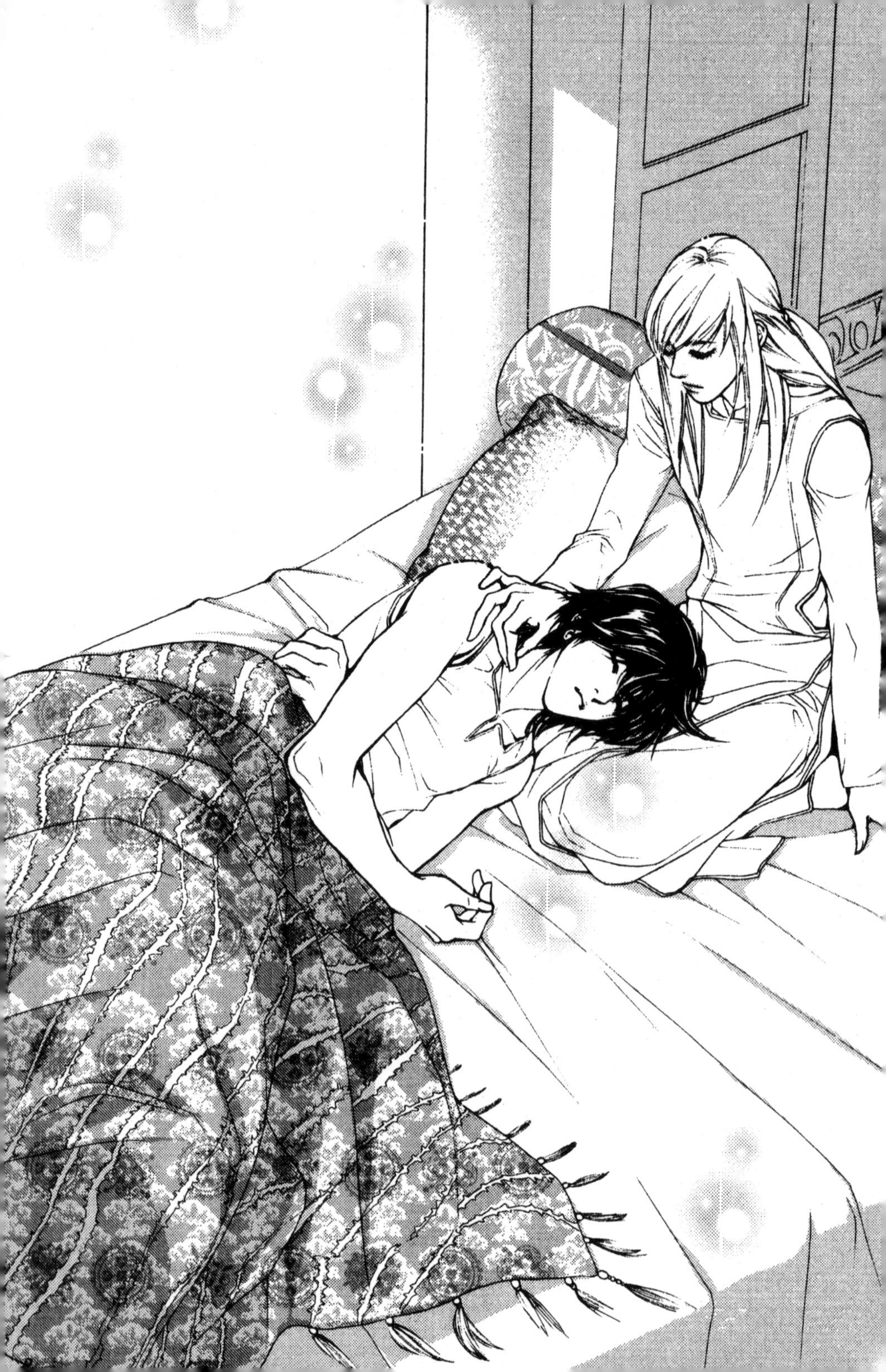

Special Commentary From
The Writer JinSeok Jeon

ONE A MAN AND A WOMAN

I FINALLY FINISHED VOLUME 4. I ATTEMPTED A SCARY STORY (WELL, SCARY TO ME) FOR THE FIRST TIME. I WONDER WHAT READERS THINK ABOUT THIS.

I'VE READ ARTICLES ABOUT KOREAN HUSBANDS LOOKING FOR RUNAWAY VIETNAMESE BRIDES OR KOREAN-CHINESE WIVES. IT MAKES ME THINK OF "THE ANGEL AND THE WOODSMAN" AS MORE THAN JUST A STORY. I'M HAPPY THAT THE STATUS OF WOMEN CONTINUES TO IMPROVE. BUT I DON'T THINK IT'S HEALTHY WHEN THE FIGHT FOR EQUAL RIGHTS TURNS INTO A BATTLE OF THE SEXES. IF EACH SIDE STEPPED BACK AND TRIED TO UNDERSTAND THE OTHER, I BELIEVE THAT WE'D HAVE A WORLD THAT IS FAIR TO ALL HUMAN BEINGS. WHEN GOD CREATED MAN AND WOMAN, HE MEANT THEM TO LOVE EACH OTHER.

I WAS TOLD THAT I POSED AS A FEMINIST WHILE I WAS WORKING ON THIS VOLUME. I'M NOT A FEMINIST. I HOPE YOU CONSIDER THIS VOLUME AS MORE OF A PARABLE FOR MEN. I HEAR THAT SCHOLARS USE "GENDER STUDIES" INSTEAD OF "FEMINISM" NOWADAYS. THIS PHENOMENON OF NOT SIDING ONE WAY OR THE OTHER COULD DEVELOP POSITIVELY INTO SOMETHING LIKE "MEN ARE FROM MARS AND WOMEN ARE FROM VENUS."

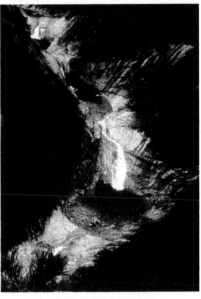

↑ SANG-PAL FALLS, WHERE AN ANGEL SUPPOSEDLY RUINED HER LIFE BY TAKING A BATH.

TWO UNIVERSAL TALE

SOME READERS MIGHT WONDER WHY "THE ANGEL AND THE WOODSMAN" APPEARS IN THIS BOOK. HOW DID SEHARA KNOW ABOUT THIS TALE?

ACTUALLY, "THE ANGEL AND THE WOODSMAN" STORIES CAN BE FOUND GLOBALLY WITH THE EXCEPTION OF PERHAPS AUSTRALIA. IT'S KNOWN AS "THE SWAN MAIDEN'S TALE" IN EUROPE AND "A BIRD WOMAN'S TALE" IN MONGOLIA. THE BIRD WOMAN CHANGES INTO AN ANGEL IN CHINA BECAUSE OF THE INFLUENCE OF TAOISM.

OTHER UNIVERSAL STORIES INCLUDE "NOAH'S ARK" AND "CINDERELLA." WHEN I WAS YOUNG I THOUGHT THE KOREAN VERSION OF CINDERELLA, "KONG-JUI AND POT-JUI," PLAGIARIZED CINDERELLA. ^^; THESE UNIVERSAL STORIES ARE VERY IMPORTANT EVIDENCE THAT THERE IS AN EXCHANGE OF CULTURE AMONG ALL THE DIFFERENT PEOPLES OF THE WORLD.

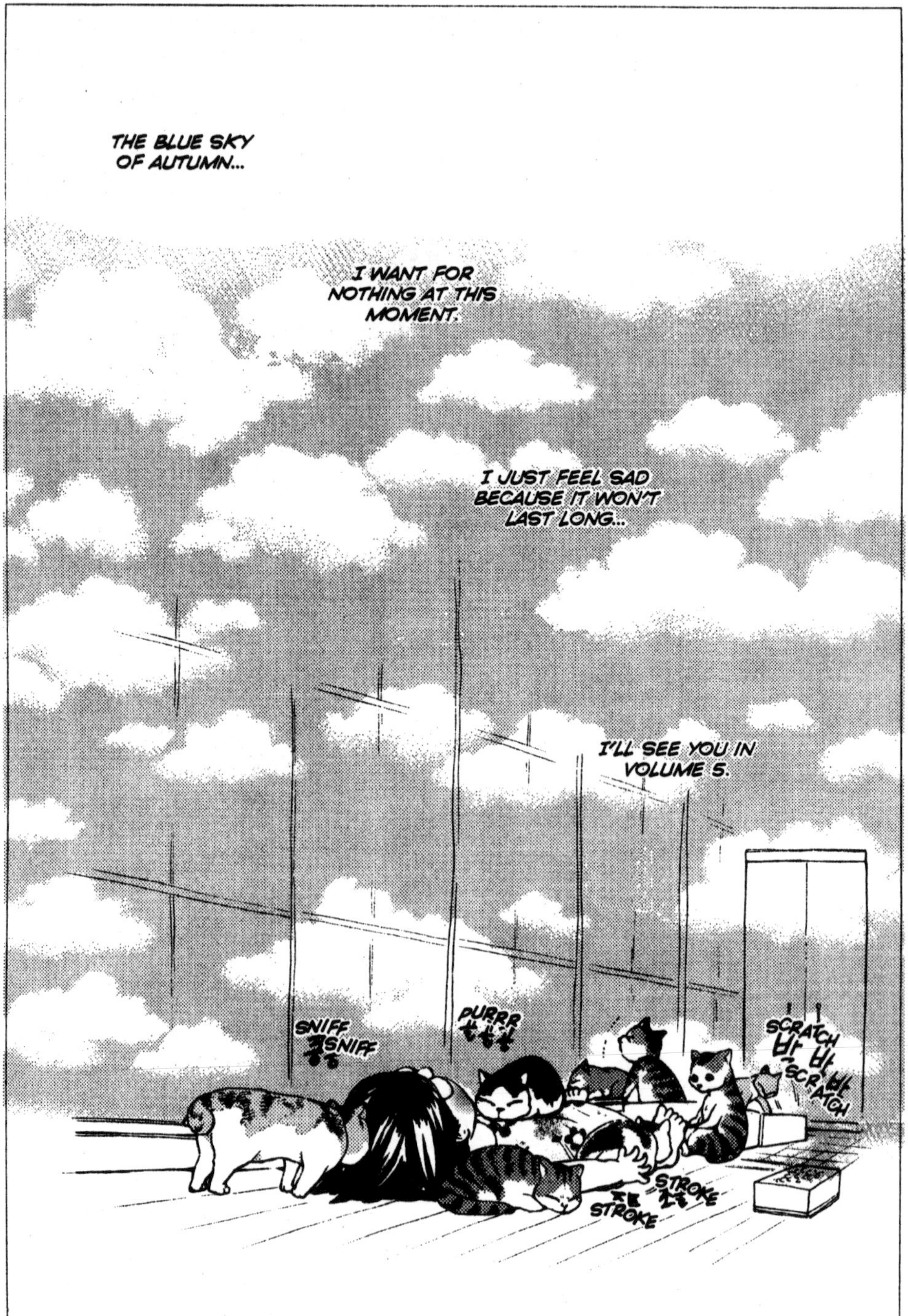
THE BLUE SKY OF AUTUMN...
I WANT FOR NOTHING AT THIS MOMENT.
I JUST FEEL SAD BECAUSE IT WON'T LAST LONG...
I'LL SEE YOU IN VOLUME 5.
SNIFF SNIFF
PURRR
SCRATCH SCRATCH
STROKE STROKE

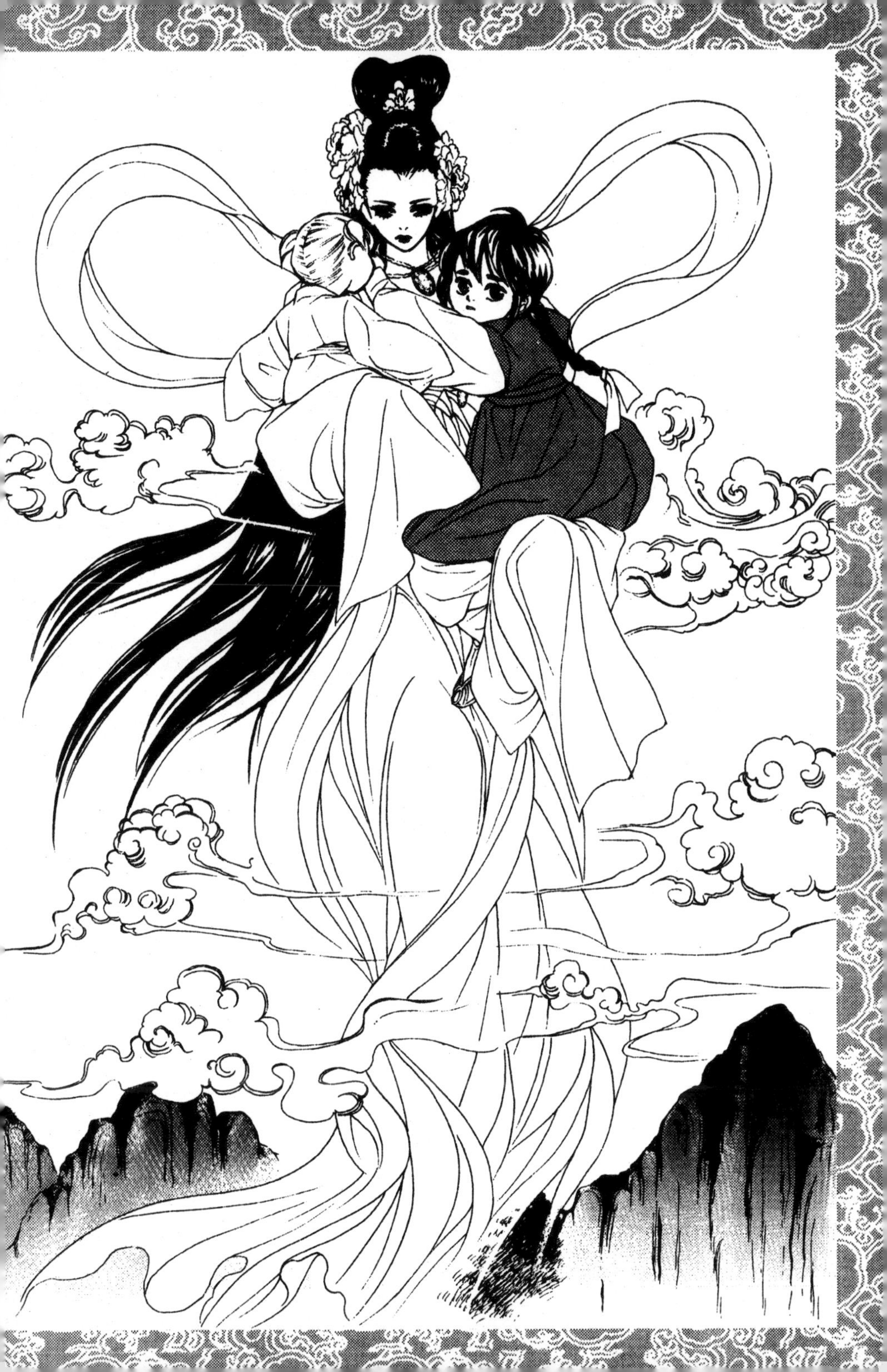

One Thousand and One Nights vol. 4

Story by JinSeok Jeon
Art by SeungHee Han

Translation: HyeYoung Im
English Adaptation: J. Torres
Lettering: Terri Delgado • Marshall Dillon

The characters and events in this book are fictitious. Any similarity to real persons, living or dead, is coincidental and not intended by the author.

Yen Press
Hachette Book Group USA
237 Park Avenue, New York, NY 10017

Visit our Web sites at www.HachetteBookGroupUSA.com and www.YenPress.com.

Yen Press is an imprint of Hachette Book Group USA, Inc. The Yen Press name and logo are trademarks of Hachette Book Group USA, Inc.

First Yen Press Edition: May 2008

ISBN-10: 0-7595-2874-8
ISBN-13: 978-0-7595-2874-1

10 9 8 7 6 5 4 3 2 1

BVG

Printed in the United States of America